Promise Renewed

Promise Renewed

Martin R. Tripole, S.J., Editor

JESUIT HIGHER EDUCATION FOR A NEW MILLENNIUM

an imprint of
Loyola Press

Chicago

an imprint of

**Loyola Press
3441 North Ashland Avenue
Chicago, Illinois 60657
1-800-621-1008**

Cover and interior design by Lisa Buckley

Background image on front cover is the title page of the 1599 Naples edition of *Ratio Studiorum*, reproduced with permission from a copy in the library of the *Archivum Romanum Societatis Iesu* in Rome.

Library of Congress Cataloging-in-Publication Data

Promise renewed : Jesuit higher education for a new millennium / Martin R. Tripole, editor.
   p.   cm.
   Includes bibliographical references (p.) and index.
   ISBN 0-8294-1292-1 (pbk.)
   1. Jesuits—Education (Higher)   2. Jesuits—Education (Higher)—United States.   3. Jesuits. Congregatio Generalis (34th : 1995 : Rome, Italy)   I. Tripole, Martin R.
LC493.P88   1999
378'.071—dc21

                                   98-36980
                                      CIP

99 00 01 02 03 / 10 9 8 7 6 5 4 3 2 1

Table of Contents

Abbreviations

AE   GC 31, Decree 28: "The Apostolate of Education"

Const   John W. Padberg, S.J., gen. ed. *The Constitutions of the Society of Jesus and Their Complementary Norms.* A Complete English Translation of the Official Latin Texts. St. Louis, Mo.: Institute of Jesuit Sources, 1996.

GC 31   31st General Congregation of the Society of Jesus, Rome, May 7–July 15, 1965; September 8–November 17, 1966

GC 32   32nd General Congregation of the Society of Jesus, Rome, December 2, 1974–March 7, 1975

GC 33   33rd General Congregation of the Society of Jesus, Rome, September 2–October 25, 1983

GC 34   34th General Congregation of the Society of Jesus, Rome, January 5–March 22, 1995

NYK   New York Province

SpEx   *Spiritual Exercises of Ignatius of Loyola.* See bibliography under Loyola, Ganss, and Puhl.

SWR   GC 31, Decree 29: "Scholarly Work and Research"

Citations from the 31st and 32nd General Congregations are taken from John W. Padberg, S.J., ed. *Documents of the 31st and 32nd General Congregations of the Society of Jesus.* An English Translation of the Official Latin Texts of the General Congregations and the Accompanying Papal Documents. Trans. Jesuit Conference. St. Louis, Mo.: Institute of Jesuit Sources, 1977.

Citations from the 33rd General Congregation are taken from Donald R. Campion, S.J. and Albert C. Louapre, S.J., eds. *Documents of the 33rd General Congregation of the Society of Jesus.* An English Translation of the Official Latin Texts of the General Congregation and of Related Documents. Trans. Jesuit Conference. St. Louis, Mo.: Institute of Jesuit Sources, 1984.

Citations from the decrees of the 34th General Congregation are taken from John L. McCarthy, S.J., ed. *Documents of the Thirty-Fourth General Congregation of the Society of Jesus.* The Decrees of General Congregation Thirty-Four the Fifteenth of the Restored Society and the Accompanying Papal and Jesuit Documents. Series III, 14: Original Studies Composed in English. Trans. Curia of the Superior General of the Society of Jesus. St. Louis, Mo.: Institute of Jesuit Sources, 1995.

Decree 1: Introduction: United with Christ on Mission (UCM)

Decree 2: Servants of Christ's Mission (SCM)

Decree 3: Our Mission and Justice (OMJ)

Decree 4: Our Mission and Culture (OMC)

Decree 5: Our Mission and Interreligious Dialogue (OMID)

Decree 6: The Jesuit Priest: Ministerial Priesthood and Jesuit Identity (JP)

Decree 7: The Jesuit Brother

Decree 8: Chastity in the Society of Jesus (CSJ)

Decree 9: Poverty

Decree 10: The Promotion of Vocations

Decree 11: On Having a Proper Attitude of Service in the Church (HPA)

Decree 12: Ecumenism (E)

Decree 13: Cooperation with the Laity in Mission (CLM)

Decree 14: Jesuits and the Situation of Women in Church and Civil Society (JSW)

Reference numbers in the text are to paragraphs within the decrees, followed by continuing paragraph numbers within the total volume, usually in brackets, as in SCM 4 [25].

Preface

The idea for this book of essays on Jesuit higher education originated in the summer of 1995, when Joe Feeney, the author of one of the essays, and I were vacationing at the Jesuit residence in Atlantic City, New Jersey. I had published in August 1994 a study of justice as it had been used in the 32nd General Congregation of the Society of Jesus (GC 32), which met in Rome in 1974–75, and my question to Joe was, where do I go from here?

The 34th General Congregation (GC 34) ended in March, and, as in 1975, issued decrees whose principles were supposed to inform every aspect of Jesuit life and apostolic activity. How that was possible was not always clear, especially in higher education. Thus, Joe suggested it might be a good idea to put together a volume of essays written by Jesuits in higher education, who would delineate the significance of the decrees in their areas of specialization. It seemed that if the principles of the Jesuit mission were important, they should be felt in education. It is with our youth most of all that we need to articulate as well as inculturate the message of the Gospel and the role it must play in the lives of future generations of Christians.

Thus was the idea for this book born, and I owe it all to Joe, who has encouraged and guided me with his expertise through this process every step of the way. This volume would never have been without him.

How were the essayists chosen? By many different standards. I especially wanted to enlist specialists across the board and in central areas of Jesuit higher education—areas that are crucial to Jesuit liberal arts education, but also areas where it would be especially challenging to articulate the concrete application of GC 34's tenets.

The areas chosen are administration, business ethics, campus ministry, classical languages, communication, computer science, economics, English, faith and justice, fine arts, history, Jesuit-lay collaboration, law, linguistics, mathematics, medical genetics, moral theology, philosophy, physics, political science, psychology, theology, and the international scene. Because of the importance of administration and philosophy, two essayists were chosen from those areas so that more than one perspective might be represented; because one of the more intractable areas for implementing the Congregation's decrees seemed to be the fine arts, two essayists are represented there as well.

Ever since the faith and justice direction was given to the Jesuit mission in 1975 indicating that justice should inform all Jesuit life and apostolic activity, many Jesuits have found it difficult to discern how precisely the new mission of the Society applied to their apostolates. This problem has been especially critical in the education mission. Thus, it was hoped this project would help considerably in responding to the needs of Jesuit teachers, and most major areas of teaching—especially in undergraduate education—are represented.

Later, I learned that a major convention of Jesuits representing the issue of higher education on the international scene was to be held in Santiago, Chile, in October 1997. It seemed important to present the concrete results of that assembly, in order to give some indication of where Jesuit education might be headed on the broader international scene. Thus our series of essays ends with a report on that meeting.

The persons selected to write these essays were chosen for a combination of factors, such as being younger, older, notable for their experience, or having a particular scholarship, reputation, or perspective. Usually more than one category applies for each essayist. It was important to get people who would know Jesuit higher education from close involvement in it, either currently or in the past, even though this would inevitably exclude notable Jesuit scholars in other institutions. I also did not want to choose essayists who might all be understood to represent a specific ideology; therefore, a wide spectrum of positions is represented, making it difficult to draw together a synthetic view from these essays, but providing, in my opinion, a much more open range of ideas, more possibilities for dialogue, and, to my delight, more possibility of confrontation.

Some areas of specialization are unfortunately missing; for example, I could find no figure in Jesuit higher education who would write on Scripture or sociology. Factored into the selection process was an attempt to represent Jesuits and schools from across the country and the various provinces. I regret that some schools are not represented at all, but including all was not possible. Jesuits were often contacted on the basis of recommendation. Some Jesuits felt unable to be a part of this project, mostly because they were already overcommitted or felt they did not have enough time to compose an essay. However, it is important to note that some also decided not to write because they were not impressed by GC 34's value to their scholarship or teaching; in other words, the decrees of the Congregation meant little to them. I regretted that these people were unwilling to present their views, because these too would have been helpful. This is not to say, however, that criticism of the decrees does not find a place in the essays herein. As the reader will see, it is freely represented here—sometimes in a clear and outspoken way, but often quietly integrated into a larger perspective on the value of GC 34. Fortunately, Jesuits are quite willing to address the shortcomings in our institutions, and offer proposals on how to correct them. Those whose fidelity to the Society and to the Church is represented in words of challenge were encouraged to be a part of this symposium.

Only Jesuits were selected: I felt it would be good to get a homogeneous grouping of essays from those who would know Jesuit life "from within," that is, from a life rooted in the many years of training to be a Jesuit, and who could reflect on how the ideals and spirituality learned from within that experience should be, could be, and are being brought to expression in Jesuit higher education. Such a perspective would be helpful to other Jesuits.

But this book is also intended—perhaps, especially—for the lay persons who constitute the majority involved in Jesuit higher education. They would want to hear how Jesuits feel about how things are going in Jesuit higher education. Because of the importance of collaboration between Jesuits and lay persons in our common ministry, a special essay is devoted to this topic. Indeed, another worthwhile project would be a volume gathering the laity's perspective on present currents in Jesuit higher education.

This volume begins with my own introductory essay on the meaning of justice in GC 34. This essay must be seen against the background of my earlier work on the meaning of justice as it was understood in GC 32. As I see GC 34, it is to be applauded, though in a qualified way, for enlarging the understanding of justice enunciated in GC 32. This new understanding makes the ministry of justice more embracing of the total apostolic life of the Society, especially education, and is more in keeping with the scriptural and ecclesial understanding of justice, especially as found in Isaiah and Paul and church documentation.

Several of the essays speak with approval, though in different ways, of GC 34's enlargement of justice; many continue to express quite admirably the importance of the Jesuit apostolate of justice as the correction of the social ills of society. A few of the essays mention the inadequacy of the social justice agenda of GC 32, and others express serious differences with the whole approach of the recent Congregations. Therefore, I suggest that the reader note with care the different perspectives on justice. This issue continues to be, I think, in need of greater clarification as we move into the twenty-first century.

Each essay begins with a summary abstract. Most of these were written by the essayists themselves; some were composed by the editor. These are helpful for getting a quick hold on what is presented in the essays, but they do not encapsulate all that is to be found in the essays, nor do they contain the richness of tone to be found in them.

A notable feature in the essays is the remarkable number of ways in which the authors find the directives of GC 34 being implemented in their areas of expertise or fields of study. There is particular influence of GC 34 in institutional programs that put into effect the ethos of the Congregation, but also in the attitudes that affect relationships between Jesuit and lay faculty, and between faculty and students. One will find here much reflection on the meaning of inculturation and the implications of interreligious dialogue. The tone of the essays is strikingly positive, and when not, strikingly penetrating. Some of the essays will surely provoke controversy.

Jesuits have also incorporated GC 34 into their value structures. They see the future of Jesuit higher education as bright, with realistic goals capable of being achieved. Not all find GC 34's directives directly meaningful to their apostolates, but perhaps they find them helpful in spirit, tone, and direction.

These essays are perhaps most outstanding for the various ways in which they call for reassertion of the justice of the Kingdom of God and for renewal of the Catholic identity of our institutions. They recognize the importance of influencing the critical, ethical, and spiritual development of our young people, as well as preparing them for significant involvement in the professional operations of our society. They want their students to become influential and constructive leaders who reflect to the world the Ignatian vision of "finding God in all things."

This volume is valuable because it indicates where Jesuits can go, what directions Jesuit education is taking and can take, what approaches can be used to increase the quality of Jesuit Catholic higher education, and, most of all, what can be done to improve the quality of life of our young people. What we can do for young people represents the be-all and end-all of our mission. This volume, therefore, is intended for anyone who is involved or interested in Catholic education. My hope is that persons of other religious orders and all those in diocesan education will find this book helpful.

Indeed, all of us have in common a commitment to what it means to be Catholic and Christian: to further the teachings of Jesus Christ, to help all, especially the young, to know him, and, if they choose, to enter into a faith relationship with him leading to service.

But for everyone, Christian or not, there is a need to grow into the principles and values that are the mark of quality in persons of good will—growth into the fullness of what it means to be human, and dedication to what is necessary to excite quality and dignity in our lives. It is for all these persons with all these purposes that this work is dedicated.

My gratitude to all the Jesuits who agreed to be involved in this project, most of whom contributed much time and effort and at considerable expense to their other projects. My gratitude also to all those who contributed their time to move this project along—they are too numerous to be mentioned. I must, however, cite Loyola Press for graciously agreeing to publish this volume, and Ruth McGugan, acquiring editor, whose kindness and support have been so valuable and appreciated. I must also single out Mr. Richard Trench, a member of the Office of Information Technology at Saint Joseph's University. He handled all the disk conversions and the multiple other problems that accompany computer operations today. He was a Godsend. Without his help, this project would never have been completed.

To the many, both Jesuit and lay, who encouraged me to continue with this project, I am most grateful. I am grateful especially to the Jesuit Community of Saint Joseph's University, who provided partial funding for this project through a grant from the Allan P. Kirby Jesuit Faculty Endowment Fund, entrusted to the community since 1964 for the intellectual and spiritual benefit of the Jesuit members of the faculty of Saint Joseph's University.

Martin R. Tripole, S.J., Editor
January 1, 1998
Titular Feast of the Society of Jesus

ESSAY 1

An Assessment of the 34th General Congregation's Understanding of Justice and Its Role in Jesuit Higher Education

Martin R. Tripole, S.J.

ABSTRACT

The author argues that the 34th General Congregation has significantly broadened and deepened the 32nd General Congregation's understanding of justice, so that it includes three meanings: first, the justifying or redemptive activity of God in Jesus Christ; second, the power of God's transforming justice as it operates in history through the evangelization of the Gospel (inculturation); and finally, justice as reform of unjust social structures. With this enlarged concept of justice, all the traditional ministries of Jesuits have a place, including that of higher education, whose purpose is to promote the intellectual and moral growth of the human person, as well as the person's community of faith with the Lord.

Introduction and Preliminary Remarks

Two hundred and twenty-four Jesuits were called to be delegates to the 34th General Congregation of the Society of Jesus (GC 34), held at Rome from January 5 through March 22, 1995. The Congregation was officially convoked by Father General Peter-Hans Kolvenbach on September 8, 1993, but preparations began as early as November 1991, when Moderators of Provincials' Conferences and members of the Jesuit Curia staff in Rome first met to draw up the themes around which material would be gathered as topics for discussion at the Congregation.[1]

The themes were separated into two main blocks: "The Challenges of Mission Today to Our *Minima Societas*" and "The Society Facing Challenges of Mission Today," or more simply, how the mission of the Society is understood today, and the ways by which the Society would go about carrying out that mission. Subthemes particularized each of these themes: those under the first theme included faith and culture, promotion of justice, and interreligious dialogue; those under the second included the apostolate of the Society, international collaboration among Jesuits, and partnership with the laity. A subtheme devoted to revision of the legislation of the Society was also a necessity, in view of the new Code of Canon Law of 1983. The background setting for all the themes was a "composition of place" made up of the events, the issues, the problems of the world, and the needs and probable direction of the world in the early part of the twenty-first century.

Throughout 1992 and the early part of 1993, a curial coordinating team of nine members chosen by Father General streamlined the presentations of the themes, submitted them for approval to the Moderators of Provincials' Conferences, and called on Jesuit "consultants" throughout the world for advice on how to develop the themes. The first theme, summarily known as the promotion of justice, was placed under the direction of Michael Czerny, social justice secretary in Rome, who wrote to Jesuits born after 1945 and chosen by the Moderators from their assistancies, and asked them to read carefully the groundbreaking Decree 4: "Our Mission Today: The Service of Faith and the Promotion of Justice" from the 32nd General Congregation (GC 32) of 1974–75, and to report to him their views on its continuing relevance through 2015. Their responses typically asserted the enormous value of that decree, the great impact it had had on the life of the Society, and the need to continue stressing its importance, even though the Society as a whole had not always responded to the decree to the degree they felt it should have.

Other consultants met late in 1992 to provide input on the subthemes. First drafts were drawn up by early 1993, and these were sent to "expert readers" for reflection and comment. By June, final essays were put together by skilled editors. These were sent to provincials, while reduced versions in tabloid or newsletter format were sent to Jesuits throughout the world. The reduced versions were to be used for reflection by Jesuits individually, as well as in community and province meetings. These tabloids did not represent official positions or "pre-decrees," but were "temporary instruments to help each Jesuit pray over the Society and its mission and contribute to our apostolic discernment."[2] Nevertheless, it can be no coincidence that the major documents to come from the congregation match the themes and subthemes.

WHY A CONGREGATION?

Why did Father General call the Congregation? The answer is given in different ways.

In a letter written to the whole Society on September 27, 1992, he indicated the Congregation would be a response to a mandate given by the 33rd General Congregation (GC 33) in 1983 "of bringing the Society's legislation into harmony with all the juridical changes which have taken place in the Church since Vatican II, as seen particularly in the new codes of Latin and Oriental canon law." But he did not wish to give the impression that the purpose of the Congregation was "purely juridical." Rather, this updating of Jesuit legislation was to be "integrated into the response which today's Society is being asked to give to the apostolic challenges of our time": to "a new quality of evangelization," to an animation of the Spirit of Vatican II through dialogue and "communion among all the forces of life," to a reaffirmation of the "Gospel choice for the poor in a new socio-economic context." The Society must respond "to the cry for the liberation of the human person" in the "many forms of slavery among us."[3]

In addition to these challenges that come from outside, the Society must respond to challenges from within: the need for vocations; for "apostolic creativity" in its structures, especially in view of the Society as aging; and for witnessing to the "true and authentic life in the Spirit" by effective implementation of the Constitutions of the Society of Jesus.

Finally, Father General added an unusual caution and directive: the Congregation must "take as its starting point the Society as it is today and will be in the immediate future." This would be necessary, he noted, to avoid a "gulf" between the delegates and the rest of the Society that "would be easily formed . . . if the deliberations about the challenges of our time were to get engrossed in lofty considerations, interesting in themselves but poorly representative of the reality and expectations of the Society's grassroots, and not directed toward the practical choices and specific decisions that need to be made." In other words, the Congregation was to take as a given the Society as it is today, and provide practical directives on the implementation of its works.

In Father General's letter of September 8, 1993, convoking GC 34, we get a simpler but more pointed presentation of the purposes of the Congregation, which are twofold: that the Society "renew its way of praying, acting and living," so that it might "meet its new apostolic challenges . . . through the renewal of the impulse generated twenty years ago by Decree Four of the 32nd General Congregation"; and that the Society rediscover "our way of proceeding" through updated legislation.[4]

In the first of the two tabloids sent to every Jesuit in May 1993, Czerny recalled that "at GC 32 [in Decree 4] the mission of the Society was characterized as 'the service of faith, of which promotion of justice is an absolute requirement,' and this mission was reinforced with 'integral evangelisation' and 'the preferential option for the poor' by GC 33." The purpose of GC 34, Czerny said, was "not to unmake these choices but to focus on the conversion and changes which they demand."[5]

Thus it was made clear to the delegates before the beginning of GC 34 that a reorientation toward faith and justice had been given to the life of the Society by GC 32 in 1975, that it was reinforced by GC 33 in 1983, and that it was not to be called into question in 1995. The reason for this concern was no doubt that Decree 4's redirection had caused some confusion and division in the Society from the time it was enacted.[6] The focus of the problem may be directed to the beguilingly simple statement Czerny cites from the second paragraph of Decree 4: "The mission of the Society of Jesus today is the service of faith, of which the promotion of justice is an absolute requirement."[7] What this statement affirms, in a way that had never been done before, is that the promotion of justice is intrinsic to the service of faith, and as a result, the service of faith may not be carried out without in some way promoting justice.[8]

The most immediate consequence of this theological and mission principle is indicated in Decree 4: Every Jesuit would be called to clarify how his life as a Jesuit promoted justice: "the promotion of justice . . . should be the concern of our whole life and a dimension of all our apostolic endeavors" (4:47).

What further complicated matters was that the decree was ambiguous about the meaning of justice: What kind of justice did Decree 4 require? By most accounts, it was social justice. Those Jesuits whose work was in that area took heart from the statement, which gave an importance to their apostolate that they felt it deserved, but others, such as those in education, whose apostolate did not directly pertain to the social ministry, felt threatened. Some Jesuits felt this was appropriate, because Jesuits in education had failed to turn the minds and hearts of their often well-heeled students to a concern for the poor and oppressed.[9] Fathers General Pedro Arrupe and Kolvenbach repeatedly denied that the decree downgraded the importance of education as a Jesuit ministry, but their efforts met with varying degrees of success.

As time went on, it seemed more and more necessary that the next time a congregation was called, it would have to try to clarify Decree 4's understanding of justice.

The Meaning of Justice for Father Arrupe and in GC 32

Before we examine justice as it was used in GC 34, it will be useful to trace briefly an important position on justice taken by Father Arrupe, who was General of the Society from 1965 to 1983, and who was a major influence in the development of the Society's views on justice in GC 32.

It would take us too far afield to dwell at length on Arrupe's role in the development of the notion of justice as formative of all Jesuit apostolates, as used in GC 32; nevertheless, some brief notations must be given to establish the fact that his influence was significant. First, most helpful in this respect is the work of Jean-Yves Calvez, S.J. Calvez was a close associate of Arrupe's. He was a member of the six-man preparatory commission set up in April, 1971; he was one of four general assistants to Arrupe at the time of GC 32; and he was a delegate to the Congregation. He was also a member of the Council of the President, a group of five Jesuits who helped Arrupe prepare the meetings and preside over the Congregation's plenary sessions.

Calvez wrote *Faith and Justice: The Social Dimension of Evangelization*,[10] a study of the development of the notion of the promotion of justice as an element of the Jesuit mission before, during, and after GC 32.

Calvez notes that Arrupe was not consistent: sometimes he spoke of justice and the social apostolate as one apostolate among many in the mission of the Society; other times he understood the social apostolate as the form of all Jesuit apostolates.

Evidence for the latter understanding may be found starting in 1966, when Arrupe set in motion "orientations which would become the perspective adopted by Decree 4."[11] In a letter to Latin American provincials on December 12 of that year, Arrupe wrote that it was "the moral obligation of the Society to rethink all its ministries and apostolates, and to investigate if they really responded to the urgent and prevailing requirements of justice and even of social equity." Arrupe pointed out, moreover, that even an apostolate "such as education at every level of its concrete form today ought to undergo reflection in the light of the requirements of the social problem."[12] Calvez notes "how great an influence [Arrupe's] personality was able to exert, as well as the orientations which he gave to the Society of Jesus, evident in the discussion and conclusions of that general congregation, particularly Decree 4."[13]

Second, a particularly revealing look into the inner workings of GC 32 is provided by a former Jesuit sociologist, Thomas Philip Faase, who was allowed to attend many of the plenary sessions of the Congregation for the writing of his dissertation, published as *Making the Jesuits More Modern*.[14] Faase speaks of the wide influence of Arrupe in spreading the social justice agenda prior to the Congregation, especially in addresses and travels abroad, including Arrupe's presentation on justice in the world at the 1971 Synod of Bishops.

Prior to the General Congregation, provincial congregations all over the world met to suggest topics for discussion at the Congregation. According to Faase, "there was concerted 'lobbying' before the various Provincial Congregations on behalf of this issue [the promotion of justice]." The Mexican Provincial Congregation came closest to suggesting what the Congregation actually adopted when it asked that GC 32 "define explicitly . . . the Society's option as regards the problems of international injustice, in such a way that all the deliberations of the Congregation regarding our way of life and apostolic mission in the world today fall within the perspective of this fundamental option." In addition, in January 1974, five Mexican Jesuits put together a sixty-page proposal regarding the promotion of justice and describing, according to Faase, "injustice in the world, economic and social inequalities, and political, military, and cultural domination," and called for the Society (in the words of the document) to "struggle against injustice, particularly at the international level." According to Faase, the proposal was condensed and widely distributed to various provincial congregations. It was subsequently included by the Jesuit Curia in Rome in a summary report of all suggestions that thereby "increased the likelihood of its gaining the attention and following that it had at the Congregation. . . . It had the full sanction and obvious backing of the Society's General."

Finally, when the Congregation got underway, an agenda of six priority topics for discussion was put together. The promotion of justice ranked fourth on the list. But, at the suggestion of the General's Council of the President, the promotion of justice was combined with the first priority to create a superseding "priority of priorities" category, which the council then presented to the general membership for approval. The supervening category was accepted by exactly a two-thirds vote of the delegates. Thus, according to Faase, the promotion of justice was made "a governing horizon." Faase considers this move "one of the most significant and influential decisions of the General Congregation, [whose] effects would be felt in many subsequent deliberations."[15]

Third, basic confirmation of Faase's presentation is found in John W. Padberg, S.J., "The Society True to Itself: A Brief History of the 32nd General Congregation of the Society of Jesus (December 2, 1974–March 7, 1975)."[16] Padberg also makes it clear that Arrupe expressed eloquently to the General Congregation "his own reflections on an option for justice," a "work" which he thought was "inescapable, that it came from the gospel itself, [and] that it flowed from the priestly character of the Society."[17] According to Padberg, this matter of the promotion of justice was one of the major issues which eventually led to the unsettling of Paul IV.

Arrupe was known as a strong supporter of the ministry of social justice in the Society. Yet he could be critical of reducing Jesuit life to action for social justice. For example, in 1976 he admonished one province that attempted to rewrite its mission statement entirely in terms of correcting social injustices. Decree 4, he argued, listed not only "socioeconomic" injustice as an evil of modern society, but also lack of faith in Christ and secularization.[18] Here Arrupe seems to correct a mistaken notion that social justice could be the comprehensive mission of the Society.

But elsewhere, Arrupe used the concept of justice as comprehensive of many apostolates. In an address to the Congregation of Procurators in 1978, he asserted that the mission "to struggle on behalf of faith and justice . . . ought to imbue the life and work of all Jesuits, not be reduced to a specific apostolate reserved to some" (here he was echoing GC 32, Decree 4:47, and Decree 2:9, "Jesuits Today"). He gave no explanation of the meaning of justice as he used it here, only that it was linked to "solidarity with the poor" and included "political engagement."[19] In this case, he understood justice as a dimension of life that must somehow inform all Jesuit life and apostolic endeavors.

What is little noted is that it was becoming apparent to Arrupe—probably already by 1976, and certainly by 1978—that Decree 4's understanding of justice had led to "exaggerations and one-sidedness" on the part of some, and "fear" on the part of others, so that he agreed to the desires of many Jesuits "for theological clarification of the relationship between faith and justice and for a more precise understanding of the concept of justice."[20]

TRANSCENDENT JUSTICE OF THE BIBLE

An important point to consider in our understanding of justice is the transcendent biblical concept of justice understood as justification, meaning God's saving covenant with his people whereby he frees them from enslavement to the forces of evil, and allows them to share in his own divine life. This concept of justice provides a theological foundation for the mission activity of the Society and, indeed, of the Church: to introduce all humankind into an experience of the justifying, or saving, relationship with God. Arrupe was of course aware of this concept of justice, and saw its importance as a foundation to all other types of justice. He developed this deeper and broader understanding of justice on at least two occasions.

The first is in a 1972 commentary on the 1971 Synod of Bishops' *Justice in the World*, where he tried to correct an ambiguity often found in the understanding of justice. The passage is worth quoting at length:

> *The most important contribution Christians can make to the promotion of justice, is, of course, to bring the reality of Christian justice into their family and professional life, and their social, cultural and political activity. "Everywhere and in all things they must seek the justice of God's kingdom."*[21]
>
> *During the past decade action for justice was conceived principally in terms of socio-economic development: the improvement of the material conditions of life of those who have less than they should have of material goods to live a truly human life. Today, without denying the continuing need for socio-economic development, thoughtful men prefer to regard action for justice as principally* liberation.
>
> *Liberation, first of all, from the inner constraints, the inner slavery of personal sin and sinful proclivities.*
>
> *Liberation, next, from the ignorance, the apathy and the fatalism, the narrow and selfish mental patterns and attitudes induced in us by our own sins or by the sins of others.*
>
> *Liberation, finally, from the unjust economic, social, and political structures, arrangements and procedures which effectively exclude so many people from human development, and even deprive them of the means to acquire this development for themselves. Liberation in this sense obviously calls for some kind of political involvement.*[22]

The second place where Arrupe develops a broader understanding of justice is in "Men for Others," a talk in which he provides one of his finest presentations on the meaning and importance of the transcendent concept of justice as justification. Here he explains sin as "a congenital inclination toward evil," a concupiscence that God in his "marvel of justification" uproots when a person is converted. But the effects of sin, Arrupe argues, continue to dominate in one's "periphery," one's way of life. Christ's grace frees us from sin not only in our inner life—"personal conversion"—but also in our periphery, our relationships with others. In our inner life, justification operates "at the very core of our person," but that justification is incomplete unless it includes "a reform of the structures at the 'periphery' of our being, not only personal but social." Finally, for Arrupe, "We cannot separate personal conversion from structural social reform."[23]

What Arrupe shows quite well in these two presentations is that there are three internally related aspects of justice that must be taken into consideration for an adequate understanding of the meaning of justice in a Christian context. First is the transcendent justice or justification foundational to all others. This is God's redemptive activity, ultimately completed in Christ, by which God liberates his people from enslavement to sin and invites them to share in his own divine life. In this sense, justice includes personal conversion, which it effects upon the inner life or core of the person.

This justice then comes to expression in two forms in history: one form is understood as liberation from the "mental patterns and attitudes" induced by sin in our lives in our relationships with others. I would call this understanding of justice comprehensive, in the sense that it includes the effects of God's justification as it operates within history, as it permeates human culture through the lives of his followers, and thereby touches the life of every human person.

The other form is justice as it is understood in its most specific form: "structural social reform," God's justice expressed in human efforts upon specific social structures to overcome economic poverty and political oppression. Thus, as Arrupe shows, the foundation of all justice resides in God's justification of his people, but its effects must be felt in the comprehensive transformation of human history and culture (inculturation), and in specific efforts toward the reform of unjust social structures.[24]

For many Jesuits, the failure of GC 32 clearly to enunciate and maintain these three aspects of justice marred its perspective. I would argue that Decree 4 conflated the three levels of justice into the third specific form of justice (social justice), and then inflated that justice, making it the second comprehensive form of justice to be understood as liberating all human life and activity, even though it was inadequate for doing so. Decree 4 thereby made the work of social justice the standard by which all Jesuit apostolates could be validated, rather than their participation in God's justice and its transformative power in history.

Promoting social justice became the one goal of Christian living, instead of one specific apostolate among many.

It is unlikely that Arrupe ever intended to promote this conflation-inflation exercise. However, though he argued to three levels of justice, the bulk of his discussion of justice was devoted to exposition of social justice as it would inform all Jesuit life. The fact is that in the very presentations to which we have referred, Arrupe, once having made the important distinctions among the various levels of justice, made little further use of the first and second levels in the development of his thought. The distinction among the three was probably always clear in his own mind, but by focusing so heavily upon social justice in his many addresses and writings, he may have inadvertently provided the foundation for Decree 4's conflation-inflation understanding of social justice, an understanding that is one of the lingering concerns of Jesuit spirituality since GC 32.

The Meaning of Justice in GC 34

GC 34 began with an allocution from John Paul II. The Pope reminded the Jesuits repeatedly of their "commitment to the new evangelization," a commitment that required a *"renewed dedication"* to carry out the command of the Lord to "'proclaim the Gospel to every creature' (Mk 16:15)." For John Paul, this command, which is "an essential aspect of the Church's mission," is also a "fundamental aspect" of the Jesuit mission as rooted in the *Formula of the Institute*,[25] which states that the chief purpose of the Society is to defend and propagate the faith.[26]

The Pope reminded the Jesuit congregants that evangelization also calls them *"to promote the full communion of all Christians,"* and to work against any forces that oppose that goal.[27] He recognized and accepted that "the Society is deeply committed to social work" (he mentions justice only once in his talk), but he reminded the delegates that such work "should never be removed from the global service of the evangelizing mission of the Church," which is geared toward the "salvation of every person" in the light of "our supernatural destiny."[28] It will be necessary, he states, to find a "balance between the need for the inculturation of the Gospel" and the integrity of the message contained in it.[29] Finally, he reminded the delegates that the "dynamism of the new evangelization" will be found only in their communion with the first evangelizer, Jesus Christ.[30]

Did the delegates take these words to heart? After a careful reading of the decrees, one may respond with a yes. Something remarkable has indeed occurred in the decrees of GC 34, something that its organizers may not have anticipated. Though the precise meaning of formulae is not always clear, which makes the message of GC 34 sometimes ambiguous and even confusing, a major redirection of the Society seems on the whole to be intended by these decrees when they are viewed in their totality. There is an explicit attempt to enlarge the understanding of the mission of the Society beyond that understanding set in place by GC 32 in Decree 4. GC 34 reaffirms Decree 4, but does so by going beyond it to formulate a theological and apostolic framework that notably deepens and broadens its perspective. GC 34 has taken what GC 32 initiated, but refashioned it to produce something that is not only more theologically sound, but also more appropriate to the total mission of the Society, and thereby more supportive of the Society's apostolate of higher education.

FIRST FIVE MISSION DECREES

GC 34's main mission statements are contained in the first five decrees.[31] They present the basic spiritual, theological, ecclesial, and evangelical principles that the Congregation wanted to enact. They also set the foundation for much of what follows in the remaining twenty-one decrees. Yet, even among these five, the most important for the new mission theology in GC 34 are Decree 2: "Servants of Christ's Mission" (SCM) and Decree 4: "Our Mission and Culture" (OMC). SCM also serves as a summation of the remaining three. It places Jesuits exactly where they should be: with Ignatius at La Storta outside Rome, where he was called to be a servant of Christ carrying his Cross, laboring with him "under that same Cross until his work is accomplished" (SCM 4 [25]).

It is our contention that a broader and more theologically correct direction is given to the understanding of the Society's mission in the introductory decree and in three out of the four governing decrees on "Our Mission." This understanding includes the three levels of justice as we have presented them, including (1) the transcendent foundational justification of God, which (2) is comprehensively expressed in history through processes of inculturation, and, finally, (3) particularized in efforts to transform specific social and political structures. Unfortunately, this larger perspective is not consistently followed, as we shall see, in Decree 3: "Our Mission and Justice" (OMJ). The end result is a thrust that is theologically and apostolically sound, but not consistently maintained.

JUSTICE IN SCM

The major problem with GC 32's Decree 4, as noted above, was its conflation of the promotion of justice to socioeconomic and political action, which was then inflated and made the measure of all apostolic life and activity in the Society. We have argued that the transcendent biblical concept of justice is the only justice capable of being this measure.

SCM repeats the formulary from GC 32's Decree 4, which has now become renowned—"the service of faith, of which the promotion of justice is an absolute requirement" (4:2)—but gives the formulary new meaning.[32] The justice to be promoted is not limited to social action categories. It is variously identified as "the justice of the Kingdom" (SCM 2 [16], 14 [39], 15 [40]); "the justice of God's Kingdom" (11 [36], 16 [41]); "the justice willed by God" (3 [24], 13 [38]); "that justice of the Gospel" (3 [24], citing GC 33, Decree 1:32); or "God and his justice in the world" (18 [46]). The service of faith is linked repeatedly to the promotion of justice in one of these expanded forms (3 [24], 14–16 [39–41], 20 [48]).

This use of justice can only be understood as identical with the transcendent biblical concept of justice as justification—the full panoply of God's saving activity toward the world, which achieves its fullness in Jesus Christ (SCM 5 [30]).[33] The promotion of this justice, which SCM explains as the Jesuit mission, is set "within the total evangelizing mission of the Church" whose mission Jesuits share (3 [24]), a mission to proclaim God's love and realize his Kingdom in this life and "in the life to come." It is a justice that is "the embodiment of God's love and saving mercy" (3 [24], citing GC 33, Decree 1:32), a justice that is aligned with "salvation" and "reconciliation to a world that is still broken by its sins" (5 [28]), a justice that is "the entry of the human family into peace with God and with one another" (13 [38]).

We are told repeatedly, and with emphasis, that various key concepts must be understood to have an enlarged meaning, so that a fuller perspective on justice may be brought into play; for example, that human acts of justice look to the "fullness" of the Kingdom where justice and not sin will prevail (SCM 10 [35]); that we are to live by God's Gospel "in all its implications" (11 [36]); that we have to work for—in the words of John Paul II in *Redemptoris Missio* 15—"liberation from evil in all its forms" to realize "God's plan of salvation in all its fullness" (10 [35]).

Finally, the decree explicitly states that the Congregation is going beyond the dimensions of the Jesuit mission "to which Decree 4 drew attention." The "aim" of our mission, which is "received from Christ," is the "service of faith," as Decree 4 stated, but the "integrating principle" of that mission is now said to be not simply the ambiguous promotion of justice, but "the inseparable link between faith and the promotion of the justice of the Kingdom" (SCM 14 [39]). The service of faith, moreover, as "directed towards the justice of the Kingdom," is "dynamically related" to evangelization, which includes, as "integral dimensions" of it, the "inculturated proclamation of the Gospel" and "dialogue with other religious traditions" (15 [40]). Thus, when the promotion of justice is addressed, it must now be understood as referring chiefly to the promotion of God's Kingdom by inculturation of the Gospel and interreligious dialogue (18–19 [43–47]).

With the clear intention of admitting that the Congregation has come to new insights since previous congregations, SCM ends by stating the following:

In the light of Decree 4 and our present experience, we can now say explicitly that our mission of the service of faith and the promotion of justice must be broadened to include, as integral dimensions, proclamation of the Gospel, dialogue, and the evangelization of culture. They belong together within our service of faith—they are "without confusion, without separation"—because they arise out of an obedient attentiveness to what the Risen Christ is doing as he leads the world to the fullness of God's Kingdom. (SCM 20 [48])

The delegates admit to a "profound, and Spirit-inspired" experience of *"sentire cum ecclesia in missione"* (union with the Church in mission), with the Jesuit "charism" set more securely inside "the Church's evangelizing mission" (SCM 20 [48]).

One cannot exaggerate the importance of these statements, which lead to a new formulation of the Jesuit mission. We have here a language, a goal, a theology, and a foundation for apostolic mission significantly broadened beyond that of GC 32.

PROMOTION OF JUSTICE AN "ABSOLUTE REQUIREMENT" IN GC 34?

The reader will recall that an inseparable link was made in GC 32 between the service of faith and the promotion of justice, which was said to be an "absolute requirement" of the service of faith (4:2). The source of this absolute requirement is the 1971 Synod of Bishops' *Justice in the World,* which has been interpreted to affirm such a requirement. But Charles M. Murphy has shown that there are good reasons to question whether the bishops ever intended to make so strong an assertion.[34]

Avery Dulles, S.J., has argued that this absolute requirement "seems excessive." As we noted in *Faith Beyond Justice,*[35] he asserted that a better formulation would be that taken from the Final Report of the 1974 Synod of Bishops, namely that "the promotion of justice is an integral part of the priestly service of faith," meaning thereby that justice pertains to faith in its completeness, but is not essential to its existence. This, Dulles says, allows for the "possibility of faith being served" without necessarily being "engaged in the transformation of social structures."[36]

But now that SCM has enlarged the meaning of justice, Dulles' objections are no longer operative. Once SCM applies the transcendent understanding of justice as the justice of God's Kingdom to Decree 4's statement, the statement is theologically sound. When the promotion of justice is understood as promoting God's justification of humanity for his Kingdom, it is obvious that the proclamation of such justice is intrinsic to the service of the faith. The statement is virtually tautological. SCM's clarification of Decree 4 demonstrates how easily the problem created by that statement is resolved, once justice is rooted in its transcendent foundation.

SCM'S JUSTICE AND THE FORMULA OF THE INSTITUTE

Some have also questioned whether GC 32's requirement of the promotion of justice for all Jesuit ministries (4:47) had sufficient warrant in Ignatius' *Formula of the Institute* (*Formula*),[37] which would be essential if such promotion were made the measure of all apostolic activity. GC 32 had failed to show such a warrant. What SCM shows is that, when justice is rooted in its transcendent understanding as the justice of God's Kingdom, a mission to promote justice finds ample support in the *Formula*. For these reasons, this clarification is without doubt the single most important section in all the decrees to substantiate the promotion of justice as the heart of the Jesuit mission.

According to the *Formula*, the aim or purpose of the Society of Jesus is "the defense and propagation of the faith" and "the progress of souls in Christian life and doctrine." The *Formula* enumerates the works that the Society is to use to arrive at this goal. Those listed as primary are "ministries of the Word and ministries of interiority, ministries of sacramental service, teaching catechism to children and the unlettered." Those placed at the end of the list are "works of charity, according to what will seem expedient for the glory of God and the common good" (*Formula* [3], as cited in SCM 7 [32]).

When SCM seeks warrant in the *Formula* for the promotion of the justice of God's Kingdom, it is able to correlate that understanding of justice with the *totality* of the above activities.[38] Thus, SCM asserts that the foundation for the justice of Decree 4, understood now as the justice of the Kingdom, resides in all the ministries listed in the *Formula*, since all—including the ministry of the Word, the ministry of sacramental service, and the works of charity—serve "the defense and propagation of the faith," and thus the promotion of the justice of God's Kingdom.

Therefore, SCM continues to insist, as GC 32 did, that the promotion of justice is the standard against which every ministry in the Society must be validated (SCM 14 [39]). However, because justice now stands for the justice of the Kingdom, there is no longer a problem. We are simply being told that all ministry is validated insofar as it promotes the coming of God's Kingdom. This is also the standard of validation for all ministries of the Church. Therefore, any Jesuit ministry that serves the coming of God's Kingdom, including the apostolate of higher education, is no longer at risk of being excluded.[39]

MEANING OF JUSTICE IN OMJ

Unfortunately, Decree 3: "Our Mission and Justice" does not follow through on these deepened insights regarding justice.[40] OMJ does admit that "the justice of the Kingdom" is the transcendent understanding of justice which must be our ultimate guide (OMJ 4 [53]), but then gives that understanding of justice no further role in the decree.

OMJ appears to make two advances beyond GC 32, but in fact, does not. First, for OMJ, the promotion of justice is no longer an absolute requirement, but "an integral part of our mission" (1 [50], 3 [52]). This would appear to be an advance beyond Decree 4, which made the promotion of justice an "absolute requirement" of our mission.[41] However, SCM affirms that the promotion of justice is an absolute requirement because it understands justice as the justice of God's Kingdom. Therefore, the fact that OMJ corrects Decree 4 by making justice only an integral part of the mission indicates that OMJ not only continues to understand the justice of Decree 4 as social justice, but is out of step with the other mission decrees.

Second, OMJ broadens its concept of justice to include "other dimensions of this struggle for justice" beyond those of "the socio-economic and political orders" (OMJ 5–6 [54–55]). These other dimensions include: "Respect for the dignity of the human person" and "the full range of *human rights,*" including "economic and social rights"; "freedom of conscience and expression and the right to practice and share one's faith; civil and political rights; . . . and rights such as development, peace and a healthy environment." In addition to these personal rights, there are what are called "'rights of peoples,' such as cultural integrity and preservation, and control of their own destiny and resources" (6 [55]).

OMJ includes the rights to human life against the "culture of death" (an expression borrowed from John Paul II): "abortion, suicide, and euthanasia; war, terrorism, violence, and capital punishment," as well as drugs, AIDS, and poverty. OMJ supports a "culture of life" providing ethically and morally acceptable alternatives to the above (OMJ 8 [57]).

Thus OMJ enlarges the meaning of action for justice to include, not just action in the socioeconomic and political orders, but action in support of human life, and so seems to be employing what we have called the second level of justice understood as the comprehensive power of God's transformation of history and culture through human action (inculturation). The fact is, however, that OMJ is arguing only from a specific understanding of social justice to an expanded version of that same justice. It is attempting to inflate the socioeconomic concept of justice to make it include, which it cannot do, the comprehensive form of God's liberating justice in history, rather than seeing that comprehensive justice as the expression of God's transcendent foundational justice, which is justification. As a result, the promotion of justice in OMJ begins to mean something more than socioeconomic and political action, but it never escapes the limitations indigenous to action for social change.

How do we know that OMJ never gets beyond an inflated concept of social justice? Because OMJ establishes a criterion for acceptance of apostolic mission no different from Decree 4's, evidenced in this key declaration (which is certain to get wide usage among social action advocates):

. . . every Jesuit in his ministry can and should promote justice in one or more of the following ways: (a) direct service and accompaniment of the poor, (b) developing awareness of the demands of justice joined to the social responsibility to achieve it, (c) participating in social mobilization for the creation of a more just social order. (OMJ 19 [68])

Thus, while OMJ says that the promotion of justice as social action is only "integral" to the service of faith and not an absolute requirement, in point of fact the decree treats social justice as if it were a requirement.

The issue of contention that existed with GC 32's understanding of justice thus remains in this one decree, namely, that God's justice as justification, and our participation in its transformative power in history and culture, must be primary to the mission of any religious institute, and that these are not reducible to action for social change, however broadly that concept might be inflated. The value of many ministries is found in the intrinsic worth of the ministry itself, and not in how that ministry may be reduced to extrinsic social worth. But that is the reduction OMJ makes when it insists on a social dimension as the criterion of acceptability for every Jesuit mission. This decree is especially reductionistic when it is applied to the apostolate of Jesuit education, since the primary value of that education is intrinsic to the educational experience itself: to foster the growth of the person in Christian humanism and in a faith experience with the Lord.

OMJ tries to substantiate its requirement that social justice be a part of every ministry by arguing that "forming 'men and women for others' is appropriate not only in our educational institutions, but in ministries of the Word and the Spiritual Exercises, in pastoral apostolates and communication" (OMJ 20 [69]). But if such an argument is applied to education and spiritual apostolic activity, it is myopic, narrowly pragmatic, moralistic, and shows no understanding of the intrinsic worth of these ministries; for while intellectual and spiritual ministries certainly do have social and moral formative power that should be fostered for the service of others, it is reductionistic to make that formative role necessary to the measurement of their worth.

INCULTURATED EVANGELIZATION

GC 34 advances beyond GC 32 not only in that it makes God's justice as justification foundational to all mission activity, but also in that it understands that justice to have a comprehensive transformative power to play in history and human culture. Understood in this way, this second level of justice is synonymous with inculturated evangelization.

Inculturated evangelization directs apostolic activity toward the intrinsic renewal of the human person and every aspect of human culture. OMC defines "culture" as *the way in which a group of people live, think, feel, organize themselves, celebrate, and share life. In every culture, there are underlying systems of values, meanings, and views of the world, which are expressed, visibly, in language, gestures, symbols, rituals, and styles.* (OMC 1 [75], n. 1)

Because culture touches such profound levels of human experience (OMC 23 [107]), we must go there, according to the decree, for the creation of a truly human and Christian society.

Inculturated evangelization focuses on a world that is absorbed in secular and rationalistic values that "refuse spiritual transcendence" (OMC 24 [108]). It challenges that world through witness and dialogue to become open to the "possibility and reality of God" (22 [106]). Its eventual goal is to work within a culture "in such a way that the line of development springing from the heart of a culture leads it to the Kingdom" (8 [87]).

Inculturating the Gospel is "a form of *incarnation* of the Word of God" throughout human experience (OMC 3 [77]), at the same time as it embeds a culture in God's *"mystery of salvation"* (14 [98]), the *"Paschal Mystery"* (3 [77], 15 [99]), where "the Gospel as Christ's explicitly liberating presence" (8 [87]) frees a culture from the "negative features" of sin and enters it into "the freedom of God's Kingdom." In other words, inculturation is precisely where God's justification takes place in history. The Gospel challenges a culture to "remove all those things which inhibit the justice of the Kingdom," so that the "Word of God" can "exercise a power within the lives of the people" (3 [77]) and bring them to the moment of authenticity in the "discovery of God" (7 [86], citing the discourse of Father Kolvenbach to the Congregation, 6 January 1995).[42]

Vatican II and Paul VI both noted that the split between the Gospel and culture is one of the serious problems of our day (*Gaudium et Spes* 43; *Evangelii Nuntiandi* 20, cited in OMC 2 [76]). The Ignatian vision is especially geared toward overcoming this split, because its mission is directed both "towards the mystery of God and the activity of God in his creation." For Jesuits, it is never "a question of choosing either God or the world; rather, it is always God *in* the world, laboring to bring it to perfection so that the world comes, finally, to be fully *in* God" (OMC 7 [86]).

Inculturated evangelization is, like the promotion of the justice of God's Kingdom, especially open to the apostolate of education, and OMC notes this.[43] One of the ways in which the union between the immanent and the transcendent justice of God is made clear is precisely in Jesuit education, which has "a crucial role to play in linking Christian faith" to contemporary culture (OMC 28,7 [125]). From earliest times, Jesuits have "linked Christian catechesis to an education in classical humanism, art, and theatre," so that students might be able to integrate both faith and culture (10 [89]). Through Jesuit education, the "ministry of evangelizing culture" can provide a "sense of the divine mystery" by bringing to light "God's activity in those cultures" (9 [88]). Thus, Jesuit education becomes one of the noblest forms of inculturation and, thereby, contact with the justifying power of God.

Finally, OMC recognizes that the secular forces of opposition to inculturation are great, in that the countercultural values of the Gospel are often seen as "marginal" to or "disruptive" of social life (OMC 5,1 [80]). Nevertheless, the tone of this document, as with all of the decrees, is optimistic: History shows a "long process of enlightened human growth" in which God is preparing his creatures "for the loving acknowledgement of his truth" and the "transformation promised in Christ" (18 [102]).

The insights of this decree are completed by Decree 5: "Our Mission and Interreligious Dialogue," where dialogue with believers of other faiths who share many of our Christian values is understood as a major moment in the process of evangelization. GC 34 considers interreligious dialogue "an integral element of the Church's evangelizing mission" (OMID 5 [133], citing John Paul II's "Address to the Pontifical Secretariat for Non-Christians," 28 April 1987), and a way by which we can cooperate with God in his "ongoing dialogue with humanity" (5 [133]).

Final Accolades, Cautions, and Concerns

The decrees of GC 34 represent on the whole a stunning development in the self-understanding of the Society and its mission. As is clear from the above, the delegates have put together profoundly insightful theological, spiritual, and socially relevant documentation on the nature of the mission in ecclesial and ministerial life, and future generations of religious will have much for which to be grateful. At the same time, there are elements in the decrees that give reason for caution and concern.

First, in spite of what we have said above, the decrees do not clarify and differentiate the various uses of "justice" as much as would be desirable. Justice is in fact never defined; it is only described in different ways, and its meaning is often ambiguous. Because justice has been used in so many different ways since 1975, the decrees needed to state with precision the various meanings of the term, and how precisely the word is being used in any given context. This is not done.

SCM at one point produces this especially unhappy blending of faith-justice-culture statements where each is said so to include the other that their individual meanings become hopelessly entangled. To say there is

> *No service of faith without*
> *promotion of justice*
> *entry into cultures*
> *openness to other religious experiences*

> *No promotion of justice without*
> > *communicating faith*
> > *transforming cultures*
> > *collaboration with other traditions*
> *No inculturation without*
> > *communicating faith with others*
> > *dialogue with other traditions*
> > *commitment to justice*
> *No dialogue without*
> > *sharing faith with others*
> > *evaluating cultures*
> > *concern for justice* (SCM 19 [47])

is to indicate a state of circumincession that does nothing to clarify the use of the terms, but seems rather designed to overcome conflicting contentions about their meanings and relative importance. When everything includes everything, is anything being said? Everyone is able to find in the decrees whatever one wants at this point, in which case the decrees are more open to political manipulation than to conceptual clarification.

Second, there was a need for theological balance between immanence and transcendence after GC 32, and GC 34 is a major step toward that. Kolvenbach indicated as much when he highlighted in his final statement to the press that GC 34, while continuing to stress the need to promote social justice, "underlined more emphatically the spiritual character of the promotion of justice" than GC 32 had done.[44] The decrees themselves stress that a balance needs to be maintained between the transcendent and immanent dimensions of Jesuit mission (OMC 21 [105]). Unless such a balance is maintained, there is a danger of Christianity becoming a secular humanism, and the primacy of the interpersonal relationship with Christ becoming marginal.

Third, two lingering concerns relevant to Jesuit education may be noted. The first concern is that there is an apparent conflictive ecclesial issue created by GC 34 in emphasizing *Jesuit* promotion of inculturation and perhaps of social justice, in view of the fact that Vatican II made it abundantly clear in *Apostolicam Actuositatem* that the apostolate of inculturation belonged primarily to the laity: "The apostolate of the social milieu, that is, the effort to infuse a Christian spirit into the mentality, customs, laws, and structures of the community in which a person lives, is so much the duty and responsibility of the laity that it can never be properly performed by others" (13).[45] If that is the case, why are others trying?

It would seem, therefore, that the primary effort of the Jesuits, insofar as inculturation and the social justice apostolates are concerned, would be to foster the growth of those missions among the laity.

Evidence that the delegates to the Congregation were aware of the supportive role proper to the Society regarding these apostolates may be found in Decree 13: "Cooperation with the Laity in Mission" (CLM). This decree distinguishes the Jesuit ministry from that of the laity, and states that Jesuits "must increasingly shift the focus of [their] attention from the exercise of [their] own direct ministry to the strengthening of laity in their mission" (CLM 19 [353]). The decree indeed speaks of Jesuits in "a supportive role" to the laity (18 [352]), offering themselves "in service to the full realization" of the mission of the laity (1 [331]) (at times this seems to be in regard to a mission that was once more properly seen as belonging to the Jesuits [4 (334)]). At other times, however, the Jesuit relationship is expressed in terms of a "companionship" (7 [337]) or a "cooperation" with the laity in their mission (1 [331]), as well as of a "partnership" (2 [332]) or "collaboration" (11–12 [341–42]), "coresponsibility" (13 [343]) or "cooperation" with laity "in works of the Society" (5 [335]).

In areas involving Jesuit *service* to the laity in the laity's mission, the nature of the laity's ministry is described in general categories, but it includes the laity's call to be "concerned for faith, justice, and the poor, [as] they evangelize the structures of society" (CLM 6 [336]). Jesuit service includes the offering of "our spiritual and apostolic inheritance [and] *our educational resources,*" including "pastoral and theological training" (7 [337]; emphasis added).

Areas where Jesuits *cooperate* in "Non-Jesuit Works" as a way of "witnessing to the Gospel and to Ignatian spirituality" include "social development and welfare centers, educational and research institutions, seminaries and religious institutes, international organizations, labor unions, ecclesial base communities and grass-roots movements" (CLM 14 [344]).

Works where laity collaborate with Jesuits in the Jesuit ministry include "Jesuit educational institutions, parishes, social center, retreat houses, and the Jesuit Refugee Service" (CLM 11 [341]).

These statements indicate that the ministries of inculturation and the social apostolate are looked upon by the Congregation both as a *shared* ministry, where Jesuits and laity cooperate with each other either in works of the Society or in the laity's own proper mission, and at other times, and perhaps in other places, as a ministry of Jesuit *service* to the laity in the laity's proper ministry.

By stressing both cooperation and service, the Congregation may be reflecting the uneasiness or uncertainty of a transitional phase in Jesuit spirituality, where there is a new awareness of the need to emphasize the importance of the mission of the laity as the Church becomes more and more a Church of the laity, while at the same time recognizing both the continuing importance of the Society's own traditional apostolates, and the diminishing manpower to maintain these apostolates.

Could the mission of service to the laity in the laity's ministry reflect the distinction between the ordained priesthood and the priesthood of all the faithful—the former more ecclesially oriented, the latter more dedicated to life in the world—while the notion of shared ministry reflects the view that these ministries of inculturation and social justice are common to ordained priests as well as the laity by reason of their common baptism? If this is the case, it becomes more urgent than ever to distinguish in what ways the ministry of the ordained priesthood differs from that of the priesthood of all the faithful, lest a blurring of lines, already resulting from Vatican II, make Jesuit vocations increasingly difficult to come by.[46]

The second concern relevant to Jesuit education is whether the Church's religious institutions, as opposed to the state's political structures, should identify themselves so closely with the ministry of social justice.

David O'Brien recently tried to figure out why the Church should exist today. He did not think evangelization provided the answer (I would disagree), but he thought that the struggle for justice was not the answer either: "The post-Vatican II church struggled toward a justice-and-peace answer. In practice, almost everyone has given up on 'action on behalf of justice' as the answer. . . ."[47]

While no one should question the importance of such action, one may question whether there are not root issues plaguing society today that might more profitably be investigated by the Church and its religious institutions.

It seems that John Paul II is arguing that the sacredness of human life is the fundamental value at issue today. If religious education could concentrate on restoring an awareness of and respect for that sacred value, it would get to the root of the problem that leads to unjust social structures. The deeper levels of faith in God and principles of morality are in jeopardy today; without establishing conviction on those levels, the Church's impact in resolving derivative issues can only be temporary and minimal.

If the ministry of the Church is to focus on what is necessary today to bring about the justice proper to inculturated evangelization, it seems necessary to look to the causes of violence in our society and the disintegration of the moral order. Publications of every social and religious persuasion are absorbed with this problem. Our society may not be more united than on the need to do something about the rampant violence that is tearing the world apart.

Gil Bailie tells us that the "world in which we live is in the grip of an anthropological crisis of unimaginable proportions." For Bailie, the moral and cultural unraveling of Western society is moving so fast that we are approaching "the abyss of uncontrollable violence."[48] This seems more than what a ministry of social justice would be able to address.

While some data show that violence is down in the United States among the adult population, there is still a serious problem of "homicide by young people of young people."[49]

Even the popular press is alert to the problem: We are "unwittingly destroying the fabric of our society," with the "daily carnage" that afflicts the young every day; "American children are 'terrorized' every day in almost every way."[50]

A 1995 meeting of the Connecticut Christian Conference board of directors concluded that "at its root the violence that is plaguing America's children is a spiritual issue." The conference admitted that "we have failed to commend effectively the teaching and example of Jesus to this generation of children and youth," and they called for an exploration of "new possibilities of evangelism of children and youth," so as to "reach out to them in creative ways that offer good news, instill Christian values and provide a sense of hope and belonging."[51]

The disintegration of the family and its values is not simply an American problem. A recent report from the Population Council in New York, entitled "Families in Focus," states that "trends like unwed motherhood, rising divorce rates, smaller households and the feminization of poverty are not unique to America, but are occurring worldwide."[52]

This is not a problem of social justice; it is a problem rooted in the failure of Western culture to accept, promote, and live by fundamental human and Christian values. Correcting this problem is the mission of inculturated evangelization. The Jesuit mission, therefore, could well refocus here, and in its teaching establishments, where structures are already in place, the Jesuit mission may best be used to promote the justice for which the world so desperately longs.

A NEW FORMULA FOR THE SOCIETY

A major insight of GC 34 was to define inculturated evangelization of the Gospel as the mission of the Society. This leads to the possibility of a clearer formulation of the Jesuit mission: "the service of the faith through the promotion of inculturated evangelization." If Jesuits share the mission of the Church (SCM 3 [24]), we should identify who we are by that mission.

In doing so, we must keep in mind the Society's statement that

> *the educational apostolate in all its ramifications, recommended in a special way by the Church in our day, is to be valued as of great importance among the ministries of the Society. . . . For this work, when carried out in the light of our mission, contributes greatly to "the total and integral liberation of the human person, leading to participation in the life of God himself."*[53]

As such, Jesuit education is not simply the inculturation of human values, as important as that is, nor even of Christian values, as necessary as that is, but the transmission of the experience of God's justification in the encounter with Jesus Christ. Paul VI clarified this point so well:

> *Evangelization will always contain—as the foundation, center and at the same time summit of its dynamism—a clear proclamation that, in Jesus Christ, the Son of God made man, who died and rose from the dead, salvation is offered to all men, as a gift of God's grace and mercy. . . . a transcendent and eschatological salvation, which indeed has its beginning in this life but which is fulfilled in eternity.*[54]

ENDNOTES • TRIPOLE

1. This account of the introductory process is taken largely from Michael Czerny, S.J., "Whence the Themes . . . ?" *CIS* 75 (1994): 4–9.
2. Ibid., 9.
3. These and all following excerpts from Father General's letter come from Peter-Hans Kolvenbach, S.J., "To the Whole Society: The 34th General Congregation," *Acta Romana Societatis Iesu* 20 (1994): 788–91.
4. Peter-Hans Kolvenbach, S.J., "To All Major Superiors," *National Jesuit News* (October 1993): 8.
5. Michael Czerny, S.J., "Challenges of Mission Today to Our Minima Societas," *CIS* 75 (1994): 10–19 at 10.
6. Cf. Martin R. Tripole, S.J., *Faith Beyond Justice: Widening the Perspective,* Series IV, 14: *Studies on Jesuit Topics* (St. Louis, Mo.: Institute of Jesuit Sources, 1994), ch. 1: "Jesuits Divided," 7–21.
7. "Our Mission Today: The Service of Faith and the Promotion of Justice," Decree 4 of the 32nd General Congregation of the Society of Jesus, in *Documents of the 31st and 32nd General Congregations of the Society of Jesus,* ed. John W. Padberg, S.J. (St. Louis, Mo.: Institute of Jesuit Sources, 1977), 411–38. All citations from these congregations are taken from this volume, with decree and paragraph from the decree noted in the text.
8. Much of the rest of the decree justifies this assertion with theological arguments, as well as arguments from Jesuit history and ecclesial statements. Discussion of all of these points is presented at length in Tripole, *Faith Beyond Justice.*
9. Cf. "Men for Others: Training Agents of Change for the Promotion of Justice," Father Pedro Arrupe's Address to the International Congress of Jesuit Alumni of Europe, Valencia, Spain, 31 July 1973, in Pedro Arrupe, S.J., *Justice with Faith Today, Selected Letters and Addresses II,* ed. Jerome Aixala, S.J. (St. Louis, Mo.: Institute of Jesuit Sources, 1980), 123–38. In this talk, Arrupe so strongly criticized alumni of Jesuit schools for their lack of concern for justice that the president of the group immediately resigned in protest.
10. Jean-Yves Calvez, S.J., *Faith and Justice: The Social Dimension of Evangelization,* trans. John E. Blewett, S.J. (St. Louis, Mo.: Institute of Jesuit Sources, 1991 [1985]).
11. Ibid., 26.
12. *Acta Romana Societatis Iesu* 14 (1966): 791; author's translation from original in Spanish; cf. Calvez, *Faith and Justice,* 27.
13. Calvez, *Faith and Justice,* 28.
14. Thomas Philip Faase, *Making the Jesuits More Modern* (Washington, D.C.: University Press of America, 1981).
15. Ibid., 54–60.
16. John W. Padberg, S.J., "The Society True to Itself: A Brief History of the 32nd General Congregation of the Society of Jesus (December 2, 1974–March 7, 1975)," *Studies in the Spirituality of Jesuits* 15/3–4 (May–September 1983): 20–26.

17. Ibid., 26.

18. Pedro Arrupe, S.J., "To a Certain Provincial Superior," *Acta Romana Societatis Iesu* 16 (1976): 1097–98.

19. Pedro Arrupe, S.J., "Report of Father General on the State of the Society," 27 September 1978, *Acta Romana Societatis Iesu* 17 (1978): 451–80, nn. 8–10 at 455–56.

20. Ibid., 455.

21. Arrupe is citing Vatican II, *Apostolicam Actuositatem* 7. Note that Vatican II understands justice here as the justice of God and not human forms of it.

22. Pedro Arrupe, S.J., *Witnessing to Justice* (Vatican City: Pontifical Commission Justice and Peace, 1972), 41; reprinted in Arrupe, *Justice with Faith Today,* 79–120. This publication appears to have been the important talk that Arrupe gave before the bishops at the 1971 Synod; cf. Faase, *Making the Jesuits More Modern,* 55, and Calvez, *Faith and Justice,* 27.

23. Arrupe, "Men for Others," 130–32.

24. These three aspects of justice were experienced within the covenant or treaty relationship of love and fidelity between God (Yahweh) and his people, or among human beings as a lived expression of that covenant relationship within the community.

    According to J. P. M. Walsh, S.J., the justice that was exercised by God's people toward others (what I am calling the second aspect of justice) was a reflection of the justice that they experienced from their life of friendship with God (the first aspect). The polity of Israel (the second aspect) represented the acceptance of a "vision and form of life," which Israel knew in its allegiance to and recognition of the sovereignty or justice of God (the first aspect). The justice of God was exercised in life by "concern for the other," by responding to the cry of the poor, the needy, and the powerless (the third aspect). See J. P. M. Walsh, S.J., *The Mighty from Their Thrones* (Philadelphia: Fortress, 1987), 61–63, 179, 174.

    Scriptural texts support the existence and meaning of each of these three aspects of justice:

    (1) The transcendent conception of justice as God's justification of his people. More recently, Scripture scholars refer to this understanding of God's justice as his righteousness or uprightness, but all four terms are roughly equivalent. See Raymond E. Brown, S.S., *An Introduction to the New Testament* (New York: Doubleday, 1997), 576. This justice has its origins in the Hebrew Scriptures, where it is the "quality" of God "whereby he acquits his people, manifesting toward them his gracious salvific activity in a just judgment." This is the basis for Paul's understanding of justice: he "sees God providing a new mode of salvation for humanity as justification by grace through faith in Christ Jesus—as a part of his plan of salvation history." See Joseph A. Fitzmyer, S.J., "Pauline Theology," in *The New Jerome Biblical Commentary*, ed. Raymond E. Brown, S.S. et al. (Englewood Cliffs, N.J.: Prentice Hall, 1990), 82:39; cf. also Brown's New Testament study, 565. Scholars find this understanding of God's justice thoroughly explicitated in Romans; for example 3:21–26, where the *New American Bible* (New York: Catholic, 1992) explains the justice or righteousness as "Divine mercy" whereby God "declares the guilty innocent, and makes them so. God does this . . . through forgiveness of their sins, in virtue of the redemption wrought in Christ Jesus for all who believe." For further scriptural use of this concept of justice, cf. Gen 15:6; Ps passim, for example 98:1; Is passim, especially 11:5; 30:18; 45:8; 56:1; Heb 2:4; Lk 18:14; Rom 1:17.

    (2) Justice as a comprehensive force of transformation of history through the activity of God's justified: explicitated especially in Rom 12:1–13:14. NAB commentary: in this text Paul "explains how Christians can function, in the light of the gift of justification through faith, in their relation to one another and the state," and under 12:1–8: Christians "present their *bodies as a living sacrifice*" and "are liberated for the exercise of good judgment as they are confronted with the many and varied decisions required in the course of daily life." Brown sees Rom 12–14 as made up of Paul's "suggestions to the Roman Christians about how they should live in response to the mercy of God," in their "different gifts/charisms, among which are prophecy and *teaching,* and an emphasis on love" (*Introduction to the New Testament,* 571; emphasis added). Cf. Is 42:4–7; 1 Cor 12:4–11; Eph 4:1–7, 11–12; 5; 1 Pt 4:11.

    (3) Justice as social righteous action toward the economically poor and politically marginalized or oppressed.

In the Hebrew Scriptures, God is known as the protector of the poor, which motivates his people to do the same. According to John Donahue, S.J., concern for justice toward the powerless and the poor is rooted in Israel's reflection on the events of salvation history, such as the Exodus and the covenant at Sinai. The laws of Israel, such as the Deuteronomic legislation of Dt 12–26, show that for Israel, "religious belief must be translated into law and custom which guide life in community and protect the vulnerable." Indeed, for Israel, how the community treated the marginal was the "touchstone of 'right relationship' to God." See John R. Donahue, S.J., "What Does the Lord Require?: A Bibliographical Essay on the Bible and Social Justice," *Studies in the Spirituality of Jesuits* 25/2 (March 1993): 19–25 at 25.

The incompleteness of the biblical understanding of justice without social justice is forcefully presented by S. C. Mott, who notes that "God's saving concerns" include "the morality of the social order," and not merely "the salvation of individuals or small groups of individuals." When the New Testament speaks of the reign of God, it "sums up the hope of the Old Testament" that would include not only a "new relationship of faith and obedience to God but a new social order." According to Mott, Jesus' words and actions "challenged the whole social order," including the "inequalities of status" or social position in society, and thus called for the establishment of "a new age." See S. C. Mott, "The Use of the New Testament for Social Ethics," *The Journal of Religious Ethics* 15/2 (Fall 1987): 225–60 at 230–31, 236. Cf. Is 11:4; Jer 21:11, 22:3,16; Prov 31:9; Dt 10:18, 16:18–20.

25. This is the founding document of the Society of Jesus, written largely by Ignatius of Loyola and his first companions in 1539. It formulated the basic code, rule, and way of living for the new group, and serves as the measure for all Jesuit apostolic activity. In 1540, it was incorporated into a papal bull by Paul III, which established the Society of Jesus as a religious institute of priests, and was only slightly modified and given its final form in a bull by Julius III in 1550. Because this rule, or formula, was incorporated into papal bulls, it can never be modified by the Jesuits without papal approval.

26. "Allocution of Pope John Paul II, 5 January 1995," in John L. McCarthy, S.J., ed., *Documents of the Thirty-Fourth General Congregation of the Society of Jesus* (St. Louis, Mo.: Institute of Jesuit Sources, 1995), Appendix 1, 247–54 at 249, n. 4.

27. Ibid., 250, n.5.

28. Ibid., 252–53, n.7.

29. Ibid., 250, n.4.

30. Ibid., 252, n.7.

31. These include an introductory decree and four decrees on "Our Mission." They are as follows:
    Decree 1: Introduction: United with Christ on Mission (UCM)
    Decree 2: Servants of Christ's Mission (SCM)
    Decree 3: Our Mission and Justice (OMJ)
    Decree 4: Our Mission and Culture (OMC)
    Decree 5: Our Mission and Interreligious Dialogue (OMID)
    References to decrees will be made in the text, as in SCM 4 [25], where the first number is the paragraph from the decree, and the second the continuing paragraph in the total volume of decrees.

32. SCM also stresses that the mission of the Society is to serve the faith (SCM 11 [36]). OMJ admits among Jesuit "failures" in the last twenty years that "justice has sometimes been separated from its wellspring of faith" (2 [51]).

33. In a letter written to me 18 September 1995 (and used here with permission), the Reverend John McDade, S.J., a delegate at the Congregation from the British Province, explained that the use of justice "in the final paragraphs of *Servants* [SCM]" is dependent on the thinking of Bernard Lonergan, even to the point of borrowing certain expressions from him. An editorial of McDade's in *The Month* 28 (May 1995): 170–73 also affirms this point.

The dependence is found in Lonergan's conjunction of faith in God with efforts to change the world. For Lonergan, it is only through faith in God that a foundation is established for overcoming the world's evil. The change is effected "by the charity of the suffering servant, by self-sacrificing love." See Bernard Lonergan, *Method in Theology* (Toronto: University of Toronto, 1994 [1971]), 117; cf. SCM 13 [38]. For

Lonergan, faith and "human progress" go together: "To promote either is to promote the other indirectly." In faith, the human person finds the knowledge, love, and power of God not only to resist social decline and decay, but to construct structures of freedom that redound to human good as well as to the glory of God (ibid.). It is this understanding of faith, which is real only when it is activated by the grace of God through Christ to transform human culture, that lies at the root of the understanding of justice in SCM.

As I understand the use of justice in the final paragraphs of SCM and its roots in Lonergan, it is consistent with the three aspects of justice as I outline them in this article.

34. See Charles M. Murphy, "Action for Justice as Constitutive of the Preaching of the Gospel: What Did the 1971 Synod Mean?" *Theological Studies* 44 (June 1983): 298–311. I examine this issue at length in *Faith Beyond Justice*, 45–49.

35. Tripole, *Faith Beyond Justice*, 52–54.

36. Avery Dulles, S.J. "Faith, Justice, and the Jesuit Mission," in *Assembly 1989: Jesuit Ministry in Higher Education* (Washington, D.C.: Jesuit Conference, 1990), 19–25 at 23–24.

37. Ibid., 22.

38. Decree 4 had listed all of these activities as well (4:17), but never explained precisely where in these activities lay warrant for its concept of the promotion of justice. Since its understanding of justice was largely social justice, only the *Formula*'s reference to "works of charity" was able to provide this foundation. Calvez understands it this way in his own defense of Decree 4 (Calvez, *Faith and Justice*, 123–26). The problem then was: how could justice as a work of charity, listed in last place among the activities of the Society, be made normative for all apostolic life?

39. In case there be any doubt about the acceptability of all Jesuit ministries in the apostolate of the Society, Decree 6: "The Jesuit Priest: Ministerial Priesthood and Jesuit Identity" makes it clear: "In the light of our tradition, we can say that no ministry which prepares the way for the Kingdom or which helps to arouse faith in the Gospel is outside the scope of Jesuit priests" (15 [172]).

40. Part of the reason for this is that the decree on justice was put together by a committee completely separate from the committee that wrought consistency among the three other decrees on mission (Decrees 2, 4, and 5).

41. Only in Decree 7: "The Jesuit Brother" (2 [196]) and Decree 14: "Jesuits and the Situation of Women in Church and Civil Society" (8 [368]) is there an explicit affirmation of our mission as the service of faith in which the promotion of justice is an absolute requirement. But in neither case is there discussion of the meaning of justice, nor are theological implications drawn.

42. Twice OMC asserts that culture can also do something for the Gospel: "culture brings something new to the richness of the Gospel" (2 [76]); and the Gospel can "be seen in a new light: its meaning is enriched, renewed, even transformed by what these cultures bring to it" (13 [97]).

43. One of the delegates to the congregation has written that GC 34 may be understood as "more inclusive" than GC 32 because, with the crucial role it has given to culture, it provides a "more obvious place for traditional Jesuit apostolates like educational institutions, parishes and retreat houses, which specialise in the promotion of evangelical values." See Gerry O'Hanlon, S.J., "Jesuits Renewed for Mission," *Tablet* 249 (8 April 1995): 473–74.

44. Kolvenbach's final statement to the press, March 22, 1995, by e-mail.

45. Walter M. Abbott, S.J., ed., *The Documents of Vatican II* (New York: Guild, 1966), 504. Cf. also *Lumen Gentium* 31 (57–58):

> But the laity, by their very vocation, seek the kingdom of God by engaging in temporal affairs and by ordering them according to the plan of God. They live in the world, that is, in each and in all of the secular professions and occupations. They live in the ordinary circumstances of family and social life, from which the very web of their existence is woven.
>
> They are called there by God so that by exercising their proper function and being led by the spirit of the gospel they can work for the sanctification of the world from within, in the manner of leaven.

46. In this respect, Decree 13's statement that Jesuits "must increasingly shift the focus of [their] attention from the exercise of [their] own direct ministry to the strengthening of laity in their mission" (19 [353])

seems to create certain problems, perhaps unforeseen, at the time of the Congregation: (1) Why would the Jesuit delegates focus so much attention upon inculturation and the social action ministries as if these were direct ministries of the Society, if the focus of their attention should be shifting to how they might strengthen the mission of the laity? (2) Why would prospective members to religious institutes such as the Society of Jesus spend years in training for the ordained priesthood, only to be told, after ordination, that the focus of their attention must now shift to strengthening the apostolate of the lay state from which they had just come? and (3) Many of the essays in this volume will show how much Jesuits recognize the importance of their role in education in fostering the ministries of inculturation and social justice among the laity. Nevertheless, by making the promotion of these apostolates so distinctive of their own mission, Jesuits may not be stressing this role enough, thereby weakening the laity's perception of their own distinctive ministry in the life of the Church.

47. David O'Brien, "American Culture Key to Understanding Lay Shifts," *National Catholic Reporter,* 8 October 1993, 30–31 at 31.

48. Gil Bailie, *Violence Unveiled: Humanity at the Crossroads* (New York: Crossroad, 1995), 4, 25, 259.

49. Marie Simonetti Rosen, "Professor Alfred Blumstein of Carnegie Mellon University: A LEN Interview," *Law Enforcement News* (30 April 1995): 10–13 at 10.

50. Claude Lewis, "Terrorizing of Children Beyond Oklahoma City," *Philadelphia Inquirer,* 24 May 1995, A13.

51. Connecticut Christian Conference, "Gun Violence Against Children and Youth," *Origins* 25 (25 May 1995): 17, 19–21 at 17 and 20. According to the conference, "homicide is the second leading cause of death for children 10–14 years of age" (19).

52. Tamar Lewin, "Family Decay Global, Study Says," *New York Times,* 30 May 1995, A5.

53. John W. Padberg, S.J., gen. ed., *The Constitutions of the Society of Jesus and Their Complementary Norms* (St. Louis, Mo.: Institute of Jesuit Sources, 1996), Norms 277; citing GC 32, Decree 2:11.

54. Paul VI, *Evangelii Nuntiandi* 27 (On Evangelization in the Modern World), (Washington, D.C.: USCC, 1976).

The Mill and the Old Mill Stream:
A View from the Deanery

J. Robert Barth, S.J.

ABSTRACT

Changes in society and in the Society have given us new challenges: peace and justice, diversity issues, internationalization, interreligious dialogue, collaboration with the laity in ministry, the empowerment of women, information technology and communication, and the environment. In all these areas, Jesuit colleges and universities can respond in important ways, through creative initiatives and innovative programming, to the needs of the Church and the world.

> *"D'ye think th' colledges has much to do with th' progress iv th' wurruld?"*
> *asked Mr. Hennessey.*
> *"D'ye think," said Mr. Dooley, "'tis the mill that makes the wather run?"*

The wisdom of Peter Finley Dunne and his Mr. Dooley is hardly known today, much less honored, but the above thoughtful exchange might help to keep us from getting above ourselves. The power of colleges and universities to influence the world has sometimes been wildly overestimated. And yet, for those of us who are true believers in higher education, hope occasionally dims but is never quite extinguished—even in these turbulent times that have been called "postmodern."

Let's not underestimate the difficulties, though. Living in times when the pace of change is faster than it has ever been, when all stable values seem to be called into question, some of us may feel that the reassuring stability of the *Ratio Studiorum* is only a distant and largely irrelevant memory. In fact, I might well have begun these reflections on GC 34 from the dean's office with a warning from the pilot: "Ladies and gentlemen, please fasten your seat belts, as there may be some turbulence ahead." Or, to translate it from airline-speak into something more candid: "Hang on, folks, we're in for a rough ride."

Well, perhaps. More stately, though, and I believe more accurate, would be Cardinal Newman's dictum from his celebrated *Essay on the Development of Christian Doctrine:* "In a higher world it is otherwise, but here below to live is to change, and to be perfect is to have changed often."[1] God knows Jesuit higher education in the United States is not perfect, but we're alive and therefore changing. We've certainly changed often in the past, and it has usually been for the better. We opened our classical curriculum to business and the professions late in the nineteenth century, and the result has been generations of Jesuit-trained business executives, doctors, lawyers, and teachers who have brought to their work a deeper awareness of ethical values and social responsibility. We embraced the social sciences early in this century, and so contributed to society an army of people dedicated to social work, community service, and public life. Later in the century we opened the doors of our colleges and universities to women, and thus enriched not only society and the professions but our own institutions with the gifts of countless remarkable women who are at last finding their proper place in the life of the community and the nation.

But GC 34 tells us—not just us in higher education, but the whole Society—that the modern world offers us new challenges. In my reading of the documents of GC 34, these challenges are most sharply focused in the call of Decree 3: "Our Mission and Justice" (OMJ): "In response to the Second Vatican Council, we, the Society of Jesus, set out on a journey of faith as we committed ourselves to the promotion of justice as an integral part of our mission" (1 [50]). As it is expressed in Decree 2: "Servants of Christ's Mission" (SCM), there is "no service of faith without promotion of justice" (19 [47]).

The needs seem to be all around us. The natural environment is violated daily by the careless excesses of industry and business. The poor, in our own cities and around the world, call out for food and shelter and education. Refugees in many lands seek a home, and even in our own country many are homeless. Racial and ethnic prejudice still dominates the life of many countries, and festers even in our own. Whole classes of people are marginalized in society, whether because of age, social condition, religious tradition, or sexual orientation. Women still struggle to win an equal place in society, and the economic divide between rich and poor grows wider every day. We have no need to search for injustices to fight against; they're all around us.

But what can the colleges and universities do in the face of all these needs? "D'ye think 'tis the mill that makes the wather run?" No doubt Mr. Dooley is right, but the miller can in some measure direct the course of the stream, control the force of its flow, harness its energy and put it to use. The grain will at last become flour and the flour, bread.

Postmodern Changes Influencing Higher Education

A helpful preliminary question is, I think, what in the complex equation of postmodernity has changed that would affect our ministry in higher education? GC 34 offers us, in some detail, an answer to this question.

One significant change has been in the Society itself. As Decrees 1 through 3 make clear, the Society has been called in modern times to return to an important dimension of our original charism. Decree 2 points back directly to the *Formula of the Institute,* with its insistence on the service of faith as the aim of our mission. But there can be no genuine "service of faith" without the "promotion of justice" (SCM 15 [40]). GC 34 makes its own the words of GC 32: "The service of faith and the promotion of justice . . . must be the integrating factor of all our ministries" (SCM 14 [39]). Decree 3 then spells out eloquently the needs of the world for justice, underscoring the calls of previous congregations: "working for peace and reconciliation through non-violence; working to end discrimination against people based on race, religion, gender, ethnic background, or social class; working to counter growing poverty and hunger while material prosperity becomes ever more concentrated" (OMJ 5 [54]). But it goes on to point to "other dimensions of this struggle for justice," especially "the growing international consciousness of the full range of *human rights,*" including "economic and social rights to the basic necessities of life and well-being; personal rights such as freedom of conscience and expression and the right to practice and share one's faith; civil and political rights to participate fully and freely in the processes of society; and rights such as development, peace, and a healthy environment" (OMJ 6 [55]). The consciousness not only of the Society of Jesus, but of the world, about injustice is perhaps higher than it has ever been.

The Society has also become, as Decree 2 points out, "a body more diverse than ever before" (SCM 2 [16]), and the composition of the Congregation itself—drawn from every corner of the world—heightens "our awareness of the diversity of cultures in both the world and the Society" (Decree 4: "Our Mission and Culture" [OMC] 1 [75]). Thus the brilliant and moving document on "Our Mission and Culture" challenges us to use these newly diverse resources to bring the values of the Gospel to bear on the needs of different societies throughout the world. The notion of "inculturation" has rarely been so clearly and eloquently articulated: "The process of inculturating the Gospel of Jesus Christ within human culture is a form of *incarnation* of the Word of God in all the diversity of human experience. . . . When the Word of God becomes embedded in the heart of a culture, it is like a buried seed which draws its nourishment from the earth around it and grows to maturity" (OMC 3 [77]). This respect for the particularities of an individual culture is both a challenge and a resource for us.

A related development has been the Society's—and the world's—increasing awareness of the international dimension of our problems and our resources. Decree 3 points to the international character of the problems we face in the pursuit of justice, while Decree 21, on "Interprovincial and Supraprovincial Cooperation" (ISC), suggests how the Society can use its international network to work together to address these problems.

Still another crucial development is the dramatic call for interreligious dialogue in Decree 5: "Our Mission and Interreligious Dialogue" (OMID), building on the strong foundation of Vatican II and the encyclicals of John Paul II: "General Congregation 34 encourages all Jesuits to move beyond prejudice and bias, be it historical, cultural, social, or theological, in order to cooperate wholeheartedly with all men and women of goodwill in promoting peace, justice, harmony, human rights, and respect for all of God's creation" (OMID 2 [129]). Particular mention is made of our relationship with Judaism (which holds a special place because of our "shared history"), with Islam, with Hinduism, and with Buddhism, while the phenomenon of fundamentalism in many religions, including Christianity, calls for special openness, patience, and sensitivity.

Two of the most compelling documents of GC 34—and arguably among the most relevant for higher education—are Decree 13: "Cooperation with the Laity in Mission" (CLM), and Decree 14: "Jesuits and the Situation of Women in Church and Civil Society" (JSW). GC 34 accepts the now common prediction that the Church of the new millennium will be called "the Church of the Laity." Our role, therefore, is to work in solidarity with the laity as they fulfill their mission in the world, responding to "the call to ministry flowing from the grace received in baptism" (CLM 1 [331]). Jesuits are called, after all, to be (in the words of Father General Kolvenbach) not only "men *for* others" but "men *with* others" (CLM 4 [334]). The splendid document on women, perhaps because it was the least expected, caused the greatest public comment in both the religious and secular press, and has already evoked a high level of dialogue on Jesuit college and university campuses.

One of the most striking changes in this "postmodern" world is in the arena of communication and information technology, where change is measured in weeks rather than years and time in nanoseconds. Decree 15: "Communication: A New Culture" (CNC) is a modest document that barely touches the surface of this complex cultural reality. While it does point to some of the dangers inherent in the new electronic media and the "information revolution," it does not do justice to the new possibilities for good in these new tools. Clearly, though, this is an area in which Jesuit colleges and universities, like every institution of higher education, are already deeply engaged.

Finally, in the briefest of all the documents, Decree 20: "Ecology" (EC), GC 34 recommends to Father General the study of a matter increasingly and urgently of concern to the world today. We look forward to the results of this study, which are to be communicated to the Society to help us set a course in response to the dramatic and urgent environmental needs we face as stewards of God's creation.

Clearly, ours is a far different world—in its problems and in its possibilities—even from the world of GC 32 in 1975, much less Ignatius' world of the sixteenth century.

However, the spirit of the Society is the same: flexible, alert to changing times, open to the needs of God's people—especially needs not being met by others. As Jerome Nadal wrote in his journal soon after Ignatius' death, "The Society has the care of those souls for whom either there is nobody to care for or, if somebody ought to care, the care is negligent. This is the reason for the founding of the Society. This is its strength. This is its dignity in the Church."[2] And to this end, from very early in its history, the Society's institutions of learning had a unique role to play. As John O'Malley observes, "The schools inserted them [the Jesuits] into secular culture and civic responsibility to a degree unknown to earlier orders."[3]

The Role of the Dean in Higher Education

I must come at last to the question most pertinent to me: what is the role of a dean in all this? Is the view from the deanery different from that of any other window in our ivory tower? In Trollope's Barchester novels, the deanery tended to be an office rather more quaint and eccentric than energetic and effective. Let me explain first, then, how I conceive the place of the dean—in my case, that of an arts and sciences dean—in a Jesuit institution.

One common faculty perception is, I suspect, that the proper job of the dean is to pay the bills and stay out of the way. Some deans try to do more than that—so goes this view—but if they do they're overstepping the bounds. Having been a faculty member for over twenty-five years, in secular and Jesuit institutions, I can understand this perception. In my view, however, the dean is—at least ideally—a faculty member who has a special leadership role to play among his colleagues; a member of the administration, the dean remains at the same time a member of the faculty. The faculty appointment the dean commonly holds is not merely an insurance policy in case of burnout or meltdown; whether the dean routinely teaches or not, this faculty status has symbolic significance. It is important that the dean is both management and labor.

What then does the academic dean in fact do? The dean is of course a manager, who has responsibility for such tasks as hiring, approving budgets, setting salaries, supervising curriculum and other academic programs, and generally assuring that faculty and staff have what they need to do their work and that students receive the advising and other academic services they reasonably expect. In this way, the dean is primarily an "enabler" for the academic community he or she serves.

But the dean needs to be a "prompter" and a "cheerleader" as well. Occasionally the dean needs to play the sheepdog, nipping at the heels of recalcitrant or laggard members of the flock, urging them on to better efforts; more often the role is that of cheerleader, recognizing and encouraging the accomplishments of colleagues.

At times the dean is an initiator of new ideas, whether for programs or research or curricular changes. At other times the dean can recognize and nurture the ideas of faculty members, department chairs, or administrative colleagues. Creativity and openness to change are, to my mind, among the hallmarks of the successful arts and sciences dean.

It is perhaps through these latter qualities—creativity and openness to change—that academic deans at American Jesuit colleges and universities will be most influenced by GC 34. However, in all of his or her roles the dean can exercise considerable influence in making the ideals of the Congregation a lived reality in our academic communities.

But none of us—whether president, dean, campus minister, professor, or any other member of an academic community in a Jesuit institution—lives and works in the abstract. Our academic careers are in very particular institutions: some large, some small, some regional in their constituency, some national; some exclusively undergraduate, others with extensive graduate and professional schools; geographically diverse, from Seattle to Mobile, from Los Angeles to Boston. It would be foolhardy to try to generalize about such a rich and diverse array of institutions, each with its own history and traditions, each with a particularized mission within the overarching rubric of Jesuit higher education. I write out of my own experience at one of these institutions, Boston College, in the hope that my reflections will find resonances with the experience of colleagues in other places. Let me only add that my reflections will include not only what I have done myself but what my view from the Dean's Office tells me about how Boston College has addressed, or is trying to address, the issues of GC 34.

Let me approach this complex reality in the order in which I sketched out the principal concerns of GC 34: greater awareness of justice issues, such as poverty, violence, discrimination, and human rights; a new consciousness of diversity in the human community; internationalization; interreligious dialogue; the new role of the laity; the status of women; advances in communication and technology; and environmental problems in our stewardship of creation.

Justice

Serious attention to issues of justice has, of course, always been part of a Boston College education, as it has been at every Jesuit institution. Ever since Father Kolvenbach's visit to Boston College some ten years ago, however, this concern has been given new and sharper focus. Our institution—like so many others he has visited over the years—has taken to heart his challenge to "educate men and women for others." This motto has, for most of us here, been set side by side with Boston College's founding motto "Ever to excel."

One of the most distinctive programs that focuses on such concerns—the PULSE Program—was founded over twenty-five years ago under the leadership of Father Joseph Flanagan and Professor Patrick Byrne. A yearlong, twelve-credit course grounded in the philosophy and theology departments, it begins in the classroom, typically with such philosophers as Plato and Aristotle as they address issues of justice, then the challenge of the Old Testament and the Gospels, continuing perhaps with Augustine and Aquinas, and moving on to more modern considerations of the just person and the just society. Once the semester is well begun, after five or six weeks, each student (typically they are freshmen and sophomores) then goes out into a prearranged placement in a service agency—one of some forty with whom we cooperate throughout the greater Boston area—to work for about ten hours a week. It might be a soup kitchen, a halfway house for ex-prisoners, a retirement home, or an inner-city tutorial program, but what is important is that it is hands-on work with people in need. They come to know not only those in need, but also the professionals who serve them. In the light of this experience, students then return to the classroom to reflect together on what they have seen and learned—and on how their experience might effect their lives: the decisions they make, the careers they are preparing for, the roles they will play in their families and in society. PULSE is invariably, for some three hundred students each year, a life-changing experience.

Our Faith, Peace, Justice Program is an interdisciplinary minor for undergraduates, consisting of a six-course sequence, usually taken during junior and senior years. Grounded deeply in theology and philosophy, it also draws on the expertise of such departments as political science and economics. Although it does not include the hands-on dimension of PULSE, it is a solid academic experience, culminating in a senior seminar and a lengthy research project that has the merit of focusing a student's academic work during senior year on the relationship between one's faith and the crucial issues of peace and justice.

A more recent program that includes issues of social responsibility, now six years old, is the Capstone Program for seniors begun by Professor James Weiss of the theology department. It is a one-semester seminar that allows students during their final year to try to integrate what they have learned, especially in the light of how they go about making ethical decisions important for their future lives: about family, careers, their responsibility to society, and their relationship with God.

In addition to these special programs, other dimensions of our curriculum touch importantly on issues of justice. As in other Jesuit institutions, our core curriculum includes two semesters of theology, during which such concerns have an important place, and two semesters of "Philosophy of the Person." Here, and elsewhere in the core curriculum and in the majors, social justice concerns are being given increasing prominence. One of the dean's responsibilities is to encourage this attention and to support it in such practical ways as staffing and funding.

Other important programs at Boston College have been in support of research on issues of justice. Most visibly, the Jesuit Institute—founded by the Jesuit community as a research center of the university and headed first by Father Robert Daly and now by Father

Michael Buckley—has for the past eight years addressed many of the interfaces of faith and culture, giving special attention to such issues as poverty, the Holocaust, the AIDS crisis, inequities in health care, and the role of women in society. A more recent research center established only a year ago is the Center for Child, Family, and Community Partnerships. Drawing on the resources of all the schools of the university, including education, law, nursing, and social work, as well as arts and sciences, the CCFCP has as its mission to establish working relationships with the community outside the university, and to integrate the services—especially the research resources—that the university can offer the community. Another proposed research center, growing out of theology department initiatives, is a Center for the Study of Religion and Public Policy.

Such initiatives as these, both in curriculum and in research, are of course typical of what one can expect to find in any Jesuit college or university. Although there is much more we can do to implement GC 34's challenges to justice, the commitment is clearly deep, and the path has already been set.

Diversity

Like all colleges and universities throughout the United States, Jesuit institutions have been struggling with the issue of diversity, whether racial, ethnic, or cultural. Boston College has had its share of racial unrest among students, which has been echoed in the more temperate but very real concern of faculty members. This unrest springs out of genuine and deeply felt idealism and concern, not simply out of anger. GC 34 is clear in its mandate to the Society to deal with these concerns openly and compassionately, and to seek to "inculturate" ourselves and our institutions into the many cultures reflected in our society in a spirit of openness and respect. The temptation is of course to retreat into the familiar world of our own past experience in education, whether it take the form of religious conservatism or the canonical texts of "Western civilization." But to do so is to cut oneself off from much that is valuable, much that reflects the working of God's spirit. One can preserve the cherished traditions of the past without hardening them into dogma or viewing them as the sole reality that shapes our lives. We are called to be open to the cultural experience of African Americans, Hispanics, Asian Americans, Native Americans, and others. GC 34 reminds us that "whether we are working in our own culture or in another, as servants of the Gospel we must not impose our own cultural structures, but witness to the creativity of the Spirit which is also at work in others" (OMC 27 [114]).

Some twenty years ago, a Boston College African American student coined the acronym AHANA—representing African American, Hispanic, Asian American, and Native American—for a campus organization that would try to raise the awareness of the whole academic community about the riches of some of the diverse traditions represented here. AHANA has become over the years a respected and effective symbol of the university's commitment to respect and attend to the diversity among us. Happily, many other initiatives have followed: the Black Studies Program is well established and flourishing; Asian Studies offers a solid interdisciplinary minor; and a strong Latin American Studies minor has recently been added to the curriculum.

In addition, during the most recent study of our core curriculum, the faculty introduced a one-semester "cultural diversity" requirement, a course to be chosen from an approved list of courses in departments across the College of Arts and Sciences. As philosopher Martha Nussbaum writes in her splendid new book, *Cultivating Humanity: A Classical Defense of Reform in Liberal Education,* "it seems sensible for students to be required to study in some depth one non-Western culture . . . and from a group of courses designed to awaken conversation and reflection across cultural boundaries."[4] A modest requirement, to be sure, but meant to raise the consciousness of students about cultures and worlds other than their own. It is, at least, a beginning, though we still have admittedly far to go.

We continue to struggle at Boston College, as do other institutions, with the recruitment of AHANA students and faculty. The commitment is strong and genuine, but it is a difficult task. We have had some success with the recruitment of AHANA students—though admittedly we need to do even better—but less success with faculty. The pool in many academic areas is small, and we are all fishing in the same waters. I urge that Jesuit schools, without giving up on the recruitment effort, follow the model of institutions that emphasize attracting AHANA students into our graduate programs, in order to increase in the long term the pool of prospective faculty members available to us all.

Internationalism

The Congregation's call to take advantage of the Society's international character is insistent and unambiguous: "To exploit more fully the possibilities given us by being an international body, additional global and regional networks must be created. Such networks of persons and institutions should be capable of addressing global concerns through support, sharing of information, planning, and evaluation, or through implementation of projects that cannot easily be carried out within province structures" (ISC 14 [446]). We have made a beginning, but much remains to be done. At Boston College, for example, we have now established some forty overseas faculty- and student-exchange programs, including a dozen or so with Jesuit universities abroad, but some of them are still in their infancy. We have also begun to strengthen the infrastructure that supports them: an International Studies minor; several area studies programs, such as Irish Studies, Germanic Studies, and Latin American Studies; intensive language study; and an integrated International Studies office. Our near-term goal is for 25 percent of our undergraduate student body to have an experience of international education. Meanwhile, the number of our students coming from abroad has risen significantly, and our campus programs in support of them are strong.

The university aims as well to find ways to internationalize our research capability. In pursuit of this goal Professor Philip Altbach, a specialist in international education, has inaugurated a new Center for International Higher Education, whose stated goal is to connect universities across international boundaries, with a particular emphasis on Jesuit colleges and universities around the world. The center's *Journal of International Education* is only one of the means it will use to establish an effective network among Jesuit colleges and universities in pursuit of our common goals. Through such initiatives as this, American Jesuit institutions can hope to develop what GC 34 envisions: "networks of specialists who differ in expertise and perspectives but who share a common concern, as well as . . . networks of university departments, research centers, scholarly journals, and regional advocacy groups" (ISC 14 [446]). International education is beyond question one of the areas identified by GC 34 that is most open to imagination and experiment. As Decree 21 remarks, "In many respects, the future of international cooperation remains largely uncharted" (ISC 14 [447]).

Interreligious Dialogue

Given the religious background of so many of the conflicts that have riven countries throughout this century—places like India and Pakistan, Northern Ireland, Bosnia, Rwanda, Israel, and a host of others—it is not surprising that one of the most deeply felt documents of GC 34 is Decree 5: "Our Mission and Interreligious Dialogue." The question is an urgent one: "How do we respond to the racism, cultural prejudice, religious fundamentalism, and intolerance that mark so much of today's world?" (OMID 1 [128]).

On one level, Boston College's response is symbolized by the work of the Jesuit Institute, one of whose goals is precisely to address such issues by bringing together scholars, both local and from other institutions, for discussion of the interrelationships of faith and culture. In this, the theology department has had a leading role, especially as it has moved in recent years to expand its purview to take in the serious study of Judaism, Buddhism and other Eastern religions, and Islam. Another crucial need, however, is that of our undergraduate students. The theology department has significantly revised its core offerings to include a two-semester track called "The Religious Quest," which offers students the opportunity to study not only the history of Christianity but the central tenets of such world religions as Judaism, Buddhism, and Islam. As Martha Nussbaum remarks in *Cultivating Humanity*, "some understanding of the major world religions" is "of such fundamental importance to all political and economic interactions with the world's varied cultures that we simply cannot afford to have citizens who are ignorant of Islam, or Hinduism, or Buddhist and Confucian traditions."[5]

Even deeper, beyond the very real needs of "good citizenship," is the challenge of GC 34 "to cooperate wholeheartedly with all men and women of goodwill in promoting peace, justice, harmony, human rights, and respect for all of God's creation. This is to be done especially through dialogue with those who are inspired by religious commitment, or who share a sense of transcendence that opens them to universal values" (OMID 2 [129]).

Laity

Nothing can be more crucial for the future of Jesuit institutions of higher education than our collaboration with the laity. First of all, the demographics of the Society, as we all know, have made us more and more reliant on our lay colleagues to continue our ministry in education. In this we share in the situation of the Church itself, as the Congregation makes clear, in that we are all being called to enter the "age of the laity" that is already upon us. Nor need we lament this historical development; many among us celebrate this call of the laity to new roles of service as providential, a movement of the Spirit.

It is perhaps salutary for us to remember that this collaboration with the laity is no new phenomenon for the Society. In *The First Jesuits,* John O'Malley underscores the importance of this shared ministry in the early Society: "The extent to which the early Jesuits engaged the laity, especially young people, in helping them in their catechesis is striking. They seem altogether innocent of any concern that it should be reserved to priests, pastors, or members of religious orders."[6] The Society has yielded control of many aspects of our ministry in higher education—through lay boards of trustees, the appointment of lay people in important administrative positions, lay faculty increasingly exercising control over curricular decisions, and the like. I like to think we have done so not simply out of necessity but because our colleagues are eminently worthy of our respect and trust.

It remains incumbent on Jesuits, though, to do everything we can to pass along to our lay collaborators the spirit of the Society and the ideals of Jesuit education, if our institutions are to remain true to our Jesuit and Catholic heritage. There are two neuralgic issues, it seems to me: hiring and development.

First of all, I believe, we must find ways—difficult though it may be—to take into account in the hiring process, especially for faculty, not only research excellence, teaching ability, and general collegiality, but the likelihood that this person will contribute in some way to the mission of the institution. What I have in mind is not some Catholic litmus test, whether of orthodoxy or practice, but a discernment about the qualities of mind and spirit a candidate brings: awareness of the values of the institution, openness to the legitimate religious interests and concerns of students and colleagues, willingness to engage in dialogue on some of the interfaces of religion and culture, genuine concern for issues of social justice. A Muslim or a Jew may be just as suitable a candidate in this regard as a Catholic; an atheist or agnostic may be as open to many of the values of the institution as a believer. This is not to say that there does not need to be a significant core of active Catholics on the faculty, but that part of the vitality of the community can be precisely the rich mix of people from various religious traditions addressing the great issues of our time. GC 34 quotes the eloquent words of John Paul II: "By dialogue we let God be present in our midst, for as we open ourselves to one another, we open ourselves to God" (OMID 5 [133]). If such dialogue is, in the Pope's words, "a work desired by God," it should flourish on our campuses.

The other aspect of our challenge in lay collaboration is development: the process by which we share our tradition with our colleagues. All of our institutions have been working hard to devise and implement strategies to this end, and many of them have been imaginative and successful. Let me simply share a few that have had some success at Boston College.

We have tried, with moderate success, a number of forms of orientation of faculty and staff during their first year of employment. Off-campus weekends at the Andover Inn (hence dubbed "Andover Weekends") are held each fall, sponsored by the Office of the Academic Vice President. Usually three weekends are held, each involving about a dozen new faculty members and four or five veteran faculty members, including Jesuits. Discussions focus on Boston College as an academic community and on the values and ideals of Jesuit education, as well as on the resources available for new faculty. The weekends are popular with faculty, and now have a history of close to twenty years.

In addition, we have recently begun a more formal series of three orientation meetings on campus for new faculty, one of them focusing specifically on the Jesuit tradition in education, using the excellent video series, *Shared Vision,* produced by Saint Louis University. We believe this program has great promise for the future.

For a number of years, the Boston College Jesuit Community also hosted "Cohasset Weekends," which brought together fifteen or twenty faculty and staff at the Jesuit Community's summer house—not simply new hires but people drawn from every corner of the university—to discuss their experience of Boston College as a Jesuit and Catholic university. These weekends have lapsed in the past several years, in spite of their popularity and relative success, because of the heavy burden on the Jesuits responsible for them. They may well be resurrected, however.

Another recent initiative that has had great success is a luncheon discussion series under the aegis of the Jesuit Institute, hosted by Professor John L. Mahoney of our English department. These luncheons, now in their third year, bring together about a dozen faculty members—a different group each month—to discuss their experience of Boston College as a Jesuit and Catholic institution. Reports of these luncheons have shown them to be making an important contribution to faculty members' awareness of institutional values.

For some six or eight years now, Father James Skehan has led a growing movement on the Boston College campus to share the Spiritual Exercises with our lay colleagues. Using especially 19th Annotation Retreats, he has developed a program that has touched a significant number of colleagues—both Catholic and non-Catholic—and helped to lead them into deeper lives of faith and prayer. His book *Place Me with Your Son* has been an important tool in the success of this program. Activities centered in the Jesuit Community Chapel of Saint Mary's have also increasingly been directed to the larger academic community: for example, three very successful yearlong series of presentations on prayer by members of the academic community, Jesuit and lay; programs of sacred music; and Eucharistic liturgies planned especially for the larger community.

New on the horizon, just begun in 1997, is our new Center for Ignatian Spirituality, under the direction of Father Howard Gray, which works to find ways to make the Spiritual Exercises and Ignatian spirituality even more a living force on the campus. How it will do so remains open, but its establishment by the Jesuit Community as a formal university center analogous to the more research-oriented Jesuit Institute is seen as a major step forward in addressing the challenge of sharing our Jesuit charism with our colleagues.

It is important to note the number and variety of people involved in initiating and directing these programs: academic administration, lay faculty, the Jesuit community. We shall need the creativity and energy of us all if we are to keep the tradition alive and thriving.

Women

GC 34's extraordinary statement on the situation of women in the Church and in society came for most Jesuits as a fresh and welcome breeze. The larger challenge is, of course, to address "the legacy of systematic discrimination against women," which is "embedded within the economic, social, political, religious, and even linguistic structures of our societies" (JSW 3 [363]). This dimension of the problem must be seen as one of the many injustices abroad in the world that academic programs—like our Faith, Peace, and Justice Program, PULSE, and ethics courses in philosophy and theology—must bring into sharp focus. This will require the raising of consciousness of all of us, especially administration and faculty, about the injustices against women still prevalent in the structures of society. It must surely be one of the responsibilities of an academic dean to encourage and support the process of doing so.

Significant beginnings have already been made at Boston College, as at most Jesuit institutions. Our Women's Studies Program—an undergraduate interdisciplinary minor—is strong and active, but it needs and merits further support. Courses focusing on women's issues have been developed in such departments as sociology, English, and history. But new initiatives are surely needed.

With the aim of addressing a broader audience, a new organization was founded at Boston College five years ago—the National Association for Women in Catholic Higher Education—by Sociology Professor Sharlene Hesse-Biber. The assumption of NAWCHE was that Catholic institutions, because of their particular history and their relationship with the Church, have problems and neuralgic concerns different from those of other colleges and universities. It soon became clear that this assumption was correct, and that the new organization was addressing a genuine need; to our surprise, the first conference in 1992—at which we expected at best seventy-five or a hundred—drew some two hundred participants from more than seventy-five Catholic colleges and universities. It is our hope that eventually all our sister colleges and universities in the Catholic tradition will be part of NAWCHE, so that together we can address the issues so forcefully articulated in Decree 14.

In some degree, important first steps have been made at Boston College—as I know they have at other Jesuit schools—in opening up a dialogue with the women of our academic communities. The forums we have held on Decree 14, involving faculty, staff, and students, have been a welcome response to the Congregation's call to all Jesuits "to listen carefully and courageously to the experience of women" (JSW 12 [372]).

But action must follow. There has been solid academic programming, but there is need for more; we have made good progress in attracting and supporting outstanding women faculty members, but we must continue our commitment to the process; and—in response to the Congregation's call for "genuine involvement of women in consultation and decision making in our Jesuit ministries" (JSW 13 [378])—we still need to find a larger role and voice for women in the senior ranks of administration. John O'Malley remarks of the early Society that "the Jesuits' practice in dealing with women was much better than their talk about it. As was often the case, the vocabulary they inherited was inadequate for the reality they lived, or at least wanted to live."[7] Our problem today is rather that the reality may not be up to our rhetoric; the challenge for us is to live up to the splendid and moving rhetoric of Decree 14 and, very especially, to "the prophetic praxis of Jesus in his relationship with women" (JSW 6 [366]).

Communication and Technology

In the view of many of us, technology is a wild horse we are trying to tame. If we can only get a rope around that dogie and a saddle on him, we may be able to bring him under control; then, there'll be no limit to how far we can ride—maybe right off into the sunset. We've all made considerable progress, and some of our institutions are right at the cutting edge. But we need to be sure, as GC 34 insists, that we "become critical consumers" (CNC 2 [386]) of the new communication media.

The new technology is available for all our ministries, of course, but it should be the special responsibility of our institutions of higher education to address the underlying problems this technology poses. As the Congregation points out, this new world of communication is "filled with ambiguities. Its media and language are often used in manipulative and undemocratic ways for negative and ephemeral ends. In addition, it often propagates a materialist or consumer-dominated mentality that fails to promote genuine human growth or make people receptive to the gospel message" (CNC 2 [386]). What our universities can offer is not only training in the new media and technology but also serious reflection on its meaning and proper use; thus studies such as communication ethics should be given high priority.

But the colleges and universities, with their special resources, can also model some of the new possibilities offered. Such advances as e-mail have already connected us in ways unheard of a few years ago, and programs like the Center for International Education can find new modes of connection and new ways to use the connections we make in the light of our mission. Such university-based entities as the Center for Child, Family, and Community Partnerships can use technology to model new ways of supporting academic and community collaborations. Father Kevin Kersten's new Jesuit channel on the Boston College Cable Network—offering Jesuit history, theological discussion, forums on current ethical issues, and other forms of religious programming that reflect the mission and traditions of the Jesuit community—could be replicated elsewhere. And we have all profited by such innovative programs as Father Lee Lubbers' SCOLA network out of Creighton University, which has allowed us and colleges and universities all over the country to pull in live news broadcasts in virtually any language in the world around the clock. The possibilities for ministry in the new technology and communication media are limited only by our imaginations.

Environment

However brief it is, Decree 20 of GC 34 begins by casting a wide net: "The contemporary debate between development and ecology is often posed as an opposition between First World desires and Third World needs; in fact the terms refer to many interrelated problems throughout the world" (EC 1 [430]).

Our colleges and universities can contribute, I believe, to two of the issues connected with ecology and the environment: the role our Ignatian spirituality—with its strong incarnational emphasis—can play in grounding a thoughtful response to these problems; and the use of the resources of our academic disciplines to address in specific ways environmental issues—very much including raising the consciousness of our students about ecology and the demands of an appropriate stewardship of creation.

It is our hope that such research efforts as the Center for Child, Family, and Community Partnerships and our proposed Center for the Study of Religion and Public Policy will include environmental issues in their purview, and the Jesuit Institute has already begun relevant discussions in its ongoing seminar on "Science and Religion." On a different level, our newest interdisciplinary minor for undergraduates, the Environmental Studies Program, has already elicited an enthusiastic response from students and strong commitment from a number of our academic departments. Begun under the aegis of the departments of biology and geology, it has drawn support on the "policy side" from economics (several specialists in the economics of developing countries), political science, history, and English.

As the results of the study mandated by GC 34 are communicated to the Society, we trust we can find further new and innovative ways to address these issues, which are so crucial for the future of the fragile planet that has been entrusted to us.

Conclusion

Clearly, the challenges laid out for us by GC 34 are many and daunting, but the resources of our twenty-eight American colleges and universities—resources of tradition and people—are wonderfully rich. "D'ye think th' colledges has much to do with th' progress iv the' wurruld?" Perhaps, in spite of Mr. Dooley's skepticism, they do. We can certainly hope so. It may just be that the grain from our mill will become bread for the world. And perhaps, God willing, that bread will be Eucharist for us all.

ENDNOTES • BARTH

1. Quoted in Ronald Modras, *Paul Tillich's Theology of the Church: A Catholic Appraisal* (Detroit: Wayne State University Press, 1976), 200.
2. Quoted by John W. O'Malley, S.J., *The First Jesuits* (Cambridge, Mass.: Harvard University Press, 1993), 73.
3. Ibid., 374.
4. Martha Nussbaum, *Cultivating Humanity: A Classical Defense of Reform in Liberal Education* (Cambridge, Mass.: Harvard University Press, 1997), 146.
5. Ibid., 145.
6. O'Malley, *The First Jesuits,* 120.
7. Ibid., 75.

Managing Jesuit Universities After GC 34

John J. Piderit, S.J.

ABSTRACT

This essay considers Jesuit higher education in the United States as a large corporate endeavor, and it explores ways senior management can make the corporate project more effective. After discussing the appropriate role of business language and models in the realm of higher education, the author examines the limited aspirations for Jesuit influence in American society when compared with major corporations. In order to make specific what the expected outcomes of a Jesuit education should be, the author considers what a Jewish university, committed to the Jewish faith, would expect from its students and faculty. Since Jesuit universities promise benefits for a lifetime, some evidence should be offered to students and parents that such benefits are realized. The essay examines critical evaluations of laypeople about the Jesuits' lack of coordination. In a society that wishes to privatize religious justifications for acting and legislating, Jesuit universities should communicate more regularly their specific difference. In addition to writing and speaking, Jesuit universities should make greater use of nonverbal symbols to communicate their commitment to faith and justice.

Introduction

The large number of management books in print as well as the variety of business journals available suggest that many different styles of management work well. Each management consultant usually works with a single management model, selected from a variety of models. But each consultant emphasizes that his or her model must be adjusted to fit the particular situation of each institution or firm.

In this essay, I do not intend to sanctify any particular management approach. Rather, by making use of a standard management model, I want to indicate the ways in which the new emphases of GC 34 are having or should have an impact not just on my managerial priorities but also on those of other people in senior management positions at Jesuit institutions of higher education. In my role as president, I have more direct influence on senior levels of management, but, once one makes the appropriate adjustments, much of what I say applies to other levels as well. In what follows, to avoid cumbersome phraseology I frequently use the word "university" as a comprehensive contraction to apply to both colleges and universities.

GC 34 articulated views that had been discussed in various forums prior to the Congregation itself. By bringing these views together in thematic fashion in the individual decrees, the General Congregation provided a stimulus to all Jesuits and laypeople working in Jesuit institutions to modify structures to ensure that Jesuit institutions incorporate the goals highlighted by the General Congregation. The contribution of the General Congregation is not that it offers new and imaginative viewpoints, but rather that it focuses attention on matters of great importance at this time in the development of the Church and urges those associated with our institutions to respond by applying the Congregation's recommendations to the circumstances of each institution. This essay considers Jesuit higher education in the United States as a large corporate endeavor, and it explores ways senior management can make the corporate project more effective.

Systemic Areas of Management

Any large organization—whether not-for-profit or for-profit, public or private, religious or secular—involves the coordination of activities toward the achievement of common goals. An organization usually has several goals, a number of activities designed to promote those goals, and a limited amount of resources to devote to the activities. Management considers the goals, activities, and available resources and develops ways to ensure that the goals are achieved by the harmonious blending of appropriate activities and available resources.

GENERAL ORGANIZATIONAL AREAS

The most significant activity of the president or chief executive officer is to specify the goals of the organization, adjust activities to new realities, and establish policies that provide for effective utilization of resources. Under organizational goals, the president must attend to the vision of the institution, the marketing of that vision, the product itself, production and quality control, and strategy. In this essay, I treat seven major areas which any successful manager must keep in focus: (1) vision and marketing; (2) services and quality assurance; (3) strategy; (4) personnel (qualities desired and number to be employed); (5) structure; (6) human resource development; and (7) communication.[1]

Other tasks that are very important, but which I will not treat explicitly in this essay, are operations and leadership.

At their best, managers advance the goals of an organization. At a university, faculty and staff work cooperatively with administration to promote the goals of the university. Two primary goals for any university are well-educated students and new knowledge. (Through scholarly publications, the national and international community of scholars sifts purported new knowledge to determine whether it is true and significant.) Other goals for higher education include attention to alumni, neighbors, staff, and the broader community in which a university is located; stimulating students to develop their social, religious, cultural, and intellectual life; and creating a diverse community that is of value in itself and also teaches students how to live cooperatively with people of differing values.

The goals listed above apply to most universities, private or public, religious or secular. With one addition (noted below), a Jesuit and Catholic university maintains much the same goals, but achieves them within the framework of the Catholic tradition. Imparting knowledge can be achieved in a number of ways. A Catholic university has as part of its mission to share with students the wealth of the Catholic tradition, in the many ways it has been developed over the centuries. Without espousing a conservative or liberal version of Catholicism, a Catholic university tries to show students how the Catholic faith has been incultured and how it is appropriately incultured in our modern world. By sharing this tradition, the Catholic university does not attempt to proselytize its students (or faculty and staff), but rather strives through education to bring them to greater insight about the successes and failures of Christianity (and, more specifically, Catholicism) in various cultures, and to demonstrate how Christianity establishes a foundation that supports and provides unity to seemingly disparate academic disciplines.

An additional goal in Jesuit and other Catholic universities but usually not in secular universities is the formation of students. Imparting knowledge is not sufficient.[2] By a series of programs at Jesuit universities, students are encouraged to become more ethically sensitive; more generous in responding to societal difficulties, both in the United States and around the world; more aware of God's action in their lives, in part through the Catholic Church; prepared to assume the duties of being a spouse and parent; articulate in description and argumentation, and so on. These are important goals, and Jesuit universities have structures to foster this type of formation and training.[3]

MARKET LANGUAGE IN THE EDUCATION SECTOR

The use of business and market-oriented language is rejected by some faculty members, though clearly not faculty in the business school and some other professional schools. Faculty members objecting to business language resent the suggestion that either the faculty or students are to be treated in purely economic terms. They also resist the quantification of goals, which is fostered through emphasis on a bottom-line mentality that is characteristic of market thinking. Particularly objectionable is the attempt to measure the productivity of faculty members, using such standards as the net revenue generated per faculty member per student or the net surplus or deficit generated by a particular college, once all general costs are allocated.

The foregoing critique has much to recommend it. Neither faculty nor students should be treated primarily as means toward creating desired goals, such as the goal of graduating students with degrees or the goal of stimulating faculty to publish a certain number of books or articles per year, properly weighted according to classification of journals for degree of prestige. Rather, each student, faculty, and staff is a child of God, deserving respect and capable of making great contributions to society. Part of the vocation of a faculty member is to treat each student as a distinct child of God who has particular talents. Each faculty member should take pleasure in helping every student become truly educated. Students who believe that they are being helped because the professor receives an increase in annual income in proportion to the time that he spends helping them will not be affirmed; rather, these students will perceive that they are being treated as a mere means toward the end of increasing the faculty member's income. Providing economic incentives in higher education to faculty and staff is certainly acceptable, but the economic structure should not prompt a student to suspect that the university is uninterested in him or her as a student. Similar comments apply to faculty members and staff as viewed by the university. Something would be significantly wrong if faculty members or staff persons thought that the primary reason they are valued at the institution is that they generate large net revenues for the university.

Sometimes, however, market language and concepts are both appropriate and useful. If a university wants to expand services or continue to provide good services at a lower price, using standard economic analysis can indicate areas where revenues can be enhanced or costs reduced. A university does not exist to generate surpluses in each unit; on the other hand, a university cannot exist if every unit runs a deficit. The balancing act is to make administrators and others aware of the imperative to function so that the entire university does not lose money at the same time that one encourages faculty and staff to affirm their students because of their value as individuals, not because of their value as tuition-paying students. When expectations of students and society are changing and when pressure increases to decrease the cost of providing an education, market concepts can help determine areas where costs can be cut or revenues increased. But the university community should note that cost reductions or revenue increases are important because they help achieve the goal of providing students with more effective training or for generating more new knowledge through research.

Envisioning, Marketing, Producing, and Refining the Product

The four management functions examined in this section are envisioning, marketing, quality control, and strategy. In terms of a university, marketing involves not just the admissions office but also public relations and the president, through his writings and appearances. Although vision and marketing are distinct, in this essay I will treat them as linked together. Quality control refers to the systems of evaluating the services generated by universities: knowledge in individual students and new knowledge, particularly as it is made available to other researchers across the United States and around the world. Strategy refers to the emphases chosen either explicitly or implicitly by management to achieve the goals of the university. Because our focus is on the Catholic university, we will be particularly interested in the way in which GC 34 suggests an adjustment in strategy to strengthen the Catholic and Jesuit character of our universities (see JUL 8 [411] and 9 [412]).

VISION AND THE MARKETING OF JESUIT UNIVERSITIES

Marketing includes both the means one uses to make people aware of a particular product or service and the audience one targets. The group of people for whom a message is intended depends in part on the product or activity being marketed. Jesuit universities offer three services: education, formation of students, and new knowledge, as discovered through the research activities of the faculty. The nature of the product limits to a certain extent the group of people whom one will try to approach to use the service. Accepting this constraint, an institution still exercises considerable discretion in choosing the particular audience to which it will attempt to market its product.

How much influence, attained through marketing its product, should a particular Jesuit university or the group of Jesuit universities desire? Decree 2: "Servants of Christ's Mission" (SCM) offers some direction concerning the expected impact of Jesuit institutions on a particular culture.

> *The proclamation of the Gospel in a particular context ought always to address its cultural, religious, and structural features, not as a message that comes from outside, but as a principle that, from within, "animates, directs and unifies the culture, transforming and remaking it so as to bring about 'a new creation.'"* (SCM 2 [41])

This vision of Jesuits making a significant impact on society as an energizing force from within, when coupled with the openness of American society, has expanded the parameters of what I think ought to be the desired sphere of Jesuit influence.

A particularly attractive feature of American society is that individual organizations are "allowed" to attempt to stake out as much territory of influence as they desire. In order to actually have impact, each institution or organization has to offer something that other persons or institutions in society desire. This requirement is just the market principle of supply and demand, and though this principle should not and does not have validity throughout all spheres of society, where operative it offers institutions exciting opportunities for influence.

Consider a secular example of a simple product, fast food. McDonald's Corporation desires to operate in most major countries. In those countries where it already operates, it wants to be the dominant firm in the fast-food market. Consonant with this aspiration, McDonald's Corporation opens up over fifteen hundred new restaurants a year, about half of them in the United States. In order to contrast the type of influence to which McDonald's aspires with that desired by a single Jesuit university or even by the group of Jesuit universities in the United States, consider a large rectangle. Let the area within the rectangle represent actual influence by any group in American society, with different parts of the flat-surface rectangle representing different geographical and perhaps qualitative areas of influence.[4] Suppose one shades the rectangle yellow wherever McDonald's has an impact—as judged by consumption of McDonald's goods and services. A Jesuit university produces education, student formation, and research services. If one were to consider all the Jesuit universities as a group and color their area of influence in blue, the size of the area would, I propose, be considerably less than the yellow of McDonald's.

The Jesuit justification for the smaller area of influence is twofold. First, the direct goal of Jesuit universities is to educate leaders in society, who, in turn, are supposed to have an impact on others. Second, though the Jesuit emphasis is on traditional educational services through the usual array of subjects, the true goal is to educate all our students in matters of faith and justice.[5] But even with such an expansive goal, which is much broader in scope than providing fast food to Americans, the actual as well as the hoped-for area of influence is modest. American Jesuits, as revealed by aspirations for influence by Jesuit institutions of higher education, appear to be content with desiring a relatively small colored area of influence. Put competitively, Jesuits are less ambitious for the Church than people in commerce are for their products. GC 34 decrees touching on evangelization have prompted me to expand my hoped-for areas of impact both for my own institution and for our Jesuit institutions as a group. I think we should seek to make a much greater impact on various sectors in society, by energizing society with components of the Catholic tradition that fit well within the modern spirit or Zeitgeist of the United States.

This reflection on the limited extent of marketing by Jesuit institutions does not mean that Jesuit universities do not market their product well to the targeted group they have selected. However, it does suggest that the group targeted by Jesuit universities is more modest than the mission of the Jesuits as an apostolic, evangelizing order realistically mandates. Especially in a society that dotes upon mass media, Jesuit institutions of higher education should yearn for and strategize for a much greater impact.[6]

Jesuit education has a reputation for high quality, and it is interesting to explore how Jesuit universities monitor quality to make sure that the Jesuit reputation remains well founded. Certainly, universities have various processes for monitoring quality. With respect to education, faculty members assess student performance in each class, and vice versa. Faculty qualifications are reviewed when they become members of the university. Faculty publications in books or journals are ultimately reviewed by other experts in the field, and these reviews either add to or diminish the reputation both of the individual faculty member and the institution. Quality control certainly exists in Jesuit universities; however, one can question whether it is sufficiently focused on our essential products.[7]

According to Decree 2, "Ours is a service of faith and of the radical implications of faith in a world where it is becoming easier to settle for something less than faith and less than justice" (SCM 11 [36]). GC 34 not only reaffirms justice as an important goal of Jesuit institutions but also stresses the way in which faith is at the core of justice. This dual emphasis has prompted me to review the type of quality control Jesuit universities have with respect to these goals.

Consider what Jesuit universities are willing to settle for with respect to both proximate and remote outcomes. A very proximate outcome is a class that a student has taken and in which he or she has been evaluated. Questions arise about the effectiveness of the class. Have the implications of faith been addressed in this particular class? That is a reasonable question for an institution that professes the radical implications of faith. Does a process exist for evaluating on a regular basis whether particular teachers have addressed this in the classroom? For prudential reasons, administration may not wish to ask a faculty member where in the syllabus she or he addresses the radical implications of faith with respect to the subject matter covered in a particular course. If so, alternate methods could be devised. For example, a group of interested faculty members in a particular academic discipline from various Jesuit universities could produce material about the radical implications of faith in their subject matter. For particular courses, they might even indicate questions that should be addressed, answers that have been shown to be unsatisfactory, the relationship between this course and a particular aspect of theology, and so on.[8]

What should be a desired proximate impact on students at Jesuit universities once they have finished their undergraduate degrees? To order our expectations realistically, consider an example involving a Jewish university, such as Yeshiva University in New York City, and let us focus on its mission of education and formation. Suppose I were a young Catholic man who was contemplating whether to attend Yeshiva University as an undergraduate. What would be realistic expectations on my part? I would expect that in every course I took there would be references to Jewish faith, customs, or history. Even in mathematics and science courses, I would expect that there would be references, perhaps only in the problems to be solved, to Jewish customs or practice. Some courses would have much more Jewish content than other courses. Certainly courses on the Torah would give extensive coverage of Jewish history and religious thinking. If a course in the law school were available to undergraduates, I would expect that secular law would be related to the Torah. Undergraduate or graduate courses, such as in history or political science, would also have segments that focus on the Jewish experience and the Jewish approach to government. In fact, in history courses I would expect that the teacher would devote some time to the Jewish experience at each point in history. At the end of four years, I would expect still to be a Catholic, but I would also expect to graduate with a much greater knowledge of Jewish faith and history than if I had attended a non-Jewish university. But I would expect more than knowledge. I would also expect to have a much greater appreciation for Jews and a fondness for them, because I would know particular Jews and see how they strive to live their faith in a modern society.

A Catholic university should incorporate the wealth of its tradition in its academic offerings, similar to what a Jewish university would do. We should not be hesitant about presenting our tradition. Of course, academic freedom is important. But, while respecting academic freedom, the issue is: What ideals are held up for faculty in the classroom? For the undergraduate experience, our Jesuit universities should strive to find more ways to share the Catholic tradition in most of the courses that are offered. Faculty members themselves will have the best ideas about how to achieve this and what is reasonable, but sharing the tradition should be highlighted as a worthwhile goal, with proximate and long-term effects.

A remote outcome refers to educated students five, ten, twenty years after graduation. One of the goals of the Jesuit liberal arts is to educate the whole person for a lifetime. Many of us hear glowing reports from alumni/ae about the outstanding education they received at one of our Jesuit institutions. It would be useful to know how these favorable reports differ from similarly enthusiastic reports provided by alumni/ae at secular institutions. Furthermore, it is important to know how these evaluations relate to the core goals of Jesuit education. Committed as Jesuit universities are to the whole person, in addition to academic outcomes, nonstandard outcomes should be evaluated. A number of areas are important in the Catholic tradition. Compared with outcomes of students attending secular universities, are the marriages of our alumni/ae more stable? Are our alumni/ae more active in their churches, mosques, and synagogues? Are our students more committed to justice? Twenty years after graduation, do our students pray more regularly than their counterparts? Do our students contribute proportionately more to their parish or religious community than students who did not attend a Jesuit university? No individual answer or even a group of answers could provide sufficient evidence about the real education and formation that any particular student receives. Nonetheless, the statistics give an overall sense of what has been achieved.[9]

In deciding whether to send their children to a Catholic university or a secular one, parents have to weigh costs and benefits. Jesuit institutions have a wonderful tradition of emphasizing the liberal arts, which offer benefits for a lifetime. In addition, Jesuit institutions say that they help in the religious and moral formation of students. Parents and children ought to evaluate and compare pertinent statistics before selecting a university.

Jesuit universities should be vitally interested in collecting nonstandard data of the type described here. After all, the less data there are available, the more easily an institution—whether religious or secular, public or private—can claim that it holds certain things in high esteem. Most universities say that they emphasize good teaching. Do Jesuit universities offer evidence that would at least be moderately suggestive that teaching is better at Jesuit institutions? I have yet to hear of a university, religious or secular, that does not say that it teaches values. If Jesuit universities wish to claim that they do this in a preeminent way, can we cite evidence that suggests that Jesuit institutions are more effective than other universities at instilling certain values? Evidence about outcomes should make Jesuit universities more credible. Furthermore, data are highly valued in our modern culture; this is a cultural characteristic to which Jesuit universities can respond positively, by collecting and disseminating the appropriate data.

Quality control means that management is interested in evaluating the impact of our teaching, formation, and research, and that the university has a plan for gathering and evaluating such information.[10] By highlighting the core reason why Jesuits engage in our institutional ministries, GC 34 suggests both long-term and short-term projects that can substantially enhance the effectiveness of our institutions in their goal of integrating faith and culture into the regular patterns of interaction.

Strategy, the third facet of good management, is determined in large part by the specific situation of an institution. Addressing any particular situation is beyond the scope of this paper. Furthermore, although it would be possible to speak about strategies for the collective set of Jesuit institutions of higher education, this would be a rather abstract exercise, since the institutions are not organized in a way to implement a strategy that extends beyond individual institutions.[11]

Effective Management of Human Resources

There are three management areas relating to human resources: personnel (qualities desired in staff members and the number to be employed), structure, and human resource development. Just as I did not have much to say about strategy in the previous section, because it depends in large part on the particular situation of the institution, so in this section, for similar reasons, I will not address the reporting structure within a Jesuit institution. Instead, I will focus on personnel and human resource development.

HUMAN RESOURCE DEVELOPMENT

Jesuit universities have reasonably well developed programs for introducing faculty and staff into the mission of the university. Some institutions make exemplary use of the Spiritual Exercises as customized training for faculty and staff to experience, understand, and participate in the core mission of the institution. Others use weekend sessions to explore ways in which the Jesuit and Catholic heritage influences the various activities and programs undertaken by the university. Finally, a number of Jesuit universities have special institutes whose primary focus is to help infuse various areas of the university with a Jesuit, Catholic spirit. The GC 34 decrees affirm the value of such programs and encourage further programs that help faculty and staff to develop additional ways to share the Jesuit, Catholic heritage in their courses and research (see Decree 18: "Secondary, Primary, and Nonformal Education" 2 [417]).

All Jesuit universities have procedures that inform prospective faculty members about the mission of the institution and require a judgment of those reviewing the candidates as to whether a candidate will make a helpful contribution to the Jesuit, Catholic mission of the university. Since part of the mission is teaching and research, a prospective faculty member can contribute on this level even though he or she has no interest in promoting the religious goals of the university. The imprecision in the type of commitment and contribution required to the religious mission poses a problem that has been widely discussed in Jesuit universities, but which I will not attempt to resolve here. I merely suggest, in light of the previous discussion of reflecting the Catholic tradition in most academic courses, that Jesuit deans and department heads be more specific when speaking to prospective faculty members about the contribution they are expected to make to the university.

SELECTING PERSONNEL

All Jesuit universities have a procedure to attract Jesuit faculty or staff to the university. Given the relatively small number of such Jesuits and the role that religiously committed individuals play in determining the ethos of an institution, it is important to attract young laywomen and laymen who are committed to the specifically religious mission of the institution. Until twenty years ago, each Catholic religious congregation was expected to provide the religious for their own apostolate. As a result, Jesuit universities have not had a policy of attempting to attract members of women's religious congregations and orders.

Given the paucity of religious women and men who are trained for higher education, it is important for Jesuit universities to develop policies that enhance the likelihood that other religiously committed young women and men, with academic credentials at the appropriate level for each institution and department, will be hired. A variety of avenues exist by which this goal can be accomplished. However, in light of the emphasis that GC 34 places on culture, a Jesuit university should be a beacon for people who wish to pursue an academic atmosphere within a religious context.

Decree 14 calls upon Jesuits to listen closely to the aspirations of women and to deliberate whether in Jesuit institutions women have open to them the full range of faculty and management positions that are available to most of their male colleagues (see Decree 14: "Jesuits and the Situation of Women" 13,1 [374] and Decree 13: "Cooperation with the Laity in Mission" 13–13,b [373–79]). Senior management at most Jesuit institutions is committed to this principle. For example, many women have become deans and vice presidents in the past five years. Much still remains to be done, and presidents and other senior administrators will continue to look to women to fill major administrative roles. Decree 14, which received an enthusiastic response from women and men alike, enunciates principles that have gained acceptance in many sectors of society. For this reason, Decree 14 confirms changes that are already underway in Jesuit universities.

Decree 14 supports and sustains a movement to place women in significant positions. Indeed, the enthusiastic reception accorded this document suggests that the Church should work quickly to appoint women to senior management positions within the Church. In speaking of senior management, I set aside the issue of women's ordination. According to the Pope, the Church does not have the authority to ordain women. In this situation, it is even more urgent that women be given significant positions of management in the Church.

Women are made in the image and likeness of God. It would be a black mark against the Church if they were not ordained and not given substantial leadership positions (not requiring ordination). If women were not ordained and not senior managers, people both in and outside the Church would rightly question the commitment of the Church to the implications of the biblical teaching that both women and men are made in the image and likeness of God.

Jesuit universities are ready to assist the Church, both in clarifying doctrinal matters and in implementing practical changes. In the coming decade the Catholic Church at the diocesan level may, for a variety of reasons, find it difficult to create positions in which women exercise full management authority. Exercising senior management in the Church means that women will have priests and bishops reporting to them, though in such a way that the manager does not interfere with the bishops' and priests' functions. This will be a difficult transition for the Church. Jesuit universities might be able to provide assistance. One example might be granting a joint appointment on both the university and the diocese levels. Where collaboration with diocesan authorities enables the Church to use more completely the abilities of women, Jesuit universities should prepare to help.

Communication

Whether an organization is large or small, effective communication requires both listening and speaking at all levels of management (see Decree 15: "Communication: A New Culture" [CNC] 3 [387]). Furthermore, we know from sociology and communication theory that effective communication involves information exchange on a number of levels. One of the most effective modes of communication is through symbols. Administrators should be equally adept at reading symbols and at using them to advance core messages of the university. In sequential subsections, I will speak first about listening, then about speaking, and thirdly about the use of nonverbal symbols as a particular mode of communication.

LISTENING

Decree 13: "Cooperation with the Laity in Mission" (CLM) suggests a variety of ways in which Jesuits can learn from lay people by cooperating with them.

> *The Society of Jesus acknowledges as a grace of our day and a hope for the future that laity "take an active, conscientious, and responsible part in the mission of the Church in this great moment of history"* [John Paul II, Apostolic Exhortation *Christifideles Laici* 3]. *We seek to respond to this grace by offering ourselves in service to the full realization of this mission of the laity, and we commit ourselves to that end by cooperating with them in their mission.* (CLM 1 [331])[12]

An elemental requirement of cooperation is listening. Senior administrators, particularly Jesuits, should listen to the messages that laypeople are trying to communicate. To be sure, laypeople have a great variety of views, even with respect to practical changes that should be introduced within the Church. Discerning which views to cherish and cultivate requires prayer and reflection. In the comments that follow, I assume that views of laypeople are constantly being subjected to prayerful, positive reflection within the heritage of our faith, and that the president or manager must also engage these views with an equal amount of prayer and reflection within that same heritage. While acknowledging the variety of views proposed by laypeople connected with institutions of higher education, one theme has emerged in the various comments I have heard from laypeople during the past few years. Many Catholic and non-Catholic colleagues, alumni/ae, and friends of Jesuits and Jesuit institutions appear to have much higher expectations of the Jesuits than

Jesuits have of themselves. This echoes a pattern identified earlier in this essay, namely, that Jesuits aspire to influence a relatively modest share of United States culture.

The high expectations of laypeople for Jesuits and Jesuit institutions reflect their gratitude for what these institutions have done for the Church and the world. Their lofty estimation of our accomplishments is considerably higher than our recent performance warrants. For example, they assume that we Jesuits operate a much more extensive and integrated system of educational and spiritual services than we do in practice. Their positive attitude toward Jesuit management and administration might be a wonderful legacy of an earlier generation of Jesuits, among whom obedience and openness to new assignments played a much more prominent role. Modern Jesuits should not trivialize their legacy; instead, they should find ways to develop the legacy and expand this endowment, so that it can be handed on to another generation.

The management endowment can be expanded in a number of ways, corresponding to various assumptions lay people make about Jesuit management. First, lay people assume that Jesuits coordinate their respective institutional activities: high schools with universities, universities with retreat houses, universities with social works, and so on. Where such collaboration does not exist, apostolates can be mutually strengthened by undertaking some targeted joint activities. Second, although laypeople understand that various Jesuit universities compete with one another, many laypeople also assume that Jesuit universities cooperate, at least in certain areas, among themselves. The Association of Jesuit Colleges and Universities sponsors conferences for various groups of managers in Jesuit institutions. These testify to some cooperation in the Jesuit league. Even though these conferences are restricted to sharing information and making contacts, not making common policies that apply across many institutions, the regular contact afforded by these conferences does, indeed, generate various forms of cooperation. Laypeople assume that this type of cooperation takes place, but they expect more.

Many well-positioned laypeople are surprised at the inability of Jesuits to launch national educational programs that would benefit the group of Jesuit universities and high schools collectively, though perhaps not every single institution. Parents who send their children to Jesuit high schools are disturbed that the graduating seniors from Jesuit high schools do not appear to be given much preference when they seek entrance into Jesuit colleges and universities. The parents assume that the two groups (Jesuit high schools and Jesuit universities) support one another in this basic manner. Would not each Jesuit university want to give special consideration to the graduate of a Jesuit high school when one has to decide between two talented students? Some preference is indeed given, but when parents see more students from the local prestigious prep school, and less from the local Jesuit high school, being accepted into prestigious Jesuit universities, they wonder whether the Jesuits have a coordinated approach.

Substantially greater cooperation among Jesuit institutions of learning will require a new approach, I suspect, because many attempts have already been made to have groups of Jesuit universities coordinate some of their activities. What is perhaps most perplexing to laypeople is that such cooperation does not occur through some command given by Father General or through some directive collectively supported by the United States provincials. Most laypeople do not understand the workings of the Society of Jesus. They think that it is a relatively simple matter to use the Jesuit vow of obedience to promote the common good of the Jesuits and the Church. When laypeople perceive that certain things, which seem so obviously beneficial to them and even required by the religious commitment of the Jesuits, do not take place, the people are disturbed.

To be sure, other Jesuits may hear different themes from laypeople than the ones I have articulated. But the major chord that I hear from people associated with our institutions is surprise at the lack of cooperation among institutions. By training, religious are supposed to coordinate their own desires and aspirations with the good of the Church. With so many religious of goodwill working at Jesuit institutions, laypeople are surprised that cooperation and collaboration do not occur more readily and intentionally (see SCM 11 [11]).

In listening to laypeople, understanding the background from which particular groups speak is important. Colleagues who do not share the Catholic heritage sometimes make very important observations. Understanding the background from which these suggestions emanate, however, is a crucial process in evaluating the suggestion. In every instance it is necessary to place the suggestion or observation within the Jesuit, Catholic mission of the university. Outside such a context, one risks following the advice of colleagues without insuring a proper integration within the broadly conceived Catholic tradition. When committed lay Catholics suggest certain activities designed to promote the Catholic heritage, one should consider them carefully. Such suggestions emerge from a life of devotion within the Catholic heritage.

A suggestion heard a number of times from our Catholic well-wishers is concern for the future of the Jesuits in the United States. These people like and respect Jesuits; they admire what individual Jesuits and Jesuit institutions have provided. However, they suspect that something is amiss. They do not know the Jesuit way of proceeding well enough to offer concrete suggestions about how to advance major projects. But they feel that United States Jesuits are adrift. An echo of this sentiment is found in Decree 17:

> *In response to this challenge, Jesuits must continue to work hard, with imagination and faith and often under very difficult circumstances, to maintain and even to strengthen the specific character of each of our institutions both as Jesuit and as a university. As we look to the future, we need consciously to be on guard that both the noun "university" and the adjective "Jesuit" always remain fully honored.* (JUL 17 [408])

Some committed and well-motivated laypeople fear that the separation of Jesuit and university may happen without the Jesuits fully realizing what has occurred.[13]

This may appear to be a harsh message, but it comes from people who admire Jesuits and want them to succeed. Similar to parents who try to support a child when he or she is confused, our lay admirers are attempting to bolster our confidence and help us rediscover the path that has enabled us to make great progress over the past hundred years in the United States. They observe that at the present time Jesuits struggle to attract vocations. Although they realize that other religious orders also are experiencing similar downturns in the number of vocations, these laypeople expect more from the Jesuits. In some instances, the laypeople are familiar with the range of Jesuit activities and they note what they perceive as a lack of focus or determination. For example, at a time when American society appears more secular than ever, Jesuits seem to affirm too readily the spirit of the age by distancing themselves from overt religious practices. In their view, a number of individual Jesuits, as well as Jesuit institutions, do not make it sufficiently clear that they are working to advance the Kingdom of God, or that they are working to promote the greater glory of God within the institution of the Church. At a time when society lacks strong religious voices, the Jesuit religious voice is, in many instances, muted, according to this group of committed friends and admirers.

Such criticisms come from a relatively small fraction of our admirers. But many criticisms that can lead to substantially improved outcomes often originate from small groups. In this case, those making the suggestions are also thoughtful, prayerful, and committed to building up the life of the Church. Therefore, in the spirit of GC 34, they deserve careful attention from Jesuits.

Some people, Jesuits as well as lay, assert that individual Jesuits and Jesuit institutions of higher education have not displayed an adequate commitment to justice. In my estimation, this criticism holds only if one focuses on certain types of responses to the challenge of justice, such as making sure that the portfolio of stocks held in an endowment contains stocks only for those firms who are visibly just in their labor and marketing practices. Apart from focused critiques such as this, which may have merit in particular cases, most Jesuit institutions of higher education have developed many concrete programs to insure that students are attuned to the demands of justice. For example, most institutions of higher education have developed ethics courses for all students, promoted volunteer work for justice, and sponsored trips that expose students to instances of injustice. Many institutions have incorporated themes of justice into various undergraduate courses. In short, justice is a well-developed theme at Jesuit universities. Certainly, more needs to be done to secure greater representation by different ethnic and socioeconomic groups at Jesuit institutions. One the whole, however, Jesuit institutions are committed to the proper goals and are allocating appropriate resources to attain these goals.

Institutions of higher education do not change as quickly as some other institutions in society. Nonetheless, like many institutions in an open, cosmopolitan society like the United States, American colleges and universities undergo regular change. An important responsibility of the president, and of other senior administrators, is to maintain focus on the essential goals of the university during times of change. Because change requires adjustment in the daily patterns and thinking of many individuals within the institution, individuals correctly focus their attention on the individual changes that they personally experience or that their unit has to make. As a result, people are liable to miss the reason for the change or to think that one of the reasons for the change is that part of the mission of the university has been modified. In most instances, the mission remains the same but the means toward fulfilling the mission have been modified to fit better the current context both within and outside the university. An important role of the president is to show how the change affirms the central mission of the institution.

Because secular institutions of higher education are more prominent today than ever before, it is important for the leadership—Jesuit and lay—in Jesuit universities to explain the specific contribution that Jesuit institutions make to the well-being of individuals and the common good of society. Presidents, I believe, have to repeat this message regularly, changing the emphasis to suit the occasion. Although people recognize that religious institutions play a significant role in society, modern culture increasingly views religious belief as a private enterprise, which should have no impact on the public life of a society. Stephen Carter makes this point forcefully, stating that modern society has relegated religion to the status of a private hobby.[14] That is, religion can be satisfying and energizing, but it belongs within the private realm.

According to the modern approach described and critiqued by Carter, religious principles should never be used to justify policies one advocates in the public sector, and religious celebrations should remain private. If Carter is correct, spokespeople for religious groups face a significant challenge. This is certainly the case for Catholic universities, since part of the central mission of a Catholic university is to show how Christian belief has influenced culture and how it might appropriately influence both private and public living in the future. In a very important sense, evangelization is part of a Jesuit university's central mission. But evangelization must be understood in a nuanced way. A Jesuit university does not evangelize in the sense that it attempts to convert students from non-Catholic beliefs to Catholic ones. On the contrary, Jesuit universities try to support the religious beliefs of their students at the same time that they share with students the religious riches of the Christian and Catholic heritage. Part of this heritage is to show how Christian beliefs and ethical principles make people individually more genuine children of God and, when the beliefs are lived together in community, human beings reflect more clearly their status as children of

God. Understanding this aspect of the mission is vital toward achieving the mission (see Decree 5: "Our Mission and Interreligious Dialogue" 4c [131]).

SYMBOLS

Nonverbal symbols are as influential as words. The Catholic faith has a tradition of using art and artifacts effectively.[15] Since Jesuit institutions attempt to have a religious impact on society, they should be creative in using nonverbal symbols, both new and old, to communicate their message. Some concrete symbols are as simple as clerical attire, crucifixes, statues, and other religious symbols in university buildings. They are clear reminders about the distinctive project in which Jesuits and laypeople are involved. Other symbols may be more abstract, creative, or engaging. Inasmuch as these nonverbal symbols emerge from two streams, the Christian heritage and the modern media culture, they help people understand how religious faith fits into modern society.

Jesuit universities in the United States have an outstanding tradition of using nonverbal symbols of the faith to remind, encourage, and stimulate students. Prior to Vatican II, Jesuits and their lay colleagues worked hard to populate our campuses with good, artistically worthy, and culturally related religious objects of art. Vatican II required an adjustment in thinking and practice, which rendered some of the former nonverbal symbols less effective. Now that much of that adjustment has taken place, it is appropriate for laypeople and their Jesuit colleagues once again to enliven the Jesuit tradition of using art to stimulate both believers and nonbelievers alike. The Jesuit tradition in the arts stretches back to the first century of existence of the Society of Jesus. A full application of GC 34 to the modern situation would make greater use of nonverbal Christian symbols throughout the campuses, buildings, and activities of Jesuit universities.

Not only should Jesuit institutions use nonverbal symbols to communicate our commitment to faith and justice, but these institutions should also help students to achieve a critical stance toward symbols of our secular culture. Jesuit institutions of higher education should teach our students to read symbols, to evaluate their implications, and to use them effectively in their own lives. Through courses in literature, philosophy, theology, media, and history, Jesuit institutions already provide students with tools for interpreting and using nonverbal symbols. Decree 15, however, suggests that Jesuit institutions need to elevate our efforts in this area (see CNC 6 [390], 7 [391], 9 [393]).

A culture is nourished by its art and music, but the culture can also be challenged through both the fine and performing arts. By imaginative use of nonverbal symbols, Jesuit universities achieve three things: they create their own subculture, they live creatively in a larger culture, and they challenge the larger culture, at the same time that they nourish the subculture.

Conclusion

GC 34 challenges Jesuits to use positive aspects of culture to promote belief in Christ and the work of the Church. It also encourages Jesuits to think of themselves as colleagues of the laypeople with whom they serve in Jesuit institutions. In examining how these decrees apply to senior management at Jesuit universities, I have identified a number of areas where Jesuit universities—with Jesuits working with Catholic and non-Catholic laypeople to formulate a plan—are being challenged to deliver more. In most of the areas that I have addressed, Jesuit universities have already begun the process of change and are making good progress. However, GC 34 urges Jesuits and Jesuit colleagues in significant ways to become more evangelical, but in ways that take advantage of the positive components of contemporary culture. To meet these challenges, Jesuit universities will have to make significant adjustments for many years to come. To undertake and digest such changes, everyone at Jesuit universities should engage in prayer and reflection. They should also adhere to the advice that Saint Ignatius Loyola gives in the *Spiritual Exercises:* "it is necessary to suppose that every good Christian is more ready to put a good interpretation on another's statement than to condemn it as false."[16]

ENDNOTES • PIDERIT

1. I have selected a few of the major areas of concentration that are identified by Gerard Egan in *Adding Value: A Systematic Guide to Business-Driven Management and Leadership* (San Francisco, Calif.: Jossey-Bass, 1993). He considers six essential features in any effective organization: (1) strategy; (2) operations; (3) structure; (4) human resources; (5) management; and (6) leadership (p. 29). He then addresses individual subtopics under each of these categories. In some cases, I have chosen some of the subtopics, such as marketing, for consideration in this essay. Other classifications of organizational areas may be used to make sure that an organization is making progress in achieving the goals of the organization, but the taxonomy presented in the text is a useful one that avoids reliance upon transient management models. Some models are currently more popular—such as reengineering or total quality improvement—but they are not likely to be in vogue ten years from now. Management consultants provide a service by giving honest, direct advice. In order to market their services better, consultants frequently emphasize a distinctive difference in their particular service. Hence, new terms are developed periodically in order to make more relevant to the current market the value added of the management consultant. Using a model that in various forms has been used for many decades, I adopt the classic approach in this essay.

2. "A Jesuit university must be outstanding in its human, social, spiritual and moral formation, as well as for its pastoral attention to its students and to the different groups of people who work in it or are related to it" (Decree 17: "Jesuits and University Life" [JUL] 11 [414]).

3. Research at the level of secondary education shows that the emphasis on formation is a powerful factor in explaining the very positive impact of Catholic secondary schooling, even after one adjusts for the socioeconomic background of students. For an interesting and important study, see Anthony Bryk, Valerie E. Lee, and Peter B. Holland, *Catholic Schools and the Common Good* (Cambridge, Mass.: Harvard University Press, 1993). Formational elements also play an important role in Laurence Steinberg's analysis of success in educating students at the primary and secondary level. See his *Beyond the Classroom: Why School Reform Has Failed and What Parents Need to Do* (New York: Simon and Schuster, 1996). These studies suggest that formation continues to play a significant role in higher education.

4. A more nuanced example would allow for different levels of the rectangle, superimposed on one another. With each level referring to a different type of good, the first level might refer to physical goods and services, while the second might refer to public goods and services, and the third to spiritual goods and services. For simplicity, I assume that all goods and services are projected onto the same rectangular surface.

5. In terms of the rectangle with various levels, the Jesuits produce education and new knowledge, but their ultimate goal is to have these goods and services impact the two additional levels of public goods and services (justice) and spiritual goods and services (faith). Even in this more developed model, the area to which the Jesuits aspire is rather limited, compared to that of purely secular corporations.

6. Loyola University Chicago has a large, highly rated medical center, and it has recently established the Loyola University Health System with another Chicago-area hospital. Among the many good justifications for this development, one is that it increases the area of impact of Loyola's Catholic medical center and of the medical school, which is one of only five Catholic medical schools in the United States.

7. Traditionally, Jesuit high schools have exercised greater quality control than Jesuit universities. It would be interesting to explore the historical, developmental, and functional explanations for the actual differences between the two types of institutions.

8. The *Ratio Studiorum,* in its various versions, provided excellent tools for maintaining quality control in each Jesuit institution. For a discussion of the relationship between the *Ratio Studiorum* and Ignatian principles of education see George E. Ganss, S.J., *Saint Ignatius' Idea of a Jesuit University* (Milwaukee, Wis.: Marquette University Press, 1954).

9. See Robert Wuthnow, *God and Mammon in America* (New York: Free, 1994), for a discussion of the impact of Christian belief on economic practices of Christians. The evidence for a significant impact is not reassuring. Wuthnow offers a more extended analysis of this result in *Poor Richard's Principle: Recovering the American Dream Through the Moral Dimension of Work, Business, and Money* (Princeton, N.J.: Princeton University Press, 1996).

10. As indicated in JUL 10 [413], the selection of research projects undertaken at Jesuit universities should also be influenced by the overall mission. For an academic and religious treatment of this issue see George M. Marsden, *The Outrageous Idea of Christian Scholarship* (New York: Oxford University Press, 1997).

11. In recent years, some of the Jesuit universities have formed groups to explore collaboration. One such body is the Heartland/Delta group, consisting of ten midwestern Jesuit universities. Senior leadership meets to discuss common issues, and two conferences involving about four hundred faculty members and staff from the ten institutions have been held. At this point, the universities collaborate in exploring the Jesuit, Catholic heritage; ventures beyond these informational and formational issues have not been discussed.

12. Also pertinent is "the decree on cooperation with laity summons us to an attitude of listening and exchange with those who are vital partners in our service of Jesus Christ and His Church" (Decree 1: "United with Christ on Mission" 11 [11]).

13. For an account of how strong sectarian colleges and universities in the United States lost their religious heritage, see George M. Marsden's *The Soul of the American University: From Protestant Establishment to Established Nonbelief* (New York: Oxford University Press, 1994). Marsden argues that a gradual, almost imperceptible separation occurred, without the leaders of these institutions understanding the impact of their decisions on the religious heritage of their institutions.

14. See Stephen Carter's *The Culture of Disbelief* (New York: Harvard University Press, 1994).

15. See Andrew Greeley, *Religion as Poetry* (New Brunswick, N.J.: Transaction Publishers, 1996), for a discussion of the relevance of religious symbols and imagery for modern Catholics.

16. See Presupposition 22, *The Spiritual Exercises of St. Ignatius,* trans. Louis J. Puhl, S.J. (Westminster, Md.: Newman, 1951), 11.

ESSAY 4

Education for Social Responsibility: On Forming Men and Women for Others in Business

William J. Byron, S.J.

ABSTRACT

After the publication of the documents of GC 34, the author found himself looking from a new perspective at the forty-seven students who were enrolled in his course "Social Responsibilities of Business." The author was impressed with the relevance to this course of what the Congregation had to say about many things, particularly about women and the relationship of the Jesuit mission to culture. Looking at the faces in front of him in the classroom and imagining where those students will be forty years from now, he sees women at high levels of executive responsibility, and sees both men and women of cultural sensitivity feeling quite at home in a global marketplace. Many of them are now and will continue to be men and women of faith, and most of them are quite prepared to become men and women for others. As business becomes more global, education for business must take on a more global perspective. The global perspective of GC 34 and its affirmation of the faith-that-does-justice theme provide both encouragement and direction to any Jesuit whose personal mission puts him in a classroom with students preparing for careers in business.

Since 1993, I've been teaching Management 282, "Social Responsibilities of Business," in the School of Business at Georgetown University. It is a required course for seniors; they can't leave Georgetown without it.

The first class I met for this course after the publication of the documents of GC 34 totaled forty-seven students. More than half of those enrolled were female. Almost half the class was foreign born. Most of the students could handle more than one language, some as many as four. Many religions were represented in the group.

Having just read the documents from the Congregation, I was impressed with the relevance to this course of what the Congregation had to say about many things, particularly about women and the relationship of our mission to culture.

Comparisons with my own college days (at Saint Joseph's in Philadelphia) were both amusing and inevitable. No course like the one I teach now was offered then, and no women would have been there to take it, if it had been offered. All of my classmates were United States citizens, very few were not Catholic, and all, if memory serves, were born in this country. Most served in the armed forces during World War II and were attending college on the GI Bill of Rights.

Immediately upon graduation in 1950, my contemporaries who studied business put on their gray flannel suits and stepped onto lower rungs of their career ladders. Up they went swiftly and surely. Most found that their ladders were up against the right corporate walls—banks, broadcasting, insurance, manufacturing. Few thought globally; most lived, worked, and dreamed quite locally. None, to my knowledge, ever had to depend on a second language for career advancement or to bring added value to the enterprise. Now their careers are, for the most part, over; they have enjoyed success and prosperity without going very far from home.

Looking at the faces in front of me now in my Georgetown classroom and running a straight-line projection out forty years, I see women at high levels of executive responsibility (even though they themselves are not completely convinced that the "glass ceiling" will lift for them), and I see both men and women of cultural sensitivity feeling quite at home in a global marketplace. Many of them are now and will continue to be men and women of faith. Yet they know exactly what the Congregation meant by the words, "People's spiritual lives have not died; they are simply taking place outside the Church" (Decree 4: "Our Mission and Culture" [OMC] 21 [105]). It is interesting to speculate on the degree to which they will remain or become men and women for others. I asked them all at semester's end to compose a "personal mission statement" and here is a sampling of what they wrote:

1. *My initial focus is, as of right now, my own progress in success at college, finding a post-graduation job in the automotive industry, and establishing a network of connections to help me along. However, I am also focused upon ensuring that my family maintains some sort of coherence, despite the fact that they are distributed across the globe. I am there for my friends when they need someone for any reason. Keeping in mind how fortunate I am, I will commit myself to causes in surroundings from which I will not directly benefit. I will succeed by acknowledging my strengths and by using them to my advantage at all times.* (German passport; male)

2. *To live out my belief that God's presence on Earth is manifested in others and in myself. This belief imparts to me a responsibility to treat others with the utmost respect and dignity as one would treat God, and to behave as God would—to exhibit love, energy and the wisdom of experience at all times.*

I am committed to service to the communities in which I reside and in which I will reside. I am alert to opportunities to participate in the life of my communities. I am especially dedicated to the service of women, children, schools, and the natural environment. (U.S.; female)

3. *I am a focused person with a drive to succeed. In this drive, I attempt to maintain a high level of honesty and respectability. In order to achieve my goals, I maintain an air of persistence and a necessary flexibility. I am respectful and caring of others, never letting my goals blur the importance of those around me. I am the type of person who will forgo an achievement in order to help a loved one or friend.*

   I am confident that I will be able to give to the community as I develop my personal career. Currently, I believe that I am very conscious of others' needs and feel that it is impossible for me ever to lose this consciousness. (U.S.; male)

4. *I am dedicated to the many communities to which I belong. I am committed to diversity, multiculturalism and equity, involving all members of society. I am committed to the understanding of different views and perspectives and exposure to different ideas, which is necessary in promoting a more diverse and all-inclusive environment in which to coexist. I do not believe in charity, but in empowerment. As a dynamic and aggressive leader I attempt to raise the level of awareness of others through exposure to different ideas and points of view. I serve as a resource, role model, and most importantly a facilitator of dialog. As a leader, my goal is to inspire and empower others to act according to their beliefs. I challenge others to think critically and come to their own conclusions. My philosophy of leadership is based on a belief in effective team work. I am a team player who assesses the individual strengths of my fellow members, and then fills the gaps. I determine the needs of the organization with which I am involved and attempt to meet those needs.* (Japanese American; female)

5. *I am a 21-year-old woman who is half Chinese and half Greek, and who grew up in Kuwait. I feel Greek, but I'm not sure what it is that makes the Greek side of my heritage so dominant. I am very interested in advertising and I would like to work in the account management department of a large advertising firm in London or New York. I want to give back to the community in any way I can. I believe that in the advertising industry there is a lot of room for socially responsible behavior. I plan to have a*

positive effect on society through the products I will promote and the methods I will use to promote them.

I will be a wife and mother. My children will come before my work and before my personal life. Through my children, I will give back to society. (Greek passport; female)

6. *I've spent most of my life thus far studying, and during the most recent years pursuing two particular paths of interest: international business and the Russian language and culture. For as long as I can remember, I have been drawn to and fascinated by Russia—its people, history, language and culture. This is actually why I began to study business. I think that business is potentially a great means by which one can help people, by providing new products and improving their living standard. It is my goal to create some sort of mutually beneficial relationship, wherein there is a sharing of resources and a fulfilling of needs. I know that although it may not be possible for one person to help the world, it is possible for one to help a few.*

During the course of my life I intend on extending my family. I think that children are miraculous creations; and although I don't know at what stage of my life or how many I want to have, I cannot wait until the day when I will be a mother. Although I have my fears, just like everyone else, I hope that I will never be afraid to reach out to others, and to give them everything I can. (U.S.; female)

7. *As a Hindu in the* bhramacharya ashram *(student phase) in life, my existence centers around learning. I am dedicated to the attainment of knowledge. The skills I have attained at school will serve me in the workplace, where I will continue the learning process. Along the way I hope to serve and aid people I come into contact with—fellow employees, employer, customers. Eventually, I want to establish my own business in India.*

My mission is to use the opportunities I have been given to serve my family and the community. I want to serve as a role model for Indian-American children and show that there is no need to sacrifice their Indian identity to assimilate into American culture. I also want to provide hope and assistance to my relatives in India who are in need. (Indian American; male)

These are just samplings of the responses my students made to an assignment to write a mission statement that would have no impact at all on their course grade, but would, if they chose to let it happen, serve as a guide and checkpoint for their progress through life. It was striking to me that issues of concern to GC 34 were alive in the minds and hearts of the students I met routinely in the classroom.

They are not unconcerned about making money, but they will be reluctant to do that at the expense of the natural environment and the rights of other persons. If the Congregation had produced a document on ecology (instead of simply recommending that Father General commission a study on "how this issue affects our lifestyle"), my students would have been positively impressed. They regard the environment as a "stakeholder" in what they and their various enterprises will do in pursuit of profit. They also agree, at least most of them agree without any hesitation, that employees, suppliers, customers, competitors, and the community wherein the enterprise is located are all, along with the shareholders, *stake-*holders in whatever these young men and women will do or decide in the organizations with which they will associate themselves once they graduate from Georgetown.

I see these students and hear their voices as I listen to GC 34 say, in the unofficial translation published by the *National Jesuit News,* "There is something happening in the diversity of human history which is truly the work of God." Here is how the official text puts it:

> *The work of God in the diversity of human history is seen in the long process of enlightened human growth—still incomplete!—as expressed in religious, social, moral and cultural forms which bear the mark of the silent work of the Spirit. In the conceptions of the mind, in the habits of the heart, in the root metaphors and values of all cultures . . . God is preparing the conditions in his creatures for the loving acknowledgment of his truth, making us ready for the transformation promised in Christ.* (OMC 18 [102])

That "something is happening" is abundantly clear. That it is the "work of God" is a realization that takes awhile to sink in. It starts to seep into consciousness as you get to know these young people better and as you become more attentive to their hopes, their fears, and their dreams.

GC 34's willingness to speak not simply about women, but about "Jesuits and the Situation of Women in Church and Civil Society" (Decree 14 [JSW]), was, in my view, a gift of the Holy Spirit. Indeed, the discontent that explains the emergence of the question of equal rights for women in the contemporary Church is, as I see it, a sign of the Spirit in our midst. There has been, over the past several decades, a feminization of Jesuit higher education in the United States. Enrollment statistics point to it, but we Jesuits are not giving the issues that underlie those statistics our full attention. The representation of women in academic majors leading to careers in business, law, medicine, science, engineering, and other occupational areas previously considered to be all-male preserves, signals their certain rise to positions of influence in those fields in the not-too-distant future. This realization affects what I do in the classroom in several ways.

Management communication is one of four emphases (along with ethics, the business-government relationship, and global consciousness) that are expected to be part of every course taught in the Georgetown School of Business. Oral presentations and weekly written assignments are integral to my courses; students are made aware that these are indispensable tools for efficient management and effective leadership. All students, male and female, know that communication skills are important, but I make a point of encouraging females to convince themselves that good communications skills are for them an early, if not first, line of defense against discrimination in the workplace. Both oral and written communication exercises are critiqued for their coherence, clarity, conciseness, and overall impression. The present generation of college students has, let it be said gently, the communications equivalent of bad breath. Overall impression is important in any communication. In the matter of writing and speaking, students must be told while still in school (and while there is still time!) if the impression is not good.

A typical written assignment would be a response, in letter-to-the-editor format, to an opinion piece or analytical report that appeared in *Business Week, The New York Times, The Washington Post,* or *The Wall Street Journal.* Students are encouraged to agree or disagree as they wish, but to state their agreement, disagreement, and a possible alternative proposal in convincing and compelling language. While watching the Winter Olympics on television a few years ago, I noticed a two-tier scoring system in the figure skating competition: one bank of scores for meeting the "required elements," and a separate set of marks for "artistic impression." It occurred to me then, and I've done so ever since, that written assignments could be given a number grade for the required elements (that number would fall directly to the academic bottom line—the grade for the course), and a letter grade for the overall or "artistic" impression (and that mark is just a message from me to the writer of the assignment; it does not affect the course grade). Grade-conscious students respond with proper alarm to a C, D, or F, even when they know "it doesn't count." Their writing then improves over the course of a single semester. The point of it all for men and women (but I'm particularly concerned that women about to break into business get the point) is that the world moves on words and numbers. They have to be able to handle both. And the difference between success and failure in whatever they want to do for others in business is going to be their ability to communicate clearly and effectively.

Two other ways the presence of women in my course (together with the Congregation's effort to heighten our concern for women) influences the course relate (1) to the issue of balancing career and family responsibilities, and (2) to an element that GC 34 identifies as part of the "situation," namely, that "women are commonly treated as objects in advertising and in the media" (JSW 2 [362]).

We discuss policy questions like those surrounding the Family and Medical Leave Act of 1993. We have reports from female members of the class on some of the workplace-life literature that relates to spousal sharing of child care and household responsibilities. ("It is really good for the guys to hear about that" is an inevitable end-of-the class comment to me by several female students.) And we talk a bit about divorce, an issue that bothers (and frightens) many students in every class I teach simply because so many have seen it happen to their own parents.

The advertising issue always gets close attention. It enables me to make a theological point before exploring the practical implications. The theological point relates to what we call the *triple concupiscence.*

The word *concupiscence* is not familiar to students; it sounds strange, so I take it apart. They are familiar with Valentine's Day references to Cupid. They know what cupidity is (and hope to avoid it). I explain that the prefix *con* simply means "with," and that *concupiscence* just means "with desire." More often than not it is taken to refer to lust, or ardent sexual desire. Their interest level rises! The triple concupiscence, I tell them, is the lust of the flesh, the lust of the eye, and the lust for power over other persons. They find it reassuring to hear that this is all part of human nature. Any normal, healthy person will recognize stirrings within that reflect a desire, rooted in one's human nature, for sexual union, possession of things that attract the eye, and for power over others. These impulses, of course, have to be contained, but there is no point in trying to deny that they exist. So we turn to Scripture.

In 1 Jn 2:15–17, the scriptural basis for reflection on this triple concupiscence is presented in words that always need a bit of explanation:

> *Do not love the world or the things of the world. If anyone loves the world,*
> *the love of the Father is not in him. For all that is in the world, sensual*
> *lust, enticements for the eyes, and a pretentious life, is not from the Father*
> *but is from the world. Yet the world and its enticements are passing away.*
> *But whoever does the will of God remains forever.*

The necessary explanation relates to John's use here of the term *world.* It is meant here to signify all that is not of God. Business students in particular have to be assured that elsewhere, for instance in his Gospel (3:16), John uses *world* in a positive sense:

> *For God so loved the world that he gave his only Son, so that everyone*
> *who believes in him might not perish but might have eternal life. For God*
> *did not send his Son into the world to condemn the world, but that the*
> *world might be saved through him.*

Throughout Scripture the world is viewed as good, as lovable, worth saving, worth working in, worth transforming. In the quotation from 1 Jn 2:15–17, where John warns the believer to be wary of the pull of these three drives that are so familiar to human nature, John wants the believer to do God's will and thus live forever with God, rather than letting natural appetites, these desires for "passing" things, run wild and pull him or her away from God.

Another widely used translation of this set of three is: "Carnal allurements, enticements for the eye, the life of empty show." Students can relate to this. They discover that the sexual harassment issues that we also discuss extensively in class relate to the first. I point out that the advertising industry plays on the second and, in the process, reinforces those selfish values that encourage sexual harassment. And the "life of empty show" or the "pretentious life," I tell them, refers to a state of mind characterized by pride and the desire to dominate. This is the arena that catches up all those superficial values, power plays, and the drive for prestige that constitute the "world's" way of measuring success. Students acknowledge that these are not the values that respect human dignity and foster self-control. They also know that these values vie for dominance in the business culture.

"Enticements for the eye" is one way of describing what the advertising industry parades in front of a consuming public. Students offer from personal experience examples of their own having been "taken in" by visually attractive (often reinforced by sexual attraction) advertisements. I ask them to consider any advertisement from print, billboard, or television, examine it closely, and ask not what this ad invites them to buy, but *what it presumes them to be.* High on the list of answers to that moment-of-truth question are words like hedonist, sex maniac, materialist, insecure, and greedy. The exploitation of the anatomy and sexuality of women to appeal to the concupiscence of the male eye is recognized by all and always figures prominently in classroom discussions about socially responsible advertising. In a section on the educational apostolate that is part of the *Complementary Norms to the Constitutions* produced by GC 34, we are told that "in this new communications-media culture, it is of great importance to educate our students to a critical understanding of the news transmitted by the media, so that they can learn to be selective in personally assimilating such news."[1] The same applies to advertising.

Student projects are part of the course. Without fail, groups want to look at tobacco and liquor ads that entice immature consumers, as well as ads that cover the gamut from automobiles to zithers and depend on sexual imagery to make the sale.

One final point concerning women and education not just for social responsibility, but for management responsibility in business organizations, can relate to the Congregation's call for Jesuits to "trust in the patronage of the Blessed Virgin Mary in their assigned tasks and activities, and everywhere show more and more clearly the role of the mother of our Savior in the economy of salvation" (*Const,* Norms 276,2, pp. 301–2). I was struck when Barbara Boggs Sigmund—wife, mother, writer, poet, and innovative mayor of Princeton, New Jersey, until she died of cancer in 1990—wrote a 1987 article in *America* calling upon the Pope to "bring back Mary" to Catholic devotional life. "Modern women in particular need her," said Mrs. Sigmund,

> *to validate female strength-in-gentleness in the world of power. We are entering that world inexorably but uncertainly, jealous of both our femininity and our detachment. We resist taking on the "pinstripes of the oppressor," but all of our archetypes of power are male ones: the warrior, the team, the old bulls and the young. We need a model of our own on the grand scale.*
>
> *So bring back Mary . . . to celebrate the need for the tough tenderness of femaleness in the life of the world, to acknowledge that charm and kindness can still entice God to dwell among us.*[2]

Jesuit educators and their lay colleagues, male and female, should see a challenge in every female face they meet in the classroom. Our women students can bring "female strength-in-gentleness" to the world of power for which we are preparing them, if we help them think about it now. Along with "eloquentia perfecta," they should be taking "tough tenderness" with them from the Jesuit campus into the world of work.

Look now into the mind of another one of my students to take the measure of this challenge:

> *If I were to describe myself as a person, the first word I would use is woman. The next description would be binational, bicultural, and bilingual. I am a very sensitive person, and, because I can empathize with others, I am a good listener. I am loyal to my friends, but quite fierce when betrayed. This fierceness never seems to outweigh my ability to forgive, however. I will have a career but will not consider myself completely successful if I do not fulfill my dreams for family life. I will get married when, and only when, I find someone whom I can stand and who can stand to be with me for the rest of our lives. Divorce is not in my plans, as I would rather not marry than divorce. Companionship is always an option. If I feel that I am prepared to bring children into the world, I will. I will raise them as my parents have me, and hopefully set an equally good example for them to follow. If this is so, I would then like to be the matriarch of a large family, like my grandmothers were in their time. This will be my legacy.* (citizen of Colombia)

Decree 26, which outlines the "Characteristics of Our Way of Proceeding" (COWP), indicates that our work as Jesuits is to "prepare our complex and divided world for the coming of the Kingdom," and that this "requires a plurality of gifts, perspectives, and experiences, both international and multicultural" (COWP 16 [550]). As the song from a Broadway musical put it so well decades ago, "If you become a teacher, by your pupils you'll be taught." The plurality of gifts, perspectives, and experiences, both international and multicultural, that can be found in a Jesuit college classroom today can, in the spirit of GC 34, enable a Jesuit to expand to some extent his mission-and-culture horizons without even leaving home!

Looking at that "complex and divided world" through the window of a course on the social responsibilities of business helps me understand better why the Congregation thought it important to say, "Our commitment to social justice and ongoing human development must focus on transforming the cultural values which sustain an unjust and oppressive social order" (OMC 28,3 [121]). Working with and learning from my students, I can readily affirm the Congregation's assertion: "One of the most important contributions we can make to critical contemporary culture is to show that the structural injustice in the world is rooted in value systems promoted by a powerful modern culture which is becoming global in its impact" (OMC 24 [108]).

The global dimension of who we are and what we do in business is inescapable in any effort to educate the young for business. Talk about downsizing and job loss at home, and you'll hear the word "global." Talk about expanding markets and maintaining a level playing field for business competitors and you'll hear a lot about international pressures on business ethics. In one class session, three students—one from Iran, another from Vietnam, and the third a Japanese national—discussed the distinction between bribery and "grease payments" in their respective business cultures. The topic for discussion was the United States Foreign Corrupt Practices Act, which became law in 1977 as part of an effort to assist United States corporations in holding their own against foreign competitors in overseas markets. Lively discussion drew enlightening perspectives from an Italian national who explained the important function of "gifts" in business relationships in Italy. It was an eye-opener for the Americans, but all students from all the nations and cultures represented in the room found common ethical ground—a place to take their stand—in a simple "graft syndrome" model: where secrecy, easy money, and the violation of trust are present, corruption is setting in. The degrees of graft are as follows: (1) a gift, which, if of modest value, may be innocent and acceptable; or, if of more than modest value, may be intended to make the recipient "much obliged" to reciprocate in inappropriate ways; (2) a bribe; and (3) extortion or a "holdup." What do these terms mean in different parts of the world? Exploring what is involved in the violation of trust opens the door to an analysis of integrity. And the further that inquiry proceeds, the more national and cultural differences are transcended and questions of what is just and fair are clarified.

As business becomes ever more global, education for business must take on an ever more global perspective. The global perspective of GC 34 and its affirmation of the faith-that-does-justice theme ("the contemporary Jesuit mission is the service of faith and the promotion in society of 'that justice of the Gospel which is the embodiment of God's love and saving mercy'" [Decree 2: "Servants of Christ's Mission" 3 (24), citing GC 33, Decree 1: "Companions of Jesus" 32 (35)]) provide both encouragement and direction to any Jesuit whose personal mission puts him in a classroom with students preparing for careers in business.

ENDNOTES • BYRON

1. John W. Padberg, S.J., gen. ed., *The Constitutions of the Society of Jesus and Their Complementary Norms* (St. Louis, Mo.: Institute of Jesuit Sources, 1996), Norms 280, p. 303. Hereafter *Const* in text.
2. Barbara Boggs Sigmund, "Five Minutes with the Pope," *America* 157/6 (19 September 1987): 30–31.

ESSAY 5

The Dialogue Between Faith and Culture: The Role of Campus Ministry in Jesuit Higher Education

John B. Breslin, S.J.

ABSTRACT

The importance of bringing faith and culture into dialogue is a hallmark of the decrees of GC 34. Campus ministers at Jesuit colleges and universities have a rich heritage to draw on for this apostolic task, both in the writings of Saint Ignatius and in the early history of the Society. The themes of *reflection, gratitude,* and *service* flow from the lived experience of the Spiritual Exercises and speak to the life experiences of contemporary students. Carefully adapted and applied, these themes can help students link learning, worship, and volunteer work in a gracious circle of Christian commitment.

[Prenote: In order to avoid an awkward shifting of tenses throughout this essay, I have maintained the "historical present" to describe my recent experience at Georgetown as university chaplain in charge of campus ministry.]

If GC 32 has become famous for its linking of faith and justice as inseparable twins in Jesuit life and ministry, GC 34, while in no way backing away from that commitment, has added another and much needed twin as a complement: faith and culture. The dynamic within each pair is different, of course, but not antithetical. Justice and faith imply one another: for the believer, faith without the pursuit of justice becomes a sham, the very thing so many of the prophets of Israel railed against. For the unbeliever, the pursuit of justice demonstrates "good faith" in two senses: it opposes to "bad faith" the honesty of the believer who does not use faith to avoid questions of injustice, and it reveals the desirability of faith as a religious value that actively promotes justice.

The dynamic between faith and culture within Christian tradition is more complex, as H. Richard Niebuhr demonstrated in his now classic study, *Christ and Culture.*[1] At one extreme the two are seen in conflict: faith rejects the merely human because the latter (identified with Paul's notion of *sarx*) cannot in principle support the divine. But in the Catholic Christian tradition with its radical incarnational bias, faith and culture may kiss, for the human, apart from sin, is seen as being fully taken up into God in Christ. This is certainly the stance of GC 34, and nowhere is it more clearly and economically stated than in the key fourth decree, "Our Mission and Culture" (OMC): "Our intuition is that the Gospel resonates with what is good in each culture" (OMC 11 [90]).

From my first reading of the documents, that sentence has impressed me as a key statement of GC 34's central affirming thrust in looking toward Jesuit mission in the twenty-first century. It certainly resonates with the thought of both Thomas Aquinas and Ignatius Loyola, who in their quite different ways saw the world as saturated with God's active presence. But they were also radical realists, not romantics. Sin is an integral part of ordinary human experience, and human culture drinks of that cup, too. So the Gospel also finds itself inevitably in conflict with "what is [not] good in each culture."

What then of the world of higher education? Where do these complementarities and polarities play themselves out in Jesuit college and university work? As the title of Pope John Paul II's apostolic constitution, *Ex Corde Ecclesiae,* suggests, the dialogue between faith and culture lies at the heart of the university project within the Catholic tradition. The high culture of western Europe had its origins in the intimate—and occasionally strained—dialogue between an established ecclesiastical institution and a fledgling academy that grew out of the former's monastic and cathedral schools. Right from the beginning, then, the characteristic Catholic principle of "both/and" marked this new development, for the medieval university cherished its academic identity not only as a place of intellectual debate and discovery, but also as the privileged venue (*magisterium*) for the Church's own reflection on its identity and mission.

The modern Jesuit Catholic university, heir to this tradition as well as to the rather more autonomous intellectual developments of the Renaissance and the Enlightenment, strives to maintain this dialogue of faith and culture in a decidedly different setting. But for that very reason, the dialogue has become all the more necessary, for little common understanding—let alone agreement—can be presupposed. Of its very nature, dialogue presupposes a mutual exchange, a willingness to learn as well as to teach, a conviction that the other party has something to contribute to one's own self-understanding. If faith has much to say to culture, it has reason to listen as well. For GC 34, such listening is a fundamental requirement for Jesuits in all their apostolic work, with a broad hint that it has not always been a hallmark of our approach! Whether we're entering into dialogue with women, with our apostolic colleagues, or with representatives of other Christian traditions and other faiths, fruitful dialogue begins (and continues) only if we have a listening ear and heart.

But this is nothing new in Christian tradition. Indeed, we can find this dialogic principle already at work in the New Testament. Near the end of his letter Paul commends to the Philippians for their reflection "whatever is true, whatever is honorable, whatever is just, whatever is pure, whatever is pleasing, whatever is commendable . . . any excellence . . . anything worthy of praise" (Phil 4:8)—or, to repeat GC 34's paraphrase, "what[ever] is good." Moreover, in a different vein, Jesus occasionally uses the realities of an agrarian economy in his parables to shock his listeners into confronting the revolutionary character of the Good News (for example, the parable of "the dishonest manager" where the "children of this world" are commended for their shrewdness in achieving their aims [Lk 16:1–9]).

Thus, from its very beginnings, *confirmation* and *challenge* shape the dialectical approach to preaching the Gospel. And so, too, they become, in an analogous way, the basis for the Jesuit Catholic university's efforts to bring the Gospel into conversation with the high and popular cultures of our day. The broad consensus about the importance of values in education, the emphasis on service, the rigorous pursuit of truth for its own sake— all of these contemporary examples point to the elements of culture that gospel faith wishes to confirm and support. Conversely, the skepticism about transcendence, the cheapening of the value of human life, the easy acceptance of the "Gospel of getting on"—these and similar views call out for constant and well-argued challenge from within the university as an intellectual community identified with the Church's mission of preaching the Gospel of Jesus (cf. OMC 24 [108]).

At a Jesuit Catholic university this dialectic of confirmation and challenge in conversation with culture should permeate all parts of the institution, from curriculum to athletics, from student affairs to financial affairs. For it is the *whole* university that participates in the institution's mission. But as in Paul's metaphor of the Christian community, every part has its own unique role to play in the building up of the body of Christ, so, too, in the university. Campus ministry serves the university and the Church by focusing the dialogue between faith and culture in a quite specific manner.

Campus Ministry's effort to do this at Georgetown University, our nation's oldest Catholic and Jesuit school, involved, not surprisingly, a process of reflection on the Spiritual Exercises of Saint Ignatius Loyola and on the Jesuit educational philosophy rooted therein. What we found were three virtues or habits *(reflection, gratitude, service)* that flow directly from the dynamic movement of the Exercises and that in turn shape the distinctive character of Jesuit education. Happily, we also found that these "Ignatian" virtues ring true as educational goals not only for other Catholics, but for Protestants, Jews, and Muslims as well in our diverse university community.

The revived interest in "virtue ethics" in the academy has contributed to this acceptance and represents a good example of what faith can happily confirm in the dialogue with culture. As Thomas Aquinas argued, acquiring virtue means acquiring a *habitus*, literally "having" or possessing a certain way of acting or being. And to achieve virtue perfectly means that this particular way of acting or being has become habitual, part of oneself, out of which a person acts spontaneously without second thoughts. The best analogy is probably physical, the way an athlete has become so attuned to her sport that she no longer needs to think through every shot or every move; instead, her body reacts spontaneously, the racquet moving toward the oncoming ball, placing the shot exactly where the player wants without a great need for conscious planning or second-guessing. Of course, in the moral sphere, what is most important is not simply the act itself but the intention behind it, and so moral habits are primarily habits of intention or habits of choice. By conscious effort over time in practicing a given virtue, we establish a disposition within ourselves to do that particular good, just as the athlete trains his body to react spontaneously to the challenges of the game.

In educational terms, reflection, gratitude, and service represent, respectively, habits of mind, heart, and will—those three faculties of the soul that the Spiritual Exercises seek to bring into play in prayer, and Jesuit education attempts to engage in developing the whole person. The role, then, of the chaplaincy is to assist the rest of the university in reforging a link that American higher education in general has severed between spirit and intellect. By translating a valid legal distinction between the operations of church and state into an academic divorce, public universities have deprived their students of a truly integrated education. Private secular universities, almost all of which were founded as confessional colleges, have effectively done the same thing over the last century.[2] American Jesuit universities, precisely because of their commitment to full academic freedom and the pursuit of knowledge in all its richness, have undertaken to promote as well the moral and religious development of all their members—students, faculty, and staff.

How then does campus ministry contribute to the whole university's task of fostering the habits or virtues of reflection, gratitude, and service, and thus to the wider task of engaging in the dialogue between faith and culture? Let me begin with *reflection,* a habit of the mind and therefore the most clearly intellectual of the three.

The Three Virtues of Jesuit Education

REFLECTION: A HABIT OF THE MIND

We found at Georgetown University that retreat programs represent one of the best ways to introduce colleagues and students to the serious practice of reflection, and one that grows naturally out of our Jesuit heritage. When Ignatius urged his first friends at the University of Paris to go and spend a month in prayer under his direction, he was introducing them first and foremost to the practice of solitary reflection. From his own experience Ignatius had learned the value of silence and solitude for nourishing knowledge of self and knowledge of God. Even in the sixteenth century the clamor of the world easily drowned out deeper thoughts. But the prospect of a month of silence and what it might reveal about our inner resources was as scary then as now, and Francis Xavier, who was to become one of Ignatius' most ardent disciples, demurred several times before accepting the invitation.

Students today are no different, and the invitation to make a five-day silent retreat creates similar anxieties among undergraduates at Georgetown and among not a few of the faculty and staff as well! But there's an interesting pattern we have discovered—and it is almost invariable—by the third or fourth day, the people who were most worried about their ability to live in silence eagerly consider extending the retreat for another day or two. What they discover from experience is an ancient ascetical teaching: namely, that eliminating distractions and curtailing abstract speculation allows us to reach that part of ourselves where our deepest convictions lie, a place otherwise almost inaccessible. Indeed, much of our busyness serves as a screen, consciously or unconsciously erected, to keep us from these deeper levels of ourselves.

Such a retreat experience is, of course, a rather special kind of reflection and indeed it depends very much on a structure of the day and a series of presentations that allow students and others to navigate these unknown waters with a certain sense of confidence. The spiritual director serves as a kind of pilot for the journey, not setting the course so much as helping the retreatant learn his or her way around the shoals. In this the director also mirrors the ideal academic role of the teacher as mentor. But most important of all, such a retreat experience is an act of faith based on the conviction that a loving God is directing the retreatants to discover their deepest desires, which is where God is to be found and where true freedom lies. Thus, this five-day exercise in reflection also introduces our students and colleagues into the core discernment process of Jesuit apostolic life and prepares them to join with us in making choices for our common apostolates. Decree 26: "Conclusion: Characteristics of our Way of Proceeding" (COWP) nicely sums up this fundamental interplay of prayer and action: "God invites us to join with him in his labors, on his terms, and in his way. To discover and join the Lord, laboring to bring everything to its fullness, is central to the Jesuit way of proceeding" (COWP 8 [542]).

Given such a foundational experience as the common heritage of all Jesuits, it is no wonder that reflection as a habit of mind has become fundamental to Jesuit educational philosophy. The effort to get beyond rote learning, which characterized humanist educational reforms in the sixteenth century, dovetailed nicely with the spirit of the Exercises and encouraged the early Jesuits to move their students in a similar way "beyond pious practices to an inner appropriation of ethical and religious values."[3] That same process continues today in our colleges and universities in a twofold way: (1) helping religiously committed students to deepen their faith; and (2) introducing the less pious to the reality of personal religious experience and its natural link with communal prayer and worship.

Providing an extensive variety of retreat programs is but one way that campus ministry can support the university's mission to promote the habit of reflection. And that habit, in turn, can help counter an often highly pragmatic approach to education as well as a hypersensate culture in which most of our students grow up bombarded by video images and sound bites from their earliest years and indeed during every day of their time on campus.

Quiet, persistent attention to ideas, fueled by the joy of discovery and freed from a calculus of immediate gain, corresponds closely to the dispositions that Ignatius urged on his retreatants as they entered into the Spiritual Exercises, and that GC 34 recommends to Jesuits (and implicitly our colleagues) who are primarily involved in intellectual labors (Decree 16: "The Intellectual Dimension of Jesuit Ministries" [IDJM]). The courage to enter requires an act of faith like Anselm's *credo ut intelligam,* a paradoxical assertion that faith precedes understanding and is its condition. But it is a paradox that faculty are surely familiar with in their own work, for who would have the courage to begin a major research project or to take on a new class of students each semester without an underlying confidence that understanding is attainable and that their efforts, despite constant setbacks, can ultimately bear fruit in a finished book or in a truly learned student?

GRATITUDE: A HABIT OF THE HEART

By gratitude I mean a habit of the heart that requires as much cultivation as does reflection, that virtue of the mind. For Ignatius it was the great gift to be sought at the conclusion of the Spiritual Exercises, what the retreatant should desire to take away as the fruit of a month's prayer. This final exercise is commonly known as the "Contemplation to Attain Love," but the motive proposed throughout for loving God is gratitude for all the gifts we have received. He suggests that we look at our lives, at the world around us, at the whole cosmos, and in each case become aware how immediately God dwells in every part of creation, not inertly or distantly like the deist's clock maker, but vibrantly, actively working on our behalf.

In the face of such generous self-giving, Ignatius suggests, one can only respond, after quiet reflection, with thanks and a self-offering of one's own. And so he proposes a prayer that is intended to sum up the experience of the entire retreat: A prayer that begins by acknowledging all I possess as gift—liberty, memory, understanding—and then offers it all back to God, asking *only* for God's love and grace in return. That "only" is ironic, of course, since to ask for love and grace, in the context of the retreat experience, is to ask for everything worth having.

How can we imagine this experience transposed from a retreat setting to the daily life of our students and our colleagues? Students, like the rest of us, crave a sense of belonging, a connection with a world larger than themselves. At the same time, they suffer from a strong temptation toward the self-absorption of the late adolescent, intensified by their focus on studies and their concerns about future plans in an unstable economic world. Inviting them to experience and express gratitude offers one of the best avenues out of their introversion.

In his posthumously published journal *Markings,* Dag Hammarskjöld noted at the beginning of 1953 a hard-won realization that issued in a summary statement: "For all that has been—Thanks! To all that shall be—Yes!"[4] I would argue that the connection between those sentences is not fortuitous, but causal, and that Jesuit education seeks to encourage exactly that linking. Opening students to an appreciation of the splendors of creation—in science, in art, in human life—offers the best antidote to their self-absorption, for it naturally redirects their attention to the gifts that surround them. Such giftedness, reflected upon, yields a thankful spirit and an attitude of affirmation.

What's more, it also serves to foster a sense of work as a calling or vocation and not just as a career, thereby introducing a vertical dimension into an otherwise horizontal enterprise. For what distinguishes a vocation from a career is a sense of purpose that lifts our eyes above and beyond the carefully laid-out track, that *carrière,* we have constructed for ourselves. And, continuing the etymology, vocations imply calls, convincing voices beckoning from within or without that give us new purpose, a goal beyond our self-interest. GC 34 puts all this quite directly in a passage concerned with our own needs as a diminishing number but that, happily, begins by taking a wider purview: "Our mission and spiritual heritage make us all promoters of vocations; vocation promotion simply means helping young people hear and respond to the stirrings of the Spirit in their hearts. Naturally, vocation promotion does not necessarily produce a vocation to the Society of Jesus. It leads to various types of a Christian response, and we must carefully respect the particular way in which the Spirit calls each person" (Decree 10: "The Promotion of Vocations" 2 [293]).

My contention is that a well-developed sense of gratitude opens us up to hearing such a call, perhaps even expecting it. For at its root a habit of thankfulness implies a personal relationship whether to parent, spouse, mentor, or friend—or, encompassing all of these, to God. Moreover, the relationship rests on the experience of "gift": something given freely, without expectation of any *quid pro quo,* and so I have simply to say "thanks." But once that channel of communication is opened, we become attuned to the possibility of altruism, to giving and self-giving as a way of life, to sharing with others what we have bountifully received. One of the sayings of Jesus we owe to Paul's preaching pushes this point even further, indeed to its counter-intuitive extreme: "It is more blessed to give than to receive" (Acts 20:35).

How better to express such thanks than through worship, which in the Judeo-Christian tradition is so explicitly a thanksgiving (*barakah,* eucharist) ritual? Providing such opportunities for worship is a principal function of campus ministry in which the experience of personal reflection finds its fruitfulness not simply in an act of private thanksgiving but in a common liturgy that remembers all that the Lord Jesus has done for us and in so doing "re-members," reconstitutes the Church here and now as the People of God at prayer.

We do this at Georgetown not only by providing a variety of Sunday and weekday Masses for our Catholic students, along with opportunities for reconciliation and a full RCIA program for catechumens, but also by offering regular liturgical services for our Jewish, Muslim, and Protestant students and staff. Having both a rabbi and two ordained Protestant ministers as long-term full-time staff members gives us great scope and makes somewhat easier GC 34's mandate to "conscientize . . . students on the value of interreligious collaboration and instill in them a basic understanding of and respect for the faith vision of the members of the diverse local religious communities, while deepening their own faith response to God" (Decree 5: "Our Mission and Interreligious Dialogue" [OMID] 9,8 [145]).

On special occasions, we offer as well interfaith services that attract a wide variety of our community to give thanks together or to remember a deceased colleague. It is in such an interfaith setting of worship, of thanksgiving that true dialogue is best fostered. By listening respectfully and reverently to the sacred texts and prayers of our colleagues and attempting to make them our own, we move toward the fourfold sharing that GC 34, quoting a pontifical document, recommends to us: "a sharing of life, a shared commitment to action for human development and liberation, a sharing of values and a sharing of human experience" (OMC 23 [107]; cf. OMID 4 [131]). In prayer, we can move beyond abstractions and stereotypes and meet on a common ground of worship.

Our educational goal in all of this is to foster the habit of gratitude, not only for its own sake, but also as a counter to the prevailing cynicism and skepticism of our postmodern world. Strong, positive experiences of worship give shape to students' weekly lives and offer a *sotto voce* rebuttal to the mood of pointlessness in much popular culture. Moreover, such experiences, in the Jesuit tradition of learning by doing, prepare them to participate in the liturgical life of their churches and synagogues after graduation.

SERVICE: A HABIT OF THE WILL

But worship as an expression of gratitude has its own dynamic, leading the worshippers to translate their prayer and praise into action on behalf of their neighbor. Saint John in his first letter captures that dynamic in his exhortation to love: "Beloved, since God loved us so much, we also ought to love one another" (1 Jn 4:11). And so we move from the habit of gratitude and the life of worship to the work of service, a habit of the will.

In the *Spiritual Exercises*, Ignatius made "service of the Divine Majesty" the primary condition for deciding on a course of action. At a hinge point of the retreat, he presents this prayer of offering "of greater worth and moment":

> *I wish and desire, and it is my deliberate decision,* provided only that it is
> for your greater service and praise, *to imitate you in bearing all injuries
> and affronts, and any poverty, actual as well as spiritual, if your Most
> Holy Majesty desires to choose and receive me into such a life and state.*[5]

Even in the most sincere and passionate desires to imitate Christ in his suffering, humanity must yield before a calculation of God's service. And what is that service for Ignatius? Put most simply, it meant working for "the progress of souls in Christian life and doctrine," as the original *Formula of the Institute* had it. That generic sixteenth-century phrase meant helping people attain the end for which they were created—the praise, reverence, and service of God. Worked out in detail it could mean setting up a house for prostitutes in Rome, helping plague victims, founding and running schools, giving parish missions, being a theological expert at the Council of Trent, writing catechisms, going to foreign lands as a missionary—all of which, and more, were projects Jesuits undertook during Ignatius' lifetime as founder and first superior general of the Society of Jesus.

Thus "service of the Divine Majesty" translated immediately into service of the neighbor, echoing the New Testament insistence that love of God and love of neighbor be inextricably joined. Ignatius could be quite ruthless in requiring that such service be the main criterion for Jesuit decision making, no matter the circumstances. For example, he insisted that the two papally appointed Jesuit theologians at the Council of Trent, Fathers Diego Lainez and Alfonso Salmerón, carry out the ordinary ministries of the Society, including preaching, giving the Spiritual Exercises, and visiting the sick and poor, while advising the bishops; indeed, as O'Malley points out, Ignatius designated these the principal reason for their being there at all.[6]

On the other hand, he could wax indignant at the suggestion that Jesuits engaged as counselors and confessors at Court should withdraw from these ministries because they might risk giving scandal or being corrupted by power and luxury:

> *[I]f we sought nothing else in our vocation than life devoid of trouble and
> risk, if we eschewed the good merely to keep out of harm's way, we might
> as well quit the world and have no dealings with people. . . . [M]erely out
> of regard for what the mob says, one should never refrain from undertak-
> ing a work that can promote the greater service of God our Lord and the
> best interest of souls.*[7]

Clearly, the idea of service for Ignatius was both comprehensive and compelling, and it constantly reasserted the unbreakable incarnational link between the divine and the human, or as he liked to say, between the "above" and the "below."

In our own day that same priority of service has taken on a new dimension and a new urgency. As we have already noted, the last three General Congregations of the Society of Jesus have reaffirmed the intrinsic bond between the divine and the human by linking the "service of faith" to the "promotion of justice" in such a way that, as the song says about love and marriage, "you can't have one without the other." Or if you try, it will be at the expense of both.

More specifically, how does a Catholic, Jesuit university like Georgetown make service an integral part of the educational experience of our students? Service and volunteer programs have become popular across the country at colleges and universities, but they have a special place at a Jesuit school, for they complete the circuit of reflection and gratitude, of mind and heart, by moving the student toward action. Love, Ignatius claimed, is best expressed in deeds. Without this movement toward active involvement in the world, the previous habits become suspect as mere mental gymnastics and emotional self-indulgence.

Many if not most of these volunteer programs at Jesuit schools began—and often remain—in campus ministry. At others, like Georgetown, they have taken on a life of their own under the aegis of student affairs. But the spiritual link remains important both for the student and for the university because service not only completes our circuit of habits or virtues but keeps it going, providing further material for reflection and gratitude. How often we have heard the surprised and humble refrain from those who do service: "I started out expecting to give and ended up receiving much more in return!" That is a reaction crying out both for serious reflection, theological, ethical, and psychological, and for renewed thankfulness. Indeed, without such a response, the experience of service loses much of its educational—and human—value.

This is where campus ministry has its unique role to play. Not necessarily to administer the service programs themselves, but to establish two important links. First, to encourage students and other members of the university community to participate in service programs as an expression of their faith: service as the fruit of prayer (reflection) and worship (gratitude). And second, to help students already committed to service to grasp the link between what they do in their tutoring or AIDS ministry or soup-kitchen work and their religious experience: service as the seed of prayer and worship.

Fruit and seed, another circuit connecting these foundational virtues. Indeed, the best way to imagine this threefold educational process might be as a gracious circle, opening upward into a spiral that draws the members of the college or university community into an ever richer experience of the love of God and neighbor. For some the starting point will be intellectual, for others affective, for still others engagement in service. Campus ministry's task is to help individuals and groups discern, according to Ignatian principles, how they can move in faith along the spiral, integrating mind, heart, and will in the process. At each stage of the journey the dialogue between faith and culture takes on flesh and bone, as deepening faith confirms or challenges the values of the dominant culture according to the promptings of the Spirit.

Conclusion

Let me conclude with another historical reminder from Father John O'Malley, S.J. In listing ten characteristics that made Jesuit pedagogy so initially successful in establishing "a new, international educational style," he concludes this way: "Further, they tried to influence their students more by example than by their words. They repeatedly inculcated in one another the importance of loving their students, of knowing them as individuals, of enjoying respectful *familiaritas* with them."[8] Today we might call it "modeling," but the truth remains: if at Georgetown or any other Catholic university we want our students to enter that gracious circle of reflection, gratitude, and service and make of it a spiral toward the divine, we must be moving in it easily and familiarly ourselves. In T. S. Eliot's image from "East Coker," we chaplains and educators in the Ignatian tradition

> *ought to be explorers*
> *Here and there does not matter*
> *We must be still and still moving*
> *Into another intensity*
> *For a further union, a deeper communion*
> *Through the dark cold and the empty desolation,*
> *The wave cry, the wind cry, the vast waters*
> *Of the petrel and the porpoise. In my end is my beginning.*[9]

ENDNOTES • BRESLIN

1. H. Richard Niebuhr, *Christ and Culture* (New York: Harper and Row, 1961).
2. See George M. Marsden, *The Soul of the American University: From Protestant Establishment to Established Unbelief* (New York: Oxford University Press, 1994).
3. John W. O'Malley, S.J., *The First Jesuits* (Cambridge, Mass.: Harvard University Press, 1993), 226.
4. Dag Hammarskjöld, *Markings,* trans. Leif Sjöberg and W. H. Auden (New York: Knopf, 1964), 89.
5. George E. Ganss, S.J., trans., *The Spiritual Exercises of Saint Ignatius: A Translation and Commentary* (St. Louis, Mo.: Institute of Jesuit Sources, 1992), 98, p. 55 (emphasis added).
6. O'Malley, *The First Jesuits,* 324.

7. Ep. 3220, "Patri Jacobo Mironi," 1 February 1553, *Monumenta Ignatiana,* series prima, "Sancti Ignatii de Loyola: Epistolae et Instructiones 1551–1553," IV (Madrid: 1906), 625–28 at 627; cited in Hugo Rahner, "Ignatius as Confessor," in Hugo Rahner, *Ignatius: The Man and the Priest* (Rome: CIS, 1977), 59–72 at 69.
8. O'Malley, *The First Jesuits,* 227.
9. T. S. Eliot, *Collected Poems, 1909–1962* (New York: Harcourt, Brace, 1963), 189–90.

A Classicist's View of GC 34 and Catholic Higher Education

Anthony C. Daly, S.J.

ABSTRACT

The author has chosen a personal focus for his essay because it makes theory concrete. The theme of the essay is that studying and teaching classical antiquity advances the Jesuit cause. The author also wants to show how GC 34 affects and might affect classicists in Jesuit institutions of higher education. The essay begins with some experiences in Jesuit education, which lead to thoughts about the teaching of language and literature. The author closes with some remarks about our Jesuit purpose as educators and some thoughts about justice.

Background

In 1959 when I entered the Society of Jesus, I lived in a firmly structured thought-world. In my Catholic milieu faith and reason were in harmony, faith was supreme, and reason was far more important than feelings or instinct in apprehending the truth.

The index of forbidden books was a hallmark of the period. So firm was the thought-world that opinions seen at variance with it were considered alien. In certain respects the general level of education was lower than it is today, and the framers of the index thought the forbidden works represented threats to the catechesis against which the ordinary person did not have adequate intellectual defenses. My point in mentioning the index is that its existence points to the firm thought-world it was trying to protect.

Catholic education was important in those days because the intellectual content of Catholicism permeated all subjects taught and learned, like salt in a stew. I experienced this in grade school and high school.

In the Jesuit juniorate or liberal arts training, literature and history were treated on their own terms. There was no overt attempt to introduce an explicitly Christian critique.

Nevertheless, the professors were all Jesuits and it was from an implicit and all-pervading Catholic perspective that we read and considered all of our subjects.

I was looking for a unified world view that would allow a subordinated and connected view of reality. One of the main sources of this preoccupation was, oddly, the Spiritual Exercises of Ignatius. He would not be classed primarily as an intellectual or an academic, and this is why the phenomenon is odd. The Exercises are primarily interested in love.

In seeking a center for his personal life, Ignatius developed a synthetic view of all of reality.[1] Because the Exercises are intended to free us for decision making,[2] they encourage an ordered understanding of all realms of life as part of the basis for making decisions.

My firm view of life and my preoccupation with synthesis were characteristics I shared with my fellow Jesuits of the period. They were characteristics fostered by our common environment. In my case they were corroborated by the intellectual character of my father. The house was full of books on all subjects, probably less than a quarter of it fiction. My father was a disciplined mind and a careful and broad reader who judged everything in harmony with his Catholic intellectual background.

In the Jesuit philosophate in St. Louis in the mid-1960s, Missouri Valley Thomism was the official point of view. Major proponents of other systems were called "adversaries," and, in the classes I attended, they were not taken seriously. Other disciplines such as psychology, literature, and the arts were considered intellectually peripheral. On the personal level, the involvement some of us had in the inner-city parishes was viewed with suspicion by the philosophical establishment. It tended to draw us away from philosophical studies. Catholicism was Thomism, and Thomism was Catholicism. The circle was complete, but stringently circumscribed.

The seams were cracking even then, and by the late 1960s at the Jesuit theologate in St. Louis there was no official theological system. Various branches of theology, moral theology, for example, or Scripture or Christology were treated independently from one another. The professors doubtless had personal philosophical views that influenced their theological positions, but what they were was not discussed. From my perspective, the firmly established, commonly held thought-world of a decade before had broken up.

Until about 1990 I found that as a faculty member at Saint Louis University I could talk to students about their courses and find that by and large their professors were synthesizing faith and learning, in history, for instance, and in literature and philosophy. After 1990 it was increasingly more difficult to find evidence that this integration was being fostered in a substantial number of courses. Intellectual Catholicism seemed to have receded into pockets and valleys on the landscape of the university.

Many of us here have lamented the lack of any university-wide provision to secure new faculty members who, in our view, could maintain the Catholic character of the university and further the exploration of a contemporary Catholic humanism. This is a controversial concern, to be sure, but it is widespread and well known to everyone in the Jesuit colleges and universities in the United States who is interested in their religious character.

Like all institutions of higher learning in our country, Jesuit colleges and universities have long been interested in the promotion of social justice as a part of their civic responsibility. Decree 4 of GC 32, "Our Mission Today: The Service of Faith and the Promotion of Justice," gave the project a new urgency and a higher profile; it did not introduce a new mission.

After GC 32 the abiding interest of Catholic colleges and universities in promoting justice in the tradition of the social encyclicals seemed ineffective or insufficient to many Jesuits. Those of us engaged in higher education were put on the defensive. Our work could not be seen as legitimate unless it could be shown to promote justice in a significant way, and there was the remote but real threat that we might be called upon to abandon our institutions, or that they would not receive the level of support from the order that they had enjoyed in the past.

As time went on, arguments were developed to show that our colleges and universities were powerful engines of justice. Inspired by ideals of antidiscrimination and cultural diversity, influential elements at Saint Louis University—forgive the constant local reference—tended to elevate the goal of the promotion of justice above all other goals of Catholic education, sometimes to the point of wholesale reductionism. New faculty members could be regarded as full-fledged Catholic educators solely because they were interested in promoting justice.

Even justice tended to be ecumenical. At a meeting here on the subject of justice in the late 1980s one of the panelists declared that we would be better served not to define justice; limiting the concept would limit our creativity. This sentiment seemed to enjoy general approval, and only one person objected.

At Saint Louis University the mission statement of several years ago devoted a few words to the pursuit of knowledge "under the inspiration of the faith" and then went on to a lengthy announcement of its goal of promoting justice. The formula "under the inspiration of the faith" had been deliberately and explicitly chosen in preference to the phrase "in harmony with the faith." The latter formula was thought to imply too close a link between knowledge and faith.

Morale was low among many of my Catholic colleagues, and although no one in the university was sufficiently in command of the facts to actually assess the religious character of the faculty at large, we felt we were in a minority, tolerated but largely ignored. The day came when I felt that much of the religious meaning of my professional life had been dissipated. The small enrollments in literature classes in my area of ancient Latin and Greek had always restricted the scope of personal influence, as did the subject matter in better-enrolled language courses. Now it seemed unrealistic to view myself as a member of a team of Catholic educators who together exercised significant intellectual influence on a great number of students.

Nevertheless, each succeeding year strengthened the general realization among Jesuits that Catholic higher education contains worthwhile elements not directly geared to the promotion of justice, and that Jesuits' abiding interest in them was legitimate. It became less necessary to defend educational objectives by enlarging the scope of justice to include all manner of things.

Effects of GC 34

The documents of GC 34 have restored the university apostolate and the broad range of activities and ministries in the Society to full legitimacy. The specifically religious character of the Society has also been unambiguously reaffirmed as its central interest.[3] Still, the effect the Congregation will have on the overall Catholic character of our colleges and universities remains to be seen. GC 34, Decree 17: "Jesuits and University Life" (JUL), maintains that "a Jesuit university must be outstanding in its human, social, spiritual, and moral formation" (11 [414]). But this is one short section of the document, and, curiously, explicit reference to intellectual formation has been left out of the formulation.

Much more space is given to explaining the prescription that the Jesuit character of a university is to be measured by its efforts to improve social and economic conditions (see JUL 7–10 [410–13]). The broader intellectual, cultural, and religious role Vatican II and *Ex Corde Ecclesiae* envision for the Catholic university as a whole is proposed by GC 34 as the individual ideal of the Jesuit working in higher education (see JUL 1–6 [404–9]).[4] The interpretation of this decree in terms of the nature and role of the Jesuit university as a whole is therefore unclear—and more important, what its actual effect will be in the United States is uncertain.[5]

Depending on how matters develop, those Jesuits and Catholics on the faculties of our colleges and universities who have lost some of their sense of teamwork as Catholic educators might regain it, perhaps in an enhanced form. In developing my thoughts about the implications of GC 34 for Jesuit higher education in the United states, I have taken the position that JUL is fully in harmony with Vatican II and *Ex Corde Ecclesiae*.[6] I take it that as far as circumstances permit, the decree wants the Jesuit university as a whole to play the same role and aspire to the same ideals that it proposes for the Jesuit working within it. I am also assuming that our institutions of higher education will take steps to maintain or secure faculties that are competent with respect to these ideals.

Many of the things I say below are general in nature and easily apply to any of our institutions. When particularities are mentioned, they always concern Saint Louis University. This is because I am most familiar with SLU. I use it only as an example, and it has seemed either impossible, disproportionately difficult, or unimportant to find parallels at other institutions.

Teaching Language

It is enjoyable and satisfying to teach a language. I have had at least one class in Latin or Greek at the elementary levels every semester since 1980. It is natural to have formed some thoughts about the value of language teaching.

Quite apart from the access to texts learning Latin or Greek gives the student, thinking in another language—even thinking isolated words and phrases—unchains us from the tyranny of a single mode of thought, a single way of looking at things at the most fundamental level. There have been and are people who think in a different way, different even in how they name and conceive and relate things. As they begin to assimilate a second language, students experience a liberation and expansion even when they do not reflect on it.

Another phenomenon occurs simultaneously. When words and phrases become relative, a person tends to focus a little more on the meaning underneath the words. The experience of learning a second language reveals things about one's first. A rich opportunity to cultivate care and exactitude in expression and thought is opened up by the experience of trying to express in a second language a thought conceived in one's first.

Humane as this teaching is in itself, it makes little personal apostolic sense when it is not seen as part of a collegial effort to develop and communicate a Catholic humanism. Hopefully GC 34 will foster this Catholic collegiality. In any case, I am lucky in the students who have enrolled in Latin or Greek—especially Greek.

The last several years I have been teaching Greek in very small classes, typically classes of five or fewer students. I have found myself making friends with nearly all of them. We have consistently found ourselves in discussions of what we think really matters, sometimes in class, but mainly before or after, or at other times. I regard these discussions as extremely valuable—they benefit the students and they benefit me. I'm with Newman—better a university in which there are no professors than a university in which there are no conversations.[7]

Teaching Literature

Literature naturally invites and furthers intellectual integration. Take, for instance, the familiar tragedy of Sophocles, *Oedipus the King*. Oedipus grew up in the city of Corinth thinking he was the son of the king and queen of that city. But one of his friends got to drinking and told him they weren't his real parents. They said they were, but Oedipus was worried enough that he consulted the oracle at Delphi. The response said nothing about the matter, but told him he was destined to kill his father and marry his mother. He ran away from Corinth to keep the oracle from coming true. In his travels he met an old man with some servants coming from another way. They got to the crossroads at the same time, an argument developed about who had the right of way, a fight started, and Oedipus killed the old man and most of his servants. Oedipus didn't know it, but the old man was Laius, his true father, the king of Thebes.

When Oedipus got to Thebes the mythical monster, the sphinx, was killing anyone who could not answer her riddle. Oedipus answered it, the sphinx left Thebes, and as a reward Oedipus was named king of Thebes and married the queen, Jocasta, who was, of course, his true mother. Every step he took to avoid killing his father and marrying his mother only brought him closer to doing so. As the truth begins to dawn on him, he exclaims to Zeus who controls fate, "O Zeus, what have you decided to do to me?"

The truth becomes clear and Oedipus decides nothing in life is sweet to him anymore and he wants to cut himself off from the world because of his shame and disgrace. He blinds himself. If he could he would stop up his ears as well. Then he would be sealed off from the world and the bitterness of his life. He asks to be exiled and left to die on the mountainside where he had once been left to die as a baby.

This tragedy stimulates reflection, discussion, analysis, and comment whenever it is read or produced. Zeus, who contrived the downfall of Oedipus, does not love us—he has his plan for us, but his plan very well may be to destroy us. If this is true, life may not be a good thing at all—it may in fact be evil.

Sophocles makes explicit a foreboding many of us may feel but only dimly recognize. Why else would anyone make up a story like this and others find it interesting? Many of us feel an unspecified guilt we cannot avoid, no matter how careful and earnest we may try to be. We feel we will inexorably be found out and punished because we feel the guilt. Left unchecked, these feelings can make life bitter.

Speculation along these lines draws us deeply into the human condition. All great literature does this. It brings us to the pressure points where Catholic education can have telling effects.

There is, of course, much more to *Oedipus the King:* the themes, for instance, of a feeling of worthlessness, of alienation, of passivity before life, of the self-fulfilling prophesy, and of the evil of servitude to others against your better judgment that ultimately destroys our purchase on reality.

There is the supreme art of the poet and playwright Sophocles. One does not read ancient literature or any literature with a view to scoring points for Christianity, nor should an instructor in literature drag in Christian themes just for the sake of doing so. To do this would be to study theology rather than literature.

But when it is appropriate, and this depends on personalities and circumstances, I think students of literature have a right to expect the faculty to foster broad speculation. It is a form of intellectual integration that has been a hallmark of the Jesuit version of Catholic education.

What is intellectual integration? In simple terms I believe it is thinking about how things we experience in life fit together. It is integration because it draws experiences and ideas and facts together into one organic whole. It is intellectual because it is done by thinking and by having insights. It can be worked out consciously, formally, and methodically—we can sit down and write about it, or talk about it. It can also happen informally and automatically.

Everybody practices intellectual integration at least informally, even people who conclude that no integration is possible, that life is chaos, that it is absurd. For even this conclusion is an integration of various experiences.

If experiences are to be understood as fitting together into an intelligible whole, they have to be centered on some guiding idea, some central reality that explains the meaning of the whole and all its parts. For Christians, this is God and Christ.

We should make no mistake: education is not indoctrination, or maybe I should say that on the college level, in this country, in this day and age true education is not indoctrination. We faculty members should not think that we are directly causing our students to think this or that. In a secondary way we may be. But it is always under this format: we propose a view or a fact and the student either accepts it or not. Better to say the student either rejects it or modifies it. Or maybe the most accurate way to put it is that the student modifies it and fits it one way or another into his or her view of the world.

At any rate, students are free, and we the faculty want to foster that intellectual freedom. To the extent that we are successful in doing so, we are unsuccessful in directly causing our students to think what we might want them to think. We need to convince them that what we are proposing is true and worthwhile.

The study of literature is especially useful and good in promoting intellectual integration. This is so because literature presents the view of the world entertained by its author in a way that appeals to the imagination and the emotions as well as to the intellect, and which casts abstract insights and understandings in the form of the concrete and particular. This is especially true of the play and the novel and the motion picture. It is true in a different way of poetry—not to rehearse all of the forms of literature.

Literature is an art form with purposes other than serving as a vehicle for intellectual integration. High on the list of these other purposes is entertainment, providing enjoyment. Also high on the list is the way literature has of letting us get to know somebody else. We can enter into the mind of a character in a novel more thoroughly, more easily, and more quickly than we normally can in the case of our ordinary acquaintances. We come to know the mind of the author, too, because the author has said something very studied and complete to us, something on a level we rarely reach in living conversations. So we should be just as adamant in our refusal to teach literature solely as a vehicle of intellectual integration as we are to use it to promote Catholicism.

Learning how to appreciate and interpret literature can free a person from the tyranny of other people's views of the world and clear the way for the construction of one's own view. This is the case because so much of our lives is spent entwined in literature of one sort or another. Here I am thinking about songs with their lyrics reinforced with music, about advertisements of various sorts, about shows on television, and so on. Once we gain the habit of thinking about literature as literature, about what its themes are and how they are expressed, we are less influenced by the thoughts and attitudes that envelop us in the literary expressions that I just mentioned. Everyone is naturally critical of them to some extent, but the habit of literary criticism strengthens and reinforces this natural tendency and makes it much more effective in freeing us from ideas and attitudes we don't want to have. It helps us to see and evaluate, and choose or reject or modify ideas and attitudes that are presented to us.

Purpose of the Educators

Back to the Catholic mission of the university: in the *Constitutions of the Society of Jesus,* "the end of the Society and of its studies is to aid our fellowmen to the knowledge and love of God and to the salvation of their souls."[8] Father George Ganss, S.J., takes this as the fundamental purpose of all our Jesuit educational institutions. As he points out, Saint Ignatius is talking here about the final purpose, the most basic purpose, of the Jesuit educator.[9]

Jesuits are supposed to have this as a fundamental goal of their lives, including their lives in academe. Should other faculty members have the same fundamental goal in their educational activities, because it is an underlying goal of their lives? "For this the Church was founded: that by spreading the kingdom of Christ everywhere for the glory of God the Father, she might bring all men to share in Christ's saving redemption. . . . For by its very nature the Christian vocation is also a vocation to the apostolate."[10]

What about faculty members of Jesuit colleges and universities who are not Christian? Should their purpose be such that their educational activity works in harmony with the mission of the institution?

This focus is not something to be apologetic about, for to whom would we apologize? Everybody has some end in view in teaching, conscious or unconscious, and it governs the way the teaching is carried out. We have a purpose that in its persuasiveness integrates all knowledge, and not only that, it integrates life in all its dimensions. We have an answer, in principle at least, to the great puzzle bedeviling today's educators: what can be done about the disintegration of knowledge in the university, and about its sterility, its valueless emptiness?

But does this ultimate purpose of ours as faculty members make any practical difference in the classroom and in the way we go about our other duties? Of course it does. It colors the way we treat those around us. It governs what we say and do not say in class. I do not mean that it violates the canons of our disciplines, but I do mean that it governs the way we work with the canons of our disciplines.

An ultimate purpose in education that is related to the educator's own ultimate purpose in life is the thing that makes the educator an integrated person. The Jesuit university should encourage and facilitate the habit of intellectual integration in its students. It can't do this unless its faculty have this habit themselves. On another level, it is important that the faculty give an example of an integrated life. That means that their reason for being educators should be closely related to their ultimate purpose in life. There should be ample Catholic models of intellectual integration and of personal integration at a Catholic university.

Justice

JUL 7–10 [410–13] renews the call to change the structure of society so that those who are disadvantaged can have better opportunities for social and economic advancement, and so that all of us may reach "more profound levels of justice and freedom" (JUL 10 [413]). Happily, our universities have divisions that are better geared to promoting social and economic justice than are their classics departments. Yet in our own way we classicists directly promote justice and freedom.

Justice begins at home. Our immediate families, our children if we have them, or our brothers and sisters, or even our parents, have a right to expect us to be the best sort of persons we are capable of being. The case of children is the easiest to see. If we are less than we ought to be, and all of us are to some extent, our children won't get the sort of adult model for their lives that they deserve. This will be a handicap in their development.

This sort of justice can be generalized to include all of our relationships and contacts. Others deserve to encounter us as the best people we can be, and their lives are less rich to the extent that we are less than we could be. So justice is close to each of us, because to be just from this fundamental perspective we need to fulfill our human potential as best we can in our circumstances. From this point of view, the university is directly geared to promoting justice, because it is directly geared to helping us fulfill our human potential. This is especially true of the Catholic university, centered as it is on God and Christ, because the most important and central aspect of fulfilling our human potential concerns the knowledge, love, and service of God. As I have been arguing, the Catholic and Jesuit university tries on the intellectual level to foster an integration of faith with the other elements of our experience. Moreover, because we are a community with interests other than intellectual, we hope also to promote a broader integration of the personality while our students are with us.

Clearly though, the most important factor determining the degree to which our institutions are internally and fundamentally just is the extent to which our faculties are competent to foster intellectual integration from a Catholic perspective.

Suppose a university adopted a curriculum directly geared to highlight the opportunities for promoting the social and economic advancement of underprivileged groups, but in doing so neglected to address what is necessary for its students if they are to reach their full human potential as far as circumstances allow. Wouldn't such a university, even though its intentions are the very best and most sincere, actually be itself unjust to its students even as it tried to promote social and economic justice for the disadvantaged? The primary duty of a university must be to its own students, and the nature of its duty to them is to educate them. A university must first itself be just; it must be just foremost in doing its own most central duty as an educational institution. Then it will be positioned to promote social and economic justice in society at large. The social consequences, the good that can come about for society at large, if the university does its own job well, are incalculable.

Much of what I have proposed regarding the teaching function of the university is also true of its research and publishing agenda. For classicists this endeavor can be important as a stimulus to our own intellectual vitality. As such, even when it is entirely secular or strictly technical, it wears the legitimacy with which GC 34 has clothed all the limbs of Jesuit higher education. It can add intellectual credibility and luster to our institutions. Often it advances and communicates elements of Christian humanism. In all cases, "we are assured that, despite occasional appearances to the contrary, the truth we seek will ultimately be one. That truth, rooted as it is in God, will make us free" (JUL 12 [415]).

ENDNOTES • DALY

1. See "First Principle and Foundation," in *The Spiritual Exercises of St. Ignatius,* trans. Louis J. Puhl, S.J. (Westminster, Md.: Newman, 1951), 23, p. 12; and the account of Ignatius' illumination at the Cardoner in John C. Olin, ed., *The Autobiography of St. Ignatius Loyola, with Related Documents,* trans. Joseph F. O'Callaghan (New York: Fordham University Press, 1992), 39–40.

2. "Spiritual exercises which have as their purpose the conquest of self and the regulation of one's life in such a way that no decision is made under the influence of any inordinate attachment," *SpEx* 21, p. 11; cf. 1, p. 1.

3. See GC 34, Decree 2: "Servants of Christ's Mission" (SCM), esp. 14–21 [39–49]. Cf. GC 32, "Documents of the Holy See," in *Documents of the 31st and 32nd General Congregations of the Society of Jesus,* ed. John W. Padberg, S.J. (St. Louis, Mo.: Institute of Jesuit Sources, 1977), 546–48; and GC 34, "Allocution of Pope John Paul II," in *Documents of the Thirty-Fourth General Congregation of the Society of Jesus,* ed. John L. McCarthy, S.J. (St. Louis, Mo.: Institute of Jesuit Sources, 1995), 252–53.

4. See also "Declaration on Christian Education," 10–12, in *The Documents of Vatican II,* gen. ed. Walter M. Abbott, S.J., trans. ed. Joseph Gallagher (New York: Guild, 1966), 648–51 (further reference to Vatican II is from this edition); *Ex Corde Ecclesiae, Apostolic Constitution on Catholic Universities,* 1–30, 38, 43, 46, 48–49, in *Origins* 20 (4 October 1990): 265, 267–76.

5. The ambiguity may be partly a result of international differences that are hard to accommodate in a general decree. See JUL 4–5 [407–08].

6. JUL 3 [406] refers with approval to *Ex Corde Ecclesiae* and similar documents.

7. See John Henry Newman, *The Idea of a University,* ed. Frank M. Turner (New Haven, Conn., and London: Yale University Press, 1992), Discourse VI: "Knowledge Viewed in Relation to Learning" 9, pp. 105–7.

8. John W. Padberg, S.J., gen. ed., *The Constitutions of the Society of Jesus and Their Complementary Norms* (St. Louis, Mo.: Institute of Jesuit Sources, 1996), [446], p. 179.

9. George E. Ganss, S.J., *The Jesuit Educational Tradition and Saint Louis University* (St. Louis, Mo.: Saint Louis University, 1969), 19.

10. "Decree on the Apostolate of the Laity" 2, in Abbott, *Documents of Vatican II,* 491.

ESSAY 7

Teaching Communication in the Light of GC 34

Paul A. Soukup, S.J.

ABSTRACT

The author looks at the field of communication from its understanding in Church documents, Jesuit responses in GC 34, and his own work as validating and clarifying these two. For the Church, Christ is the "perfect communicator" in his self-emptying in culture "because he established perfect unity and justice," and "gave a voice to the voiceless." As companions of Jesus, Jesuits are called to do the same. Communication is both a tool of evangelization and an environment. In GC 34 communication becomes both act and world: as act, it is a tool for engaging the world "with Ignatian boldness" in embracing new ways of thinking and in a willingness to operate new technologies; as world, it calls for understanding and critique. A Jesuit university "acts as bridge to the community," correcting distorted images of the world created by the mass media, and fostering dialogue with the world and education of the whole person. Communication departments should "include issues of justice in the curriculum," and foster that engagement with the culture that sides with the "mis- or underrepresented," and brings "an intellectually sophisticated research capability to the problem."

Teaching can engross us, capturing our attention and affection, but at the same time it can shrink our world to the boundaries of our campus. GC 34 provides a healthy balance to this with its call to look outward again at our Jesuit identity, mission, and challenge. The Congregation offers the hope of renewal of what we do by a return to why we do it. To paraphrase a bit, we would do well to echo the Congregation and ask:

>   I. *What is it to be a Jesuit today?*
>   II. *What is it to be a Jesuit university today?*
>   III. *What is it to be a Jesuit university communication department today?*

For someone like myself, teaching communication in a Jesuit university, the questions provide the impetus to look at my teaching in the light of the Congregation.

What Is It to Be a Jesuit Today?

The Congregation calls us "servants of Christ's mission." It describes that mission in terms of service of faith, promotion of justice, evangelization of culture, entry into dialogue, and openness to others. None of these characteristics stands alone, but in the words of Decree 2: "Servants of Christ's Mission" (SCM), they fit into a pattern of Jesuit living:

> *No service of faith without*
> > *promotion of justice*
> > *entry into cultures*
> > *openness to other religious experiences*
> *No promotion of justice without*
> > *communicating faith*
> > *transforming cultures*
> > *collaborating with other traditions*
> *No inculturation without*
> > *communicating faith with others*
> > *dialogue with other traditions*
> > *commitment to justice*
> *No dialogue without*
> > *sharing faith with others*
> > *evaluating cultures*
> > *concern for justice.* (19 [47])

For a student and teacher of communication, the Congregation's emphasis on culture and communication both makes good sense and challenges me to look again at how I do what I do. In some ways the Congregation's documents invite me to ask on behalf of us all how we act and what we should do. For me, however, they do this within a larger framework, one partly erected by the Church's ongoing reflections on communication and partly built by the field of communication studies. In this structure, three sets of complementary themes take shape. The first, from Church documents, describes the challenge of communication. The second, from the Congregation, examines Jesuit responses. And the third, from communication, validates and clarifies the other two.

The great Church documents on communication describe Christ as the "perfect communicator" because he emptied himself to enter human culture fully, because he established perfect unity and justice (communion) through love, and because he gave a voice to the voiceless.[1] As companions of this Jesus, we Jesuits emulate his communication through an engagement with culture, through the work of evangelization, through our willingness to create communion with all men and women, and through a commitment to justice born of that communion.

Writing in *Redemptoris Missio* (Mission of the Redeemer) (1990), Pope John Paul II remarks that in our contemporary world we should treat culture seriously and broadly. Just as Saint Paul brought the gospel message to the Athenian Areopagus in the first century, so we too must bring the Gospel to our world. The places that call for evangelization include the "areopagus" of communication.

> *The first Areopagus of the modern age is the* world of communications, *which is unifying humanity and turning it into what is known as a "global village." The means of social communication have become so important as to be for many the chief means of information and education, of guidance and inspiration in their behavior as individuals, families and within society at large. In particular, the younger generation is growing up in a world conditioned by the mass media. . . . [S]ince the very evangelization of modern culture depends to a great extent on the influence of the media, it is not enough to use the media simply to spread the Christian message and the Church's authentic teaching. It is also necessary to integrate that message into the "new culture" created by modern communications. This is a complex issue, since the "new culture" originates not just from whatever content is eventually expressed, but from the very fact that there exist new ways of communicating, with new languages, new techniques and a new psychology.*[2]

On the one hand, this cultural place and the people who dwell there stand in need of evangelization. On the other hand, the Gospel and its ministers must seek inculturation into this new cultural world.

The cultural world of communication creates a complex whole that engulfs all people. It not only forms a part of each human culture, but also, in our age of multinational enterprise and global networks, cuts across individual cultures. Moreover, as John Paul II recognizes, communication constitutes both a tool and an environment. As a tool, it forms a means of evangelization. It describes an activity that all engage in—whether in conversation, in preaching, in teaching, in writing, or in the mass media. As an environment, communication describes the context of our lives, complete with its set of definitions and explanations for how the world works.

James Carey, the former dean of the College of Communication at the University of Illinois, suggests a similar distinction of functions to clarify the complex world of communication. One function he names "transmission": handing on knowledge, getting a message across, imparting information. But, more importantly, people also engage in what Carey terms "ritual": creating and sustaining a community. Here communication consists of the "construction and maintenance of an ordered, meaningful cultural world that can serve as a control and container for human action."[3] In this light, communication is the "representation of shared beliefs," what "draws persons together in fellowship and commonality."[4] His example of the newspaper as a ritual makes his point clearer: Seeing communication as a ritual "will, for example, view reading a newspaper less as sending or gaining information and more as attending a Mass, a situation in which nothing new is learned but in which a particular view of the world is portrayed and confirmed."[5] Communication, then, becomes both act and world, an experience, perhaps best known in the kinds of ritual processes through which we interact and know the world. This "culture" consists of both the set of ideas, which we take for granted more often than not, and the practices through which we make those ideas our own—reading the paper, watching television, listening to the radio. In all of these we cooperate with the communication industry to produce and reproduce this new culture.

GC 34 echoes this view in Decree 15: "Communication: A New Culture" (CNC), noting that it could equally describe communication either as a sector of Jesuit work or as a dimension of all Jesuit ministry (CNC 3 [387]). Similarly, it regards communication as a tool (CNC 4–5 [388–89]), which the Society should embrace, and as a culture, which calls for greater understanding (6 [390]) and for an honest critique (5 [389]).

Moreover, the Congregation has identified a number of Jesuit activities that touch upon the world of communication: dialogue (Decrees 2, 4, 5), inculturation (Decree 5), evangelization (Decrees 2, 4), intellectual reflection (Decree 16), university teaching (Decree 17), action on behalf of justice (Decree 3), collaboration in ministry (Decree 13), ecumenism (Decree 12), and the situation of women (Decree 14). Each of these has a communication component and, in fact, most call for us to hone our communication skills in ways we have not before.

Perhaps three examples will make this clear. First, to collaborate effectively— whether in evangelization, teaching, social ministry, or ecumenism—we must learn the art of interpersonal communication and dialogue. This includes learning to listen, learning to express ourselves clearly, and, perhaps painfully, learning to let go of our "rights" to direct our own work or to protect our own thinking. Second, to deal effectively with the new culture of communication, we must incorporate media education in our lives and works. This includes gaining a sense of how communication media work to represent and reproduce the world, gaining a sense of the economic and political structures of these media, and gaining a sense of their visual and narrative patterns—what Pope John Paul termed the "new languages" of communication. Third, to engage our world with an Ignatian boldness, we must embrace a new way of thinking that incorporates communication at every level. With the rapid convergence and growth of communication media and techniques, this includes a willingness to express ourselves with new technologies, a willingness to link existing works to new forms, and a willingness to confront the injustices, exploitation, and blindness that these media incorporate and foster.

These things, then, form a context of Jesuit ministry. We are companions and communicators all. What does it mean to be a Jesuit? To be a Jesuit, to serve Christ's mission, requires that we communicate in two complementary ways. First, we create and transmit messages; second, we engage the culture of communication through participation, reflection, analysis, and critique. To be a Jesuit today, in other words, includes taking our place in fellowship and commonality with the world, unafraid to give witness to the Gospel in a new language that we must make our own.

What Is It to Be a Jesuit University Today?

Viewed through the lens of communication, the educational sector of Jesuit ministry provides a privileged place for the engagement with culture that the Congregation describes. Education itself—like the communication industry—produces and reproduces culture; however, its intellectual requirements add rigor and critique to the cultural process. Here we can expect to find a place for the discernment that Decree 4: "Our Mission and Culture" describes:

> *Our ministry of evangelizing culture will be a ministry of consolation when it is guided by ways that bring to light the character of God's activity in those cultures, and that strengthen our sense of the divine mystery. But our efforts will be misguided, and even destructive, when our activity runs contrary to the grain of his presence in the cultures which the Church addresses, or when we claim to exercise sole proprietorial rights over the affairs of God.* (9 [88])

Part of the Ignatian educational process includes evaluating and critiquing culture, not only with the tools of intellect and science, but also with those of faith.

Focused narrowly on communication questions, the work of the Congregation suggests to me that a Jesuit university will have at least four characteristics. In writing this, I do not mean to suggest that other elements do not have a place—even a defining place—in Jesuit universities. My perspective emerges from the optic of the doubled sense of communication described above: a culture within culture, and both a tool and an environment.

First, a Jesuit university will promote genuine dialogue, living out what Hans-Georg Gadamer[6] describes as a fusion of horizons. By honestly preserving and describing culture, it allows the past to speak to the present; it allows the young to meet the old; it allows the marginalized a voice; and it allows serious reflection on differences. A place of learning, it takes culture seriously, including the popular culture of mass communication.

Second, a Jesuit university fosters what most of our schools call "the education of the whole person." Ignatian pedagogy refuses to focus only on the intellect. This it does, but it also seeks to engage the interpersonal, social, ethical, spiritual, psychological, and emotional dimensions of students' lives. How students live in society, how they think critically, how they express themselves, how they recognize and confront injustice, how they relate to others and to God all form part of that education of the whole person. Because of this, a Jesuit university cannot ignore the pedagogical role assumed by the means of social communication, which, as Pope John Paul notes, have become "for many the chief means of information and education, of guidance and inspiration in their behavior as individuals, families and within society at large" (*Redemptoris Missio* 37). A Jesuit university can no more ignore this aspect of our contemporary culture than it can avoid the classical works defining Western civilization.

Third, a Jesuit university acts as bridge to the community, bringing the community into its intellectual world and bringing its students into the community. We find a good example of this characteristic in the many service learning projects undertaken in Jesuit schools. Not only do these recognize different learning styles but they also recognize that the university should encourage many voices, including those of the poor. All too often students come to the university with an image of the world formed by the mass media—an image distorted particularly in regards to women, the poor, the old, and religion. The university experience acts as a corrective to such false images and as an introduction to the civic context. A university's connection with its community extends both its commitment to dialogue and its commitment to educating the whole person.

Finally, a Jesuit university has a rhetorical orientation. In a communication culture, it gives witness to the value of communication and it teaches communication: writing, speaking, argumentation, dramatic and artistic expression, the use of new technologies. It teaches criticism, the evaluation of argumentation, and logical thinking. It also acknowledges what Aristotle named *ethos* and *pathos*—a concern for character and an empathy with others. Communication becomes a way of living.

These things form part of the structure of a Jesuit university today by providing the means for the discernment of culture described by GC 34. To be a Jesuit university today directly involves communication: mastering its tools and engaging its culture.

What Is It to Be a Jesuit University Communication Department Today?

As a part of a Jesuit university, the communication department takes on the characteristics described above. However, it adds things more specific to its own area of study. Like any other department, the communication department must teach the basic curriculum, whether that encompasses speech, rhetoric, journalism, interpersonal communication, public relations, television, advertising, film studies, multimedia, or some combination of them. But GC 34 suggests that there is more to it than this. As noted above, a number of Jesuit activities include communication dimensions (dialogue, inculturation, evangelization, intellectual reflection, university teaching, action on behalf of justice, collaboration in ministry, ecumenism, the situation of women); some of them fit as well into a departmental curriculum.

In order to reflect the values and goals of the Congregation, communication departments at Jesuit universities should stress at least three things within their general curriculum. I base this observation on my experience at Santa Clara, where we do these things—perhaps not as well as we should, but we have tried to include them. In addition, at their annual meeting, representatives of the Communication Departments of the Association of Jesuit Colleges and Universities (AJCU) have discussed ways to respond to GC 34. Other schools no doubt have their own approaches to the same challenges.

First, it seems to me that we must include issues of justice in the curriculum. These might enter our teaching under several headings:

(A) Communication policy debates. (What role should the government take, for example, regarding violence on television? Regarding ownership of telecommunications facilities? Regarding access to the Internet?) Such debates are natural elements in the curriculum given the United States Telecommunications Act of 1996, which raises many of these issues.

(B) The political economy of the media. (How do ownership patterns and profit margins influence communication practices in different countries? How does economic or political power flow from the media?) In a world where we too often consider mass media as mass entertainment, we do well to realize the other roles they play in society.

(C) The right to information and communication. (How do groups and individuals utilize communication? What restrictions apply?) Although some have treated these questions in Cold War terms, the Church raised them as serious issues, both at the Second Vatican Council and in later documents (*Inter Mirifica* [Decree on the Means of Social Communication], *Communio et Progressio* [Pastoral Instruction on the Means of Social Communication]). Decree 15 (CNC) offers a perspective for examining such questions of justice:

> *But we must also look critically at the authoritarian methods and unjust structures of communication and information organizations themselves. . . . Freedom of the press and information must be promoted in countries where they are nonexistent or threatened by state control or ideological manipulation. An equitable flow of communication between industrialized and developing countries needs to be established.* (5 [389])

While the Congregation raises the questions, communication departments form natural places to seek the answers.

Second, and related to the first, we must include questions of representation in the curriculum. Because the communication media so influence culture and ways of thinking, distorted images of individuals or groups can cause serious damage. We already recognize how this happens with women (as does Decree 14) and minorities, but the phenomenon deserves more study in terms of other cultures, religions, and political systems. Perhaps more than other areas this one gains strength from the connections of Jesuit universities to their communities. For many of the mis- or underrepresented, their contact with a Jesuit university may be the only contact they have with an institution that will take their side and bring an intellectually sophisticated research capability to their problem. This same concern for the underrepresented flows over into questions of interpersonal communication, because many of our students have no ordinary contact with the poor or with groups different from themselves. A respect for the dignity of others flows from contact with others.

Third, we must explore the connections between communication and culture as a first step toward that engagement with culture described by the Congregation. Cultural studies models already hold an honored place within communication curricula, though many times we have not articulated them in as sophisticated a way as demanded by the complex interaction of media, institutions, individuals, and groups. Communication departments may well benefit from more collaborative or interdisciplinary work in this area in particular. Additionally (and I hope not surprisingly), a communication ethics (so briefly alluded to in Decree 15: 5 [389]) may well play a dominant role here, though it, too, has remained underdeveloped.

These three curricular areas show great promise in the communication departments of Jesuit schools. We have begun to address them, and there is much room for growth. There exist other areas inspired by the Congregation, which some schools pursue. These include media education, not so much for our own students (who study these topics throughout the curriculum) but as an outreach program. Decree 15 (CNC) indicates the importance of such programs:

> *In the new media culture, it is important to educate media users to understand and make creative use of communication techniques and language, not only* as individuals but also as participants in the social dialogue. (CNC 6 [390], emphasis added)

In the context of academic life in the United States, we all too easily lose sight of that social dialogue. Here the Congregation serves us well to remind us of a goal for our teaching that extends beyond the campus. Another possibility that the Congregation presents to communication departments arises from the themes of ecumenism and evangelization. While communication scholars do not have the competence to work in such fields, we do have valuable expertise to support those who do. While other university units (departments of theology or religious studies, campus ministry, and so on) and diocesan offices take on active roles in ecumenical dialogue and in evangelization, the communication department might explore ways to offer support.

The AJCU Communication Group already does a great deal to promote collaborative study and work in communication across campus boundaries. The annual conversations about curriculum, about addressing questions of justice, about service learning, and about intellectual work help us to maintain the focus encouraged by the Congregation. But, as usual, there is more we might do. I have often thought that we could strategically develop a clearly articulated national (or international) "Jesuit school" or approach to communication study, perhaps along the lines of the Centre for the Study of Communication and Culture at Saint Louis University.

Finally, the Congregation can influence a personal research agenda. In response to the Society's priorities, I have more or less consciously chosen to look at two areas that fit well with the Congregation: religious communication and the interplay between culture and communication. This latter focus also has a religious component, particularly in terms of evangelization. For example, I now work with the American Bible Society on their Multimedia Translations Project, which attempts to provide biblical materials in nonwritten formats. To do this, the task group draws on communication research about culture, literacy, visual communication, audience studies, and so on. Our overall intent is evangelization, and what we learn here may help to address the larger question of the evangelization of culture.

To be a Jesuit university communication department implies a willingness to teach the traditional communication curriculum in a different way, highlighting some themes over others. It implies addressing questions of justice, dialogue, and culture in a serious intellectual fashion. And it implies that each of us on a faculty find ways to make that commitment our own.

Conclusion

GC 34 has renewed the desire of the Society to walk as companions of Jesus, to join together as servants of Christ's mission.

> Like that of Ignatius, our way of proceeding is both a pilgrimage and a labor in Christ: in his compassion, in his ceaseless desire to bring men and women to the Father's reconciliation and the Spirit's love, and in his committed care for the poor, the marginalized, and the abandoned. (UCM 5 [5])

We do this in many ways: our diversity enriches the body of the Society. I hope to do it as a teacher of communication—a member of a communication department at a Jesuit university. As I have sketched here, the Congregation gives us the opportunity to integrate our life and work, to look beyond the confines of the campus to the world Christ—and Ignatius—so loved.

ENDNOTES • SOUKUP

1. Pontifical Council for Social Communications, *Communio et Progressio* (Pastoral Instruction on the Means of Social Communication) 11, in *Vatican Council II: The Conciliar and Post Conciliar Documents,* ed. Austin Flannery, O.P. (Collegeville, Minn.: Liturgical, 1975 [1971]), 293–349 at 247; Pontifical Council for Social Communications, *Aetatis Novae.* (A New Era: Pastoral Instruction on Social Communications on the 20th Anniversary of *Communio et Progressio.*) (Vatican City: Libreria Editrice Vaticana, 1992); Paul VI, *Evangelii Nuntiandi.* (On Evangelization in the Modern World) (Washington, D.C.: USCC, 1976), 45.

2. John Paul II, *Redemptoris Missio* (Washington, D.C.: USCC, 1990), 37.

3. James W. Carey, "A Cultural Approach to Communication," in James W. Carey, *Communication as Culture: Essays on Media and Society* (Boston, Mass.: Unwin Hyman, 1989 [1975]), 13–36 at 18–19.

4. Ibid., 18.

5. Ibid., 20.

6. Hans-Georg Gadamer, *Truth and Method,* trans. G. Barden and J. Cumming (New York: Seabury, 1975 [1965]), 273ff.

GC 34, Higher Education, and Computer Science

Dennis C. Smolarski, S.J.

ABSTRACT

The author focuses on the impact of GC 34 on the scientific and technical disciplines. From its origins, Jesuit education understood study in the physical sciences and mathematics as necessary for the well-educated person who would "play a significant role in the world," and for the "salvation of souls." The author sees his field of computer science "in direct continuity" with the Ignatian vision. For both religious and laity, the computer world has built up a network of connections having vast implications for the formation of "a new culture in our world." The author distinguishes between the "pragmatic norm" that identifies appropriate means for desired goals (which Ignatius fostered), and pragmatism, which demands immediate application to current issues. He wonders whether the latter is, in fact, a disguised curse for the sciences as well as for religious life; for example, he fears that certain explanations and implementations of the recent emphasis in Jesuit spirituality on the promotion of justice may unintentionally become obstacles to the rigor required for scientific study and the long-range contribution abstract sciences may make to society. The author reflects upon the vast untapped areas for advancement in computer knowledge and their ethical implications.

Introduction

It is an understatement to say that we live in an age of computers, and neither the Catholic Church nor the Society of Jesus can isolate itself from the influence computers have in our world. In actuality, neither has. The Vatican has its own homepage on the World Wide Web and "publishes" documents on CD-roms. During GC 34, the Society of Jesus issued news reports by e-mail, which were distributed worldwide via a computer in Korea. Some delegates to the Congregation brought laptop computers on which the Congregation's documents were written and rewritten. Since GC 34, a Jesuit-only e-mail distribution list (the "virtual recreation room") via a computer at Le Moyne College in Syracuse, New York, has provided contact and conversation for Jesuits worldwide, and a similar list enables scholastics in East Asia to communicate with each other. Moreover, e-mail addresses of many Jesuits are now included in the common catalog of the United States Jesuit Assistancy.

On one level, attempting to address the relationship of the Society of Jesus to computer science is like trying to address the relationship of contemporary Christianity to the telephone. The computer is yet another technological wonder, like so many in the past—the clock, the printing press, the engine, the automobile, the telephone—that causes us to rethink established ways of doing things and makes us wonder how we ever managed without them. Yet, because of their complexity, computers are used in myriads of ways, a claim that few, if any, other technological or scientific inventions can make.

But there is another level at which the relationship of the Society of Jesus to computers should be the subject of reflection—the level of a self-contained academic discipline. It is at this level that I will focus my comments on what I see as the vision of GC 34 and the impact this vision can and should make on higher education, particularly on scientific and technical disciplines.

The Constitutions of the Society of Jesus and Academic Disciplines

Before examining the documents of GC 34, let us first look at the *Constitutions of the Society of Jesus,* for it is here that we find Ignatius' thoughts on academic disciplines appropriate for study by Jesuits and in Jesuit universities.

It is not surprising that the *Constitutions* make no mention of computer science. But what might surprise some is the mention of disciplines commonly considered to belong to the world of science and technology. In part 4, chapter 5, entitled "What the Scholastics of the Society Should Study," Ignatius lists logic and natural philosophy (what are commonly called the biological and physical sciences today) as required areas for study, along with theology and Scripture.[1] In chapter 12 of this same part, entitled "The Subjects Which Should Be Taught in the Universities of the Society," he lists natural sciences, logic, physics, and mathematics (cf. *Const* [450, 451]).

The subject areas mentioned in the *Constitutions* should be seen in the context of the *trivium* (grammar, rhetoric, logic) and the *quadrivium* (arithmetic, geometry, music, astronomy). In Ignatius' time, these seven disciplines had been considered for several centuries as foundational subjects and were taught in a *collegium* by the lower faculty of the liberal arts.[2] Without a solid basis in these foundational subjects (which, in a sense, focused on basic skills), a student could not hope to succeed in any of the specialized faculties of a Renaissance university.[3] And, as I eagerly point out to students who claim to have a "math phobia" or who question the relevance of science for a humanities major, four of these seven areas dealt with subjects now usually taught by mathematics or science instructors. (Note that "logic" and "logic design" are standard courses taught in mathematics, computer science, and computer engineering departments as well as being taught in Aristotelian format in philosophy departments.)

Our contemporary Western categorization of human knowledge into distinct fields may also obscure the breadth formerly considered under one title. Current divisions in scientific and technical disciplines were not clear-cut until well into the nineteenth century, and even today, in some institutes of higher education, there is a certain fluidity of departmental affiliation for scientists whose research builds upon and bridges several fields. Centuries ago, individuals who focused on physics or astronomy often made advances in geometry and other areas of mathematics. Should such individuals be considered "astronomers" or "mathematicians" or both or neither? For me, the mere mention of scientific fields in the *Constitutions* reflects Ignatius' insight into the complexity of God's creation. It also indicates how varied the fields were that Ignatius considered necessary for the human mind to study to be well educated and able to play a significant role in the world. In reality, students who learned "physics," "natural science," and "mathematics" may have been exposed to much of the technical knowledge known in the sixteenth century.

For proof that some early Jesuits were, in fact, very well trained in what we might call "cutting edge" scientific and technological fields, we need only look at the lives of two Jesuits. One was Matteo Ricci (1552–1610) who won esteem at the courts of China because of the astronomical equipment he brought from Europe and his scientific acumen. The other was Christopher Clavius (Christoph Klau) (1538–1612) whose mathematical calculations, coupled with astronomical observations, produced the Gregorian calendar and whose legacy to mathematical notation includes the decimal point, the square-root sign, and parentheses. Clavius was also a friend of Galileo and served on a committee of Jesuits who revised the *Ratio Studiorum* to mandate the teaching of geometry in all Jesuit schools.

But we should not look at the academic subjects in Jesuit documents or the expertise of certain Jesuits independently of the motivation for studying various disciplines. Ignatius expressed his mind in part 4, chapter 5 of the *Constitutions* when writing about the required courses for scholastics. He states:

> *Since the end of the learning which is acquired in this Society is with God's favor to help the souls of its own members and those of their neighbors, it is by this norm that the decision will be made, both in general and in the case of individual persons, as to what subjects* [Jesuits] *ought to learn, and how far they ought to advance in them.* (*Const* [351])

Ignatius is clear: All knowledge is to be used to benefit others—"to help the souls," using the language of the sixteenth century. We know, moreover, from reflecting on his activities, that the phrase "helping souls" or "the salvation of souls" never referred exclusively to religious matters. Ignatius' actions showed he had a more holistic view of the human person and what it meant to "help souls" when he and his companions took care of the sick and dying, fed the hungry, and sheltered the homeless. Moreover, for Ignatius, any discipline that helped reach the "end" was worth learning and teaching.

Ignatius repeats his vision at the beginning of chapter 12, in writing about the disciplines taught in the universities:

> . . . the end of the Society and of its studies is to aid our [neighbors] to the knowlege and love of God and to the salvation of their souls. . . . (Const [446])

I admit that in this same paragraph, Ignatius puts principal emphasis on theology, but he also sees other disciplines as necessary to assist the study of theology as well as in themselves.

> Moreover, since both the learning of theology and the use of it require (especially in these times) knowledge of humane letters . . . there should be capable professors. . . . (Const [447])

> Likewise, since the arts or natural sciences dispose the intellectual powers for theology, and are useful for the perfect understanding and use of it, and also by their own nature help toward the same ends, they should be treated with fitting diligence and by learned professors. . . .(Const [450])

Noteworthy in this paragraph is the comment that "the arts or natural sciences . . . by their own nature help toward the same ends" (emphasis added). Although in Ignatius' writings theology was a focal point for a university, and understanding theology was aided by studying other subjects, Ignatius also saw other disciplines as independently leading "toward the same ends," which is, ultimately, helping others, especially those unable to help themselves. The "norm" to be used to determine which branches to study and to teach is this simple end: "the salvation of . . . souls." In a sense, this can be seen as an academic formulation of the Ignatian gift of "finding God in all things."

These paragraphs suggest to me that the study and teaching of computer science is in direct continuity with the vision of Ignatius rather than being on any periphery. Our contemporary culture is interwined with computers as backbones for communication, information storage, technological advances, commerce, scientific and nonscientific research, and recreation (to name but a few fields in which computers are used). Because of their utility in so many areas, computers can be of great value in "helping souls." Thus, it seems perfectly in line with Ignatius' sentiments that the formal study of something as much a part of our comtemporary culture as computers should have a place, even an honored place, in contemporary Jesuit higher education.

GC 34, Science, and Technology

If the software I used to scan an electronic version of various documents of GC 34 (available on the World Wide Web) worked correctly, the word *computer* does not appear in any decree. But the related words, *science* and *technology,* which do occur, indicate that the Congregation grappled with issues related to modern technology. For example, in Decree 4: "Our Mission and Culture" (OMC), the difference between scientific and faith answers to modern questions is discussed (22 [106]); and in Decree 16: "The Intellectual Dimension of Jesuit Ministries" (IDJM), references to science and technology and the autonomy of science are found (4 [397]). (The Congregation also mentions science and technology in four other decrees.)

For me, the decrees of GC 34 realistically refer to the role of science and technology (and thus, to the world of computers) in our contemporary world. They portray science and technology as aspects of contemporary human life, aspects that cannot be overlooked as Jesuits adapt their ministries in an everchanging world. Because science and technology are so intertwined with the world in which we live, it is most appropriate that they be studied in Jesuit schools in various ways, both in how they affect people in their daily lives as well as in abstract and foundational ways.

SUMMARIZING GC 34

There are probably as many ways of summarizing GC 34 as there are Jesuits and others who have examined its decrees. Let me propose my own: *GC 34 has called Jesuits to reflect on the CONTEXT of their vocation and, in a particular way, to engage themselves with CULTURE and COMMUNICATION, in a spirit of COLLABORATION.*

Let me unpack the four key words a bit:

Context: The decrees of GC 34 invite me to reflect, once again, on what it means to be a Jesuit, being a companion with Christ on mission (cf. Decree 1: "United with Christ on Mission"), and being someone who must also ponder the implications of "The New Context" of the Church and the World (cf. Decree 11: "On Having a Proper Attitude of Service in the Church").

Culture: Given a renewed look at the context of communal Jesuit life and ministry in many decrees, GC 34 focuses on culture in Decree 4 (OMC) (and mentions culture in fourteen other documents).

Communication: The Congregation responded to the proliferation of forms of communication by Decree 15: "Communication: A New Culture."

Collaboration: The Congregation advises that Jesuit ministries can no longer be seen as the private domain of individual Jesuits (Decree 13: "Cooperation with the Laity in Mission").

When I look at the Congregation's focus on *culture, communication,* and *collaboration* (beautifully captured in the verses found in SCM 19 [47]), I see my academic discipline of computer science reflected. For several reasons, I do not think I am stretching for any connections. Our contemporary culture is dominated by an evergrowing reliance on technology, which itself relies on computers. A new age of communication has dawned with the birth of the Internet and the availability of electronic treasuries of information as close as a computer connected to a modem and the ability to communicate instantaneously via e-mail with people on the other side of the world. And the networking of unknown numbers of computers, all "collaborating" with each other, as well as the trend toward "distributed computing" and "parallel processing," are images of what Jesuits are called to do in their ministries. In the sense that GC 34 invites me to look ever more at our culture, a culture I am deeply involved in through my work with computers, I see its thrust and spirit influencing me and challenging what I do in my apostolic work in a university.

SCIENCE

Members of my Jesuit community often ask me computer questions. Both they and I get frustrated when they ask about WordPerfect 6.0 and I say I know nothing about that word processing program, and they respond with "But I thought you taught computers." Computer applications are no more "computer science" than the United States Declaration of Independence is English grammar. Certainly word processing software is an application of computer science, just as documents originally composed in English use English grammar. But one does not do justice to any "science" by reducing an entire discipline and methodology to a small application or identifying the underlying science with its popular applications.

Most of us would agree that the ability to *drive* a car is distinctively different from the ability to *fix* a car, or to design a more efficiently running car, or to determine the route needed to get a car from point A to point B. Similarly, designing a new television camera or set is different from operating a camera, writing a television script, or being a television actor or talk show host. Driving a car, being a television actor, and using a computer for word processing are primarily utilitarian interactions with modern technologies. But designing a more efficient engine or a smaller television camera, pondering new computer architectures, designing new computer languages, creating new computer algorithms that are provably faster than existing ones are all in the realm of theory and are foundational for the advancement of science and technology.

It is important to acknowledge such distinctions because of common misperceptions of what sciences and engineering disciplines can or cannot do, and how "practical" or "impractical" various aspects of these disciplines are. Because of certain misunderstandings about the nature of "computer science," some researchers now refer to their discipline as "computational science" or "scientific computation" to emphasize that using physical "computers" is secondary to the scientific study of the "computation" that computers enable humans to do. It pertains to sciences to observe the natural world, organize what is observed, and abstract theories based on the observations. Sciences formulate hypotheses, test them, and assert the truth of laws or the falsity of propositions. These theoretical aspects are critically necessary for the future of scientific knowledge, yet because they are often so technical and abstract, they tend to be overlooked and even ignored by many people, who focus on "But what good is it?"

The Pragmatic Norm vs. Pragmatism

In all Jesuit apostolates, the legacy of Ignatius, as clarified, enhanced, and adapted by General Congregations in response to contemporary challenges, should provide the ambience in which ministry takes place. Without being motivated and guided by Jesuit traditions, it would be difficult to continue calling certain apostolic activities "Jesuit." The *Constitutions* and decrees of General Congregations give Jesuits the ends for apostolic work as well as various means to help achieve those ends. This pragmatic norm of identifying desired goals and using appropriate means to achieve them has been a long and honored Jesuit tradition.

But I admit to having hesitations about certain "practical" ways of interpreting congregational decrees. For example, I am uneasy with those who would propose, as a result of GC 34, numerous and explicit changes in content or in pedagogy for *every* course in academic institutions *without exception.* I have misgivings about urging Jesuits to respond to decrees of Congregations by significantly redirecting their energies of research and scholarship toward issues that relate only to contemporary problems. In a sense, I worry about well-intentioned individuals who take a naive, almost fundamentalistic, approach to implementing GC 34 (or any other General Congregation, for that matter). In the long run, in certain disciplines, the *magis,* "the greater good," may in fact be achieved, particularly for future generations of the human race, by dedicated, solitary research in, for example, an obscure and very abstract science, producing results that may not seem to have any applications for decades.

I agree that looking toward the future can be an excuse to avoid grappling with the present and that focusing on the theoretical can be an escape from involvement with the "nitty-gritty." Yet I am also convinced that "pragmatism" (in the sense of demanding that something have immediate utility) can be one of the greatest enemies of the growth of science and technology.

Many might agree with me when I suggest that the pursuit of knowledge and truth as well as praise given to God begins with *wonder*, something which, in itself, is not very practical. Yet, unless I can look at creation, look at the "work of human hands," look at human history and current problems, and then stand back and marvel and reflect on them, I cannot grow in knowledge about the world in which I live, nor can I grow in praise of the God who is the origin of all that is and guides it in loving providence. My experience is that much of science and technology begins in wonder and in asking, "Why?" But the answer to the "Why?" or the "Why not?" often leads to years of seemingly fruitless research, experimentation, and frustration, much of which has no immediate practical usefulness.

Though wonder and awe may not be very practical, they are at the core of what it means to be human! When I stand back and marvel at the coherence, the beauty, the abstract truth I find in mathematical proofs or computer-generated numeric results, I sometimes find myself echoing Saint Augustine's sentiments, if not some of his words, as recorded in the *Confessions:* "O eternal truth. . . . Late have I loved you, O Beauty ever ancient, ever new."[4] To use the image of Exodus (3:2) and echo the words of Elizabeth Barrett Browning, some people look at a bush and want to pluck blackberries (albeit perhaps to satisfy their hunger), but scientists often stand in awe before a barren bush, overwhelmed at seeing its "flames."

It is not for its own sake that Jesuits engage in science, but as a means to an end. That end is "the salvation of souls" or, in different words, knowledge of God and of God's creation. Science is pursued in the hope that, directly or indirectly, with some insight and inspiration, someone may one day utilize new discoveries as building blocks to construct a better world. In this sense, basic scientific research admirably fulfills the "pragmatic norm" long used by Jesuits, yet often not what many would term very "practical." Much scientific research and study focuses on providing a firm foundation for the future, rather than providing immediate solutions for today's transitory crises.

Discovering more about black holes in intergalactic space will not in itself provide jobs for inner-city teenagers or bring an end to the warring between the Hutus and the Tutsis. Taking an elementary course in organic chemistry will not immediately enable a student to discover a cure for HIV or cancer. Learning about the syntax of C++ and the different parameter passing schemes of FORTRAN-90 or Ada will not enable a freshman to write a program to predict the next tornado. But rigorous scientific work, at both foundational and advanced levels, provides the language and tools better to understand God's creation.

I firmly believe that the pursuit of truth and beauty, the experience of wonder and awe, whether in the physical sciences, in abstract mathematics, in music, in art, or in data generated by computer simulations, can both draw a person through creation to the Creator of all and, in the long run, contribute to the betterment of society. In its own way, such earthly progress does assist in building up the Kingdom of God, while remaining distinct from it. Although the Kingdom is in our midst (cf. Lk 17:21), we continue to pray that it may come in its fullness (cf. Mt 6:10), the Kingdom of peace and joy of God's Spirit (cf. Rom 14:17). The Second Vatican Council's *Constitution on the Church in the Modern World* (*Gaudium et Spes*) tells us (n. 39) that we must distinguish earthly progress from that of the Kingdom of Christ.[5] Nevertheless, the Council also states that earthly progress that improves human society is of vital concern to the Kingdom of God—and basic scientific research is central to such earthly progress.

Decree 16 and the Jesuit Intellectual Tradition

Decree 16 of GC 34 focuses on the intellectual dimension of Jesuit ministries and, in a sense, its very existence is a counterbalance to exaggerated emphasis on the pragmatic. The decree refers to the high esteem given to intellectual labor by the Society from its foundation (IDJM 1 [394]). It also mentions "vigorous spiritual and intellectual formation for young Jesuits" (3 [396]) and "competence"(4 [397]) and recognizes "the specific characteristic of each of the various scholarly disciplines, including science and technology" (4 [397]). To summarize, this decree stresses seriousness and rigor in undertaking any and all academic disciplines.

I find this decree particularly heartening because the world of science and technology is a world foreign to so many people (Jesuits included!), is often misunderstood, and sometimes is obliquely criticized by nonscientists. Scientists are regularly caricatured as absentminded professors living in a world far removed from the day-to-day struggles of much of humanity, and many people believe that the caricature is the reality. Oftentimes, the give and take, the different approaches, and the intrinsic nuances that are part of many disciplines are absent from sciences and other technical fields. Some scientists are even criticized for their exactitude and rigor, for being more comfortable with chemicals or computers than with conversations with a colleague or companion. It is true that, in general, one cannot discuss various personal feelings or opinions about a mathematical theorem—it either is true or false and can be proven to be one of the two. A computer program "works" if it is accepted by a computer and does what its author claims it will do, no matter what the input. The mind-set needed to work in fields requiring such exactitude is a talent that God has not given to everyone, but it is necessary for the growth of scientific knowledge. Unfortunately, some critics see such a mind-set as more properly belonging to machines than to humans and thus denigrate the value of possessing such expertise.

People generally agree that some types of scientific research can be lonely and specialized, dry and at times boring, and even those who would never think of changing their fields acknowledge that they must often be content with delayed gratification. In other words, the type of affirmation and consolation that many people receive from sustained interpersonal interactions common in the social sciences, the humanities, or pastoral ministry is frequently absent in the work done by other scientists. Perhaps this is why such technical fields are less attractive for many younger Jesuits now than they had been in decades past. Yet, the solitary and abstract aspects of science should never mean that such scientific work is any less significant in the contribution it may make to society's well-being, in bringing about a more just world, in aiding the "salvation of souls," in assisting God's Kingdom to come.

Lest it seem as if I am "protesting too much," the context of my words is the anxiety and confusion I felt after GC 32. At that time, the focus of the Society was rightly on issues regarding faith and justice, in response to that Congregation's Decree 4. But, certain explanations of justice seemed to imply (perhaps unintentionally) that foundational scientific work was a second-class citizen in Jesuit schools. Blanket statements that insisted that *all* courses and *all* research must have some justice component seemed to rule out mathematics and many of the sciences, according to some of the examples of justice presented. In many schools, faculty were encouraged to revise courses to include an experiential justice component for students, such as working with underprivileged or underserved individuals. Yet in certain technical subject areas, such interaction would amount to tokenism and could even be counterproductive to the rigor, intensity, exactness, and seriousness particularly necessary in many scientific or technical courses. Hence, my concern is that GC 34 not be interpreted in any sort of naive or fundamentalistic way that may once again unintentionally slight the valuable work that is done in scientific and technological courses and related research.

GC 34 and Computer Science: Opportunities and Challenges

In 1987, E. D. Hirsch, Jr., published *Cultural Literacy: What Every American Needs to Know*,[6] in which he suggested that deficiencies in contemporary education were mass producing young adults who were "culturally" illiterate. High school and college graduates might be able to read or write, but they were ignorant of a common body of images, references, and quotations that were considered second nature to most of their parents. Hirsch considered such people to be minimally functional in contemporary society and its inherited culture since they were ignorant of basic, age-old traditions of the culture.

In a similar vein, in an interview with Nobel physics laureate Leon Lederman published in the *Chicago Tribune* on October 6, 1996, Professor Lederman worried about a possible lack of "science literacy" in future generations. He states: "We must ask ourselves what are to be the major functions of schools. . . . We're increasingly addicted to technology, yet the gap between what people know and should know is increasing."[7]

Perhaps here is where a fundamental opportunity exists to respond to GC 34—Jesuit schools requiring *all* students (not merely engineering or science majors) to become computer literate. For me this means much more than "practical" things such as using a computer to write a term paper or to play solitaire or even to "surf the Net" for information for a term paper. If our culture is evermore becoming one that is interwined with scientific and technological advances and with computers everywhere we look, it behooves everyone to understand the fundamentals of how computers work, to understand what it means to "develop an algorithm," struggle with the challenge of tearing a problem apart and organizing its solution into "bite-sized" instructions that can be encoded in an appropriate computer language, and to see how data storage and communication via computers enable persons literally to have the entire world at their fingertips, making treasuries of information easily available.

At the same time, GC 34 implicitly calls Jesuits to continue the tradition of scientific research in this relatively new science of computers. For instance, new computer architectures that are, in effect, a whole army of interconnected computers, raise new questions on the level of theory. Such parallel architectures may require, as one example, rethinking older approaches to problem solving, with, perhaps, the development of new computer languages for new types of problems. On the level of practice or computer applications, I suggest that we are also asked to dream about what may be possible with computer technology, something that is quite available, yet still is very much in its infancy. Implementing such dreams may take years of work and the collaboration of many disciplines. For example, "distance learning" via television has existed awhile in some places, but the dream of "distance medical treatment" has only recently been achieved via interactive computers (with microtelevision cameras). Medical specialists can now assist rural doctors miles away in diagnoses and treatment, saving lives, energy, and expense. The use of computers for artificial intelligence and to simulate human learning is also in its infancy, but its eventual maturation, through new computer languages and deeper insights into how humans think, could lead to another technological revolution. The ways in which computers will be used in the next millennium will be limited only by our feeble imaginations.

The growth of the internet and the accessibility that schools and individuals have to it provides other challenges. The opportunities afforded by the explosion of Web browsers and homepages since they first appeared early in 1994 means that new ways of communicating information are possible and adaptations may need to be made in the ways that course materials are made available to students.

The rapid changes in the world of computers and the relatively brief time since the end of GC 34 means that I (and I assume others) am still slowly getting my footing as to how to respond appropriately and adequately. I am not quite sure whether I am really responding to GC 34 or whether I am responding to the opportunities offered by my discipline and hoping that I can find something to justify my actions in the documents of GC 34! A Jesuit should not need the *Formula of the Institute,* the *Constitutions,* or the decrees of a General Congregation to justify service to the sick and dying, nor should he need a General Congregation to justify being involved in scientific research. But it is heartening to know that one's personal expertise (ultimately a God-given gift) is seen as valuable in the context of the Society's traditional charisms, as refined and renewed by General Congregations.

Basically, I see GC 34 acknowledging that my activities in the world of science and technology are valuable. It tells me that our modern culture, a culture intimately bound up with technology, is an opportunity-filled new vineyard in which to labor *ad majorem Dei gloriam.*

The presence of computers also raises the issue of how they are used by individuals and by society, and thus creates a locus for new ethical reflections. Although I emphasize my belief that these sorts of "applied" reflections on computers and society are separate, and independent, areas of academic research, yet given the Society's traditions, it seems most appropriate that Jesuit universities should become prime centers for such scholarly reflection. And the questions that can be raised are numerous. For example, how much should society let computers do for them (fire ICBMs)? What obligations do corporations have toward employees who are no longer needed after "computerizing" a plant? How foolproof should a computer program be before being released (for example, could "star-wars" defense satellites ever be guaranteed to work correctly)? Are we seeing the beginning of a new social class and elite—those who are computer literate with e-mail accounts and Web access? How do we teach about computers, yet instill values that keep alumni of Jesuit schools from becoming the world's best "hackers" or developers of new "viruses"? Will those who are computer literate encounter difficult cultural barriers when dealing with non-technologically-centered peoples? What about new privacy issues when information about individuals is gathered on electronic databases? Will the increase in internet connections from homes isolate individuals further (producing high-tech "couch potatoes") and contribute to the deterioration of society? (This last question reflects the focus of a conference sponsored by Computer Professionals for Social Responsibility in March 1997.)

These are only a few of the questions that the new technology raises. Because my area of expertise is in developing faster computer algorithms to solve standard numerical problems, these questions are out of the range of my competence, and so I hesitate to offer any answers. (I candidly admit that when I wander too far from the theoretical to the practical, I often stand on shaky ground.) Yet just as advances in biology and medicine raise new questions for bioethicians, so the use of computers raises new ethical and legal issues that, in turn, raise questions not covered by current laws. These issues cannot be ignored and need scholars to reflect on them who are knowledgeable about computers and competent in grappling with moral and ethical issues.

Concluding Reflections

On the one hand, I see relatively little changes occurring in my elementary computer science courses as a direct result of GC 34. This does not mean that changes will not take place, though. But the changes that I will continue to make may often be based on the evolving nature of my discipline and the opportunities that new technology provides. I will make more use of the Web to communicate assignments and information to students. In introductory courses, I will try to incorporate more study of and reflection on societal issues. But, in most of the elementary courses I teach, it seems to me more important to stress again and again basic scientific skills and methods, such as clarity of thought, logic, testing of hypotheses, preciseness in manipulating symbols (for example, algebraic correctness), analysis of processes, discovery of errors, and exact adherence to linguistic syntax. Without these, very little advanced progress can be made in the world of computers.

On the other hand, I think GC 34 tells me that I, as a Jesuit, should have no misgiving about being immersed in the world of science and technology, for these are integral components of our contemporary culture. The academic rigor I try to convey in my courses is appropriate to discovering the truth that is part of the computer science. I should not feel guilty about stressing the importance of locating semicolons correctly in a C++ program because, without such exactitude, if the program runs at all, the answer will most likely be incorrect. (For those who think such exactness is not needed or that computers themselves can detect all such simple syntactic errors, I point out that the undetected substitution of a single period for a single comma in a running FORTRAN program necessitated the destruction of the Mariner I rocket in 1963 at the cost of around $18.5 million.) I should continue to encourage students to learn the foundations as well as they can, for, if they try to build on sand, their skyscrapers will surely collapse.

My personal research will also not change much, but I can look at it in a new light. Abstract research is part of a long and honored tradition in the Society. Most of the undergraduate students in my classes (to say nothing of my Jesuit brothers in my community) couldn't care less about my area of research (which deals with solving, via iterative methods, linear systems with large, sparse matrices, and developing techniques that are faster than the dozen or so other methods commonly in use). Yet those scientists who use such methods tell me that having speedier methods could be very useful in research in weather prediction, fluid-flow problems, or interstellar space simulations (none of which I understand!).

Ultimately, GC 34 encourages me to be glad in my work as a teacher, convey to my students my own joy in my field, and show them that competence and integrity are foundational to any academic field. By my presence as a religious and a priest, I hope I am demonstrating to them that all things (including theoretical mathematics, science, technology, and the world of computers) are part of God's world and can be used to better that world for God's greater glory.

1. John W. Padberg, S.J., gen. ed., *The Constitutions of the Society of Jesus and Their Complementary Norms* (St. Louis, Mo.: Institute of Jesuit Sources, 1996), cf. [351]; hereafter, *Const* in text.

2. George E. Ganss, S.J., *Saint Ignatius' Idea of a Jesuit University* (Milwaukee, Wis.: Marquette University Press, 1954), 123–24; cf. 57–58.

3. Ibid., 126; cf. 46–50.

4. Saint Augustine, *Confessions,* Bk 7, Cp 10.16; Bk 10, Cp 27.38, in *The Liturgy of the Hours,* vol. iv, trans. International Commission on English in the Liturgy (New York: Catholic Book Publishing Co., 1975), 1356–57.

5. Cf. *Catechism of the Catholic Church* (Liguori: Liguori Press, 1994), 2820. This paragraph references *Gaudium et Spes,* but also comments that the "distinction" between the Kingdom of God and earthly progress is "not a separation."

6. E. D. Hirsch, Jr., *Cultural Literacy: What Every American Needs to Know* (Boston, Mass.: Houghton Mifflin, 1987).

7. Leon Lederman, "On the Record," interview by Amanda Vogt, *Chicago Tribune,* 6 October 1996, sec. 2, 3.

ESSAY 9

Globalization Rhetoric and the Reshaping of Critical Perspectives

Paul D. McNelis, S.J.

ABSTRACT

The author, whose area is international economics, has a family background in social justice, which fostered his own interest in that area and attracted him to the Jesuits. He argues that the time is opportune for the Society to enter into dialogue with world "policymakers" on "the nature and role of government in regulating market economics" and "designing programs aimed at basic needs and human development." He sees good economics as one that fosters "'open societies' based on respect for individuals and shared values," in a search for the "optimal mix" between "government intervention and market determination." He finds that recent "globalization rhetoric" that blames foreigners for domestic problems is an obstacle to the creation of such societies. The main economic problems in the United States—"health care, education, and job security"—are caused by poor domestic policies, "political incompetence," and fiscal irresponsibility; in developing countries, domestic responsibility based on a "culture of private and public savings" to care for present and future generations is the paramount need. Once there is domestic responsibility, globalization will "enhance the welfare of a country."

[I wish to thank Julio Giulietti, S.J., Otto Hentz, S.J., and Kevin Wildes, S.J., for urging me to organize this essay around the theme of globalization, after listening to me attack this concept in so many discussions at table or in the haustus (snack) room.]

Introduction and Personal Background

As a Jesuit, I have been involved in professional economics since 1970, when I began graduate school during my regency at Johns Hopkins University. My father was an official of the United Mine Workers in Pennsylvania. During the 1940s he took courses at the Labor College organized by the University of Scranton. My first contact with Jesuits was through my father's friendships with Jesuits involved in labor relations and social justice involving the rights and responsibilities of unions. When I decided to become a priest, I was attracted to the Society precisely because of the Society's involvement in questions of economic justice. Early on in my formation, I was inclined to the study of economics, because this discipline examines issues intricately related to social justice. So the calls of recent general congregations, since GC 32, for Jesuits to take seriously the links between faith and justice, have been for me a welcome affirmation of many choices I have made since my early years in the Society.

In my own graduate studies and later in my teaching and research at Georgetown, I have focused my work on international economics. When I began teaching a required international economics course for undergraduate students in the School of Foreign Service at Georgetown twenty years ago, I found many of my students either terrified or bored by the abstract mathematical formulae or geometrical models used in the textbooks. To stimulate interest, and give a life rope to students "allergic" to the formalism of models, I developed several case studies of countries making changes in their international trade and financial policies.

During this period, Brazil's economic program was a strikingly clear example of the application of classic trade policies of "export promotion" and openness to trade after many years of "inward-looking" development based in high tariffs and other barriers to trade. As I read more and more about Brazil, I became more and more interested and fascinated by the country, its culture, history, and people. I had the opportunity to learn Portuguese and to do tertianship (my final program of spiritual training) there in the early 1980s, as well as to spend time there on research grants and visiting professorships. In fact, Brazil became almost a synonym for my professional life in the 1980s, as I focused my research on the inflationary explosions and the succession of failed stabilization programs during these years. Whenever I teach international trade liberalization, or inflation stabilization, I incorporate many personal experiences of people—including poor people whom I have befriended in *favellas*—who have experienced firsthand the consequences of these policies.

The World Economy in the 1990s

The world economic landscape of the 1990s is different from that of the 1980s. Most Latin American countries have reduced or eliminated inflation. Democratically elected governments south of the border have embraced economic reform and are eager to join the process of economic integration begun by the North American Free Trade Association (NAFTA).

In Asia, even Viet Nam is anxious to liberalize its economy and join the Association of South East Asian Nations (ASEAN). Only Africa lags behind, and as GC 34 points out, remains an "ocean of misfortunes" (Decree 3: "Our Mission and Justice" 12 [61]).

In this setting, there is a great opportunity for the Society to engage in a very productive dialogue with policymakers, co-workers, and students throughout the world, on the nature and role of government in regulating market economies, and designing programs aimed at basic needs and human development. Markets are here to stay and governments are here to stay. One can now discuss the comparative advantages of both markets and governments, without being caught in superpower rivalries, ideological conflicts between "neo-liberalism" or "neo-Marxism," or political labels of "conservative" or "liberal." The opportunity is there for us to address real issues involving real people, using the best analyses contemporary social sciences have to offer. One can, quite rationally, hold that governments should play a major role in the allocation of education, particularly primary education, but that the market should be "free" to determine the price and quantity of chewing gum![1]

The arguments, pro and con, for the relative roles of the government and the market in trade and finance will lead to lively political debates and differing policy outcomes in many countries. We can now learn from the experiences of different countries around the world about what works and what does not, in ways that respect the cultural differences, histories, and institutions of particular peoples.

In a recent article in *The Atlantic Monthly*, George Soros expressed fear that countries have become locked into a new tyranny of simple laissez-faire market capitalism, based on the dictates of economic theory.[2] Between the extremes of Marxist ideology and laissez-faire individualism, Soros sees the need for a middle ground in the creation of "open societies," where the rights of individuals are respected, but where society may also hold shared values.

As an economist, I am very much aware that the "science" of my field is very different from the natural sciences. Above all, in financial markets, where Soros has made his fortune many times over, an intangible subjective factor called "risk" plays a central role in the determination of prices and rates of return. Unless one assumes that all people across the world have the same subjective attitudes toward risk, and thus are identical, one has to accept the fact that market solutions may be consistent with a variety of prices and rates of return. Alternatively, one society or culture may opt for more government involvement than another, based on its shared values and attitudes toward risk. Uncertainty and subjectivity thus make economic analysis a far richer discipline than is commonly thought, and can take discussion well beyond the simple models of individualistic laissez-faire capitalism. In short, good economics may be a powerful aide in the formation of "open societies" based on respect for individuals and shared values.

Responding to GC 34

In this context, GC 34 calls us to become involved in "the transformation of every human culture" as people "reshape their patterns of social relations, their cultural inheritance, their intellectual projects, their critical perspectives" (Decree 4: "Our Mission and Culture" 25 [109]). As an economist, I am most interested in how people reshape their economic policies and institutions, as they search and learn in their respective cultures for the "optimal mix" of government intervention and market determination for allocating economic resources. As a professor, I am interested in helping students reshape their "critical perspectives" as we study how countries search and learn in the economic-policy arena.

To gain the critical perspective that GC 34 calls for, one has to examine rigorously the prevailing economic myths, appearing either in the media or in political rhetoric. For this reason, I set "globalization" as a theme for a seminar I taught during the 1997 spring term at Georgetown for advanced undergraduate and beginning graduate students in interdisciplinary programs in various M.A. programs.

There is no doubt that globalization is a popular "buzzword" across the political spectrum. Speaking on the tenth anniversary of the United States Catholic Bishops' pastoral letter, *Economic Justice for All,* Archbishop Rembert Weakland, for example, told us at Georgetown in the spring of 1997 that "globalization would be a central theme" were the letter written today.[3] In the same vein, Lester Thurow of the MIT Sloan School of Management warns that a "global economy" means that "anything can be made anywhere on the face of the earth and sold everywhere else on the face of the earth."[4] On the other hand, Ross Perot warned of the "great sucking sound" of job losses from the United States to Mexico after the NAFTA ratification, an obvious consequence of the "globalization of trade and labor." Patrick Buchanan spoke in the past presidential primary season of the threats of immigration and foreign competition to American labor. Meanwhile, many programs in higher education are marketed on the basis of equipping students to compete better in the ever more competitive "global business environment."

As an economist who has indeed quite a bit of global experience I am not very happy with this rhetoric of globalization. In my judgment, "globalization rhetoric" has become a major obstacle for helping people reshape and evolve their critical perspectives on economic policies and institutions in public debate and discussion. Globalization rhetoric, however well intentioned its proponents may be, may do damage to the creation of "open societies."

My response to GC 34, in my teaching of undergraduate courses in international economics, has been to show that "globalization" is a misleading and dangerous way to understand how policies and cultures evolve across countries.

Globalization Rhetoric Is Misleading

Globalization is not a new process. In terms of raw imports and exports as a percentage of total national product, the United States is no more "globalized" today than at the end of the Carter administration. True, the absolute quantity of international goods and services has increased, but so has the absolute quantity of domestically produced goods and services. So yes, in a trivial sense, the world is more global, in the sense that people consume more foreign goods than before, travel more internationally, have more information about foreign events. But people also consume more domestically produced goods, travel more domestically, and have more information about domestic events. Proportionally, our consumption of global goods and services is about the same.

While the United States is an open or globalized economy, perhaps no economy is as globalized as was the British economy in the nineteenth century. In terms of movement of peoples and resources across borders, oceans, and continents, the globalized economy of nineteenth-century Britain is unparalleled.

Of course, as a former colony of this global economy, the United States was also globalized. Where did our workers come from? Just ask yourself where your great-grandparents were born. How did the United States build its industrial base? Within decades after Adam Smith wrote *The Wealth of Nations,* boutique investment houses opened up in Scotland to finance "infrastructure development" (canals and railroads) in the new "emerging market" called the United States.

So globalization is nothing new as far as international trade in goods and services. What about investment and the mobility of capital? Again, there is little evidence that movement of capital across borders is more pronounced now than it was decades or centuries ago. Speculative foreign investment flows are hardly new. "Tulip bubbles"—exorbitant price increases reflecting speculative investment by France in Mississippi tulip shares—were studied in the eighteenth century by the Irish economist Richard Cantillon.

More fundamentally, if capital is really so mobile, we would find a declining correlation between national saving and national investment throughout the world. If countries could not come up with sufficient savings in their own country to finance investment projects, in a world of highly mobile capital they could finance their investment projects by borrowing from foreigners. Thus, saving-investment correlations would be progressively lower. The evidence, so far, is to the contrary: countries that are high savers also invest a great deal. Capital inflows simply supplement domestic saving rather than take its place. My advice to policymakers is not to count on foreign capital to finance long-term investment. Domestic saving remains the key for longer-term growth and development. Foreign capital is like a good dessert after a meal: it cannot take the place of a good main course, which is provided by domestic saving.

Fundamentally, globalization is limited by a very obvious factor: geography. Sure, Brazil has much better beaches than the United States. But Brazilian beaches will not put the Jersey shore out of business! Many of the services that are so vital to the quality of life have to be local. We are creatures of space.

Issues in the United States Economy

The main issues plaguing the United States economy, namely health care, education, and job security, relate to the nontraded, nonglobalized sectors of the economy.

The rising costs of health care, and the restructuring of the health insurance industry, are hardly caused by globalization. We do not see Japanese *keiretus* or combines setting up health maintenance organizations in the United States, or competing with Blue Cross or Blue Shield.

The Clinton administration tried to face the issue of health-care financing in its first term. Unfortunately, the two leaders of the Clinton health-care team, Hillary Clinton and Ira Magaziner, did not bother to consult with the foremost experts on health-care economics, Henry Aaron of the Brookings Institution and Alan Enthoven of Stanford University, both Democrats and veterans of the Johnson administration. Blame for the current health-care mess should be placed where it surely belongs: political incompetence or lack of resolve to take on domestic special interests.

The falling standard of education, especially primary education, is another example of lack of competence or resolve among local political leaders, and of course, taxpayer "revolts." Again, we do not see foreign firms setting up schools in local communities to drive down the quality of local private or public schools.

Finally, lack of job security caused by well-publicized corporate downsizing is a matter of domestic deregulation or technology, rather than foreign competition. The shake-out in the airline industry, which led to the demise of Pan Am and Eastern Airlines, for example, was caused by the liberalization of domestic airfares and emergence of start-up low-cost airlines. Much as many would like it, we do not see Singapore Airlines, for example, flying the shuttle between New York and Washington, or Cathay Pacific flying between New York and Chicago! The downsizing of Sears is another example: low-cost retail outlets, such as K-Mart, forcing Sears to restructure and change its ways.

Technology is the other major factor. The development of digital voice recognition systems, for example, is forcing AT&T and other phone carriers to lay off the traditional telephone operator in favor of the digital system. Is this phenomenon any different from the introduction of automatic elevator systems, which caused the layoff of elevator operators in large office buildings decades ago?

Thus, the development of competition and new technology is nothing new in United States economic history. John L. Lewis, the longtime head of the United Mine Workers of America and founder of the Congress of Industrial Organizations (CIO), appreciated the importance of technology for the welfare of labor. When newer, more mechanized methods of extracting coal were proposed, which would force reduction in the number of workers employed in the mines, Lewis did not oppose this. Instead, Lewis bargained that benefits from industry to the union be based not on the number of workers employed, but on the tonnage of coal extracted by industry. Thus, the union benefited from the new technology, and the increased union revenues were used to pay for retirement, education, and widows' pensions.

Globalization rhetoric in the present context of the United States economy is dangerous. Instead of focusing on the important issues—how we manage health care, education, deregulation, and technology—globalization rhetoric allows us to blame foreigners, particularly immigrants, or bash foreign competitors, especially the Japanese. We thus let politicians off the hook, and allow them to con us with promises of tax cuts, of getting something for nothing from the government.

Immigrant bashing, of course, in nothing new in United States history. Particularly troublesome to me, however, is that immigrants represent today a solution to a major economic problem, rather than being a problem. It is no secret that we have an aging population, that the present generation of baby-boomers in the work force will be succeeded, upon retirement, by a small number of workers. Thus, there will be fewer people working and paying into Social Security to finance the baby-boomers in their retirement.

A simple solution is to change the demographics of the labor force through immigration. These immigrants will join the work force, pay taxes and Social Security contributions, and thus, help mitigate the shock of the "graying" of America.

Japan bashing has been in vogue since the 1980s. Somehow, the large trade deficits of the United States are a result of the devious nature of the Japanese and their "unfair" trade practices. Again, this is an example of globalization rhetoric allowing us to take the heat off of politicians.

Until 1980, the United States had a slight trade deficit with Japan. After the 1981 Reagan tax cuts, and ensuing budget deficits, the deficit increased more than fivefold in two years. Did the Japanese character change so much in two years?

The Reagan tax cuts gave empirical validation to the long-standing "twin deficit hypothesis"—that fiscal deficits cause trade deficits. The "cause" of the large United States trade deficits since 1980 is not the devious nature of our foreign competitors, but our own reluctance to balance our fiscal budget. In short, our reluctance to pay taxes. Make no mistake about it, this is neither a Democratic nor Republican proclivity. Every politician wants to go before the electorate and "courageously" promise to cut taxes, especially for the working middle class, in order to maximize votes.

The United States is the lowest taxed among the industrialized countries in the world. Yet we give in to the illusion that tax cuts are the way to go for long-term growth and prosperity. This charade, of course, has produced large trade deficits. Globalization rhetoric allows politicians to shake off responsibility and avoid making important decisions, and to blame the "devious and unfair" foreigners.

Issues in Developing Countries

Globalization rhetoric in Latin America and many devolving countries relates to three issues: (1) the debt crisis, (2) multinationals, and (3) the role of the International Monetary Fund (IMF) and the Washington consensus in the shaping of domestic economic policies.

THE DEBT CRISIS

Debt crises are nothing new to Latin America. As in the 1970s, there was a wave of lending to Latin America in the 1920s, the economic crisis of the Great Depression, a subsequent default, with unexpected growth benefits for the countries in question. The key difference between the debt crises of the 1980s and the 1920s is that the debts of the 1920s were in international bond markets, whereas the debts of the 1980s were international bank debts.

Whether one defaults on a debt or not is a strategic decision: what are the likely consequences for debtors and creditors? If one owes $10 to each of 1,000 creditors, a default means one has gained 1,000 mildly irritated creditors. However, if one owes $10,000 to one bank, a default means one has a very dangerous enemy! So the decisions of the Latin American countries to default on their bond debts in the 1920s and to "reschedule" their bank debts in the 1980s are reasonable decisions, in the face of an international economic recession.

The international banks did indeed write off much of their debts by the end of the decade, through the spread of the Brady plan from Mexico to other countries. The Brady plan wrote off a fixed percent of the nominal debt, and fixed the interest rate for the remaining debt at rates below the market.

What really "resolved" the debt crisis for most of Latin America, however, was the fall in United States interest rates. There really is no more "debt crisis" in Latin America. Some countries have made strong adjustment programs, others have not. Some have opened to trade, others have not. Yet, for all of them, debts are no longer a problem. What do they have in common? The fall in United States interest rates. More than any other action, be it IMF accords, World Bank loans, or international bank negotiations, the fall of United States interest rates in recent years from double-digit levels to about 5 percent has significantly reduced the debt burden on Latin America.

But is this phenomenon anything new? In the nineteenth century, when the British pound was the key currency for international trade and financial accounting, decisions by the Bank of England had the same effects throughout the world. Now the dollar is the international accounting standard for Latin American and most of Asia. So changes in dollar interest rates, or the value of the dollar against major currencies, will have strong effects throughout the developing world.

The "hegemony" and "power" of the Federal Reserve is not due to any international conspiracy of bankers and policymakers, but simply to the use of the dollar as a medium of account for international settlements—nothing more, nothing less.

The 1980s are often referred to as the "lost decade" of growth and development for Latin America. But was the debt crisis a cause or an effect of the economic crisis? Unfortunately, economic downturns are a recurring phenomenon. Recent studies have shown that the amplitude and duration of business cycles in countries across the world have little to do with the relative openness of these countries to international trade or finance. In other words, recessions will take place across countries whether they are "globalized" or not. If countries caught in a major unexpected downturn have a large quantity of external debt, default or "rescheduling" of debts is reasonable, to be expected, and nothing new in international economic relations.

MULTINATIONALS AND CAPITAL FLOWS

Multinational corporations, of course, are a favorite scapegoat in developing countries. The growth of multinational investment, known as foreign direct investment, was really a phenomenon of the 1960s. Investment in developing countries in the 1970s and 1980s took the form of interbank lending. In the 1990s, investment has taken the form of portfolio investment in stock and bond markets, primarily by pension funds in the United States and Europe. Thus, the people who are sending money to the "emerging markets" today are not multinationals, but the local schoolteachers or nurses or factory workers who have put some of their savings in pension funds.

Multinationals in many countries are opposed by two erstwhile enemies: local capitalists and political xenophobics of the left and right. Local capitalists fear the competition from multinationals, whereas xenophobics resent foreign presence. While multinationals are far from altruistic, most workers in Latin America would prefer to work for a multinational than for a domestic capitalist enterprise. At the very least, multinationals are subject to the scrutiny and criticism of the international press, whereas domestic capitalists are not.

One of the great tragedies of Brazil in the post-oil shock 1980s was the large amount of resources squandered on local capitalist enterprises by the government for developing homegrown computers and for using alcohol as a substitute for gasoline. The resources could have been more effectively and more wisely used on basic domestic needs: education, health care, and nutrition for the poor. But this did not happen, as domestic capitalists and leftist xenophobic leaders played off governments against threats of foreign multinational competition in informatics and energy.[5]

Again, multinationals are not new on the world scene: one only has to think of the great trading companies of centuries past, such as Nobel House or the East India Trading Company. As a proportion of total investment flows, multinational foreign direct investment has been steadily decreasing. Overstating the importance of multinationals through globalization rhetoric can only result in the repetition of many of the tragic mistakes made by Brazil in the 1980s.

THE ROLE OF THE IMF

The International Monetary Fund, along with its sister organization, the International Bank for Reconstruction and Development, popularly known as the World Bank, were created on the instigation of John Maynard Keynes after World War II.

The *raison d'être* of the IMF was to maintain the post-war Bretton Woods system of fixed exchange rates, through short-term loans to countries under fixed exchange rates facing difficulties in their balance of payments. The World Bank, by contrast, was to give longer-term development infrastructure loans to developing countries.

Of course, the Bretton-Woods system of fixed exchange rates no longer exists. What is the *raison d'être* of the IMF? Helping to "manage" the debt crisis of the 1980s and providing technical assistance to monetary institutions of the Eastern European transition economies of the 1990s were functions the IMF readily assumed since the demise of the Bretton-Woods system. But neither of these is a function which the IMF was set up to do.[6]

Many analysts have contended that IMF involvement in multilateral negotiations among debtor countries, private banks, and the IMF actually delayed a resolution of the debt crisis during the 1980s. Similarly, technical assistance to transition-economy central banks and monetary authorities could easily come through private-sector consulting firms. One adage has it: physician, heal thyself; IMF, privatize thyself.

The "clout" that the IMF and the World Bank have enjoyed over many countries lay not so much in the amount of monies they were able to provide; rather, the existence of the "stand-by agreement" with the IMF and a "structural-adjustment loan" with the World Bank served as signals, or "*Good Housekeeping* seals of approval," for renewed lending by private banks in the aftermath of the debt crisis in the 1980s.

In the 1990s, however, developing countries are awash in capital inflows. Brazil, for example, has a reserve base of $60 billion to defend its exchange rate. Similarly, the capital that does flow to most developing countries is in the form of stock and bond purchases, not by private banks but by pension funds from the United States and Europe. Unlike private banks, pension funds diversify across a wide set of countries. While the managers of these funds do indeed make use of IMF reports and evaluations for their investments, they make use of far wider sources of information for assessing risk and return. Similarly, the World Bank is coming to realize that the capital for infrastructure development, such as telecommunications and electricity, can be raised more efficiently and cheaply by many countries, through private capital markets.

The IMF and World Bank are institutions that have seen their day. If there is any powerful institution in Washington that can have strong and immediate effects on developing countries, it is the Federal Reserve, not the IMF! As long as Mr. Greenspan keeps United States dollar interest rates low—which means that Americans balance their fiscal deficits—Latin America will be in a *buena situación.*

Private capital will flow to those countries, which yield reasonable return for reasonable risk, to the aging baby-boomers in the "North." Reasonable return for reasonable risk, of course, is a direct result of reasonable and responsible policy in developing countries.

This foreign capital, as pointed out above, is not a cause of longer-term growth, but rather a supplement to the domestic saving, which alone can sustain development. Domestic savings, of course, presume public savings—that people pay taxes for government services and social programs—and a sense of intergenerational justice: that people will defer consumption to improve the welfare of future generations. Developing a culture of private and public saving, based on an ethic of public responsibility to the needy of one's own generation and for the welfare of future generations, is the paramount task of political economy across the world. Bashing the IMF or the World Bank misses the point, and enables politicians to deflect their most important responsibilities.

Conclusion

The main point I try to get across to my students is that globalization is not only misleading but dangerous. Focusing on globalization can lean to xenophobia, or blaming foreigners for domestic problems, enabling domestic politicians to shake off responsibility for making courageous decisions, like getting people to pay taxes and save more. But there is another danger: globalization rhetoric can lead to a feeling of helplessness and hopelessness, that somehow economic reality is "out of control" or "beyond control" of domestic authority, that there is a "new international order" or "system" that limits development and progress among peoples. What I teach again and again is that the tools of domestic economic policy—such as taxation, policies to promote savings, expenditures on education and health care—subject to the budget constraints faced by any household or government, are powerful tools for promoting longer-term development. If the nontraded sector of a country is a "good place to be," globalization in the form of further investment by foreigners will surely come and enhance the welfare of a country. My advice, then, is for public leaders to chill out on globalization rhetoric, to think locally and act locally and responsibly, on behalf of domestic basic needs.

ENDNOTES • MCNELIS

1. Singapore, of course, is heavily involved in both markets: chewing gum is outlawed, and there are heavy subsidies to education.
2. George Soros, "The Capitalist Threat," *Atlantic Monthly* 279/2 (February 1997): 45–48, 50–55, 58.
3. Rembert G. Weakland, "Economic Justice for All: Ten Years Later," *America* 176/9 (22 March 1997): 8–10, 13–19, 22 at 15.
4. Lester C. Thurow, *The Future of Capitalism: How Today's Economic Forces Shape Tomorrow's World* (New York: Morrow, 1996), 9.
5. Indonesia may make the same type of mistake. The minister of trade and technology has been lobbying for a superfund for the development of an Islamic-Asian aerospace industry.
6. My own dissertation advisor from my Hopkins days, Jürg Niehans, used to refer to the IMF as an "empty shell," referring to the "egg-shell" architectural style of its main building, and the loss of its *raison d'être*.

ESSAY 10

What Is the Tune of an English Pied Piper?

Joseph J. Feeney, S.J.

ABSTRACT

The author presents a beautiful, fascinating, and informative introduction to disquieting developments in postmodern literature and literary criticism, especially political criticism and poststructuralism, and wonders if GC 34 can speak to this world with "its underlying disillusionment and parody, its fragmentation and fluidity, its lost linkage of mind, language, and 'the real.'" He finds a basis for dialogue in such parallels as their mutual indictment of "injustice and ill-used power." He finds his own scholarly life "only marginally connected" with the "focus of GC 34." The author finds God present in his own "human and intellectual quest," and sees "the needs and integrity" of his research "in creative tension with the urgings of GC 34." Finally, in his teaching, he accepts GC 34's call to present material from the viewpoint of the marginalized. He is "above all, a humanist," and never abandons the primacy of teaching everything that "the fullness of our common humanity" includes, a perspective which, in his view, GC 34 does not adequately emphasize.

The hat: I begin with the hat.

I wear several: Jesuit, priest, scholar, professor of English. Even within my field, the hats are multiple: humanist, text-reader, teacher of writing, culture-commentator, specialist in some areas, dabbler in contemporary criticism. Each hat is a different color, but after twenty-six years I've combined everything into one single hat, pied, multicolored, a Joseph's hat, a hat of Hamlin.

And the tune: this is also a medley, of many themes, multiple keys, bits of sonata, bits of rhapsody, some formal development, some improvisation. It is sad, and happy, and angry, and poignant, and funny, and longing. As a Pied Piper, I whistle in my field and lead my students. Like my hats, my music has long since fused into a single rich tune that I pipe over and over as I wander over the centuries and through Britain, Ireland, and America.

I am asked here to describe this Piper's tune: what is the song I play as Jesuit professor and scholar? It has always been a humanistic tune, a tune of life on earth and hopes of heaven. Has this tune been modulated by GC 34? Have I learned new themes? Transcribed old melodies to fresh keys? Composed new transition-passages? Finally, how does the field of English—my source of music—present itself, from the perspective of the Congregation?

I will rove widely as I investigate and judge my field itself, the Congregation's perspective, and my own work as scholar and professor. For order, I offer this structure: (1) the current state of literature and literary criticism, and an interpretation in terms of GC 34; (2) my role as scholar, with a similar interpretation; and (3) my role as teacher, specifically of undergraduates, again with an interpretation. I end with a few final comments. GC 34, I shall argue, is wise in urging a dialogue with culture, keenly accurate in reading the signs of the times, firmly countercultural in offering hope and order to fragmented contemporaries, and farsighted in expanding the faith-justice definition of GC 32, though Jesuit humanism is still not adequately affirmed.

Literature and Literary Criticism Today

Ours is an era of criticism. Even as literature enjoys a rare abundance of styles and approaches (and, as postmodern, sometimes self-destructs), literary criticism dominates the field.

Literature itself, though, is fertile with old and new styles. Nineteenth-century romanticism lives in the subliterary supermarket novels of the Harlequin and Silhouette series. Nineteenth-century realism thrives in John Updike's Rabbit series, *Rabbit, Run* (1960), *Rabbit Redux* (1971), and *Rabbit at Rest* (1990), as he satirizes American culture. Faulkner and the modernists of the early twentieth century reappear in Louise Erdrich's *Tracks* (1988) and George Mackay Brown's *Magnus* (1973), which reject linear narrative for a series of fragments that the reader must link together. Brown's poems, and Harold Pinter's and David Mamet's plays, similarly reject old structures and narratives for a modernist collage.

Postmodernism, however, is the signature movement of the last third of the century. With parody as its essence, it is epitomized in John Fowles' brilliant novel *The French Lieutenant's Woman* (1969). Written in rich, Victorian prose of orchestral grandeur, it quickly captures the reader's affection and credibility—he or she *cares* for, *believes* in, the characters—then subverts itself by telling the reader, at the beginning of chapter 13, "I do not know. This story I am telling is all imagination. These characters I create never existed outside my own mind." Moreover, writes Fowles, "I must give [my characters] their freedoms," and in any case "we are all in flight from the real reality." In chapter 45, he again trumps the reader: "The last few pages you have read are not what happened, but what [Charles] spent the hours between London and Exeter imagining might happen."[1] The novel ultimately offers three different endings—freedom again, with "truth" as the reader's choice. A final blow to credibility is Fowles' assertion, as the no-longer-omniscient author, that his nineteenth-century fictional hero *and* Fowles himself as a very real twentieth-century author are sitting together at the same time in the same compartment in the same nineteenth-century English railway-carriage. In postmodernism, the impossible takes place, the author asserts it with full authority, and the reader loses trust in both novel and novelist. The postmodern novel thus parodies the traditional novel and the traditional author. It is also self-referential: instead of being turned outwards toward life, the reader is turned inwards to the novel itself, having to face fiction's artificiality and the possibility that reality itself is an artifact. In the postmodern condition, freedom and creativity have no bounds, while tradition, credibility, consistency, order, and meaning are called into question. The main character of Julian Barnes' *Flaubert's Parrot* (1985) epitomizes the contemporary puzzlement about history, truth, self, and life as he says his own life "is pure story, whatever you may think."[2]

Criticism and critical theory, though, are in some ways more central than literature. Since the 1960s they have caught the interest of academe and affected the way people read the literature of *all* centuries. Contemporary criticism is best understood in two broad groupings: political criticism and poststructuralism.

Political criticism, with "cultural politics" implied in each case, re-reads literary texts from the perspective of an oppressed minority; its major forms are feminist, African American, postcolonial, and gay-lesbian. Feminist criticism (it has many varieties) begins with "the realization that the literary canon is androcentric, and that this has a profoundly damaging effect on women readers."[3] It works to oppose patriarchal power, subvert male abstraction, promote the experiential over the theoretical, explore the uniqueness of a woman's "voice," and urge a more fluid, personal critique of writers, books, and readers. African American criticism likewise demands "the right to define itself, its own terms for order, its very own presuppositions," recognizes that "hermeneutic systems are not universal, color-blind, apolitical, or neutral," and turns "to the black tradition itself to develop theories of criticism indigenous to our literatures."[4] Postcolonial criticism offers third-world cultures an opportunity to counter "a repressive ethnocentrism" in Western thought and literature and "to undermine the imperialist subject." Rejecting the domination, power, ownership, and authority of the imperialist West, postcolonial criticism both "draws attention to questions of [individual] identity . . . in relation to broader national histories and destinies" and shows the traditional canon as itself "strange," provisional, and contradictory.[5] Gay-lesbian criticism, again opposing the domination of a majority, calls itself "an epistemological empowerment to counter the 'idea of heterosexuality.'"[6] In language and content it celebrates the body, subverts heterosexist ideology and suppositions, and seeks to discover homoeroticism in unexpected texts. Other minorities have their own criticisms—Native American and Chicano/a, for example—and some writers combine several approaches, as in

Barbara Smith's *Toward a Black Feminist Criticism* (1977), which "exposes the total silencing of the black lesbian writer."[7] All these schools, I add, work to expand the traditional "canon" of literature—the list of works accepted as literature and taught in schools.[8] Through such critical approaches, minorities insist on the right to define themselves in their own terms, to collect and read their own stories and poems, to choose their own language and structures, and to devise their own aesthetics. Critical schools and theories thus empower minorities against domination, and their proliferation produces a variety of theories that reflects postmodern freedom.

Other approaches to criticism, dating from the late 1960s and collected under the word "poststructuralism," are more general, more nuanced, and harder to describe. Often comic and antiheroic, they mock "the scientific pretensions of structuralism"[9] because, for them, language and signs are essentially unstable. Roland Barthes, rejecting the authority of an author as source of a text and of its meaning, wants a reader to play with a text and discover its "virtually infinite 'voices.'" Jacques Lacan questions language's ability to refer to things or to express ideas or feelings. Jacques Derrida, undermining Western philosophy since Plato, demonstrates how to "deconstruct" a text by showing how the text "*transgresses the laws it appears to set up for itself.* At this point texts go to pieces, so to speak." Michel Foucault introduces the role of power—political, economic, ideological, and social—and argues that power is gained through discourse. Discourses can never be "objective," though; "there are no absolutely 'true' discourses, only more or less powerful ones."[10] Such, in highly oversimplified form, is poststructuralism.

Postmodern critics and theorists similarly affirm the primacy of language ("the dominance of the sign") and its loss of contact with reality, noting how the "decentering of language itself has produced a great deal of playful, self-reflexive, and self-parodying fiction." Jean Baudrillard asserts, and indicts, today's superficial "culture of 'hyperreality,' in which models determine yet undermine the real" and the media define what is "real." Jean-François Lyotard, scorning the "totalizing claims of reason" and reason's dire effect on culture and politics, denies the "truth claims" of language, praises difference and heterogeneity in literature and politics, and explores the "unsayable" and the "invisible."[11]

A clear summary of postmodern criticism and of its links with poststructuralism is offered in Raman Selden and Peter Widdowson's *A Reader's Guide to Contemporary Literary Theory*:

> *It is evident that there are as many "postmodernisms" as theorists. However, there is little doubt that the* Weltanschauung *we have described overlaps the world-view implied by most poststructuralist thinkers and critics. The questioning of all "depth models," the decentring of the world and the self, the rejection of elitist aesthetics and experimental formalisms, the disruption of all discursive boundaries, the obliteration of the frontiers between high and*

*low culture and between art and commodity, and the resistance to meaning
and interpretation are all also themes of poststructuralism.*[12]

Such is the state of literature and literary criticism at the end of the twentieth century: play and parody reign, outsiders demand power, and intellectual systems have collapsed to the point where even meaning is fluid.[13] Can the Jesuits' GC 34 speak to this situation?

Postmodernism and contemporary criticism call out for Jesuit culture-commentary and intellectual engagement; this is the "existential dialogue" with culture called for by GC 34 (Decree 4: "Our Mission and Culture" [OMC] 5 [79]).[14] This dialogue, of course, involves listening and conversation by both sides. Jesuits need to understand—and recognize the appeal of—postmodernism, with its underlying disillusionment and parody, its fragmentation and fluidity, its lost linkage of mind, language, and "the real." On the other hand, postmodernists—many of them our students—may find through us a needed healing and hope.[15] Such a dialogue fulfills "the simple Ignatian desire to help people in Christ" and is correlatively willing "to be helped by people" in understanding today's world (Decree 1: "United with Christ on Mission" [UCM] 6 [6]). An important aspect of "our ministry towards atheists and agnostics" (OMC 23 [107]), this dialogue is also an opportunity for "the transformation of culture" (OMC 5 [79]; Decree 2: "Servants of Christ's Mission" [SCM] 17 [42]).

The Congregation, furthermore, is keenly accurate in reading "the signs of the times" in "the world of today" (Decree 5: "Our Mission and Interreligious Dialogue" [OMID] 9,4 [141]; UCM 8 [8]) with regard to social justice and postmodernism. Contemporary political criticism—feminist, African American, colonial, and gay-lesbian—parallels GC 34's "committed care for the poor, the marginalized, and the abandoned" and its concern about "social structures which exclude the poor" (UCM 5 [5]; SCM 9 [34]). The document on "Jesuits and the Situation of Women in Church and Civil Society" (Decree 14) itself reflects the feminist approach in literary and cultural criticism. And postmodernists, I am convinced, are deeply wounded humans; work with postmodernists offers Jesuits a place "at the crossroads of cultural conflict" where they can "be present, in solidarity and compassion, where the human family is most damaged" (SCM 2 [16], 4 [26]).

GC 34 is also firmly countercultural in responding to the "fragmentation caused by sin" in "modern and postmodern culture" (OMC 16 [100]; 20 [104]). Both GC 34 and political criticism indict dominant groups for injustice and ill-used power. Moreover, in facing the sin-based fragmentation of contemporary culture, GC 34 offers postmodernists and poststructuralists a new order—or at least a blessed chaos—by offering faith in God and hope in "the very meaning of human existence" (Decree 17: "Jesuits and University Life" [JUL] 2 [405]).

My Role as Scholar

I now grow more personal as I ask, "How can GC 34 speak to my scholarly research and publishing?" To answer, I must—with apologies—write about my work.

My earliest mature research—my dissertation—was a response to the then "Province Plan" of the Maryland Province. Reacting to Vatican II and GC 31, the Maryland Province formulated its own four "apostolic goals" in the fall of 1969: Racial Justice, Economic Opportunity, Christian Unity or Ecumenism, and World Peace.[16] As a direct consequence of the "Province Plan," I chose to write my dissertation on a peace issue: "American Anti-War Writers of World War I: A Literary Study" (1971). My earliest postdissertation research had a social justice dimension: I wrote on the novelist Jessie Fauset, an African American and a woman, in *The CLA Journal* (1974, 1979), *Minority Voices* (1980, 1980), and (more popularly) in *The Crisis* (1983) and *The Philadelphia Inquirer* (1983). In the same period I did short, literary essays on Hawthorne and Twain, and a longer, broader one in *American Studies* (1982) on urban modernization in the novels of Charles Brockden Brown. In response to GC 32, I also wrote a short piece for the *National Jesuit News,* "Coping with a 'Centrifugal Century': Faith/Justice in the Classroom" (1978).

In 1977 I published my first essay on Gerard Manley Hopkins and began a new scholarly life. This essay—to my surprise, the bubbling source of a stream of essays—grew by chance, from a note on the bulletin board at Campion Hall, Oxford, announcing a seminar on the centennial of Hopkins' ordination. Unable to attend the seminar at Saint Beuno's College, Wales, where Hopkins had been ordained and I had done tertianship, I still wanted to celebrate the poet-as-priest (though I had done no graduate work on Hopkins), and I wrote an essay for *America* (1977) on Hopkins and the priesthood. It turned out to be the first of forty essays on Hopkins—thirty-one scholarly, nine popular.

These essays are varied. Two are editions of newly discovered Hopkins letters, published in *TLS: The Times Literary Supplement* (1995) and, with annotations and fuller introductions, in *The Hopkins Quarterly* (1996). Two are catalogs of major Hopkins archives: of the Harry Ransom Humanities Research Center at the University of Texas at Austin, in *Hopkins Lives: An Exhibition and Catalogue* and *The Library Chronicle of the University of Texas at Austin* (both 1989), and of the Bischoff Collection at Gonzaga University in *The Hopkins Quarterly* (1996). Other essays deal with Hopkins' poetry, his life, his creativity, his 1989 centennial celebrations, and with parallels between Hopkins, Bruckner, and Mahler as postromantic artists. Perhaps my most groundbreaking essays situate Hopkins in the context of nineteenth-century Jesuit life, dealing with his third-year theology examination, his frequent reassignments, and his relationships with Jesuits. In 1994, I also became coeditor of *The Hopkins Quarterly* with a colleague and friend at the University of Toronto.

In the years since 1977, besides my work on Hopkins, I've done scholarly and popular essays on contemporary poets, novelists, playwrights, and a composer, on post-modernism, on the contemporary religious imagination in America, on the centennial of James Joyce, and on Jesuit education. Some deal with racism (on British plays, in *America, The Month,* and *The Philadelphia Inquirer*); some deal with faith and religion (on British and Irish plays, in *America* and *The Month*); some deal with the culture of post-modernism (in *America* and *Conversations on Jesuit Higher Education*); but many are literary, biographical, or historical studies. Most of my scholarly, journal-based work does not directly deal with the GC 34 issues of faith/justice/Gospel/dialogue/culture (SCM 19 [47], 20 [48]); my popular essays are more relevant here.

I write all this not to proclaim myself but to sketch the background for a Jesuit scholar's reflections on GC 34. Given that most of my scholarly work does reflect its stresses, how do these documents challenge me? What can I do? And what do I find myself unable to do? I ask these questions while remembering the words of Peter-Hans Kolvenbach, S.J., who writes that the Congregation asks Jesuits "to allow ourselves to be shaken up by what might be asked of us."[17]

What am I challenged to do as a scholar? First, I am again called to GC 32's "service of faith, of which the promotion of justice is an absolute requirement," even as I note GC 34's more ample statement that "the integrating principle of our mission is the inseparable link between faith and the promotion of the justice *of the Kingdom*" (SCM 7 [32], 14 [39]; emphasis mine). I am also called to respond to GC 34's more ample assertion that "our mission of the service of faith and the promotion of justice must be broadened to include, as integral dimensions, proclamation of the Gospel, dialogue, and the evangelization of culture" (SCM 20 [48]). As an American, I also note how "Jesuits in North America are dealing with the challenges of new forms of cultural and economic deprivation" and "work in close cooperation with many others in trying to influence the complex structures of society where decisions are made and values are shaped" (SCM 2 [22]).

What can this call mean to me as a scholar? What can I do—or not do—specifically in view of my field and my own publishing history? First, I can continue to write popular articles: they have a broader readership and touch more directly on the priorities of GC 34. I plan, for example, an essay on David Hare, a British playwright with a strong sense of social justice, on the occasion of his fiftieth birthday in 1997. Other popular essays are sudden responses to sudden ideas: I've written on sport, ordination, and the three hundreth anniversary of my native Germantown in Philadelphia. My articles dart where my interests dart, and I hope—and expect—that these interests will often reflect GC 34. A good number of essays, I suspect, will deal with belief and culture.

As a Hopkins scholar, though, I find myself more limited—and, in truth, am at peace with these limitations. Some urgings of GC 34 have already been satisfied: a Dutch scholar, for example, has done a fine study of Hopkins' social thought.[18] I plan a short essay on Hopkins and Northern Ireland, but this is not on social justice; it will simply situate two poems in their social, geographic, and linguistic contexts. I will then do a longer work on the playfulness of Hopkins; an unusual perspective, it will offer a fresh view of him and his work, but is only marginally connected with the faith/justice/Gospel/dialogue/culture focus of GC 34. Perhaps more relevantly, I hope afterwards to continue my work on Hopkins' spirituality. But who knows what other topics will suggest themselves?

To reflect more broadly: after a scholar has developed an expertise and a reputation, he works best when a topic catches his attention and curiosity, and when there is a scholarly place for work in that area. Scholarship has a dynamism of its own, and does not easily let itself be turned by external forces, even by GC 34. My publishing peers expect a scholarly integrity of me—a certain "objectivity." At best, then, the needs and integrity of my field should—must—remain in creative tension with the urgings of GC 34. And I am at peace: for a Jesuit, there is a sure "incarnationalism" as I write about a seemingly "secular" topic. For a scholar, the Jesuit tradition—even the Jesuit mysticism—of "finding God in all things" translates itself into essays on Hopkins' playfulness, on the verbal sparkle and inventiveness of Hopkins or Joyce, on how Charles Brockden Brown's novels show how "modernization" was affecting Philadelphia as early as the 1790s.

A few closing thoughts on scholarship. In a very real way, I also carry on a dialogue with my fellow Hopkins scholars—many of them my friends—all over the world. I am thus in dialogue with agnostics and atheists (OMID 3–4 [130–31], 5–6 [133–34]), and often the credibility of belief, of the Church, and of myself as priest is a subtext in our conversations and letters. I would, of course, gladly change my research direction should the Society ask me, but I don't think such a change would be wise. With all the limitations—perhaps unfreedoms—of my work as a scholar, I still suggest to many that God is present in the human and intellectual quest. In this, I rest content before God and the Society.

My Role as Teacher

How can GC 34, finally, speak to my teaching? And, more specifically, to my teaching of undergraduates?

As a teacher I am, above all, a humanist. For me, the goal of undergraduate English teaching—the teaching of literature—is to show students the fullness of our common humanity in its joy and pain, tragedy and triumph. Nothing—truly nothing—dare intrude upon this scope. A professor must not shrink literature's compass: it is simultaneously a work of pure art, an artist's act of self-expression, and a reader's opportunity for entertainment, for new experiences, and for moral learning (including the need for social change).[19] Given the breadth of literature, I avoid any exclusive or exclusionary slant in course content or critical approach, whether it be feminist, African American, colonialist, gay-lesbian, or even Christian.

That being said, though, because teaching literature includes everything human, I recognize that a teacher must inevitably make choices about what to include, omit, stress, and balance. Here lies the relevance of GC 34: it suggests certain themes to stress, certain issues to raise, certain choices in books or courses, even certain critical approaches for sometime use. GC 34 surely has the right to urge me to present material from the viewpoint of the poor, to use books by women and Blacks, to raise issues of justice and faith, and to employ the critical approaches of the powerless. I gladly accept this advice for *aspects* of a course, though not as an exclusive focus. Given such understandings of undergraduate teaching, I must teach a field or a book *in itself,* even as I offer different perspectives on it. Clearly, these "perspectives" can well be influenced by GC 34. Thus, as in my scholarship, I live with—and enjoy—a creative tension: I must preserve the integrity and richness of my field itself—here, humanity—*and* also express my own enthusiasms and the perspectives of a believer, a priest, and a Jesuit who hears the urgings of GC 34.

What do I do in practice? Because my literary field is American and modern British and Irish literature, I easily dialogue with contemporary culture. (In graduate school, I chose these areas for this precise reason.) In my American courses, for example, I do African American and feminist books, and touch on poverty and injustice in such novels as Crane's *Maggie: A Girl of the Streets* (1893) and Steinbeck's *In Dubious Battle* (1936) or *The Grapes of Wrath* (1939). In the modern British and Irish novel, I deal with the absurdity of Beckett's *Murphy* (1938) and the postmodernism of Fowles. I've also devised courses on the contemporary religious imagination in America and on modernism and postmodernism in literature, art, architecture, and music. At appropriate points I also introduce contemporary criticism—political, poststructural, and postmodern—both for its own value and to keep my students up-to-date. But I still teach mainly in the humanist tradition, and (whatever the hazards of definition) choose works recognized for their literary quality.

As a teacher of undergraduates, I also pay close attention to my students. Teaching a humanity, I never forget the men and women who sit before me. Thus develops another healthy tension: the books themselves, the students' needs, my own enthusiasms and values, and the urgings of GC 34. As I ponder GC 34, I find that my current students stand more in need of faith and hope than of an urging towards justice. Some may need a push or pull towards justice, but many already volunteer or do service-learning courses; the many who are postmodernists, though, need reasons for faith and hope—in GC 34's terms, words on "Change and Hope" (OMC 25–26 [109–10]). These, the sometimes anguished students I deal with, are my own suffering poor.

As professor of literature, I stand in a tradition that marked Jesuit schools from 1548—Renaissance humanism, in its full human and divine scope. GC 34 helps to keep me honest to "the signs of the times" and the needs of the poor, but, I gently urge, I must also proclaim the fullness of the human and therefore of the divine. This is "the service of faith," but admittedly underplays justice. Yet, as a Jesuit priest teaching a "secular" subject, I am again showing students how to "find God in all things."

Some Comments in Conclusion

In its twenty-six documents, GC 34 spendidly synthesizes the present apostolic needs of the world, the Church, and society. It has "been well received by the Society," Father Kolvenbach writes, and "Jesuits have been satisfied that the General Congregation has succeeded in speaking forcefully and precisely on our way of proceeding and advancing together . . . [on] the road we are to walk today. While there is nothing particularly new in this task, many aspects of our work, prayer and lifestyle have been given new life."[20] Particularly important is GC 34's often eloquent redefinition of "our mission of the service of faith and the promotion of justice" to include the "proclamation of the Gospel, dialogue, and the evangelization of culture" (SCM 19–20 [47–48]).

Even with this new definition, though, the heritage of GC 32, GC 33, and GC 34 still seems to underplay the Jesuit tradition of Renaissance humanism and its mode of "finding God in all things." I illustrate my point by offering two readings of Hopkins' poem "Pied Beauty":

> Glory be to God for dappled things—
> For skies of couple-colour as a brinded cow;
> For rose-moles all in stipple upon trout that swim;
> Fresh-firecoal chestnut-falls; finches' wings;
> Landscape plotted and pieced—fold, fallow, and plough;
> And all trades, their gear and tackle and trim.
>
> All things counter, original, spare, strange;
> Whatever is fickle, freckled (who knows how?)
> With swift, slow; sweet, sour; adazzle, dim;
> He fathers-forth whose beauty is past change:
> Praise him.[21]

Both readings—pre- and post-GC 32—would work closely with the text: its form, its language, its rhythm, its punctuation, its visual vividness, its vibrant action (the autumn chestnut is red *when* it falls and cracks open), its sudden surprise that rosy-speckled trout also "swim." How, then, might I read the poem differently *before* and *after* GC 32? Before,

I would see it as a pure celebration of nature, and beauty, and action, and God. (Thus I taught—and still teach—the poem.) After GC 32, I might well worry about including some aspect of "the promotion of justice [which] is an absolute requirement" of "the service of faith" (GC 32, Decree 4: "Our Mission Today: The Service of Faith and the Promotion of Justice" 2 [48]). Should I mention the human toil needed to make the "landscape plotted and pieced" and stress the work of the farmer who directs the plough and folds-over the soil? Should I comment on the long hours, hard work, and nineteenth-century injustices in "all trades," whatever "their gear and tackle and trim"? Even as I write, though, the questions seem otiose, for they knock the poem out of kilter.

Yet these questions still nag this humanist who tries to take seriously GCs 32, 33, and 34. The expanded definition of faith-justice in GC 34 surely supports those Jesuits who proclaim the Gospel, evangelize culture, or engage in religious dialogue, but in my judgment it still does not sufficiently restore the pre-GC 32 breadth of perspective—and holy humanism—for the professors of literature who teach the modern British and Irish novel, or who proclaim poems that just cry out, "Hurrah!" I recognize that no one expects GC 32–34 to touch on every poem I teach, but I still sense that, after GC 32, pure incarnational celebration has grown less central to the Society's understanding of a Jesuit professor. I find this a loss, for incarnationalism is the theology behind both my scholarly "objectivity" and the humanism of my teaching.

For this reason, I am grateful for GC 34's statement that "dedicated Jesuits engaged in university work . . . are committed, in the most profound sense, to the search for the fullness of truth" (JUL 12 [415]). I am grateful also for the broad understanding of the document "The Jesuit Priest: Ministerial Priesthood and Jesuit Identity," where "integral evangelization" is "concerned with the good of the whole human person." Jesuits should minister not only to the "voiceless and powerless" but to "those whose values are undermined by contemporary culture, those whose needs are greater than they can bear." Thus, "no ministry which prepares the way for the Kingdom . . . is outside the scope of Jesuit priests." In sum, "Jesuits bring to their ministerial priesthood a profound respect for the ways in which God is already at work in the lives of all men and women. . . . Jesuits try to see what God has already done in the lives of individuals, societies, and cultures, and to discern how God will continue that work. . . . [Thus, the] Jesuit ministerial priesthood . . . is always aimed at building up the human person in the individual character of each one's life of grace" (Decree 6: "The Jesuit Priest: Ministerial Priesthood and Jesuit Identity" 10 [167], 12 [169], 15 [172], 20–20,1 [177–78]).

And so I pipe on with glee as I wear my pied and funny hat. After GC 34, the hat has a few new insets, the tune some new transitions, but I've been piping GC 34's music for a long while. The old hat still fits well, and the tune comes easily to my fingers. So I whistle merrily, piping scholars towards truth, piping general readers towards justice, and piping students towards a full humanity and a life in God.

That is the tune of an English Pied Piper.

1. John Fowles, *The French Lieutenant's Woman* (Boston, Mass.: Little, Brown, 1969), 95, 97, 339.

2. Julian Barnes, *Flaubert's Parrot* (London: Pan, 1985), 160.

3. Patrocinio P. Schweickart, "Reading Ourselves: Toward a Feminist Theory of Reading," in *Falling into Theory: Conflicting Views on Reading Literature*, ed. David H. Richter (Boston, Mass.: St. Martin's, 1994), 269.

4. Henry Louis Gates, Jr., "Canon-Formation, Literary History, and the Afro-American Tradition: From the Seen to the Told," in Richter, *Falling into Theory*, 173, 174, 177.

5. Raman Selden and Peter Widdowson, *A Reader's Guide to Contemporary Literary Theory* (Lexington, Ky.: University Press of Kentucky, 1993), 188–96.

6. Gregory W. Bredbeck, "B/O—Barthes's Text/O'Hara's Trick," *PMLA* 108 (1993): 274.

7. Selden and Widdowson, *A Reader's Guide*, 231.

8. A good, short introduction to this issue is Wendell V. Harris, "Canonicity," *PMLA* 106 (1991): 110–21.

9. On structuralism, see Selden and Widdowson, *A Reader's Guide*, 103–24.

10. Selden and Widdowson, *A Reader's Guide*, 125–27, 130–41, 144–49, 158–61.

11. Ibid., 174–85.

12. Ibid., 187–88.

13. There are, to be sure, many critics of postmodernism; from a religious perspective, cf. the journal *Christianity and Literature*, passim; and from a political perspective, Terry Eagleton, *The Illusions of Postmodernism* (Cambridge, Mass.: Blackwell, 1996). Also interesting is a major political critic's rejection of political criticism: see Frank Lentricchia, "Last Will and Testament of an Ex-Literary Critic," *Lingua Franca* 6 (1996): 59ff.

14. GC 34's definition of culture changes a bit in the document on "Our Mission and Culture." A footnote to OMC 1 [75] gives an anthropological definition: "'Culture' means the way in which a group of people live, think, feel, organize themselves, celebrate, and share life. In every culture, there are underlying systems of values, meanings, and views of the world, which are expressed, visibly, in language, gestures, symbols, rituals, and styles." The document mostly employs this understanding, but the section on "Our Mission and Critical Postmodern Culture" focuses (appropriately, but more restrictively) on the beliefs and values of "modern and postmodern culture," on "unbelievers in a secular and critical culture," on those who "find many answers in science which earlier generations could derive only from religion," and on "cultures today [that] are inclined so to restrict religious faith to the realm of the private and the personal, even regarding it as a strange eccentricity, that it is difficult for the Gospel to 'animate, direct, and unify' contemporary secular culture" (OMC 19 [103], 20 [104], 22 [106], 23 [107]). I deal with the second understanding and its presuppositions.

15. I argue this need in my essay "Can a Worldview Be Healed?: Students and Postmodernism," *America* 177/15 (15 November 1997): 12–16.

16. Jesuits of the Maryland Province, "A Plan for Renewal: A Community of Apostolic Men," II (December 1969): 10.

17. Peter-Hans Kolvenbach, S.J., letter "To All Major Superiors" (n. 96/16), 8 November 1996.

18. Sjaak Zonneveld, *The Random Grim Forge: A Study of Social Ideas in the Work of Gerard Manley Hopkins* (Assen/Maastricht: Van Gorcum, 1992).

19. I have argued this point in "Is Literature Still Human? Beyond Politics and Theory," *America* 173/16 (18 November 1995): 26–27, republished in the electronic database *SIRS Renaissance* (Boca Raton: SIRS, 1996).

20. Kolvenbach, "To All Major Superiors."

21. Norman H. MacKenzie, ed., *The Poetical Works of Gerard Manley Hopkins* (Oxford: Clarendon, 1990), 144.

ESSAY 11

A Faith-Justice Look at GC 34

Arthur F. McGovern, S.J.

ABSTRACT

The author reflects upon the formative elements in his own commitment to a "faith-inspired promotion of justice" strongly reaffirmed by GC 34. His early studies of Marx and liberation theologians awakened him to "the integral connection between faith, promotion of justice, and social analysis." He notes GC 34's, as well as John Paul II's, emphasis upon the need to transform "social structures," in solidarity with the poor. Marxist theology, the author argues, is still of value in its analysis of "power relations that can result from control over means of production." Examples the author provides of the ill use of power are stunning. He also discusses his efforts to awaken the consciences of his students to social justice and women's issues, and how important being involved in committee work at a university can be to serve the promotion of justice.

"The mission of the Society of Jesus today is the service of faith, of which the promotion of justice is an absolute requirement" (GC 32, Decree 4: "Our Mission Today: The Service of Faith and the Promotion of Justice" 2 [48]). This frequently cited declaration from GC 32 received a strong reaffirmation in GC 34. I have chosen faith-justice as a theme for my personal reflections on GC 34 because a faith-inspired promotion of justice has served as a focal point for most of my writings and a good bit of my teaching—for the past twenty-seven years as a professor of philosophy at the University of Detroit (U of D), now the University of Detroit Mercy (UDM). My writings (on Marxism and Christianity, on liberation theology, on social-business ethics, and on Catholic social teachings) reflect this emphasis most. A yearly course on peace and justice issues serves as a primary locus for discussing social-justice problems, but they arise in some other courses as well.

Initially I labelled my essay "A Cross-Disciplinary Look at GC 34" because much of my work, again the writing especially, has carried me beyond the realm of "traditional philosophy." I also hesitated to use faith-justice as a heading because it may suggest a level of social "activism" to which I cannot lay claim. While I have, over the years, worked in some activist groups (on hunger issues, Central American human rights, race relations), other Jesuits and laypeople whom I admire have taken far more direct and active roles in the promotion of justice. I remain primarily an "educator," and some of my reflections, especially in the last section on "other" university activities, reach beyond the faith-justice issue. The faith-justice title should, then, take into account these qualifications.

My reflections focus primarily on GC 34's Decree 3: "Our Mission and Justice" (OMJ), but later draw upon Decree 14: "Jesuits and the Situation of Women in Church and Civil Society" (JSW), and on Decree 17: "Jesuits and University Life" (JUL).

The directives for this paper asked for reflections on the "impact" of GC 34 on one's work as a scholar and life in the classroom. The Congregation will undoubtedly stimulate some new apostolic directions, but its long-range effects will take time to measure. Only in retrospect could we fully evaluate the impact of GC 32's statements on the promotion of justice, an impact noted by GC 34. "The promotion of justice has been integrated into traditional ministries and new ones, in pastoral work and social centers, in educating 'men and women for others,' in direct ministry with the poor" (OMJ 5 [54]). Nearly every Jesuit university now includes in its mission statement some reference to the promotion of justice.

While documents can impact our values and direct or redirect our life and work they more often tap into values already formed by life experiences. As I look back at my own life three value-shaping experiences, all of them in my early twenties, continue to play a major role in my apostolic work as a Jesuit. First, as a college student at Georgetown, a personal experience of being loved and valued led to my vocation as a Jesuit and stirred in me a youthful idealism of wanting to affirm others. As a Jesuit novice the great gift of the Spiritual Exercises of Saint Ignatius and the discovery of the humanity of Jesus wonderfully enriched this idealism. Second, also as a student at Georgetown, I encountered my first jarring experience of injustice. A group of Sodality members, looking for an opportunity of service, visited a rural community in Maryland. Parishioners pointed in pride to a new red brick schoolhouse. A hundred yards away I saw what I took to be a dilapidated chicken shed. "That," they replied, "is the school for the colored children." My awareness of racial injustice, deepened later by experiences in working with Friendship House, the Catholic Interracial Council, and community-organizing groups in Chicago, had its roots in that first experience. Third, Father Joe Wulftange, the most influential teacher I had as a Jesuit seminarian, insisted—counter to the prevailing method of "refuting adversaries"—that we were not to criticize opposing viewpoints until we could first demonstrate that we could present their positions accurately and fairly. That lesson would greatly affect the way I tried later to approach the study of Marxism and social justice issues.

Marxism and Social Analysis

In graduate studies I decided to specialize in Marxism. My interest in Marxism developed in years before it became a more widespread method of social analysis. As a seminarian I read a great deal of classic Russian literature (Tolstoy, Dostoyevsky), which spurred an interest in Russian history; a summer course taught by Father Jean-Yves Calvez, S.J., then introduced me to Marx and Marxism. At the outset I did not approach Marxism as a tool of social analysis. I simply believed that as a doctrine that influenced hundreds of millions in Communist countries it was a philosophy and social outlook that Christians needed to understand—as objectively as possible, following Wulftange's advice. One cannot, however, evaluate Marxism without addressing the question of social analysis. Marxism developed a whole philosophical system of dialectical materialism, but the main impact of Marxism stems from its method of social analysis, a method that has influenced a host of other social critiques: liberal economic critiques, feminism, third-world dependency theories, critiques of racism, and some critical perspectives on religion.

Liberation theologians in Latin America awakened in me a deeper recognition of the integral connection between faith, promotion of justice, and social analysis (which included some use of Marxist analysis). Our Christian faith, liberation theologians have argued, reveals a God who acts in history on behalf of the poor and calls upon all Christians to work for and with the poor.[1] A true commitment to the poor, however, requires analysis of the causes of poverty, causes that liberation theologians believe result not from personal failures but from unjust "social structures" that need to be transformed. Setting aside for the moment the controversial issue of Marxist analysis, these basic connections of faith, justice, and social analysis have become integral parts of Catholic social teachings, as evidenced in Pope John Paul II's *Sollicitudo Rei Socialis* (1987), which calls us in faith to recognize our "duty of solidarity" with the poor, and a "demand for justice" that entails confronting "structures of sin" in society.[2]

GC 34 makes similar connections. It praises and promotes Jesuit efforts in working with the poor: Jesuits in Africa "struggling to overcome the global forces that tend to marginalize the whole continent"; "Jesuits in Asia and Oceana are engaged in the struggles of the poor"; "Jesuits in Latin America . . . continue to stand with the poor as they work for the justice of the Kingdom" (Decree 2: "Servants of Christ's Mission" [SCM] 2 [17, 18, 19]). Being "'friends of the Lord' . . . means being 'friends with the poor'" (SCM 9 [34]); "working to counter growing poverty and hunger" (OMJ 5 [54]); "some insertion into the world of the poor should therefore be part of the life of every Jesuit" (OMJ 17 [66]).

GC 34 implies a need for social analysis when it calls on Jesuits to address "structural" changes. "Previous congregations have called attention to the need to work for structural changes in the socioeconomic and political orders as an important dimension of the promotion of justice" (OMJ 5 [54]). The globalization of the world economy, while it can produce many benefits, "can also result in injustices on a massive scale" (OMJ 7 [56]). "In many parts of the world, even in the most developed countries, economic and social forces are excluding millions of people from the benefits of society" (OMJ 15 [64]). These statements offer challenges that Jesuits must take seriously.

The use of Marxist analysis in addressing these issues stirred up a great deal of controversy within the Church in recent decades. Much of that controversy has subsided since the collapse of Communist regimes in Eastern Europe. Marxist analysis no longer stirs the same passionate commitment in its advocates, nor does it preoccupy former critics who viewed it as both gravely misguided and dangerous. It might, however, be worthwhile to look back briefly and consider its relation, both positive and negative, to the "promotion of justice" and its influence on my own work.

Marxist analysis focuses on capitalism as its principal target. It claims that capitalism exploits workers, creates gross inequalities, and engenders an ideology to justify its system. Socialism, Marxists argue, would eliminate the inequalities and alienation experienced by workers. This sweeping critique of capitalism, critics respond, tends toward a very reductionist view of socioeconomic problems, and its expectation that socialism can resolve the problems fails to take into account all the components and values needed to promote a healthy economy and just political system.

Marxist analysis does, nevertheless, offer insights into the ways capitalism can create injustices. Marx's own greatest insight, I believe, lies in his analysis of the power exercised in social relations: those with significant concentrations of wealth and property ownership frequently dominate the economic and political structures of society. Marx failed to recognize that power relations could become even more dominant in socialist societies (as occurred with heavily centralized Communist Party rule in Communist countries). However, Marx's analysis of the power relations that can result from control over means of production remains quite valid.

Relating Social Analysis to Justice Issues

Social analysis, with a view to the promotion of justice, needs to consider concentrations of power. El Salvador has provided, in my estimation, a clear example of injustices created by concentration of power. In 1980 the wealthiest 2 percent of the population controlled 60 percent of all arable land. The per capita income in that year was $690, yet 20 families had wealth estimated at $70 to $300 million per family.[3] Father Ignacio Ellacuría, the main target of the Salvadoran army's execution of Jesuits in 1989, provided further evidence of what concentrated wealth can cause. He cited the Salvadoran government's own study, in 1976, when it "considered" land reform. In one coastal region of El Salvador 5 families controlled 30,000 acres of land from which they each gained an average income of over

$6,000 per day. Their income equaled the total income of the other 7,800 families in the area, a third of whom averaged less than a dollar a day.[4] Access to land ownership played a major part in creating this disparity, a disparity that I believe should clearly be designated as unjust.

Disparities of wealth and power affect not just third-world countries like El Salvador but raise serious justice issues for the United States and in respect to relations between nations.[5]

The El Salvador example does not prove the validity of Marxist analysis; Marx focused on the exploitation of industrial workers, not peasant demands for access to farm lands. A study of Marx, however, can generate "leads," "insights," and a different "perspective" that can help in identifying injustices and situations of exploitation. The search for just solutions, on the other hand, should also include an objective evaluation of free-market economies; social analysis, moreover, often entails studies of how different social, economic, and political structures operate in specific historical contexts.

I found that a study of Latin American history, in particular the carryover from Spain of feudal patterns of land ownership converted later into modern systems of capitalist production, proved far more enlightening than either Marxist or modernist (free enterprise) methods of analysis. The truth needed to promote justice rarely comes from any one fixed form of analysis. Using different "heuristic structures" (to borrow from Lonergan) provides greater insight. With this in mind I team taught, a year ago, a course on the "free market" with a very conservative-libertarian professor of economics, a course that offered students an opportunity to consider and evaluate both liberal and conservative viewpoints.

Studying and evaluating major figures and movements applies in all of our teaching. In teaching epistemology I have students read Descartes not because he provides the best understanding of how to resolve questions about knowing; in fact he formulated an insoluble problem by treating ideas as the direct objects of knowing. Studying him is important, however, for several reasons: he had a great influence on subsequent epistemologies; he challenges us to think about how we know; we gain insights both from this and by learning from his mistakes. These same reasons, I believe, hold true for studying Marx and Marxism in relation to social justice issues.

Thus far I have focused on the issue of changing "structures." Séamus Murphy argues that we need a wider notion of justice than simply working with and for the poor and one that deals with more than working to bring about "structural" changes. Justice, he says, should include social injustices to women, ethnic minorities, and the unborn; individual acts of justice or injustice; and the need to develop justice virtues, values, and attitudes.[6] Martin Tripole adds to this a much more critical judgment about the Society of Jesus' whole emphasis on the promotion of justice.[7] While I agree that justice does involve more than just direct work with the poor and changing structures, I also believe that the

Society has rightly focused on a concern for marginalized people who suffer most from injustice in the world.

Teaching on Social Justice Issues

For the past seventeen years I have offered each year a course on peace and justice issues. In the initial years of the course, which focused on world hunger, Central America, racism, and the threat of nuclear war, I had as a conscious goal to "awaken the consciousness" of students to these problems. In more recent years, focusing on issues of welfare, sexism, racism, and violence, I have included a presentation of both conservative and liberal values because I believe students need to recognize and address conflicting approaches to these problems if they hope to resolve them. Promotion of justice requires a "prophetic" effort at times (raising consciousness) but also needs the "political" (negotiating differences to achieve workable solutions).

How have students responded to issues relating to social justice? The vast majority of students, at least of those at UDM, do not have political and social issues high on the list of their concerns. The pressures of getting through school, dealing with personal relationships, for many holding down part-time jobs, and for some caring for families preoccupy the attention of most. There has been, however, a significant increase in student "volunteer service" activities; such service was at most a very peripheral part of campus life in my college days; it now evokes the generosity of many students at UDM and other Jesuit universities. Volunteer service does not necessarily translate into the promotion of justice; it may simply reflect "caring for others" if unconnected with any social analysis. For some, however, it does at least make them aware of social conditions they may not have encountered.

The political views of students, as I perceive them, tend to change with the political mood of the nation, and the student "activist" groups most often mirror the more extreme activist views in the country. At U of D in the early 1970s the small activist groups—a carryover from the 1960s—were nearly all "leftist"; in the 1980s and 1990s the most active groups have tended to be staunchly conservative except for those who have made improved race relations a focus. A peace-and-justice course will draw mostly students of a liberal bent, which is not surprising since these are code words for liberal causes, just as "freedom, liberty, and heritage" have become code words for conservative groups.

Women's Issues

GC 34's Decree 14: "Jesuits and the Situation of Women in Church and Civil Society" stirred in me an enthusiastic response. As with many other Jesuits, the situation of women, in the Church especially, has greatly distressed me. So I welcomed with joy this document. Many of the issues concerning women are issues of justice, moreover, as the introductory paragraph states in referring to the "unjust treatment and exploitation of women" (JSW 1 [361]). The document recognizes the all-too-pervasive "dominance of men in their relationship with women" (2 [362]). It notes that Church teachings "call us to change our attitudes and work for a change of structures" (6 [366]). It acknowledges that we have often contributed to a form of clericalism that has reinforced male domination with an ostensibly divine sanction" (9 [369]). It invites Jesuits "to listen carefully and courageously to the experience of women" (12 [372]) and "to align themselves in solidarity with women," and lists a number of ways this might be carried out (13 [373–81]).

Over the years women friends have certainly made me aware of women's issues. However for the most part, except for including Carol Gilligan's views on moral development and a few similar insertions into courses, I followed the common practice of teaching from the traditional sources of philosophy—male philosophers. The recent formation of a women's studies program at UDM has moved me—gradually at least—toward change. The first step involved the "peace and justice" course. It had already included in recent years a significant focus on issues that affect women most: the feminization of poverty, violence toward women, and an explicit section on sexism. So, at the urging of the program director, it was not difficult to focus even more on women's issues for inclusion in the women's studies program.

A greater challenge faced me when I was asked if I might teach "Philosophy of Knowledge" as a women's studies course. Women philosophers have not figured in the traditional texts on epistemology. I needed a good part of the summer to study current writings on feminist epistemology. I needed to negotiate with the program director also, because I believed that the course should still include, as a course for philosophy majors for whom this would be their only course in epistemology, a study of traditional sources (Descartes, Hume, Kant, Wittgenstein). Much of feminist epistemology, moreover, assumes a knowledge of these major male philosophers and offers critiques of them. The inclusion of two books and several articles by women have, nevertheless, given the course a very new dimension—the listening to women's voices called for by the Congregation.

Working at the University of Detroit Mercy

GC 34's Decree 17: "Jesuits and University Life" recognizes "that universities remain crucial institutional settings in society" (JUL 1 [404]). Thirty years ago I returned from graduate studies in France with a new appreciation for our university apostolate. The more common works of the Society in Europe are individual apostolates. While I had no way of measuring their effectiveness I felt that our schools have the capacity for extending our apostolic effectiveness in the United States beyond what we could achieve as individuals. We have an opportunity to influence a culture of learning in our schools, affecting thousands of students. Universities provide, moreover, a base for the outreach of our spiritual and intellectual endeavors.

"For the poor they [universities] serve as major channels for social advancement" (JUL 2 [405]). I feel great pride in being associated with the University of Detroit Mercy. For many years, as the University of Detroit, it struggled financially to survive with a discouraging pattern of declining enrollment. The image of Detroit as crime-ridden and violent hurt us; so also has a subtle form of racism. In the late 1960s the university, responding to racial upheavals in the city, undertook a noble and bold move. It created a "Project 100" program to admit disadvantaged students (mostly African American) along with a learning center to help them meet university standards. This program, now named the University College Program with a significant number of Caucasian students added, continues its great work. The African American student body continues to grow through regular admits and now constitutes about 40 percent of our undergraduate enrollment. Profiles of our undergraduate students also indicate that we have a large proportion of relatively poor (economically poor) students.

A conversation with a journalist (about Bosnia!) serves as an illustration of the subtle racism noted above. At the beginning of our conversation the journalist remarked that he was an alumnus of U of D and added that fellow alumni friends perceived a decline in the quality of education being offered. Later in the conversation he asked: "Your student body is about 80 percent Black now, isn't it?" I corrected him but then asked if he saw a connection between that perception and his earlier comment about the quality of education. He was honest enough to respond: "You're right."

The University of Detroit began to stabilize in the 1980s. The consolidation with Mercy College took place in 1990 with the great distinction of having the first woman president of a Jesuit university, Sister Maureen Fay, O.P., a woman who has created new optimism in the university, with a more stabilized enrollment and a much sounder financial base (if still very modest in terms of endowment). The university has also significantly expanded its outreach programs to the city, including a Detroit Collaborative Design Center directed by a Jesuit, Father Terry Curry (NYK). The university has attracted, moreover, some very gifted Jesuits for whom social justice is of great concern. The city of Detroit has profited by a dynamic new leadership and its administration has much closer ties to the university. A Leadership Development Institute, funded by a Kellogg Foundation grant, has stimulated more volunteer work in the community. More, however, is needed, especially efforts to tie the experience of working with the poor and disadvantaged with a greater degree of social analysis and strategies for change.

"Jesuit universities must, in various ways, strive to do even more in order to embody this mission of service to the faith and its concomitant promotion of justice" (JUL

8 [411]). Jesuits have numberable ways of contributing to the mission of our universities and helping to strengthen their Jesuit identity. Having Jesuits identified as truly good teachers and scholars advances the mission as do courses they teach that promote both faith and justice. Celebrating campus liturgies, directing student and faculty retreats and counselling all contribute to the service of faith. Jesuits can also promote the mission of the university by serving on committees. My final set of reflections will focus on this because committee work has been a significant part of my life.

The Value of Committee Work

Most Jesuits recognize the importance of administration as a Jesuit apostolate, and I greatly esteem those who have accepted the difficult challenge of serving as presidents, vice presidents, deans, and chairs of departments. Less attention has been given to committee work, and chairing committees in particular, but I have found this work a very important way of contributing to the Jesuit Catholic mission of a university.

A great deal of my work at U of D and UDM has involved chairing or co-chairing committees (the University Core Curriculum Committee, the Minority Affairs Committee, Mission Effectiveness, the Leadership Development Institute, among others). The lessons I learned from chairing the University Core Curriculum Committee served especially to show me both the importance of such work and the gifts one needs to carry out such work.

In the late 1960s the U of D dropped its core curriculum, believing that with good academic advising each student could be guided to find courses that best fitted personal needs and talents. In subsequent years, however, dissatisfaction grew and with it demands to restore a core curriculum. A couple of efforts by committees to develop a new core failed because, in my judgment, the committees worked in isolation and presented a finished product that the faculty voted down.

In the early 1980s the board of trustees mandated a core curriculum. I suggested to the vice president the kind of "process" that was needed. He agreed, but then asked me to chair a new committee. The process worked, admittedly with pressure from the board's mandate. The process involved "stages" of consultation with the faculty and deans: first, gaining agreement on some general principles, then choosing from three general models, and only at the end negotiating specific objectives and courses.

Several lessons I learned from this: (1) the need to listen to all sides fairly and objectively; (2) the value of developing consensus (never complete) by working through stages; (3) the art of negotiating differences; and (4) the important influence one can have by being willing to draft initial documents. Volunteering to write drafts of documents can play an especially significant role. If the draft is written with a view to what can gain acceptance and one is truly willing to have it revised to incorporate other ideas (being open even to the possibility of its being discarded), one has an opportunity to present values that may serve as the basis for a final document. In the case of the U of D's core curriculum this enabled me to present objectives that expressed distinctive Jesuit goals of education.

The process, however, has to be truly iterative, involving often a series of adaptations. In the case of the core curriculum this meant an initial expression of Jesuit objectives; consultation with the Jesuit community and a first revision, discussion, and modification of the objectives with lay committee members, respecting their experiences and ideas on Jesuit education; and, finally, discussion, further adaptation, and revision through general faculty meetings, plus keeping deans and administrators updated and incorporating their concerns. The six objectives finally approved each reflected Jesuit goals in education, including attention given to explicitly religious values and studies related to justice issues. A new opportunity was presented to me as a co-chair to develop a core that consolidated the objectives of Jesuit education and the values and goals of the Sisters of Mercy.

As Jesuits, if we want to retain the Jesuit identity of our institutions, we need to take an active part in articulating our mission. We must work hard, as the Congregation states, "to maintain and even to strengthen the specific character of each of our institutions both as *Jesuit* and as a *university*" (JUL 5 [408]). At the same time we must recognize that Jesuit universities are not simply "ours" but belong as well to our lay colleagues who now carry on the mission of these universities in far greater numbers than we can provide. Our policies and curricula must give expression to their sense of the university's mission.

Committee work takes a considerable amount of time, especially if one takes an active role in helping to shape goals—time that many Jesuits may need to devote to research, writing, work with students and pastoral ministries. It remains, nevertheless, a work through which at least some Jesuits can contribute significantly to the mission of Jesuit universities.

Concluding Reflections

The editor's charge in asking for this essay was to reflect on the impact of GC 34. As my initial observations indicated, the values that have shaped my apostolic work as a Jesuit evolved over my whole lifetime and came through a variety of special graces. The Congregation documents have provided a confirmation and encouragement of these values. As I look back on my life, and as I complete a term as the Jesuit rector of my community, I find myself moved deeply by a new concern. Much of this essay focused upon the promotion of justice; now I find myself giving new attention to the "service of the faith" that is linked to the promotion of justice as an absolute requirement. GC 34 also reemphasizes this connection. We are "called to be servants of Christ's universal mission in the Church"

(Decree 1: "United with Christ on Mission" 8 [8]). We are first of all companions of Jesus, "friends in the Lord." The "vision of justice which guides us is intimately linked with our faith" (OMJ 4 [53]).

In today's world, promoting the faith life of our students has become a serious challenge. Studies show a rather dramatically declining number of young people, including Catholics, attending church services. Lack of church attendance does not necessarily translate into lack of faith; many students still search for some kind of spiritual life. I fear, however, an increased secularization of society. I want young people to come to know Jesus and find it hard to envision a faith life that is sustained without some experience of church community. So I find myself wanting to devote more time to the service of faith (through retreats and spiritual workshops), while continuing to emphasize that this faith still clearly calls for the "promotion of justice" as an "absolute requirement" (GC 32, Decree 4: 2 [48]).

ENDNOTES • MCGOVERN

1. Gustavo Gutiérrez, *A Theology of Liberation* (Maryknoll, N.Y.: 1973), introduced me to liberation theology and to this faith-justice–social analysis connection. Controversy over the use of Marxist social analysis by some liberation theologians significantly influenced my writing about Marxism and Christianity and about liberation theology. It was Jon Sobrino's *Christology at the Crossroads* (Maryknoll, N.Y.: Orbis, 1978), however, that provided me with the clearest faith-justice connection. Simply summarized: Jesus proclaimed faith in the Kingdom of God, which gives us a vision of what society should strive to become, a society in which all persons are treated justly and with dignity; to be a follower of Jesus involves sharing his values and seeking to work for the kind of society envisioned in the Kingdom.

2. John Paul II, *Sollicitudo Rei Socialis* 9–10, on solidarity with the poor and the demand for justice, and 36–37 on analyzing and confronting "structures of sin" in society, published in *Catholic Social Thought*, ed. David J. O'Brien and Thomas A. Shannon (Maryknoll, N.Y.: Orbis, 1992).

3. The per capita income in El Salvador was noted in the *Economic Handbook of the World*, 1981, ed. Arthur S. Banke et al. (New York: McGraw-Hill, 1981), 140. Data on the twenty wealthiest families were given in Paul Heath Hoeffel, "The Eclipse of the Oligarchy," *The New York Times Magazine* (6 September 1981): 23.

4. Ignacio Ellacuría, S.J., cites these income figures in his essay "The Historicization of the Concept of Poverty," in *Towards a Society That Serves Its People: The Intellectual Contribution of El Salvador's Murdered Jesuits*, ed. John Hassett and Hugh Lacey (Washington, D.C.: Georgetown University Press, 1991), 105–37 at 112–13. The acreage figures I give equal the *manzanas* cited by Ellacuría.

5. See, for example, the power issues noted by David C. Korten, *When Corporations Rule the World* (West Hartford, Conn.: Kumarian, 1995): "Markets and politics are both about governance, power, and the allocation of society's resources. . . . In a political democracy, each person gets one vote. In the market, one dollar is one vote, and you get as many votes as you have dollars. . . . Markets are inherently biased in favor of people of wealth" (66).

   The world now has 358 billionaires with a greater wealth than one-half of the world's population, Jack Nelson-Pallmeyer noted in a talk for a Michigan Pax Christi conference, April 19, 1997.

6. Séamus Murphy, S.J., "The Many Ways of Justice," *Studies in the Spirituality of Jesuits* 26/2 (March 1994).

7. Martin R. Tripole, S.J., *Faith Beyond Justice: Widening the Perspective* (St. Louis, Mo.: Institute of Jesuit Sources, 1994).

"Nonlinear, image-oriented, intuitive, and affective": Reflections on GC 34 and the Fine Arts

Thomas M. Lucas, S.J.

A B S T R A C T

The author admits that the relationship of GC 34 to the fine arts is not immediately obvious. Yet GC 34 admits the early Jesuits linked catechesis to "education in classical humanism, art, and theater," and affirmed the Society's "commitment to liberal education" as a way of discovering and shaping human wisdom. The decrees provide "raw materials and tools" for art educators' creativity. GC 34 affirms the need for positive dialogue with cultures in the work of evangelization, and respect for indigenous values. In Jesuit universities, there is a need to expand fine arts curricula to include nontraditional perspectives. There needs also to be dialogue between the contemporary art world, with its often materialistic and even pagan orientation, and the values of the Gospel. A new "nonlinear" kind of religious language may be called for, to convey truth in "nonverbal and nonlinear ways." We need to enter more deeply into an understanding of modern art, if we hope to find in it the critical expression that "can contribute to the struggle for justice in an unjust world."

At first glance, GC 34's practical challenge of integrating Jesuit mission with justice, culture, and interreligious dialogue seems far removed from the esthetic and esoteric realm of the fine arts.

The fine arts certainly are highly visible signs of culture, and are often equated with it in public discourse. The artifact serves as a vehicle of cultural transmission and meaning, and increasingly, the media are identified with the message. The relationship of the arts to the arenas of apostolic mission, the struggle for justice in an unjust world, and the imperatives of interreligious dialogue are not so evident, though, and can be teased out of the fabric of the General Congregation's documents only with some effort. Nevertheless, given the Society's long—yet ambiguous—relationship to the production and study of the works of human genius, such an effort seems warranted, and indeed, quite appropriate in this collection of essays on GC 34's implications for the Jesuit grove in the forest of Academe.

First, a *caveat*. Unlike GC 31, which dedicated some seven paragraphs and four hundred words to the theme "Cultivating the Arts in the Society" (Decree 30: 1–6 [553–59]), GC 34 never pronounces directly on the relationship between the arts and the contemporary Jesuit mission. To be sure, the recent Congregation acknowledges that "the early Jesuits, in their schools, linked Christian catechesis to an education in classical humanism, art, and theater, in order to make their students versed both in faith and in European culture" (Decree 4: "Our Mission and Culture" [OMC] 10 [89]). In its document on university life, the Congregation also affirms the Society's historical and contemporary commitment to liberal education: "From astronomy to classical ballet, from the humanities to theology, Jesuits try to enter into the languages and discourse of their inherited or emerging cultures. They attempt to discover, shape, renew, or promote human wisdom, while at the same time respecting the integrity of disciplined scholarship" (Decree 17: "Jesuits and University Life" 1 [404]). GC 34, however, provides no formal analysis, no concrete paragraphs, no written artifact on art.

What the documents do provide, rather, is a cluster of themes that can serve as raw materials and tools for artists and arts educators in Jesuit universities. What kind of artifacts emerge from our manipulation of those images, forms, and patterns—what kind of pedagogical and socially responsible strategies develop from them—depends on our creativity, not that of the Congregation's delegates. We have been given tools and raw materials, no more, no less.

OMC is a nuanced reflection on the complicated interaction between belief, apostolic outreach, and evanglization of culture, and emerging global realities that challenge, undermine, and even condemn the Society's traditional missionary stance and much of its former methodology. The document points out that around the globe, Western cultural hegemony is being questioned. In the first world, multicultural awareness is developing rapidly. In the third world, there is growing appreciation of and more systematic attempts to defend the values, arts, and legacies of indigenous cultures. The religious and cultural ramifications of postindustrial society and what the Congregation calls "critical postmodern culture" are all immense, but have yet to be dealt with by the Church in any significant way. These profound cultural questions challenge not only the Society of Jesus' "way of proceeding," but create an irregular and shifting horizon against which any kind of comprehensive cultural or artistic perspective is very difficult to draw.

The Congregation's fundamental stance is to reaffirm the best of Society's tradition of active and positive dialogue with the cultures—and people—it encounters. "We must remember that we do not directly 'evangelize cultures'; we evangelize people in their culture" (OMC 27,4 [114]). Every Jesuit work of evangelization must take place in a climate of respect for the culture it encounters, whether that culture is a person's own by birth or missionary adoption (27,6 [116]). Such a respectful attitude implies a level of modesty, a readiness to learn from the cultures one encounters and to make amends, where appropriate, for cultural insensitivity and former attitudes of cultural chauvinism (12–13 [92–97]). Into this dialogue the Jesuit—and, by extension, the Jesuit institution—must bring not only faith in a God who continues to work in all creation, but also a passion for justice, and a commitment of solidarity with the poor who "show us the way to inculturate gospel values in situations where God is forgotten" (Decree 26: "Conclusion: Our Way of Proceeding" 14 [548]).

All this having been said, what are the implications for the teaching of fine arts in modern Jesuit universities?

GC 34's breadth of view suggests that, in Jesuit universities, business-as-usual instruction in Western art history and studio technique is not enough. We need to examine our attitudes and our curricula, and continue to open them up to non-Western and nontraditional perspectives. The art forms of indigenous peoples, the immensely revelatory study of crafts as well as "masterworks," the works of women and minority artists from our own culture, all need to be drawn into an expanded curriculum of art history and technical instruction.

While indeed many of the world's artistic treasures were created by "dead white males," many immensely powerful and revelatory works are the creations of women and men who are not usually included in the canon. Especially as we deal with increasingly diverse student populations, we need to heighten our sensitivities and deepen our knowledge of non-Western cultural and artistic idioms. While few of us are called or invited to immerse ourselves as fully into another culture as Giuseppe Castiglione was, his example can still inspire us. A fairly mediocre genre painter by European standards, Castiglione—or Lang Shih-ning, as he came to be called at the court of the emperor of China—got inside Chinese culture while never entirely abandoning his own, and his refined and elegant scrolls mark a rare moment of cultural fusion based on technical mastery and cultural sensitivity.

The visual arts have traditionally been perceived as a privileged, even unique, medium for exploring and explicating humanity's relationship to the transcendent. In our post-Christian Western world, though, this perception has been challenged, and sometimes rejected outright.

> [T]here is a difficult dialogue with men and women who think they have gone beyond Christianity or any religious commitment. We need to pay particular attention to them because of their influence throughout the world. Some cultures today are inclined so to restrict religious faith to the realm of the private and the personal, even regarding it as a strange eccentricity, that it is difficult for the Gospel to "animate, direct, and

unify" contemporary secular culture. We recognize that many of our contemporaries judge that neither Christian faith nor any religious belief is good for humanity. (OMC 19 [103])

It could be argued that this passage from OMC was written with the contemporary art scene in mind. Materialistic, hedonistic, often unabashedly pagan in its orientation, the art world, because of its high visibility and cultural weight, is a natural target for the Society's values-oriented ministry.

In many diverse programs, Jesuit universities serve as a training grounds for young artists and critics. What should set our programs and institutions apart from others at private and public institutions is a commitment to the cultural dialectic that the Congregation defines as a fundamental descriptor of all collaborative Jesuit ministries. This dialectic proposes a deeply engaged, and engaging, conversation between the values of the Gospel that undergird our educational institutions and the contemporary milieu where the visual arts play a crucial role in explicating the culture. It is a dialogue in which we must be both profoundly open to what we encounter and yet confident enough of our own presuppositions that we can be critical of what is incomplete, flawed, or wrong. This dialogue presupposes a familiarity with the modern social sciences as well as theology and philosophy. Because it makes real demands on us as well as our students and colleagues, it is dangerous, challenging work:

> *The problems of working in these contexts need no elaboration here, because the boundary line between the Gospel and the modern and post-modern culture passes through the heart of each of us. Each Jesuit encounters the impulse to unbelief first of all in himself; it is only when we deal with that dimension in ourselves that we can speak to others of the reality of God.* (OMC 20 [104])

The Congregation proposes that the work of dialogue is, moreover, one that requires what might be understood as a kind of "remythologizing" of the Gospel's message and values. "[W]e cannot speak to others if the religious language we use is completely foreign to them. . . . Only when we make sense of our own experience and understanding of God can we say things which make sense to contemporary agnosticism" (OMC 20 [104]). The hermeneutic process alluded to here suggests that a new kind of religious language, informed by what GC 34's document on communication calls "a new culture, one that is nonlinear, image-oriented, intuitive, and affective in its understanding of the world" (Decree 15: "Communication: A New Culture" 1 [385]), needs to emerge from reflection on our own personal and collective experience. "Nonlinear, image-oriented, intuitive, and affective": adjectives that surely resonate with the artistic experience.

In his late-Renaissance schools, Ignatius proposed mining the lore of antiquity "like the spoils of Egypt," because he believed that every product of human genius can be useful in the dialogue between the values of the Gospel and culture. As modern teachers of art and art history, we need to find in the new mystical languages of Rothko and Frankenthaler a compliment to and expansion on the traditions of Renaissance religious expression. We need to absorb the vocabularies and critical insights of Daumier, Köllwitz, and even Warhol if we are going to teach our students how the visual arts can hold up a critical mirror to contemporary culture. We need to internalize and then make explicit the passions of Rivera, Picasso, and Motherwell if we want to show our students that art has something important to contribute to the struggle for justice in an unjust world.

   Much of what we do as arts educators in Jesuit universities is hidden work. It is a work that begins in our own silent experience of wonder, of wonder at beauty perceived, at truth conveyed in nonverbal and nonlinear ways, at revelation taking place through the works of our hands, through human creation. If we find ways "ever ancient, ever new" to share that wonder with our students, our work will contribute to the dialogue between our mission and culture, between beauty and beauty's Lord.

Evoking Justice in the Pursuit of Art:
The Fine Arts, the Constitutions, and GC 34

Kevin Waters, S.J.

ABSTRACT

The author shows how a composition written by a French composer imprisoned by the Nazis is a seminal work for its bearing on faith and justice. He points out how the congregations and *Constitutions* see study of the arts as part of a growth in understanding of reality and of different cultures. He finds his role as an educator of fine arts to be both "maker and teacher"—to create symbols that give pleasure as well as create "multiple relationships" with one's world. Art can also share in the work of evangelization, of "finding God in all things." The author's own teaching of the philosophy of art is designed to provoke a discovery of beauty and an understanding of culture in his students, and he gives examples from their writings that illustrate how remarkably insightful they can be. The author's own musical compositions probe the depths of human experience where art, reason, and faith meet in a common experience of the God who is Beauty.

Olivier Messiaen, imprisoned by the Nazis in occupied France from 1940 to 1942, composed while there "Quatuor pour la Fin du Temps" (Quartet for the End of Time), a seminal work in the field of fine arts for its bearing on discussions of faith and justice. Out of the anguish and despair spawned by the devouring beast of war, Messiaen turned to Saint John's "Apocalypse" for inspiration and succor.

> *I saw a mighty angel coming down from heaven. He was wrapped in a cloud, with the rainbow round his head; his face shone like the sun and his legs were like pillars of fire. . . . His right foot he planted on the sea, and his left on the land, . . . and standing on the sea and the land raised his right hand to heaven and swore by him who lives for ever and ever, . . . :*

"There shall be no more delay; but when the time comes for the seventh angel to sound his trumpet, the hidden purpose of God will have been fulfilled." (Rv 10:1–7)

The quartet's musical language, in the composer's own words, "is essentially transcendental, spiritual, Catholic. Certain modes, realizing melodically and harmonically a kind of tonal ubiquity, draw the listener into a sense of the eternity of space or time. Particular rhythms existing outside the measure contribute importantly toward the banishment of temporalities. (All this is mere striving and childish stammering if one compares it to the overwhelming grandeur of the subject!)"[1]

Searching his soul, his history, and his very creativity in his quest for God's justice, Messiaen found an adequate answer through his formulation of the quartet. Adequate because it lends sufficient comfort through faith to recognize in some measure God's way of working through us. In Messiaen's program notes for the eighth and final movement of the quartet, "Praise to the immortality of Jesus," he refers to what he calls the second glorification of Jesus, since the first is found in the fifth movement, "Praise to the eternity of Jesus." "Why this second glorification? It addresses itself more specifically to the second aspect of Jesus—to Jesus the man, to the Word made flesh, raised up immortal from the dead so as to communicate His life to us. It is total love. Its [the violin's] slow rising to a supreme point is the ascension of man toward his God, of the son of God toward his Father, of the mortal newly made divine toward paradise."[2]

Jesuit Educators and the Fine Arts

GC 34 embodies through Decrees 3 and 4 the character of the Congregation. These decrees describe both the thrust and ambit of the Holy Spirit's apostolic mandate to us at this moment in human development. One cannot escape the responsibility that we are to be "forming 'men and women for others' . . . in our educational institutions," nor that the "Christian message is to be open to all cultures, bound to no single culture and made accessible to every human person through a process of inculturation" (Decree 3: "Our Mission and Justice" 20 [69]; Decree 4: "Our Mission and Culture" 2 [76]).

The fact is that the culture most foreign to us, paradoxically, is our own. Our common language, developed over a multiplicity of years, races to catch up with linguistic change. Yet, "every Jesuit, in order to be apostolically effective, must be aware of and well versed in the language and symbols, as well as the strengths and weaknesses, of modern communication culture."[3] A perennial aim for the Jesuit educator of the fine arts is in consort with other Jesuits to buttress the foundations of our teaching on the *Constitutions* and the Congregations.

Jesuit educators are charged in common by the *Constitutions:* "A solid education should be fostered in literature, in the arts, in sciences, also in social sciences, the better to understand reality and to undertake the analysis of it; and also in history and in various aspects of the culture of the region where the apostolate will be carried on, as well as in modern means of social communication" (*Const,* Norms 95, p. 157). Amplifying this charge, GC 33 specifies that "research . . . in every branch of human culture is . . . essential if Jesuits are to help the Church understand the contemporary world and speak to it the Word of Salvation" (Decree 1: "Companions of Jesus Sent into Today's World" 44 [47]). In the fine arts, research implies having at one's fingertips a ready catalog of major works, trends in style, and significant understanding of both our own culture and its current interface with cultures not our own, either in time or place. No easy charge this, but the challenge pursued holds unfathomable spiritual and intellectual treasures. To participate in a Christocentric world of belief and rational discovery by grasping it oneself then telling another about it is at the heart of evangelization.

Though Beethoven's *Fidelio* holds common ground with Luigi Dallapiccola's *Il prigioniero* in depicting absence of trial and unjust imprisonment, it is easier for me to teach the nineteenth-century *Fidelio* than the twentieth-century *Il prigioniero.* The musical idiom of Beethoven needs little explanation to the ordinary listener. This not only because of Beethoven's oft-performed symphonies, but from the familiarity with tonal music surrounding them on either side for nearly two centuries. Dallapiccola, a composer of our own time, writes in a contemporary idiom that breaks new ground.[4] His territory is unfamiliar and even alien to many listeners. He shares the burden of contemporary art, which finds itself an immigrant in a new land. His language and customs are unknown here, except by those of his own kind. Genuine inculturation places the need to understand and make at home the newly arrived as much on the shoulders of the immigrants' land of destiny as it does on immigrants themselves.

It is my duty as an interpreter, familiar with two languages, two cultures, to bridge any ravine or chasm between the two. That, in essence, has always been the province of the effective teacher, following the guidance provided by the *Constitutions:* to see that those authors are critically studied, whose works have had "greater influence on present-day cultures," whether it be our own culture or a culture necessary for our apostolic understanding and effectiveness (*Const,* Norms 105, p. 163).

The vocation of the Jesuit educator of fine arts inevitably means maker and teacher. By nature, artists make vases, verses, dances, and song. The art object stands as both symbol and thing: something enjoyable or intellectually pleasurable in itself, and something that creates multiple relationships connecting with our thoughts, feelings, and all our activities. Therefore, it is in the nature of the fine arts to teach. But in common with other fields, the fine arts are also taught by masters to apprentices. The master artist has the compelling twofold mission to teach through his art and also simply to teach others his art.

Sometimes the instructional aspect does not directly relate to master and apprentice because art in and of itself contains vital didactic energy. Let me cite from Jesuit history the story of Brother Bernardo Bitti.[5] The Aymara Indians of Peru, in an area near Lake Titicaca, heard the gospel message for the first time at the Jesuit mission in the village of Juli during the latter part of the sixteenth century. After Brother Bitti arrived there in 1587, the Aymaras also saw the major icons of faith, the images of Christ, Mary, and the saints, through his medium of painting. Brother Bitti was sent from Rome to Lima because an urgent request had been made to the generalate by mission superiors for an artist—a painter—to assist in the evangelization of the Aymaras. His paintings done in tempera are said to manifest the delicacy of the followers of Michelangelo and Raphael. Though probably less known than either Brother Giuseppe Castiglione, the Jesuit painter at the court of the Chinese emperors, or Brother Andrea Pozzi, whose best known work is the *trompe l'oeil* ceiling of Rome's Sant'Ignazio, Brother Bitti was considered the finest Jesuit painter of his generation.

In heeding the request from Peruvian superiors, Rome sent Brother Bitti on a mission for the explicit purpose of evangelization. He was to evangelize through his art, through his religious paintings.

The Ignatian charism to find God in all things, which permeates the proceedings of the General Congregations after being seeded in the Spiritual Exercises and *Constitutions,* strongly resonates in the Jesuit educational mission. Wilfred LaCroix, S.J., suggests that Saint Ignatius had in mind an educational system that adapted to times and places with a curriculum that was equally adaptable.[6] LaCroix quotes this passage from the *Constitutions* to reinforce his suggestion: ". . . although the order and hours which are spent in . . . studies may vary according to the regions and seasons, there should be such conformity that in every region that is done which is there judged to be the most conducive to greater progress in learning."[7] LaCroix explains further that for Saint Ignatius the overall goals "were timeless in the sense that they were to be always at least formally present. What would count as expressing and furthering the goal of preparing the student to act well in the society will change, but the goal must not."[8]

How I Understand What I Do

Using the general norm that the Jesuit educator has as a goal that we are to prepare "the student to act well in the society" according to the "regions and seasons," allow me to explain how I understand what I am to do.

One of the courses that I teach is philosophy of art, which makes an analysis of beauty, creativity, and taste according to the theories of Aristotle, Plato, Aquinas, and some contemporary philosophers. Jacques Maritain's staple work, *Art and Scholasticism,* serves as a primary source. Among the essays students are asked to write for the course is one on a topic extracted from Maritain's text: "Tradition and discipline are the true nurses of originality; art has a fundamental need of novelty: like nature, it goes in seasons."[9]

Coping with the paradox, how one balances tradition with novelty, requires considerable reflection on the part of the student. Sometimes it comes in the form of a strange analogy, such as this description of the Yankees by one of my students, Brett Allbery:

> *The tradition and discipline of the Yankees has been to assemble a team that works hard and gives it their all, night in and night out. This year, the Yankees have thrown all that out the window in favor of players who are more exciting to watch; they are much more egotistical and rude ballplayers, and they could care less for the fans, those who are paying them to play. But to their credit, the Yankees this past season assembled a team that had tradition and discipline (hardworking, scrappy players like the old days) and novelty (much more flamboyant, cocky, and arrogant). That balance helped them win the World Series in 1996.*

But it is Maritain's mirroring of the *Constitutions* in his statement about "seasons" that also holds interest. The seasons of the year bring changes that are sudden and dramatic, even though they are for the most part expected. A devastating flood, a catastrophic hurricane or drought, though anticipated as possible within the season, may occur only once in a hundred years. So, too, with the arts whose change may be gradual and projected because of noticeable trends. They also may be a total surprise, such as the publication of Joyce's *Ulysses*, the exhibition of Picasso's *Guernica*, or the riotous premiere of Stravinsky's *Rite of Spring*.

The Fine Arts and Culture

The cultures of our time, both our own and those intersecting our own—how do we assimilate, communicate, and make them large for ourselves and our students? What is their place in the Jesuit apostolate in higher education, in our curriculum, if we are to follow GC 34 and the *Constitutions?*

Always seeking the mean, Saint Ignatius, according to LaCroix, conceived of a curriculum for Jesuit schools that neither looked exclusively to studying the past nor cast aside the past in favor of the future.

> *Many educators of the time* [Reformation], *like those of the declining University of Cologne, clung to an exclusive philosophical and theological program with a lack of attention to the interest generated by contemporary*

*problems. Others, such as Erasmus, discarded medieval studies and put in
their place a homogeneous curriculum of humanistic studies drawn from
ancient literature alone. By combining the worthwhile core of medieval
studies with the Renaissance humanism, Ignatius set up a system of studies that was singularly successful and admired.*[10]

GC 34 does not outline a specific curriculum to be followed in today's Jesuit university. But Decree 16: "The Intellectual Dimension of Jesuit Ministries," and the relatively brief Decree 17: "Jesuits and University Life" (JUL), enjoin Jesuits to imbue their
disciplines with theological reflection and social analysis. The Jesuit university should see
"that important debates take place about ethics, future directions for economics and politics, and the very meaning of human existence, debates that shape our culture" (JUL 2
[405]). Our culture, of course, is shaped by means other than debates. Surely the "making" of a culture also lies at the center of Jesuit education.

In the age of the *Ratio Studiorum,* the seventeenth and eighteenth centuries, Jesuit
schools included dance, theater, and music in their curriculum. A recent study, *Terpsichore
at Louis-le-Grand: Baroque Dance on the Jesuit Stage in Paris,*[11] tells how dramas and
ballets contributed to the development of French culture, from art to politics. In other parts
of the Continent, the Jesuits fostered the arts in their institutions in a variety of ways.
About 1730, the Polish Jesuits opened in Cracow the first music conservatory in Europe,
which was intended to train professional musicians for the Church and the court. Its purposes included the social responsibility of offering credentials to poor musicians so that
they would be able to secure gainful employment in their field of study.

Today that task is undertaken by Jesuit universities with degree-granting departments of music, such as Gonzaga, the College of Music at Loyola University in New
Orleans, or the Elisabeth University of Music in Hiroshima, Japan. Professional training
in the visual arts, theater, and dance has become increasingly associated with Jesuit
schools and universities in the United States during the past forty years. Several of the
schools also house permanent art collections in handsome galleries and museums. These
institutions actively engage in maintaining cultural heirlooms from a vast array of societies as well as serving the public's hunger for discovering art newly minted and waiting
to be savored as well by future generations.

Parents and teachers, confident that they instill proper habits of mind and heart in
their children and students, nonetheless doubt whether anything of importance will be
remembered, relied upon, and verified through positive experiences. No one doubts the
brilliance and disciplined strategies of Jesuit students Voltaire and Castro, but some second thoughts must have occurred to their Jesuit teachers when they observed the moves of
their culture-shaping alumni. Perhaps we have some advantage as educators in an era

when accrediting agencies emphasize "outcomes assessment." Thereby we can develop some methods to ascertain our short-term and long-term effectiveness.

The Students Discover Beauty

My course on the philosophy of art aims to foster in the student the ability of discovering beauty according to Aquinas's three criteria of integrity, proportion, and clarity of form, as described by Maritain.[12] At the end of the semester, Chris Durbin described his understanding and experience this way:

> It is one thing to simply look at a painting or listen to a symphony and think, "I like that," and quite another to be able to say and explain, "I think that is beautiful because. . . ." Prior to taking this course and thinking about what actually makes a work of art successful (in painting, music, literature, and other genres), my first and only response to a pleasing work was to decide that I enjoyed it and simply move on from there. What is more important, and what I am now able to explain to myself and to others, is why a particular photograph or novel is beautiful and worthy of attention, even if it does not particularly please me. For example, I do not care for most modern art, but before deciding offhand that a piece of abstract modern art is not worth my time, I am able now to reflect upon the relativity of beauty and look closer: perhaps the artist is conveying a vision or message that is truly new; I might ask how this work participates in—and breaks from—the tradition of art before dismissing it simply because I do not like the colors.

Having the students understand their own culture through careful reflection leads them to imagining the future with insight and clear vision. Christie Bird, a classmate of Chris Durbin, wrote the following observation:

> If a community is to thrive with a vibrant, healthy human population, it needs to value the artist more than it presently does. For the artist is perhaps the only one whose work brings pure good and inspiration to a community. The true artist touches the core of a community in a way the engineer and tradesman fail to do.

Kathleen Delaney adds these further thoughts to Christie's:

> The beauty of art feeds the soul and the spirit. We are enriched by the nourishment received through art as profitably as we are nourished and

sustained by food grown through the skill of the farmer. Without the beauty of art we would be fixed in the doldrums of survival rather than in the joy of living.

The composer of absolute music—chamber scores and orchestral works—occasionally turns to music with text in order to "speak" with another voice. Several years ago, after composing two large works, one for orchestra and the other for string quartet, I desired to work on an opera. As a result, I met Ernest Ferlita, S.J., and collaborated with him on some theater pieces and a couple of operas. Two of these, *Mask of Hiroshima* and *Edith Stein*, are rooted in the horrendous events in Germany and Japan at the time of World War II.

Humanity, in its search for justice, knows best its counterclaim through acts, little and large, enmeshed in both careless and carefully planned incivilities. Well-executed art describes woundings from slight hurts to major atrocities in a concentrated fashion incapable of being handled by the brevity and superficiality of the daily news media. Further, the news easily forgets even the recent past in its hunger for reporting what is happening just now.

The wellsprings of my creativity as an artist goad me to imagine, mold, intensify, and bring to light a convincing work of art. If the audiences of *Mask of Hiroshima* or *Edith Stein* have greater yearning for justice because they now better perceive soul-devouring injustice, a purpose of Ferlita's and mine has been attained.

In an analysis of Maritain's notion of beauty as one of the divine names, my student Donna L. McKereghan wrote: "Poetry, taken in the most universal sense, is caused by Beauty, while art tends toward it. Poetry is the expression of Beauty, which is its cause, and the poem . . . is a result of the superabundance of Beauty. Beauty is the cause of poetry; poetry is the cause of poems and art. Poems express beauty while art tends toward it, as its end."

For believer, philosopher, theologian, and artist, God's name is Beauty, according to some of Thomas's richest language.[13] God's name is also Just. Awards overflowing with comforting grace await those who contemplate the two names often and together.

ENDNOTES • WATERS

1. Olivier Messiaen's program notes appear in his preface to the musical score and are reprinted in full for the RCA Victor CD recording of "Quatuor pour la Fin du Temps," (7845-2-RG) performed by Tashi and produced by Max Wilcox and Peter Serkin.
2. Ibid.
3. John W. Padberg, S.J., gen. ed., *The Constitutions of the Society of Jesus and Their Complementary Norms* (St. Louis, Mo.: Institute of Jesuit Sources, 1996), Norms 303,1, p. 310; hereafter *Const* in text.

4. Dallapiccola blends Italianate lyricism with Germanic formalism as found in the twelve-tone schema of Arnold Schoenberg, Anton Webern, and Alban Berg.
5. J. De Mesa and T. Gisbert, "Bitti, Bernardo," in *The New Catholic Encylopedia* (New York: McGraw-Hill, 1967), II, 596.
6. Wilfred L. LaCroix, S.J., *The Jesuit Spirit of Education: Ignatius, Tradition and Today's Questions* (Kansas City, Mo.: Rockhurst College, 1989), 45.
7. Ibid., 45, citing Const [454].
8. LaCroix, *The Jesuit Spirit of Education,* 45.
9. Jacques Maritain, *Art and Scholasticism* (Notre Dame, Ind.: University of Notre Dame Press, 1974), 45–46.
10. LaCroix, *The Jesuit Spirit of Education,* 46–47.
11. Judith Rock, *Terpsichore at Louis-le-Grand: Baroque Dance on the Jesuit Stage in Paris* (St. Louis, Mo.: Institute of Jesuit Sources, 1997).
12. Maritain, *Art and Scholasticism,* ch. 5: "Art and Beauty," 23–37.
13. In addition to Maritain's *Art and Scholasticism* and *Creative Intuition in Art and Poetry* (Washington, D.C.: National Gallery of Art, 1952), an excellent treatise on Beauty according to Saint Thomas may be found in Umberto Eco's *The Aesthetics of Thomas Aquinas* (Cambridge, Mass.: Harvard University Press, 1988).

ESSAY 14

The Teaching and Practice of History and the Recent General Congregations

Robert M. Senkewicz, S.J.

ABSTRACT

This essay attempts to place GC 34 in three contexts: (1) the controversies surrounding the nature and scope of historical interpretation in the United States for the past thirty years; (2) GC 31, 32, and 33, especially the pronouncements of those gatherings on the faith-justice issue; and (3) the efforts of an individual Jesuit to teach history in a Jesuit university over the past two decades. The author finds that these three contexts complement each other. Both American historiography and the Jesuit documents, in their emphasis on social reality, urge us to a greater explicit focus on issues of faith, belief, and unbelief. Approaching faith and belief through a rigorous social analysis brings us an awareness that the 1965 call of Paul VI to the Society of Jesus still constitutes a present challenge to all Jesuits.

Introduction

I have been invited to reflect on how my teaching of history has been affected by the Society of Jesus' most recent General Congregation. The theme itself warrants a certain amount of digging through its components. There is more involved here than classroom teaching, although that is certainly an important and necessary part of the picture. The theme inevitably goes beyond considerations of the manner and style of pedagogy. But teaching affords a good place to begin.

One of the best teachers I have ever encountered was Father Joe Frese, S.J. Almost three decades ago, he came up twice a week from Fordham University to teach us at Shrub Oak, the Jesuit house of philosophy studies in the New York Province. Joe was supposedly teaching us about the American Revolution, but, as is the case with all brilliant teachers, the explicit subject matter was the least of what we learned from him. Whether he was shuffling his index cards as he took us through the technicalities of the Stamp Act, or detailing the precise number of acts a British soldier had to perform to fire and reload his musket successfully, he gave us, above all, a passion for knowledge. The way one teaches, he showed us by example, is fundamentally affected by one's stance toward the subject—in his case, toward the past. Moreover, he always insisted that his own stance was not the only one, or even the best one.

We found that the "real distinction," so important in our philosophy classes, had less force in Joe's. He taught us that historians had largely abandoned von Ranke's search for "how it really happened" for good reasons. He made us see that history had little of an essentialist nature, and that the human messiness of many people, including the historical actors we studied, the scholars who wrote the books we used, and the teacher in front of us, affected both how and what we studied.

This is an important point to make. In these days the very process of historical interpretation itself is often denigrated in rather absolute and extreme terms. Some people argue, for instance, that the United States Constitution ought to be understood only through the "original intent" of the eighteenth-century founders. They further allege that such an intent is discoverable through an objective study of history—as if it were possible to extract anything but the most Procrustean intent from the many tens of thousands of pages penned by the many hundreds of eighteenth-century people involved in framing, ratifying, and implementing that deliberately vague document.[1]

In the same vein, on the fiftieth anniversary of the dropping of the two atomic bombs, it proved tragically impossible for our country to engage in a sophisticated public discussion on the varieties of historical interpretations concerning those events. Attempts to question, or even nuance, the official narrative (that the dropping of the bombs was a Good Thing because it prevented an American invasion of Japan in which more Americans and Japanese would have been killed than were killed by the bombs) were derided as politically inspired and illegitimate.[2] In such a context, it is necessary to insist, as Joe Frese did for the scholastics in his classes in 1968, that "history" is an irreducibly bifocal word. It points not only to the past, but also to how that past is interpreted in the present. Moreover, since the present is always changing, history, to be true to itself, also changes.

Since before the days of Herodotus, historians have acknowledged the bifocal nature of history as an entity that involves the past and the critical interpretation of it in the present. The Deuteronomic historians, for instance, had no problem in interrupting their narratives to present their own interpretative messages with great power and eloquence (for example, 2 Kgs 17:7–20, or 24:3–4). Likewise, they had little trouble in telling their readers that they could not be bothered narrating a lot of the history of their people when that history did not accord with their interpretative aims. If you really want to know what else king so-and-so did, they blithely stated, go and look it up yourself (for example, 2 Kgs 1:8, 8:23, 14:15, 18:26, and many other places)!

Historical Interpretation Inevitably Changes

The topic of this essay demands that we acknowledge at the outset that historical interpretation inevitably exists and inevitably changes. Moreover, because interpretation is an integral part of history, we also have to acknowledge that, in a real sense, history changes as well. The important issue is not whether changes occur, but how. For me, the past three Jesuit General Congregations have marked significant milestones in that ongoing change.

I began the graduate study of history in the fall of 1969. That academic year, 1969–70, was, for my generation, a watershed one. It was Cambodia, Kent State, and Jackson State. Stanford, where I was studying, shut down completely for a few days at the beginning of April, and it reconstituted itself more informally for the rest of the academic year. Most colleges and universities in California and the rest of the country did something similar.

The turmoil outside the classroom was accompanied by ferment inside as well. An interpretative framework known as "consensus" history, which emphasized the experiences and values all Americans were thought to have shared, was breaking down. This framework had matured during the Cold War. It was being challenged by a type of history that regarded itself as more inclusive, more radical, and more vanguard. It was often termed "New Left" history. Such a name was generally valid, for this history was related to the political and social ferment of the 1960s. In many important ways, it had sprung from that unrest.

One of the books we read in that first year of graduate school was entitled *Towards a New Past: Dissenting Essays in American History*. The very first essay in the book accurately caught the trajectory of the entire new history project by placing some lines from Bertolt Brecht's poem "A Worker Reads History" in a prologue to the essay itself:

Who built the seven towers of Thebes?
The books are filled with names of kings.
Was it kings who hauled the craggy blocks of stone? . . .
In the evening when the Chinese wall was finished
Where did the masons go? . . .

Young Alexander plundered India.
He alone?
Caesar beat the Gauls.
Was there not even a cook in his army?
Philip of Spain wept as his fleet
Was sunk and destroyed. Were there no other tears?
Frederick the Great triumphed in the Seven
Years War. Who
Triumphed with him? . . .

Every ten years a great man,
Who paid the piper?

So many particulars.
So many questions.[3]

Much of the new and self-consciously radical history saw itself as addressing these questions of Brecht. It did so with a great sense of mission and moral seriousness. It wanted to recover and preserve the histories of those who had been left out of the master narratives that had shaped the Cold War consensus history. This meant, above all, African Americans and women, but it soon came to include a host of other groups, such as Native Americans and Chicanos, as well. The radical history wanted to let the experiences of these peoples become the foundation for a new American history, in which racism and imperialism would be central explanatory concepts.

In 1976, when I began teaching after four years of graduate school and three more years of theology at Berkeley, it was difficult not to read the documents of GC 32 in the light of the new and radical history I had just finished studying. In my own history classes, I consciously attempted to incorporate this framework into my classes. I did so because I believed it and because I thought that this was one of the ways in which a Jesuit history teacher could live out the mandates of the Society's most recent self-definition, which I enthusiastically endorsed. I saw very little conflict between the Congregation's words and the trajectory of historical interpretation that was the legacy of the new historiography.

Like others back then, I was heavier on justice and lighter on faith. Part of this, it must be said, was because of the fashion in which my contemporaries and I interpreted the documents as we read and studied and prayed over them. While I was aware that the phrase "the service of faith" preceded the phrase "the promotion of justice" in the second paragraph of Decree 4, I also noticed that when the same decree got down to the nitty-gritty of unpacking those concepts, the sections entitled "People and Structures," "Social Involvement," and "Solidarity with the Poor" preceded the section entitled "The Service of Faith." This latter order and weight reflected itself in my classes.[4]

I tended to think that I was following the Congregation if I gave a good amount of pedagogical attention in class to the marginalized and if I spent an equally good amount of time in locating ideological and economic reasons for their marginalization. My courses on early American history paid a lot of attention to the origins of slavery, the oppression of women, the dispossession of the Native American, and the racism endemic to the development of United States manifest destiny. These were all significant themes in the historiography of the day, and I saw little conflict between being an up-to-date United States historian and a committed Jesuit teacher.

Looking back on this over two decades later, it is hard for me to see how it could have been much different. In the Society of Jesus, the emphasis on justice was, after all, the emphasis that was novel. It accordingly needed to be placed in the forefront if it was not to be trivialized or absorbed into our normal way of proceeding. Similarly, in the historical profession, the emphasis on the marginalized and neglected was the emphasis that was novel. It also had to be placed in the forefront if it was not to be harmlessly subsumed into the existing celebratory paradigm of United States history. An analogous situation existed, I thought, in the lives of my students. They needed to become more directly aware that the history they had too often learned in high school—that the development of the United States was a tale of "the march of democracy," for instance—was not by any means the whole story. For a decade or so, these three trends, religious, historiographical, and educational, converged for me. I was convinced that all these things were working together unto good.

GC 34 Broadens Jesuit Mission

Matters began to change a bit in the early and mid-1980s. They began to get more complicated. Like many Jesuits, I found the most memorable part of GC 33 to be Pedro Arrupe's message, in which the man so fully identified with justice spoke so movingly of the faith that, in his own life, was the indispensable context for everything: "More than ever, I now find myself in the hands of God. This is what I have wanted all my life, from my youth. And this is still the one thing I want. But now there is a difference: the initiative is entirely with God. It is indeed a profound spiritual experience to know and feel myself so totally in his hands."[5]

It was in that light that I read the major document of the Congregation. Concerning the faith and justice mission, I noted the Congregation's admission, "In all honesty, we must also acknowledge that this new understanding of our mission can lead to tensions both in the Society and outside of it. Some have at times emphasized in a unilateral fashion one aspect of this mission to the detriment of the other."[6] This hit close to home. It also correlated with a growing sense of unease I was experiencing, as my earlier synthesis between GC 32 and the new history was revealing itself to me as somewhat shallow.

This discontent revolved around the "identity" issue for me: how, if at all, was the type of class I was giving any different from the classes being developed and given by people who had been in graduate school when I was? Did it make any difference that I was a Jesuit teaching this particular subject? Should it make any difference? How?

A parallel set of "identity" questions was also surfacing within the historical profession. The new history had tremendously increased the number of perspectives from which United States history had to be viewed. But, with such a multiplicity of perspectives on the horizon, what did it all add up to?

When this concern was joined to a resurgent political and intellectual conservatism, it surfaced in accusations of "political correctness," or, more crudely, in accusations that the new history was attempting to inculcate hatred of the United States or of Western civilization in general.[7] When this concern was joined to certain trends in continental literary studies, it surfaced as any number of variants of the postmodernist assertion that nothing really adds up to much anyhow.[8] In addition, when this concern was reflected on by many practicing historians, it surfaced in a number of ways. Some admitted candidly that the profession had not been too attentive to its public responsibilities. Some called for the revival of a meaningful narrative form. Some paradoxically argued that we needed a clearer way to conceptualize the complexity that is a part of human existence.[9]

In the public arena, the most stark place in which these concerns and responses were played out was in the series of quincentennial controversies over the appropriateness of celebrating/commemorating/lamenting the discovery/encounter/genocide of 1492. In California, a more local, but analogous, controversy developed over proposals to canonize Junípero Serra.[10] But all of these public displays were only the tip of a much larger iceberg that had been floating through the profession for a number of years. As was the case with the Society, the historical profession's concepts and categories became more complicated.

The historiographical responses, conservative, postmodern, or pragmatic, to these enriching complications involve the explicit question of meaning. Much of the more interesting and cutting-edge historical work these days concerns the conditions of knowledge and the development and application of theory.[11] This historiographical trend roughly corresponds to at least one aspect of the Society's most recent undertakings in GC 34. That gathering's documents seem to me to manifest a maturing awareness of the complexity of the issues that the two previous congregations had opened. The recent Congregation says that the faith and justice mission must be "broadened," and that "proclamation of the Gospel, dialogue, and the evangelization of culture" are "integral dimensions" of that mission (Decree 2: "Servants of Christ's Mission" [SCM] 20 [48]). This set of statements seems to me to be a natural maturing of the religious understanding of what is implied when we take justice seriously, just as the revival of the issue of meaning in historiography seems to me to be the natural maturing of the intellectual understanding of what is implied when we take the marginalized and the excluded seriously.

Conclusion

I have not yet been entirely successful at discerning to what these new developments in the Society and in my profession are calling me. I know that I need to begin to work to include modes of belief and unbelief, patterns of meaning and lack of meaning, in my courses. This can't be done in the old way, where belief and meaning were regarded too often as the private preserve of the educated and leisured classes. Some of the social sciences, notably anthropology, have developed sophisticated ways of allowing at least a partial entrance into the world view of preliterate cultures and other types of cultures that are strange to us. These methods need to be critically employed in ways that allow the marginalized and the excluded in history to speak for themselves, and not, yet again, to be spoken for. I suspect that my future classes will need to become a lot more explicitly interdisciplinary, as I learn from colleagues in these areas and others (like religious studies) how they manage these concerns in their disciplines and classes. Moreover, I hope that the problem itself might be one that enables a deeper faculty dialogue than we have had up to now on the constellation of issues central to a Jesuit university enterprise: belief, meaning, commitment, and identity.

I know that I will have to keep experimenting with these matters. But I am finding, as I read the Society's documents in the light of my own profession, and as I find that issues of belief and meaning become more prominent in both arenas, that I am being drawn backwards. I am being led back past GC 34, 33, and 32, important as these gatherings have been, and still are, to me. I find myself pulled back to GC 31, and especially to the address of Pope Paul VI on May 7, 1965, in which he asked the Society to take the lead in the struggle against atheism of all types. He specifically mentioned, in addition to "philosophical" and "hedonistic" atheism, cultural, scientific, and social forms of disbelief.[12] It is precisely to the latter area, especially to the complex interaction of belief and unbelief in the social and cultural realms, that I find the Society's religious work, and my historical teaching, pointing. Perhaps Paul VI spoke more presciently than he knew.

ENDNOTES • SENKEWICZ

1. See Jack N. Rakove, *Original Meanings: Politics and Ideas in the Making of the Constitution* (New York: Knopf, 1996).

2. See Martin Harwit, *An Exhibit Denied: Lobbying the History of Enola Gay* (New York: Copernicus, 1996).

3. Barton J. Bernstein, ed., *Towards a New Past: Dissenting Essays in American History* (New York: Pantheon, 1968), 3. The essay was by Jesse Lemisch, and was entitled "The American Revolution Seen from the Bottom Up" (3–45).

4. Decree 4: "Our Mission Today: The Service of Faith and the Promotion of Justice" 48, 88–90, 91–95, 96–99, and 100–105, in *Documents of the 31st and 32nd General Congregations of the Society of Jesus*, ed. John W. Padberg, S.J. (St. Louis, Mo.: Institute of Jesuit Sources, 1977), 411, 425–30.

5. "Message of Fr. Pedro Arrupe to the Society," 3 September 1983, in *Documents of the 33rd General Congregation of the Society of Jesus*, ed. Donald R. Campion, S.J., and Albert C. Louapre, S.J. (St. Louis, Mo.: Institute of Jesuit Sources, 1984), 93.

6. Ibid., "Companions of Jesus Sent into Today's World" 33 [36].

7. See, for instance, Edward T. Linenthal and Tom Engelhardt, eds., *History Wars: The Enola Gay and Other Battles for the American Past* (New York: Metropolitan, 1996).

8. See, for example, the works collected in Joyce Appleby et al., eds., *Knowledge and Postmodernism in Historical Perspective* (New York and London: Routledge, 1996).

9. The December 1994 issue of *The Journal of American History* 8/3, entitled *The Practice of American History: A Special Issue,* contains essays on this whole question.

10. James A. Sandos, "Junípero Serra's Canonization and the Historical Record," *American Historical Review* 93/5 (December 1988): 1253–69.

11. See for example Jacques Revel and Lynn Hunt, eds., *Histories: French Constructions of the Past* (New York: New, 1995).

12. "Address of His Holiness Pope Paul VI, to the Members of the 31st General Congregation May 7, 1965," in *Documents of the 31st and 32nd General Congregations of the Society of Jesus,* 314.

ESSAY 15

Partnership in Mission: The Future of Jesuit Higher Education

Peter B. Ely, S.J.

ABSTRACT

The author considers the impact of GC 34's Decree 13: "Cooperation with the Laity in Mission" on Jesuit higher education. After a brief consideration of the decree itself, he discusses different meanings of cooperation, the idea of "formation of Jesuits and laity for cooperation," and the context that currently gives a special urgency to formation for cooperation for mission in Jesuit higher education. He also includes some responses from laypeople working in Jesuit colleges and universities about the impact of programs of formation for cooperation in mission on their personal and professional lives. Finally, he offers some reflections on the project of cooperation with laity in Jesuit colleges and universities, stressing in particular the importance of having each campus take responsibility for the task of formation.

Jesuits in higher education are a little like Molière's *bourgeois gentilhomme* who, after discovering he had been speaking prose all his life, now spoke it with a new enthusiasm. It isn't prose that Jesuits have discovered, but cooperation with laity in mission. Jesuits in higher education have been cooperating with laity for as long as they can remember. But now the terms have taken on a new meaning, and Jesuits are practicing cooperation with a new enthusiasm. The latest authoritative expression of the Society of Jesus' new enthusiasm about collaboration is Decree 13 of GC 34, "Cooperation with the Laity in Mission" (CLM), the first complete decree of any General Congregation on this topic.[1] This essay will explore the impact of this document on Jesuit higher education in the United States.

The Decree Itself

"Cooperation with the Laity in Mission" is the thirteenth of the twenty-six decrees of GC 34. Interest in this topic was widespread among representatives to the Congregation. Issues of partnership in mission had been raised by Jesuits from around the world as the Congregation was being prepared, and this topic received more votes from the floor commending it to full treatment by a commission than any other topic.

Underneath the widespread interest, however, lie great differences in the experience and understanding of cooperation. In the United States, for instance, collaborators or partners are often paid employees in Jesuit institutions, enjoying an equal status in terms of compensation with their Jesuit co-workers. This creates a very different situation from that of collaborators who work with Jesuits on a volunteer basis. It is much easier for Jesuits to accept leadership from lay colleagues with whom they have already been sharing equal responsibility for the institution than to imagine leadership from volunteers.

Much of the debate around this decree centered on the extent to which laypeople can be real partners, even exercising leadership roles in Jesuit institutions. The final decree makes seven references to "leadership" or "greater responsibility" on the part of laypeople and explicitly affirms that "a lay person can be the director of a Jesuit work" (CLM 13 [343]). Many delegates at the Congregation from outside the United States found this notion of lay leadership difficult to accept.

For all the differences of view that preceded the final version, this decree embodies a bold vision of collaboration. The framework of the whole document is the statement of the first paragraph that the Jesuits put themselves at the service of the mission of the laity in the Church:

> *The Society of Jesus acknowledges as a grace of our day and a hope for the future that laity "take an active, conscientious, and responsible part in the mission of the Church in this great moment of history." We seek to respond to this grace by offering ourselves in service to the full realization of this mission of the laity, and we commit ourselves to that end by cooperating with them in their mission.* (CLM 1 [331])[2]

This framework differs significantly from another way of thinking about cooperation that has probably been dominant. Collaboration has often been seen as a matter of allowing, even encouraging, laity to participate in the works of the Society as partners. Understood in this sense, cooperation subordinates the mission of the laity to that of the Society of Jesus in its various works. In our colleges and universities, large numbers of laypeople do in fact work with Jesuits, and significant efforts are being made, as we will see later in this essay, to draw them more profoundly into the animating spirit behind our institutions. CLM mentions this form of cooperation among others. But the larger framework of this decree subordinates the collaborative mission of the Society of Jesus to the larger mission of lay leadership in the Church set out in Vatican II and reiterated by John Paul II.

This larger context means that, even where laypeople are working in Jesuit institutions, Jesuit efforts at collaboration are aimed not just at making lay co-workers partners in a particular enterprise, but at encouraging their emergence as lay leaders within our institutions or outside them.

The recommendations of this decree are grouped under four headings: "(a) the Society's service to the laity in their ministry, (b) the formation of both laity and Jesuits for this cooperation, (c) Jesuit cooperation with laity in works of the Society, other works, and associations, and (d) opportunities for the future" (CLM 5 [335]).

Because the focus of this book is Jesuit higher education, it would seem we are talking principally about "Jesuit cooperation with laity in works of the Society." But the phrase "works of the Society" needs to be qualified. In what sense are Jesuit colleges and universities still "works of the Society"? The presence of laity is in fact so pervasive in Jesuit colleges and universities that arguments sometimes need to be made to support the claim that these are indeed Jesuit institutions.

Boards of trustees made up of laypersons and Jesuits—the majority are lay—govern all twenty-eight Jesuit colleges and universities. Administration, faculty, and staff of Jesuit colleges and universities are largely lay. Jesuit colleges and universities are chartered by the states in which they are located, regulated by regional and specialized accrediting associations, and supported by government funding and by private funds from corporations, foundations, and individuals. Jesuit provincials can no longer simply appoint Jesuits to these institutions but only "mission" them once they have been offered a position by proper authorities in each institution.

How are such institutions "works of the Society"? Precisely, says CLM, through cooperation between Jesuits and laypersons: "When we speak of 'our apostolates,' we will mean something different by 'our.' It will signify a genuine Ignatian partnership of laity and Jesuits, each of us acting according to our proper vocation" (CLM 20 [354]).

So in spite of these limitations on Jesuit control, the ties to non-Jesuit organizations and individuals, and the transformed meaning for Jesuits of "our apostolates," Jesuit colleges and universities are still "works of the Society." They are sponsored by the Society of Jesus, which missions Jesuits to them and influences them through a variety of associations that are largely Jesuit. The Association of Jesuit Colleges and Universities (AJCU), whose governing board is made up of the presidents of the twenty-eight Jesuit colleges and universities, is an example. All of the Jesuit colleges and universities have a core of Jesuits working in them at a variety of levels, from the president's office to the bookstore. More important, these institutions were founded by Jesuits and are still sustained by the original vision. Most of those associated with our colleges and universities, lay and Jesuit alike, are committed to retaining the Jesuit vision.

So we are talking about laypersons cooperating in "works of the Society." But what does CLM mean by "cooperation"? Are all laypeople, just by working alongside Jesuits, "cooperators in mission"?

The Meaning of Collaboration

The GC 34 document, "Cooperation with the Laity in Mission," uses the terms *collaboration, cooperation, partnership,* and *companionship* interchangeably. The term used most frequently (twenty-five times) is *cooperation.*[3] According to GC 34, such cooperation is an essential characteristic of Jesuit practice. The concluding document of GC 34 that sets out the Jesuit way of proceeding includes "Partnership with Others" among the eight hallmarks of the Jesuit way.[4] To get at what CLM has in mind in speaking of "cooperation in mission," we need to distinguish levels of cooperation.

First is the cooperation that takes place among people of goodwill working on a common project. All that is required to be in this first level is to be competent at the task assigned and willing to work with others to get the job done. Commitment to mission does not yet enter in. Much of the cooperation that brings Jesuits and laypeople together in our colleges and universities is of this sort. It is important. Without it, the other levels would not be possible. But we mean more than this when we talk about cooperation with the laity *in mission.*

The second level of cooperation takes place between people who come together out of a shared conviction about moral values. Many who teach in Jesuit high schools and universities or work in parishes, retreat houses, or other Jesuit-sponsored works share the Jesuit commitment to social justice, individual care for people, and a humanistic view of the world. These common beliefs allow for a deeper kind of cooperation than the practical concern to get a task done that characterizes level one. We are now talking about cooperation *in mission,* because these moral values are an intrinsic element of the mission of Jesuit higher education. The vast majority of people working in Jesuit institutions are cooperators in mission at least in this sense.

But a third level takes the meaning of cooperation one step deeper, into the area of shared openness to the Spirit of God at work in individual human lives and in institutions. This openness to the Spirit was the impelling energy that gave birth to the Society of Jesus in the first place[5] and has continued to guide its development. The practice of submitting one's life to the action of God's Spirit is at the heart of the Spiritual Exercises of Saint Ignatius, which Jesuits are expected to make every year. The participation of lay colleagues in the Spiritual Exercises is the key to this deepest level of partnership. For some time now, Jesuits have made available to their co-workers the rich experience of the Exercises, especially in the form of the "retreat in everyday life."

Formation for Cooperation

When CLM speaks of "formation of both laity and Jesuits for this cooperation," it is thinking of the second two levels. It is significant that CLM speaks of "formation for cooperation." The assumption is that one does not come to the institution adequately prepared for the kind of cooperation CLM is talking about. It is significant, too, that the formation is for "both laity and Jesuits." Both laypeople and Jesuits have presumed that the formation of Jesuits automatically prepares them for the cooperation needed: all they have to do is share what they have with those who do not yet have it. This presumption, to the extent that it exists, underestimates the challenge set before us.

Laypeople and Jesuits must *learn to* cooperate in mission. Two observations about the role of Jesuits: First, Jesuits have an important leadership role in Jesuit colleges and universities. In a very real sense they are bearers of the mission that has inspired the foundation of these institutions. Jesuits have been formed by the Spiritual Exercises since the beginning of their years in the Society. They have benefited from education in the history of the Society of Jesus, the teachings of the general congregations, and have listened (or not listened) to countless instructions from their Jesuit leaders and experts in the field of Jesuit spirituality. Moreover, they have tried to live out what they have learned and to model their lives on Ignatius and other holy men of the Society. Jesuits ought to have a head start when it comes to understanding the spirit of the Society of Jesus. The willingness on the part of Jesuits to exercise the leadership for which their training would seem to have prepared them is itself a challenge.

Second, the formation Jesuits have received does not necessarily prepare them to respond to the new "crisis" (meaning "opportunity") of our time. Long years of training can just as well fix the Jesuit rigidly in a tradition as prepare him to respond to what is new. The something new is an opportunity to expand the Ignatian vision beyond the limits of Jesuit life. The expanded vision will come about through cooperation between Jesuits and lay colleagues in activities that raise consciousness about the implications of the Ignatian tradition in higher education. Jesuits need formation in the skills of cooperation.

CLM calls for the formation of Jesuits *and laity*. Jesuits may resist cooperation in mission for their own reasons. So may their lay colleagues. Hiring for mission is an essential step in creating a culture of cooperation in mission. Jesuit colleges and universities, unlike some colleges and universities that insist on a Christian faith commitment, want to be open to faculty and staff with a variety of backgrounds. This openness insures diversity. It does not, by itself, insure a culture of cooperation in mission. Many Jesuit colleges and universities are now giving serious attention to hiring the kind of faculty and staff who manifest a commitment to mission.[6]

How does one "form" Jesuits and their lay colleagues for cooperation in mission? The only valid formation for cooperation in mission is to experiment in forms of cooperation and reflect on what has happened. This process of experimentation and reflection on the results of the experiment is itself integral to the Jesuit tradition.[7]

The formation of Jesuits and laity for cooperation in mission has become particularly important now in American Jesuit higher education because of developments in the recent past. A brief look at those developments will provide a context for CLM's call for formation in cooperation.

The Context of Formation for Cooperation in Mission

Three major shifts in Jesuit higher education have occurred in the past thirty years. The first was the transformation of boards of trustees from all-Jesuit composition to a mixture of Jesuits and laypeople, with the laypeople being in the majority. Jesuit colleges and universities are still adjusting to the implications of this change. In particular, Jesuits are still getting used to a new role in the authority structure of "their" colleges and universities. Jesuits, including those wishing to be presidents, now have to go through the same hiring processes as laypeople. Some Jesuits have even felt that being a Jesuit was an obstacle rather than a help in looking for a position.

The second shift is related to the first. Jesuit colleges and universities, along with other Catholic institutions, have become increasingly tied to the goals and objectives of the higher education establishment in the United States. After John Tracy Ellis's critique of Catholic universities as second-rate, presidents, deans, and department chairs worked hard to improve the professional status of Catholic colleges and universities relative to other institutions. Like immigrant parents trying to make sure their children became part of the new country, speaking English without accent, Catholic colleges and universities began to move away from what differentiated them within the realm of higher education. They wanted to be compared favorably to colleges and universities that had attained the reputation of first-rate schools.

And they have succeeded. Catholic universities and colleges, the Jesuit institutions among them, rank favorably with their peers. But success has come at a price. To continue the analogy used above, Jesuit and other Catholic universities and colleges are now a little like the children of immigrants who regret having grown up ignorant of the language of their parents and are now trying to learn it as a second language that they speak with an American accent.

So a third transformation is now under way, the child of the first two. It consists of all the efforts to reappropriate the language and culture that have been neglected in the process of adaptation to the American higher education establishment. More and more, Catholic educators are recognizing the importance of something being called "the Catholic intellectual tradition." It was once taken for granted, now it is in danger of being lost.[8] The chief characteristic of this tradition is its belief in the integration of the two dynamisms of intellect and faith.[9] Faith and intellect have a tendency to go their own separate ways. People of faith are often suspicious of science and intellectual speculation. Intellectuals, for their part, suspect that faith is intrinsically hostile to the life of the intellect.[10]

This third transformation is the context within which the formation of Jesuits and laity for cooperation in mission is taking place. What is at stake is not just some peripheral characteristics of the Jesuit educational system, but the integrity of Catholic, and therefore Jesuit, higher education itself.

During the last fifteen years Jesuit colleges and universities and the organizations that support them have begun to invest resources of time, money, and personnel to reinvigorate the vision that inspires Jesuit higher education. National and regional conferences have focused the attention of Jesuits and their lay colleagues on issues related to Catholic and Jesuit vision. Many colleges and universities have hired Jesuits and lay colleagues to run programs on campus for the development of mission-centered activities.[11] The presidents of the twenty-eight Jesuit colleges and universities (the AJCU presidents) and the provincials of the ten United States provinces of Jesuits cosponsor a National Seminar on Jesuit Higher Education, which meets three times each year on a different Jesuit campus and produces a twice-yearly journal, *Conversations*.

A Jesuit theology student, Tom Landy, received a grant from the Lilly Foundation to establish a program called *Collegium,* an annual eight-day retreat for students finishing graduate school and hoping to teach in Catholic colleges and universities, and for junior-level faculty already teaching in such institutions. A second program called *Transitions,* initiated by Tom Landy and Father Joe Appleyard, S.J, rector of the Jesuit community at Boston College, gathers young Jesuits together to explore the challenge of Jesuit higher education.

All of these programs aim to balance and integrate the intellectual and spiritual aspects of the Jesuit and Catholic tradition in education. Their fundamental purpose is to engage both Jesuits and their lay colleagues in the work of breathing life into the Ignatian vision of education so that it can function as an integrating mission on each Jesuit campus. If this work does not take place, the founding vision will become like the stained-glass windows in chapels of colleges and universities that have substituted a secular faith for the religious faith that inspired their founding.[12]

Responses of Lay Colleagues

Though lay colleagues are encouraged to read it, CLM is written principally for the guidance of Jesuits. Because we are talking about cooperation, it is helpful to know what these lay colleagues with whom Jesuits wish to cooperate think about this new enthusiasm for mission. The accounts that follow report some responses from laypersons now working at

Jesuit colleges and universities.[13] Some have made the Spiritual Exercises of Saint Ignatius,[14] some have participated in other mission-related activities.

George is a vice president in a Jesuit university. His undergraduate years at another Jesuit university during the 1960s left him alienated from his Catholicism. Later, as an administrator at a second Jesuit university, he took advantage of the president's offer to make an eight-day version of the Spiritual Exercises as a form of paid professional development. Under the direction of a skilled Jesuit, George discovered a form of Catholic faith that enabled him to believe again. In his words, "It allowed me to create a theology that worked; it humanized Christ." Christ's humanity became real for George when he was meditating on the Passion, particularly on Christ's conflict in the Garden. "He [Jesus] wasn't sure, but he made the leap." That was something George could relate to. Now at a third Jesuit university, George is part of a group of laypeople working with a Jesuit coordinator to develop an apostolic spiritual life in the midst of their work. He is also preparing to direct the Exercises himself.

Donna has been teaching in the nursing school of a Jesuit university for twenty-five years. She was surprised and disappointed when she first arrived to find a secular atmosphere on this Catholic and Jesuit campus. She welcomes the new emphasis on the Catholic and Jesuit character of the university and has participated in mission-centered programs offered on her campus, including the "Spiritual Exercises in Everyday Life."

A lay faculty member at another Jesuit university found that his involvement in mission-related activities and his ordinary contact with Jesuit and lay colleagues had brought him back from being a lapsed Lutheran to active belief in his own church. His participation in a "Western Conversations" weekend[15] pulled everything together for him. "Being at this Catholic university has taught me how to be a better Lutheran," he said. Still another faculty member found that making the "retreat in everyday life" over a period of several months under a Jesuit director enabled him to move beyond the malaise that had troubled his personal and professional life for years. He has now become a retreat director himself. An assistant professor in chemistry who participated in "Western Conversations" came back to her university having discovered, as if for the first time, that her institution had a mission. "I always knew we had a mission statement," she said, "but it didn't mean anything to me." Now for the first time, she was willing to enter into reflection about what the mission meant for her and the colleagues in her department.

Tom, a professor of economics at a Jesuit university, spoke about his experience of making the "Retreat in Everyday Life." Tom's wife of eight years had died from a cancer that spread throughout her body, even to her brain, and left her in a vegetative state during the last years of her life. After her death, Tom found himself "brooding" and felt the need to exorcise the demons of bitterness and exhaustion that afflicted him. He arranged to make the "Spiritual Exercises in Everyday Life"[16] under the direction of a

Jesuit on campus. What he found through making the retreat was quite different from what he had looked for in choosing to go through the experience. Apparently, the demons did get exorcised, but the benefits of the retreat went beyond that.

Tom was specific in describing the results. First, he found he had both a greater sense of the purpose of his life and a deepened realization that he could not himself determine that purpose but had to be open to the unexpected designs God had for him. Second, he came away with a vivid sense of Christ as teacher. It seemed to him Christ taught by asking questions about the basic issues of human life. This had application for him in his own teaching. Having always tried to go beyond the rigorous requirements of his discipline and provide ways for students to look beyond the traditional wisdom of economics to explore some deeper issues, he found confirmation of his approach in his contact with Jesus the teacher.

Finally, Tom became fascinated by the phenomenon of what happens to a group of people when their leader leaves. It happened to the disciples of Jesus. It happened to the American people when John F. Kennedy was assassinated. It happened to him when his first wife died. He was also coping with changes of leadership in his own institution and trying to figure out how to exercise the position of leadership he himself had just come into.

David works in campus ministry at a Jesuit university. He has an undergraduate degree from Harvard and a master of divinity (M.Div.) degree from Weston Jesuit School of Theology in Cambridge, Massachusetts. During his years at Harvard, David found little support for his religious convictions. After graduation and before beginning studies for the M.Div., David joined the Jesuit Volunteer Corps (JVC) and worked in California. While at Weston, he made the thirty-day retreat in its concentrated form. This experience gave to his religious life an intimate foundational experience of God's love. He considered the possibility of a vocation to priesthood but did not feel called to celibacy. David is typical of many younger men and women who, forty years ago, would have probably chosen religious life or priesthood in the Catholic Church.

David is very interested in exploring what CLM calls a "closer personal bond" to the Society of Jesus. He is, in fact, part of a group at his university exploring the shape such a closer bond might take. The essential ingredient for David in such a relationship is "an intimate experience of partnership in mission which would involve confirmation of his current commitment, guidance in his discernment about future apostolic choices, and a sense of belonging to an extended apostolic network." As a married layman, David does not have a religious structure that can provide an "objective" confirmation of his own sense of where God is leading him in service to the Church. He thinks the "closer personal bond" with the Society of Jesus might provide such a structure.

These responses give an idea of what is meant by "formation for cooperation in mission." In particular, they show the transformative power of making the Spiritual Exercises.

Common to all these responses is the satisfaction derived from finding a way to integrate personal religious experiences and career or apostolate.[17] For the secular mind this attempt to "integrate" personal religious experience and professional competence is unprofessional, introducing a kind of bias into what should be value-free activity. The Ignatian vision, however, proposes that each human activity is authentically itself only when seen in relation to God. To discover one's personal roots in the mystery of divine love and see all things as coming from that same loving power, frees a person to engage fully in life and work. The responses recorded above are testimonials of what can happen.

Concluding Reflections

The chief impact of CLM on Jesuit higher education is to confirm what has already been happening and to put cooperation with laity in our colleges and universities in the larger framework of promoting the emergence of the laity as ministers of the Gospel. This larger framework is helpful to keep people in higher education from focusing too narrowly on their own project.

Yet, if one is writing from the perspective of higher education, it is important to keep in mind why cooperation with laity in mission is so crucial for this particular "work of the Society." For Jesuit higher education is, granted all the qualifications I have discussed above, still a work of the Society. Partnership in mission is necessary because higher education can remain a "work of the Society" only through cooperation with laity in mission. Left to themselves, Jesuits cannot maintain Jesuit colleges and universities as works of the Society. Too few are available. So the choice is either for Jesuits to join with their lay colleagues in an awakened sense of mission, or to see these historically Jesuit institutions gradually become thoroughly secular in outlook.

Such cooperation, as CLM makes clear, requires that both Jesuits and their lay colleagues engage in a process of formation. The commitment to such formation must come principally from the colleges and universities in question, beginning with their boards of trustees, not from the Society of Jesus. It is not that the Society is not committed to collaboration; it clearly is, as CLM shows. However, the primary responsibility for Jesuit colleges and universities is no longer in the hands of the Society of Jesus, even though these institutions are still "works of the Society." They are in the hands of their trustees and those to whom the trustees entrust them—administrators, faculty, and staff.

This suggests that formation of trustees is a key element in cooperation in mission. Trustees do not run colleges and universities. They know less about what is going on in the institutions than those who work day by day in offices and classrooms, but they do have ultimate responsibility. Formation for mission may not begin with them—as a matter of fact, the initiative for these programs usually begins with interested Jesuits and lay colleagues working at the institution—but it has to work its way up to them.

Even more important than the trustees are the faculty and staff. For cooperation in mission to take place, each college and university needs a core of Jesuits and laypeople who are willing and eager to enter into this project as part of their professional and personal commitment to the institution. Hiring and advancement are crucial. How many Jesuits does it take? How many Catholics? How many Christians and other religiously motivated co-workers? Most people talk about a "committed core" or a "critical mass." Dedication and strategy are more important than numbers; but personal religious commitment on the part of a significant number is crucial. Religiously affiliated institutions have the right to take religious commitment into account in hiring and promotion.

Faculty and staff of Jesuit colleges and universities have already begun to reflect on CLM. Just knowing that the Society of Jesus at its highest levels puts such emphasis on cooperation with the laity underlines the importance of the experiments now going on and heightens the sense of urgency of a movement already under way.

ENDNOTES • ELY

1. GC 31 (1965) and GC 33 (1983) both speak of collaboration with laity but as a subordinate theme in other decrees.
2. The nineteen quoted words in this statement are from Pope John Paul's Apostolic Exhortation, *Christifideles Laici 3.*
3. The terms *collaboration* and *partnership* occur in CLM only five times each.
4. Decree 26: "Conclusion: Characteristics of Our Way of Proceeding," heading for 15 [549].
5. See Father Joseph Conwell's work, *Impelling Spirit* (Chicago, Ill.: Loyola Press, 1997).
6. Gonzaga University in Spokane has devoted several years to developing a "mission centered hiring process," which is described in a brochure available from the university.
7. The famous *Ratio Studiorum,* or "Plan of Studies," of the Jesuit educational system was finalized in 1599 after fifty years of experimentation and reflection expressed in a series of documents. The final form of the *Ratio* was used as a guide for Jesuit education for the next 350 years. Getting back to the process of experimentation and reflection is part of the renewal of the Society of Jesus. For an excellent treatment of the development of the *Ratio Studiorum* see James F. Farrell, S.J., *The Jesuit Code of Liberal Education: Development and Scope of the Ratio Studiorum* (Milwaukee, Wis.: Bruce, 1938).
8. *Conversations,* a journal of Jesuit higher education subsidized jointly by the presidents of Jesuit colleges and universities and the provincials of the ten American Jesuit provinces and published by the National Seminar on Jesuit Higher Education, has devoted two issues to this topic: "Catholic Identity" (6 [fall 1994])—see especially David J. O'Brien's article, "Conversations On Jesuit (And Catholic?) Higher Education: Jesuit Sì, Catholic . . . Not So Sure" (4–12, 30)—and "Catholic Intellectual Life" (8 [fall 1995]). In her article, "The Best of Times, The Worst of Times: Catholic Intellectual Life in Today's Academic Setting" (14–19), Monica Hellwig describes five characteristics of Catholicism: (1) its deep respect for the cumulative wisdom of the past, (2) the intrinsic continuity of faith and reason, (3) the presence of the sacramental principle, (4) redemption as a communal, not just an individual, enterprise, and (5) universality of outreach.
9. Pope John Paul II speaks of this integration in the papal document *Ex Corde Ecclesiae,* which is itself the fruit of intense and often contentious collaboration between Church officials and Catholic university

administrators: "A Catholic University's privileged task is 'to unite existentially by intellectual effort two orders of reality that too frequently tend to be placed in opposition as though they were antithetical: the search for truth, and the certainty of already knowing the fount of truth'" (*Ex Corde Ecclesiae*, Introduction 1; citation from John Paul II, "Discourse to the Catholic Institute of Paris," 1 June 1980, *Insegnamenti di Giovanni Paolo II* vol. 3/1 [1980]: 1581).

10. For an impressive treatment of how the tension between intellect and faith affected the development of Protestant colleges and universities in the United States over several centuries, see George M. Marsden's book, *The Soul of the American University: From Protestant Establishment to Established Nonbelief* (New York: Oxford University Press, 1994). In chapter 22, "Liberal Protestantism Without Protestantism" (409–28), Marsden contrasts the Catholic idea of a university expressed by John Henry Newman and the Jesuit John Courtney Murray with the ideas implicit in the development of Protestant institutions of higher education. For Newman and Murray, theology was central; in the Protestant universities, theology had become marginalized.

11. The program I am most familiar with is Gonzaga University's "Council for Partnership for Mission." It is one of many on Jesuit university campuses. Established in 1985, the program is now organized under a charter and operates through several committees having to do with hiring for mission, spirituality, orientation of new faculty and staff, continuing development, and students. Each committee sponsors a variety of activities each year. An executive committee coordinates the operation of the whole program. The organization has evolved. For some time the program was directed by two co-coordinators, one Jesuit, one lay. Now it is directed by one layperson with Jesuits cooperating in a variety of roles. More information can be obtained by writing to Dr. Michael Carey, Gonzaga University, Spokane, Washington 99258.

12. Note the subtitle of Marsden's book cited above: *From Protestant Establishment to Established Nonbelief.* Marsden is convinced that secular belief is just as dogmatic and pervasive as religious belief.

13. These responses have come through personal interviews and conversations held over a period of years. I have changed the names of individuals interviewed.

14. The *Spiritual Exercises* refers to a book written by Ignatius of Loyola containing the fruit of his own spiritual journey at Manresa, where he first developed a method of praying and of disposing himself to find God's will in his life. The book is written in such a way as to help others to make similar discoveries in their own lives.

15. "Western Conversations" is a weekend program for faculty members of the six western Jesuit universities. Over a period of three years each of the participating schools sent ten different faculty members to six weekend retreats on one of the six campuses. Each weekend began with a substantive presentation, which was followed by reflection in large and small groups. Now that each of the universities has hosted a weekend, the program will continue in a slightly modified form.

16. The Spiritual Exercises can be made by going away from one's ordinary occupations and devoting anywhere between eight and thirty days full time to the experience of the Exercises. This is what I call the "concentrated form." One can also make the "Spiritual Exercises in Everyday Life." For people with family obligations and job responsibilities that cannot easily be put aside, this is the more convenient form. Saint Ignatius himself foresaw this possibility in the nineteenth of the "Introductory Notes," or "Annotations," of the *Spiritual Exercises.* Hence, the retreat in everyday life has sometimes been called "the nineteenth annotation retreat."

17. The choice one makes between the terms *career* and *apostolate* is itself significant. "Career" is the usual secular way of designating the path followed by one's job opportunities and choices. My "career" as a lawyer, for instance, might cover the time from my first job as a clerk to my final appointment as chief justice of the Supreme Court. To think of this same path as an "apostolate" puts it in the context of a religious call to be an apostle (messenger) of the saving message of Christ. I might well consider my career as a lawyer an opportunity to follow a call to service of the Gospel through the practice of law. Seeing one's life work as an apostolic call is the kind of result that typically emerges from the experience of the Exercises.

ESSAY 16

And Justice Shall Flourish in His Time

Robert John Araujo, S.J.

ABSTRACT

The author opens with an account of what drew him to give up a successful legal career to enter a religious and teaching life: the realization that the justice sought in his profession "was not ultimately man's, it was God's." More recently, he has faced the question how as a Jesuit he can convert our culture of death to one of life. Most of his time is devoted to touching the hearts and minds of those who can establish both God's and man's justice in the future, based on a tradition that has its origins in the Bible. The author confronts head-on a position trumpeted by some legal educators, that Catholic law schools that wish to attain status should abandon a distinctive Catholic character. He finds legal education "strategically situated" to inculturate "God's concept of justice," as encouraged both by Vatican II and GC 34. It is the vision of justice linked with faith that must distinguish Jesuit legal education. It must be committed to the proposition that the truth that is sought "is the transcendent and the objective—which is God."

A Pilgrim's Journey in Search of Justice

During the last twenty years, the life of this pilgrim[1] has undergone dramatic transformation—a result, in large part, of leaving one way of life in order to become a member of the Society of Jesus. At first, the story of this pilgrim sounded so strange to many of the people with whom he had gone to school or practiced law. They asked: Why would a successful lawyer leave the practice of law to become a Jesuit? Why would an individual who had become accustomed to comfortable living, to vast travel opportunities necessitating commodious lodgings, splendid dining opportunities, and the finest in transportation leave these certainties for the uncertainties of religious life in an apostolic order?

The answer, while somewhat indeterminate, is solidly rooted in his understanding of what the legal profession was about: the seeking and obtaining of justice in this world—

justice not just for one or for some, but for all. If each of us is created in the image of God, is not each entitled to one's due, the *suum cuique?* The answer to this last question slowly but certainly evolved. One day the realization came that the justice this pilgrim assumed existed at the heart of his profession and his life—the two seemed indistinguishable—was not ultimately man's, it was God's. At the heart of seeking and doing justice, then, is the realization that all is dependent on the transcendent truth that is God.[2]

Now, to the skeptic, these discoveries seemed to be the rantings of some lunatic rather than the mild-mannered but efficient and effective corporate (formerly government) counsel many had come to know and, if not like, then respect. But, the more the pilgrim sought to understand who he was and what his life was supposed to be, the more he kept encountering head-on the freeing truth that is God—and his justice, which is both simultaneously true and ultimate. Mind you, this pilgrim was neither selfish nor corrupt, but his perception of justice was narrow, was centered on a few objects identified with imperfect vision. The justice he was beginning to see was that viewed from a different perspective—that of some of the oldest law that man has known.

It eventually came to the pilgrim that he, like so many others, was a disciple of Christ called to a vocation to be on mission with the Son. But what made this vocation different from that of so many other Christians was that his vineyard was to be that of the Society of Jesus—that life and labor of being one of God's conscious instruments sent out to His people to engage them in reflection on who they are and what their ultimate destiny is (Decree 1: "Introduction: United with Christ on Mission" [UCM] 14 [14]). But could the pilgrim be sure that the journey he was to embark on was authentic? Prayer helped and began to supply answers to the question, Why leave what you know and understand? The voice of God is not necessarily found in thunder or earthquake or fire—it is often found in the quietest of places (1 Kgs 19:11–14), and that is where the pilgrim discovered the comfort and consolation to put one life aside and to pursue this new journey.

But as he began this journey, new questions arose: toward what apostolic activity should he—with guidance from the superiors—direct himself? Should he pursue in some way what he did in his former life? The answer evolved slowly but surely: yes! It was mutually agreed that the pilgrim would use his former profession to further the works of the Society. But then came a further question: in what venue? Again, after an abundance of prayer and discussion, an answer emerged: the world of the classroom. It was, and remains, in the classroom that the pilgrim has sought ways in cultivating the Society's mission of "the service of faith, of which the promotion of justice is an absolute requirement" (GC 32, Decree 4: "Our Mission Today: The Service of Faith and the Promotion of Justice" 2 [48]).

Jesuit and Catholic Legal Education As Distinctive

As the pilgrim of the preceding story, I am most interested in both the concept and practice of justice, and I am encouraged by the work of GC 34 and the application of its deliberations to my work. Significantly, the members of the Congregation identified each Jesuit, regardless of the specific apostolic assignment, as united with Christ on mission (UCM 8 [8]). Without being presumptuous, we identify with the work of Jesus. In borrowing from the "Allocution of the Holy Father" to the members of GC 34, Decree 1 specifies that the Society of Jesus was called to address its contribution to the "new evangelization" (UCM 12 [12]). Yet, as followers of Ignatius and companions of Jesus, our work in evangelization is not so much new as it is the continuation of the labor of Christ that has characterized the work of the apostolic orders throughout the Church's history. As Decree 1 concludes, the Society of Jesus is identified by "the mysterious work of God" carried on by Ignatius and those who have followed him (UCM 14 [14]).

As lawyer, as academic, as priest, as Jesuit, my participation in this "mysterious work of God" calls me along with every other member of the Society to be a servant of Christ in his ongoing mission. In a more particular way, every Jesuit is asked to cooperate with others so that we, as God's disciples, can influence in a positive and faithful way "the complex structures of society where decisions are made and values are shaped" (Decree 2: "Servants of Christ's Mission" [SCM] 2 [22]). But as Jesuits addressing the problems of these structures and the decisions made within them, what kind of world do we have in these labors? As the Holy Father has noted, the culture of the late twentieth century is one of death rather than life. If this is true, each Jesuit must ask the question, What more can be done to convert the culture from one of death to one of life?

Most of my work in this regard is indirect: as teacher, I spend most of my time working with those who will be doing the decision making and the shaping in the future rather than the present. Yet, Jesus as teacher did much the same. A great deal of his work was devoted to informing the minds and touching the hearts of others to encourage them to live in right relation with God by living in just relations with the neighbor. It is, after all, the decision-making process and the shaping of public values that often determine how members of society live with one another. Do the public policies and values developed and enforced by public institutions foster or hinder the right relationship between members of society regardless of the members' role, regardless of their participation in decision making and value shaping? These are the questions that repeatedly confront me as I engage the law students of today who will become the practitioners, judges, and legislators who make these decisions and shape these values for tomorrow.

As a teacher of the law, I share many responsibilities with most of my colleagues in the legal teaching profession. Regardless of religious or secular affiliation, we teachers of the law prepare tomorrow's lawmakers, power brokers, and ministers of justice.

As a servant of Christ's mission, I am also quietly and humbly engaged in the divine enterprise of "bringing salvation, justice, and reconciliation to a world that is still broken by its sins" (SCM 5 [28]). This is a duty that I share with a small number of my teaching colleagues.

However, I am mindful that the views of many of my other teaching colleagues are reflected by Professor Mark Tushnet. He has suggested that "Catholic legal education is primarily legal [that is, secular] education; . . . [I]f a law school associated with a Catholic university seeks to become or becomes a national law school, it will find it extremely difficult to sustain activities in a strong way that either signal or embody its Catholic affiliation."[3] Does this mean that my version of legal education is doomed to failure, or, in slightly more hopeful terms, tolerated as long as it remains outside of the mainstream? My response is a robust "No!" Its vitality can take on considerable strength if we think for a moment about the tradition on which shared notions of law and justice are built and how they are related to the formation of lawyers—be that formation at a so-called "national" or "local" school.

The late legal scholar and Oxford faculty member J. M. Kelly, in commenting on law examinations at Oxford and how one might achieve first-class honors, said "it would have been possible for the candidate . . . to write first-class answers even if suffering from the delusion that the world began around the year 1930."[4] Professor Kelly correctly noted how pitiful this prevalent attitude is, and argued that "the jurisprudence [that the students] are taught ought, therefore, to give a humane foundation to what will be their life's profession; instead of which, it seems to me, they are nowadays mostly given a sort of course in mental and moral athletics, sweating around a cinder-track of mid-twentieth-century legal analysis and late twentieth-century political issues."[5] When I think about the long tradition that has affected the growth of Western law (beginning with the Decalogue, the Roman tradition, and the codification of canon law), I share the lament made by Kelly.

If the legal profession is indeed interested in and involved with the search for and practice of justice for all as is suggested by the inscription over the United States Supreme Court building in Washington,[6] is there any justification for excluding the pre-1930 contributions made to the concept of justice beginning with the biblical tradition? After all, a quick perusal of the Pentateuch, the prophets, and the New Testament reveals an ongoing interest in and concern with the seeking of justice in this world—both God's and man's.

THE GREAT COMMANDMENT AND LAW

As twentieth-century pilgrims and disciples, we have been reminded of the intersection of God's justice with our own. In the promulgation of the *Pastoral Constitution on the*

Church in the Modern World (*Gaudium et Spes*), the Church's leadership addressed the subject of justice on at least twenty-four occasions.[7] The frequent acknowledgment of this issue in *Gaudium et Spes* brings the Great Commandment into the law of the contemporary world. When that first-century lawyer asked Jesus what was the greatest commandment, Jesus replied, "You shall love the Lord your God with all your heart, and with all your soul, and with all your mind, and with all your strength, . . . [and] you shall love your neighbor as yourself. There is no other commandment greater than these" (Mk 12:30–31). Jesus made the connection between the first commandment concerning love of God and a second, love of neighbor. The two are inextricably related—one cannot love God without being concerned for the neighbor, and what better way to do this and to treat the neighbor justly than to love the neighbor as *Gaudium et Spes* so often expresses.

Clearly, the members of GC 34 were appropriating the Great Commandment and the work of the Second Vatican Council when they noted that the Society of Jesus, through all its apostolic work, must express its commitment to the Gospel through "the promotion of justice for all" (SCM 8 [33]). The authors of Decree 2 added that "justice can truly flourish only when it involves the transformation of culture, since the roots of injustice are embedded in cultural attitudes as well as in economic structures" (SCM 17 [42]). However, the values of any culture are formed by its members; therefore, it is the hearts and minds of those who comprise the culture who must adopt God's justice in their own lives so that in turn it can be reflected in their culture. Moreover, how might the wisdom of God's way, especially those concerning justice, be incorporated into this culture? One avenue is through the process of education. In a particular way, legal education is strategically situated to cultivate God's concept of justice and related Gospel values.

COMMITMENT TO SERVICE

Some of my teaching colleagues, whether they believe in God or not, often suggest that the mission of legal education that is part of a Jesuit university includes the following: (1) rigorous academic work that cultivates and challenges the mind; (2) care for the whole person; and (3) a commitment to service and social justice. Applaudable as these elements are, they are really no different from the educational mission of many other schools that have secular foundations.[8] As Christian, as Catholic, as Jesuit, legal education sponsored by the Society or legal education that relies on the name of the Society of Jesus must, like the promotion of justice, not "be separated from its wellspring of faith" (Decree 3: Our Mission and Justice" [OMJ] 2 [51]). If "the vision of justice which guides us is intimately linked with our faith [by being] deeply rooted in the Scriptures, Church tradition, and our Ignatian heritage . . ." (OMJ 4 [53]), so must be legal education which claims the modifier "Jesuit" as part of its *raison d'être.*

Although other legal educators may make similar claims about challenging academic work, concern for people, and the commitment to service, and while at the same time we disciples recognize that we share some mutual interests with our secular colleagues, we must also acknowledge that the Christian understanding of justice transcends "the notions of justice derived from ideology, philosophy, or particular political movements, which can never be an adequate expression of the justice of the Kingdom . . ." (OMJ 4 [53]). For some, justice constitutes embracing those ideologies, philosophies, and political movements that give comfort to abortion and euthanasia—elements of the culture of death identified by the Holy Father in his encyclical *Evangelium Vitae.*[9] As the members of the Congregation correctly noted, human life is a gift of God that must be respected from "its beginning to its natural end"; therefore, it is particularly urgent for disciples everywhere, including Jesuits, to devote their apostolic energies to the "culture of life" that is far better suited to God's justice (OMJ 8 [57]).

HUMAN RIGHTS

At the heart of the Western legal tradition and its conception of justice is the notion of human rights as developed by political philosophers such as John Locke. While Christian disciples share some of Locke's notions, we must simultaneously acknowledge that respect for the dignity of the human person and protection of human rights is not simply a product of the Enlightenment; it is both the command and wish of God who created each of us in his image. As the members of GC 34 pointed out, "Respect for the dignity of the human person created in the image of God underlies the growing international consciousness of the full range of *human rights*" (OMJ 6 [55]; emphasis in original).

Yet, as educators who teach the law, what must I and my colleagues who also call themselves disciples do to ensure that human law reflects more of God's Great Commandment and the social teachings tradition of the Church? Although many elements of the postmodern world skeptically question the existence of disciples who, out of their faith and reason, search for God's objective truth, the duty of the late-twentieth-century disciple is to meet, counter, and dispel this perspective. One forum for doing this is the very forum in which the voice of skepticism and disbelief has taken root: the American university.

While every Jesuit is called to the intellectual apostolate (Decree 16: "The Intellectual Dimension of Jesuit Ministries" [IDJM] 1 [394]), which is especially helpful to "the promotion of justice with the proclamation of faith" (IDJM 3 [396]), the university apostolate is particularly well suited for the opening of the mind that leads to the conversion of heart. It is in the academy where the Society's "mission is constantly exposed to the judgment of others in conversations, in scholarly publications, and in the media" (IDJM 5 [398]). By engaging the skeptical intellect in dialogue about justice, the Jesuit is well suited to use the shared awareness of contemporary circumstances to introduce both colleagues and students who are tomorrow's community leaders to "the voice of God" (IDJM 9 [403]).

If the academy is the place where kindred intellects come together to debate the great issues that confront the human family, it is the Jesuit educator who, through his participation in the academic labor, can share in the moulding of how individuals and societies can address the problems that divert the progress of mankind and the common good (Decree 17: "Jesuits and University Life" [JUL] 1 and 2 [404 and 405]). As a legal educator, the particular demands of my work concentrate on how the legal profession and the formation of its prospective members will implement the promotion of reconciliation and the protection of the innocent that are the realization of God's justice in this world.

Two Tasks for the University Apostolate

The members of GC 34 posed two specific tasks for Jesuits engaged in the university apostolate. While the questions are distinct, how we Jesuits address them must be inextricably related. The first task focuses on "a challenge from the structure of universities." The second concerns the challenge from faith and justice.

Since the evolution of separate incorporations of Jesuit universities from Jesuit communities that began in the late 1960s, the nature of Jesuit universities has undergone dramatic transformation. While academic excellence has generally increased at these institutions, the Jesuit and Catholic soul of these institutions has also been greatly modified. This modification has had its good qualities, such as the incorporation of laymen and women into positions of responsibility. Consistent with the spirit of *Gaudium et Spes*, the laity have responded to the call to carry out the "secular duties and activities" that are properly theirs.[10] For the laity involved with the formation of those about to enter the powerful establishment of the legal profession, "it is generally the function of their well-formed Christian conscience to see that the divine law is inscribed in the life of the earthly city. . . ."[11] This is so because the unity of the human person is such that the faith-related moral conscience cannot be divorced from participation in the daily events of worldly human existence.[12]

While Jesuit educators must be open to working with their lay colleagues, we cannot forget that the underlying spirit of these universities where many diverse lives intersect cannot be abandoned. The adjective *Jesuit* (which must also imply "Catholic") and the noun *university* must remain compatible and not at odds with each other. The members of GC 34 concluded that the "University" must be committed to "fundamental autonomy, integrity, and honesty . . . [as] a place of serene and open research" (JUL 6 [409]). But if the Jesuit and the faithful lay colleague are to be committed to the freedom of healthy inquiry, the institution and the rest of its members must be equally committed to the proposition that the truth that is sought and the knowledge to be achieved is the transcendent and the objective—which is God.

Thus, the adjective *Jesuit* serves as the essential ingredient that directs the purpose of this academy and the goals of truth and justice that are sought. As the General Congregation recognized, the university must "act in harmony with the demands of the service of faith *and* the promotion of justice" (JUL 7 [410]; emphasis added). This is why the members of the Congregation asserted that if the university is to remain Jesuit, "periodic evaluation and accountability to the Society are necessary in order to judge whether or not its dynamics are being developed in line with the Jesuit mission" (JUL 9 [412]). Ultimately, the goal of the university is not the adherence to a particular world view or the ideology of the day but rather is directed to "the search for the fullness of truth . . . [and] that truth, rooted as it is in God, will make us free" (JUL 12 [415]).

CATHOLICITY VS. NATIONAL PROMINENCE?

As a legal educator who has labored to cultivate both faith and reason, I have tried to combine practical wisdom with spiritual development. In doing this, I have come to see and better understand the particular challenges that confront the legal academy that claims to be Jesuit and Catholic. One of the more obvious tasks I have encountered is dealing with teaching colleagues. If a law school affiliated with a Jesuit university aspires to national prominence, according to Georgetown Law School's Mark Tushnet, the members of the faculty "will be drawn predominantly from other, primarily secular, national law schools. . . . "[13] If this is the case, Tushnet further suggests that these faculty who pass on the tradition of the law to future generations of lawyers "are unlikely to be comfortable if their institution defines its mission as providing Catholic leadership."[14] Recalling that Professor Tushnet holds the view that "Catholic legal education is primarily legal education,"[15] his solution for the Jesuit school that wishes to achieve and maintain national status is to create an institute in which "academically qualified" Catholics could teach and write in areas where the interests of the Church coincide with secular specialties[16] (of course, I do not see why any mission-qualified academic would be precluded from doing the same). But Tushnet hastens to add that such a program could very well lack appeal and interfere with national-status ambitions, and he suggests that a program that fails to generate such appeal is "likely to confirm the narrowness of the law school's aspirations, thus confining it to the same status as local law schools, which are thought to have similarly narrow aspirations."[17]

The position and attitude of Professor Tushnet have been echoed by his colleague at Georgetown Law, Professor William Eskridge. Professor Eskridge has contributed his views in his recent book, *Dynamic Statutory Interpretation,*[18] where he discusses the 1987 case of *Gay Rights Coalition v. Georgetown University.*[19] Eskridge notes that the university's

Catholic connections have "little impact" on what he perceives to be the "educational experience and academic dialogue at [Georgetown] Law Center."[20] He continues by stating:

> *The courses are completely secular; the professors usually take positions on controversial issues such as abortion, gay rights, public aid to parochial schools that are contrary to Catholic doctrine; the traces of religious influence in our scholarship is as likely to be Jewish or Protestant as Catholic; school programs are secular; faculty hiring and student admissions are with few exceptions unaffected by religious considerations; and funded student groups regularly advocate activities that are contrary to Catholic teaching, though such advocacy is sometimes met with administrative resistance.*[21]

He furthers his commentary on the Gay Rights Coalition case by arguing that if the university were to mandate as a condition of his employment that he would have to endorse Roman Catholic theology, he would be "unhappy" because he disagrees with much of it.[22] But he adds that he would be more "upset" if he

> *had to open up my house and host meetings in which Catholic priests on the faculty inveighed against gay and lesbian intimacy. The latter would be a greater invasion of my freedom because it would be more concrete and more in my face than an abstract endorsement (as to which I could make a mental reservation).*[23]

I do not believe that I or most other Jesuits and lay colleagues who support the Jesuit and Catholic mission of institutions of higher education would expect a test of confession from every member of the university community or investigations into domestic living arrangements. On the other hand, the university—and the Jesuit and lay members who support and labor on behalf of its distinctive mission—have a right to form the image of the institution as not being the secular place that Professors Eskridge and Tushnet believe that it is or must be. As Justice Frankfurter once said in his concurring opinion in the academic freedom case of *Sweezy v. New Hampshire*,[24] an institution has definite rights in determining what will be taught, how the subject matters will be taught, who will teach, and who will be taught. The freedoms accorded to individuals are also granted to institutions. Moreover, for those of us attempting to carry on the work of the Catholic intellectual tradition in the context of the apostolic work of the Society of Jesus, law schools in Jesuit universities must also have a role in this tradition that unifies rather than separates faith and justice.

Yet, one could raise the same questions about appeal regarding the variety of programs that many so-called "national" schools seem to be pursuing today. As Judge Harry Edwards of the United States Court of Appeals for the District of Columbia Circuit has noted, *our law schools and law firms are moving in opposite directions. The schools should be training ethical practitioners and producing scholarship that judges, legislators, and practitioners can use. The firms should be ensuring that associates and partners practice law in an ethical manner. But many law schools—especially the so-called "elite" ones—have abandoned their proper place, by emphasizing abstract theory at the expense of practical scholarship and pedagogy. Many law firms have also abandoned their place, by pursuing profit above all else. While the schools are moving toward pure theory, the firms are moving toward pure commerce, and the middle ground—ethical practice—has been deserted by both. . . . My view is that if law schools continue to stray from their principal mission of professional scholarship and training, the disjunction between legal education and the legal profession will grow and society will be the worse for it.*[25]

JESUIT RESPONSE: BE CLEAR ABOUT WHO WE ARE

One response to the view of Professor Tushnet and the concerns raised by Judge Edwards is this: if law schools that call themselves Jesuit are to be true to their mission of producing good lawyers—who are first of all good people—we must be clear about who we are, where we have been, and where we must go. The first charge of who we are raises the question of identity. In identifying what Jesuit legal education is about, we must be certain that we teach and seek the justice that is God's—a justice that can be incorporated into man's if we accept the premise that law is both objective and transcendent and seeks to obtain the *suum cuique* for each and every person at whatever stage of life.

Second, we must be clear about where we have been. Having a sense of history means that we acknowledge proudly the tradition that the law is an institution designed to promote the Great Commandment of living in right relation with God by living in right relation with the neighbor. Both the culture in which we live and the norms that we develop can and must take account of the fact that the truest form of justice incorporates both God's will and our own.

Third, we must be clear about our destiny. The direction in which much of the academy of the late twentieth century seems to be directed is that all views, all beliefs, all cultures are equally valid. As a result, a strong form of relativism encroaches upon the university, including law schools. However, neither the university nor its law school can afford in this day to hold onto the view that all human perspectives are equal in quality and legitimacy. Indeed, some of these perspectives, as I have noted earlier in this essay, do not take account of precious human interests at the antipodes of life that are threatened by the norms of many contemporary cultures. The university that claims a Jesuit heritage must be willing to discuss such views but, ultimately, it cannot afford to adopt them as its own, for such action would negate the reality that each person is precious because each reflects the image of its Divine Maker.

Conclusion

The call to discipleship in the Society of Jesus and all other Christian vocations remains strong today. However, in the current age, the challenges to seeking and observing God's justice in this world are becoming increasingly potent. Nonetheless, it is through our holy desire and openness to God's leading spirit that his justice and truth shall prevail. We might take courage from another disciple of an earlier age, Thomas More—the patron saint of the common-law legal profession. As was said of More, he died King Henry's loyal subject, but God's first. Might it be said of us that while we conclude our earthly lives as loyal subjects of our contemporary culture, we were and remained God's first?

ENDNOTES • ARAUJO

1. With due respects to Fathers Ignatius and Gonçalves da Câmara.
2. "Then Jesus said to the Jews who had believed in him, 'If you continue in my word, you are truly my disciples; and you will know the truth, and the truth will make you free'" (Jn 8:31–32).
3. Mark Tushnet, "Catholic Legal Education at a National Law School: Reflections on the Georgetown Experience," in *Georgetown at Two Hundred: Faculty Reflections on the University's Future*, ed. William C. McFadden, S.J. (Washington, D.C.: Georgetown University Press, 1990), 321–34 at 322.
4. J. M. Kelly, *A Short History of Western Legal Theory* (Oxford: Oxford University Press, 1992), xi.
5. Ibid., xii.
6. The inscription over the main portico reads: "Equal Justice Under Law."
7. *Gaudium et Spes* 9, 21, 26, 29, 30, 34, 35, 38, 39, 55, 63, 66, 69, 72, 73, 75, 76, 77, 78, 81, 83, 86, 90, and 93.
8. By sampling a variety of law school Web sites, I came across the following selection of mission statements that reflect this common concern: Boston College states that "we believe that the best legal education is both intellectual and ethical . . . , education for service to others, and respect for each individual." Duke University claims that its mission "is to prepare students for responsible and productive lives in the legal profession. As a community of scholars, the Law School also provides the leadership at a national and international level in efforts to improve the law and legal institutions through teaching, research, and other forms of public service." Creighton University is

> committed to a comprehensive and value-centered education [that will] produce ethical lawyers who will zealously and competently represent clients within the bounds of the law and, at the same time, recognize their duty to improve society. . . . [A]ll faculty members are committed to excellence in teaching, research, and community service. . . . Our mission, then, is to provide the men and women of our student body intellectual challenge, academic rigor, and an opportunity to develop a foundation of moral values for life-long serice in the law. . . .

Georgetown's mission is quite explicit: "It is an educational institution dedicated to the principle that law is but the means, justice is the end." Harvard, the "oldest existing law school in the United States," provides "comprehensive and enlightened training to prepare its graduates for law practice, for public service . . . [and] seeks to make substantial contributions toward solving complex social and international problems." Yale "is devoted neither to the *vita activa* nor to the *vita contemplativa*. It is devoted to something more difficult and demanding than either. It is devoted to the endless task of building a bridge capable of carrying traffic in both directions, in order that our public life be shaped by reason and thought, and our scholarly pursuits by a moral urgency born of the passionate conviction that law really matters." Loyola of Chicago "devotes itself to examining the origins and the service component of our legal system and the legal profession, to treating students as individuals ('education on a human scale'), and to producing not just 'good lawyers' but good people who are lawyers." Marquette generously addresses both its mission and the mission of other Jesuit university–affiliated law schools by asking the question, "Why not consider a Jesuit law school?" The answer Marquette supplies is this:

> To meet the complex challenges of the 21st century, lawyers must be prepared to serve their clients with a high degree of professional competence, an enduring commitment to social justice, and a deep devotion to public service. The 14 Jesuit law schools in the United States are especially able to offer their students a legal education rooted in the values that produce such lawyers. Our programs of study share a disinct Jesuit heritage, one which values the pursuit of academic excellence, acquisition of knowledge for the betterment of society, care and concern for the individual, and preparation for public service.

Yet, as the literature of secular institutions demonstrates, so do non-Jesuit and nonreligiously-affiliated law schools. One ought to be wary of phrases like "Jesuit heritage" and "Jesuit tradition" often found in the catalogs of the law schools affiliated with Jesuit universities. To my knowledge, none of these schools elaborates on what this tradition and heritage are. It is not some relic from the past brought out to entertain loyal alumni and benefactors; it is a vibrant alernative to higher education both for today and the future. As Margaret Steinfels has argued, "A tradition is not a browned and dried-up certificate of deposit in the bank of knowledge, but a locus for questioning a framework for ordering inquiry, a standard for preferring some sets of ideas over others; tradition is the record of a community's conversation over time about its meaning and direction." See M. Steinfels, "The Catholic Intellectual Tradition," *Origins* 25 (24 August 1995): 169, 171–73 at 172.

9. As the Pope stated in par. 12 of this encyclical,

> This reality is characterized by the emergence of a culture which denies solidarity and in many cases takes the form of a veritable "culture of death." This culture is actively fostered by powerful cultural, economic and political currents which encourage an idea of society excessively concerned with efficiency. Looking at the situation from this point of view, it is possible to speak in a certain sense of a war of the powerful against the weak: a life which would require greater acceptance, love and care is considered useless, or held to be an intolerable burden, and is therefore rejected in one way or another. A person who, because of illness, handicap or, more simply, just by existing, compromises the well-being or life-style of those who are more favoured tends to be looked upon as an enemy to be resisted or eliminated. In this way a kind of "conspiracy against life" is unleashed. This conspiracy involves not only individuals in their personal, family or group relationships, but goes far beyond, to the point of damaging and distorting, at the international level, relations between peoples and States (*Evangelium Vitae*, Vatican trans. [Boston, Mass.: Pauline Books, 1995]).

10. *Gaudium et Spes* 43, in *The Documents of Vatican II*, ed. Walter M. Abbott, S.J. (New York: Guild, 1966).
11. Ibid.
12. Ibid.
13. Tushnet, "Catholic Legal Education," 326.
14. Ibid.
15. Ibid., 322.
16. Ibid., 330.

17. Ibid.
18. William Eskridge, *Dynamic Statutory Interpretation* (Cambridge, Mass.: Harvard University Press, 1994), esp. 190–95.
19. *Coalition v. Georgetown,* 536 A.2d 1 (D.C. 1987).
20. Eskridge, *Dynamic Statutory Interpretation,* 190.
21. Ibid.
22. Ibid., 195.
23. Ibid.
24. *Sweezy v. New Hampshire,* 354 U.S. 234, 263 (1957) (Frankfurter, J., concurring).
25. Harry T. Edwards, "The Growing Disjunction Between Legal Education and the Legal Profession," *Michigan Law Review* 91 (1992): 34, 41.

Intercultural Odyssey

Walter A. Cook, S.J.

ABSTRACT

The author sees GC 34 as validating Jesuit higher education and its efforts in social justice. From its origins, Ignatius determined that Jesuits should be assigned primarily to the intellectual apostolate. This is a work of justice understood, however, not simply as social justice, but as a virtue that is person-oriented. The war against ignorance has the long-range effect of overcoming poverty by educating "self-sufficient" people who train others in self-sufficiency. GC 34 also demanded "intercultural awareness" in Jesuit educational work, not only because of our shrinking world, but because "God is working in each culture." Learning the language of a culture allows one to discover "God's activity" in that culture. The author surveys the fascinating outreach of his experience as a linguist and various experiences of inculturation of the Gospel message throughout the world. He concludes that GC 34 rightly applied will introduce every Jesuit to an "intercultural odyssey" of bringing the Christian message to and finding God at work in every culture bringing it into his Kingdom.

Introduction

Jesuits from around the world convened in Rome in January 1995 for GC 34. According to Decree 4: "Our Mission and Culture" (OMC) [75], "General Congregation 34 has brought together Jesuits from the cultures of Asia, the former Communist countries of Eastern Europe, the European Community, Africa, North America, Australia and Latin America; this composition has heightened our awareness of the diversity of cultures in both the world and the Society." The General Congregation was intercultural not only in its composition but also in the decrees it promulgated. What will be the effect of GC 34 on the various missions of the Society of Jesus? In his closing address, the general of the order, Peter-Hans Kolvenbach, S.J., asks: "Why try to delude ourselves? It is conversion or the absence of conversion which is the deciding factor for the living-out of this congregation, for the future of all that this general congregation has elaborated, clarified, and decided."[1]

In assessing the future impact of GC 34 on the various Jesuit ministries, the intercultural nature of the Congregation must be taken into account. All ministries must be evaluated in terms of the position of modern Jesuits as "inhabitants of the global village" (Decree 15: "Communication: A New Culture" 4 [388]). Jesuits in education include not only Xavier University in Cincinnati, but Saint Xavier's University in Calcutta; not only Loyola University in Chicago, but Loyola School in Jamshedpur, India. Many Jesuits in America have no experience of a culture other than their own.

What is culture? "'Culture' means the way in which a group of people live, think, feel, organize themselves, celebrate, and share life. In every culture, there are underlying systems of values, meanings, and views of the world, which are expressed, visibly, in language, gestures, symbols, rituals, and styles" (OMC 1 [75], n. 1). The Congregation suggests that working in an intercultural environment requires a sensitivity on the part of the Jesuit educator to other cultures.

The primary impact of this Congregation on Jesuit higher education is the clear vindication in Decree 17 of Jesuit higher education and its effect on social justice and the preferential option for the poor. The secondary impact is the demand for intercultural awareness in Jesuit missionary and educational work. Because of Decree 17's emhasis on the intellectual apostolate, and the emphasis in Decree 4 on the recognition of the values inherent in other cultures, this congregation encourages the members of the international Society of Jesus to embark together on an intercultural odyssey.

Jesuit Education and the Promotion of Justice

For Jesuit educators, Decree 16: "The Intellectual Dimension of Jesuit Ministries," Decree 17: "Jesuits and University Life" (JUL), and Decree 18: "Secondary, Primary, and Non-formal Education" firmly establish the apostolate of university and secondary education as a prime mission of the Society of Jesus, while vindicating the valid concern of GC 32 for the service of faith and promotion of justice: "Jesuits have been engaged in university teaching, research, and scholarly publication almost since the foundation of the Society. From astronomy to classical ballet, from the humanities to theology, Jesuits try to enter into the languages and discourses of their inherited or emerging culture" (JUL 1 [404]).

In his search for the *magis,* the greater good for the greater number, Ignatius of Loyola, the founder of the Society of Jesus, very early determined that the majority of Jesuits should be assigned to the intellectual apostolate. John W. O'Malley, S.J., quotes a letter from Juan Alfonso de Polanco, which says that "generally speaking there are [in the Society] two ways of helping our neighbors: one in the colleges through the education of youth in letters, learning, and Christian life, and the second in every place to help every kind of person through sermons, confessions, and the other means that accord with our customary way of proceeding."[2] College teaching was established as a major category of Jesuit activity. By the time Ignatius died, the Society was operating thirty-five or more colleges, and by the time of the suppression in 1773, the Society had over eight hundred colleges.[3] This commitment to education was summed up in a letter from Pedro de Ribadeneira to Philip II of Spain: "All the well-being of Christianity and of the whole world depends on the proper education of youth."[4] Jesuit education was aimed at the formation of youth, and "much of what they taught related only indirectly to the Christian religion as such."[5] Jesuit education did not have social justice as its primary goal.

GC 32, with its emphasis on faith and social justice as its primary aim, unfortunately caused a division between those involved in the promotion of social justice and those involved in strictly secular secondary and higher education. Martin Tripole, S.J., suggests that "by making the promotion of justice the integrating dimension of all apostolates, not only is the legitimacy of many other apostolates such as education called into question, but also the primacy of the service of the Gospel as the truly integrating principle of all apostolates is threatened."[6] Part of this division was a result of the unique interpretation of justice as social justice. As Séamus Murphy, S.J., points out: "It is legitimate to have different notions of justice for different ministries."[7] Social justice is object-oriented, with social reform as its goal; personal justice is person-oriented, with the formation of youth as its goal. In "'growth ministries' such as, education, spirituality, psychological care . . . justice can be interpreted as a matter of 'e-ducating' and empowering persons."[8] With a clear distinction between justice as a goal and justice as a virtue, all members of the Society can be reconciled to a faith that does justice. The final paragraph of Decree 17 concludes with the words: "GC 34 sends a warm word of greeting and encouragement to all those Jesuits dedicated to make authentic and currently fresh this long-standing but sometimes challenged Jesuit commitment to the university apostolate" (JUL 12 [415]).

Jesuit Education and the Preferential Option for the Poor

Most Jesuits are educators, not social workers. Ignorance is the enemy, not poverty. The early Jesuit schools, by educating both clergy and laity, changed the face of Europe. Even in the missions they founded overseas, education through Jesuit schools had first priority, especially among the poor and illiterate.

The short-range view is that Jesuits should be directly involved in social work, but this work, while valuable, has severe limitations. The long-range view is that education, while basically a war against ignorance, is also a war against poverty, for it makes people self-sufficient. As a saying attributed to the Peace Corps puts it, "Give a man a fish and he has food for a day, teach him to fish and he has food for a lifetime." Although many overseas programs offer direct aid to the poor, the Peace Corps endeavors to make people self-sufficient by training them in how to grow food, protect their health, build housing, and begin small businesses. Even our welfare programs recognize that their goal is to get people off welfare by training programs, not simply to continue everlasting dole. The Gospel tells us "the poor you have always with you," but education can limit the number of people entering the ranks of the poor, and in the long run has more permanent effect than the more direct assistance to the poor.

A further value of education is training people to work for others, so that although the teacher's influence is on the students, the students in turn offer their services to the poor, thus multiplying the effect on defeating poverty: "Forming 'men and women for others' is appropriate not only in our educational institutions but in ministries of the Word and the Spiritual Exercises, in pastoral apostolates and communication" (OMJ 20 [69]). Well-trained "men and women for others" can multiply the effects of the war against poverty. Even those belonging to the "me generation"[9] who have personal prosperity as their major goal often end up contributing charitable donations to the war against poverty.

Although Jesuits are always well educated, they should be schooled in the ways of poverty: "During their formation, young Jesuits should be in contact with the poor, not just occasionally, but in a more sustained manner" (OMJ 18 [67]). This is currently the practice in most novitiates, where young Jesuits are sent to hospitals, AIDS clinics, or poor schools. Moreover, the Congregation suggests that all Jesuits, including educators, need poverty experience: "Some insertion into the world of the poor should therefore be part of the life of every Jesuit" (OMJ 17 [66]).

Intercultural Education

The Congregation not only vindicates Jesuit educators in Decree 17, but also emphasizes the importance of education in Decree 4. This decree sets the standard for Jesuits worldwide in all their ministries, requiring each Jesuit, in whatever ministry, to be aware of the cultural values of the people among whom he works: "As an international apostolic body, the Society is uniquely able to draw upon a range of cultural experience in its ministries . . . , contributing in this way to the Church's mission, at the service of God's plan to bring together all peoples into the communion of his Kingdom" (OMC 28,9 [127]). It is not only Jesuit missionaries, but Jesuit educators that have to be concerned about intercultural values: "The call to inculturated evangelization is not simply for those working in a land other than their own. All of our works take place in a particular cultural setting with positive and negative features that the Gospel must touch" (OMC 27,6 [116]). Jesuits in education may tend to be myopic in their relation to culture, regarding the cultural milieu in which they work as the only culture with which they are concerned. "Our educational institutions, in particular, have a crucial role to play in linking Christian faith to the core elements in contemporary and traditional cultures" (OMC 28,7 [125]).

But the world is shrinking, and our educational world is expanding. The former all-male colleges have given way to coeducational institutions in which the teacher must be aware of male-female cultural differences. The former all-Caucasian colleges have given way to an ethnic mix of black and white, and with recent immigration to the influx of Hispanic and Asian students. The colleges are multicultural institutions, in which the teacher must be aware of the values of each culture, and what each adds to the Kingdom of God. Often our universities are lightning rods for the most intelligent of the Asiatic and Arabic communities. Our schools educate Muslims, Hindus, Buddhists, Jews, as well as Christians of all varieties. The mix is intercultural, and the Congregation, itself a mixture of cultures, calls for intercultural awareness.

The Congregation suggests that this awareness is based on the premise that God is working in each culture in human history: "The work of God in the diversity of human history is seen in the long process of enlightened human growth—still incomplete!—as expressed in religious, social, moral, and cultural forms that bear the mark of the silent work of the Spirit" (OMC 18 [102]). It also lists our failures in recognizing our intuition that the Gospel resonates with what is good in each culture: "Jesuit evangelizers have often failed to insert themselves into the heart of a culture, but instead have remained a foreign presence; in our mission, we have failed to discover the treasures of humanity: the values, depth, and transcendence of other cultures, which manifest the action of the Spirit . . ." (OMC 12 [93–94]). What the Jesuit educator has to offer is not the imposition of a Christian presence on the cultures with which we come in contact, but a dialogue that finds the best elements of a culture by which God has prepared a people for membership in his Kingdom. We do not seek to put God into their world, we seek to find God already in their world.

Linguistic Science

The Congregation has particular impact in education in the field of linguistic science. When one is introduced as a linguist, the first question is, How many languages can you speak? The question is irrelevant. Many classes of people study language: classicists, poets, communication engineers, historians. What makes linguistics a special science is its viewpoint. Linguistics, as a science, studies all language, spoken or written, ancient or modern, with a view to discerning the structure of language.

Linguistics is, in essence, an intercultural science. The members of a culture represent that culture most directly in their language. To a linguist, all members of the human family are essentially the same in their human desires and their need to communicate them. In the Tower of Babel that our world represents, all languages and their corresponding cultures are seen as equal opportunities to learn about the human desire to communicate.

Jesuit missionaries throughout history learned the languages of the country in which they worked, believing that their ministry of evangelizing culture should be guided by ways that bring to light the character of God's activity in those cultures: "This intuition is what has led Jesuits to adopt such a positive approach to the religions and cultures in which they work. . . . It is also what prompted Jesuits outside Europe to express a profound respect for indigenous cultures and to compose dictionaries and grammars of local languages, and pioneering studies of the people among whom they worked and whom they tried to understand" (OMC 10 [89]).

My personal experience verified what I had read about Jesuit missionaries. From 1953 until 1962 I worked for the Jamshedpur mission among the Munda people, located in the Chota Nagpur plateau in southern Bihar. The Mundas were a tribal people, animist in religion, in a simple rice culture, living in mud huts with none of the trappings of modern civilization. With no phones, no TV, no radio, no cars, their proudest possession was often a lantern or an umbrella. A German Jesuit, John Hoffman, had composed a grammar of the language and a twelve-volume encyclopedia of the Munda culture. Through his pioneering work, missionaries were able to learn the language and appreciate the tribal culture. One of Hoffman's major informants for the encyclopedia was Menas Orea, a patriarch of some eighty years, who, as resident headman of the village of Bandgaon, was always willing to help the missionaries in their study of the language. With the help of Hoffman's monumental works and eight years of field experience speaking the language, I was able to write my doctoral dissertation at Georgetown on the Mundari language.

The Congregation recommends that every Jesuit experience a culture other than his own: "An experience of a culture other than our own will help us grow into a vision . . . more objective about our own native cultures" (OMC 28,6 [124]). My own experience with the indigenous cultures of India certainly colored my vision of the world and its cultures. Witnessing the mass poverty of Calcutta, where thousands of sick, deformed, or dying litter the streets in their "City of Joy," influenced my notion of poverty, as did the poverty of the rice culture, so completely dependent upon each yearly monsoon, where a good monsoon means food for the year, but a bad monsoon or excessive flooding means widespread starvation.

Analagous effects were produced in those missionaries who labored in the cultures of Central and South America, or who witnessed starvation and the spread of AIDS in the countries of Africa. America certainly has its own poverty, but the whole notion of poverty is enriched by the realization that poverty, AIDS, homelessness, and desperation are not limited to the streets of America.

Teaching Linguistics

In June 1962, on leave from the mission, I enrolled in a course at Georgetown University called "Linguistics for Missionaries." I had no idea what linguistics was (I couldn't even spell it). But by 1965, within three years, I had both the M.S. and the Ph.D. in linguistics, writing my doctoral dissertation on the Mundari language, which I had learned in the Jamshedpur mission. As soon as I graduated I was offered a position in the linguistics department at Georgetown. Within that department I was known as a backdoor linguist, one who had acquired field experience in learning languages before learning how to learn languages.

Linguistics has many branches. Theoretical linguistics deals directly with the structure of language, not its application. Applied linguistics deals with the teaching and testing of languages, with English as a second language, and with bilingualism. Sociolinguistics deals with language in the social context, with language variation, conversational postulates, male and female differences, as well as with pragmatics, the meaning of language in context. Computational linguistics deals with natural language processing, machine translation, artificial intelligence, and other applications of linguistics to the computer. My area of expertise was theoretical linguistics. My early teaching involved phonology, the study of sound; morphology, the study of word forms; and syntax, the study of grammar, and later branched into semantics and computational analysis. As a grammatical model I used the system of Tagmemic Analyis, advocated by the Summer Institute of Linguistics, inherited from my first linguistics course.

The Summer Institute of Linguistics was set up by the Wycliffe Bible Society, and had as its goal the formation of linguists who would travel to various parts of the world and learn even the unwritten languages. Their fundamental apostolic goal was the translation of the Bible into all the languages of the world as a means of spreading the Gospel. In this work the poor, forgotten, illiterate peoples of the world received first priority. This involved learning the language of the culture, translating the Bible into that language, and training the people in literacy programs so that they could read it. These linguists offered all of us a concrete example of how abstract linguistic theory could be put at the service of the Gospel.

Kenneth L. Pike, a leading linguist of the Summer Institute of Linguistics and former chairman of the linguistics department at the University of Michigan, in his personal synthesis of scholarship and devotion, describes the ideal Christian scholar: "He should be vigorous in devotion—with complete trust in God. He should be vigorous in scholarship—using his mind. He should be vigorous in friendship—including being friendly to those who are unfriendly to him."[10] To Pike and his fellow linguists in the Summer Institute of Linguistics, there is no contradiction in the love of Christ and the love of scholarship. Although Jesuits in linguistics may not have the translation of the Bible into all languages as their primary goal, they can remain sympathetic to any effort that brings us into contact with other cultures, and the working of God within these cultures where Christianity is unknown.

Linguistic Outreach

The graduate program of the School of Languages and Linguistics at Georgetown University began awarding the doctoral degree in linguistics in 1964. The graduate linguistics program at Georgetown grew to a point where we were averaging twenty Ph.D.s a year, producing over five hundred doctorates in linguistics by 1992. About half of these students were from the Middle East, including all of the Arab nations, or the Far East, including China, Taiwan, Japan, Korea, Indonesia, Thailand, and the Philippines.

A typical Egyptian student would complete college in Cairo or Alexandria, then apply for the doctoral program in applied linguistics, where he or she would be trained in language teaching, language testing, bilingualism, and English as a foreign language. This student would then return to six years of service in his home university. In this way the methodology taught at Georgetown University was spread throughout a myriad of cultures. Although these students were on the whole not Christians, their Jesuit education carried the message that Christianity was open to all cultures: "The Christian message is to be open to all cultures, bound to no single culture and made accessible to every human person through a process of inculturation, by which the Gospel introduces something new into the culture and the culture brings something new to the richness of the Gospel" (OMC 2 [76]).

The local outreach of the linguistics department had more immediate effects. At Georgetown University in the academic years 1968 and 1969, there was instituted a Teachers Fellowship Program, sponsored by the National Defense Education Act. The plan was to take thirty active teachers from local schools, primarily in the District of Columbia, offer them the opportunity to attain a master's degree in a single year, and send them back to their schools. The direct approach had been to send outside teachers to the schools, which often evoked the response, "Whitey, go home." But by training their own teachers to teach better, the result was multiplied by thirty well-trained teachers returning to their own poverty-ridden schools. Many of these teachers rose to be reading specialists or supervisors, enhancing their own role in the school system.

The personal outreach of the linguistics faculty was also impressive. Professors traveled to Asia and elsewhere, lecturing in universities where our graduates had been assigned. In this capacity I travelled to India, the Philippines, Japan, Taiwan, Thailand, Indonesia, and South Korea, lecturing at the Ateneo de Manila, Sophia, and Keio Universities; Fu Jen University in Taiwan; Chulalongkorn and Thammasat Universities in Thailand; Atma Jaya and Sanata Dharma Universities in Indonesia; and Seoul National, Pusan National, and Sogang Universities in South Korea. The linguistics training also helped me to assist in English training programs at Colegio San Ignatio in Puerto Rico, at Universidad Centro-Americana in Managua, Nicaragua, and to Khmer teachers of English in Site II Camp in Thailand.

During my thirty years as a professor of linguistics I directed or read seventy-five doctoral dissertations, dealing with Spanish, French, German, Arabic, Persian, Chinese, Japanese, and Thai, mostly in the areas of semantics and computational linguistics. In May 1992, I retired from my position as professor at Georgetown University. As professor emeritus, I continued to direct Ph.D. dissertations in linguistics and continued writing academic textbooks, while retaining my connections with Asian and Middle Eastern students.

Intercultural Adaptation

It is not always easy to know how to adapt the Christian religion, with its strong Western bias, to the cultures of Asia. Jesuits have had their successes, and they have had their failures. Xavier learned that he could not make any progress in Japan as a mendicant preacher, but only as a respected European envoy. Matteo Ricci, in China, adopted Mandarin costume and language to teach science and religion at the imperial court of China. Modern Jesuits in Asia are well aware of the cultures in which they perform their apostolic work.

In India, a predominantly Hindu culture, priests in the pre–Vatican II era said mass in Latin in full Roman vestments, with only the ministry of the Word in the vernacular. Today the priest in the villages sits on a prayer rug, wrapped in a prayer shawl, before a low table with a crucifix, a single candle, and a corporal. The mass is in the native tribal language or the national Hindi language. This mass incorporates traditional Eastern methods of prayer, making the priest closer to the people, and the language is understandable even to the illiterate. Partly as a result of incorporating the culture into the liturgy, church attendance is up, and so are vocations to the religious life.

In Indonesia, a predominantly Muslim country, the Church continues to expand, with increased church attendance and an increase in vocations. One of the most striking examples of inculturation was the Good Friday services. In the church on the campus of Universitas Sanata Dharma, in Yogyakarta, a life-sized crucified Christ was laid out on a low table in the sanctuary. At the time of the kissing of the crucifix, there was no kissing of the feet. But the people approached the crucifix and showered rose petals on the crucified Christ, in much the same way as they scattered flower petals in family funerals. The following Easter Sunday Mass was triumphal, and as they left the church people greeted each other with *Salamaat Pascha,* or welcome to the Pascal feast.

In Korea, a predominantly Buddhist country, there is a strong Christian tradition, carried to Korea from the imperial court of China, and witnessed by the hundreds of martyrs at

Chol-du-san (head-chop hill) in Seoul. At the Mass of the Last Supper at Sogang University in Seoul, the choir swayed and sang joyously to the accompaniment of the ever-present Korean drummers. On Good Friday students acted out the stations of the cross with full costume. The nailing to the cross was accompanied by the heavy drums, and the crucified Christ clung to wooden pegs as the cross was lifted, making a very realistic panorama. The story is age-old, but the performance was typically Korean. In Korea also, church attendance is up, and vocations are on the increase.

When we Jesuits view our American Church in comparison, we may feel discouraged at the diminishing church attendance and the lack of vocations to the priesthood. But at the same time, in countries with dominant non-Christian cultures, the Church continues to expand. There is a lesson to be learned from this: that God's Kingdom is spread in God's own way. Viewing the international scene, there is no cause for despair. He must increase and I must decrease, but God will reach all his people in his own good time.

Conclusion: Jesuit Mission

What is a Jesuit? "A Jesuit is essentially a man on a mission, a mission he receives from the Holy Father and from his own religious superior, but ultimately from Jesus Christ . . . . Jesuits remain 'ready at any hour to go to some or other parts of the world where they may be sent by the Sovereign Pontiff or their own superiors'" (Decree 26: "Conclusion: Our Way of Proceeding" 23 [55], citing *Const* [588]). For Jesuits who are priests, this mission is their ministerial priesthood, in education, social work, and missions throughout the world: "From their Ignatian tradition, Jesuits bring to their ministerial priesthood a profound respect for the ways in which God is already at work in the lives of all men and women" (Decree 6: "The Jesuit Priest: Ministerial Priesthood and Jesuit Identity" [JP] 20 [177]). For Jesuit educators, this insight "encourages us to become involved in disciplines which, although they may have no explicitly Christian perspective, are nevertheless central to the way in which human beings understand themselves and the world around them . . ." (JP 20,2 [179]). Whether Jesuit educators teach theology, philosophy, linguistics, sociology, mathematics, or astronomy, they train students to think, to be more human, to be more capable and insightful in their own lives, and more generous in their service to others. In order to do this, Jesuit priests around the world must be aware of the process of inculturation.

Father Pedro Arrupe drew attention to the importance of inculturation for the contemporary Jesuit mission: "Inculturation is the incarnation of Christian life and of the Christian message in a particular cultural context, in such a way that this experience not only finds expression through elements proper to the culture in question, but becomes a principle that animates, directs and unifies the culture, transforming it and remaking it so as to bring about a 'new creation'" (OMC 13 [97]).[11]

If we are to put into practice the decrees of GC 34, then every Jesuit, and particularly Jesuit priests, must embark on an intercultural odyssey, bringing the Christian message to the heart of the cultures within which they exercise their ministerial priesthood, whether at home or abroad. This requires an awareness of the way in which God is working, and has been working, within the culture to bring it eventually into his Kingdom. It requires an understanding of, and a dialogue with, the values inherent in that culture to transform that culture into a new creation. If we have this intercultural awareness, and understand the cultures within which we work, God will give the increase in his own time.

ENDNOTES • COOK

1. Appendix 4, "Homily of Father General at the Closing Mass, 22 March 1995," in *Documents of the Thirty-Fourth General Congregation of the Society of Jesus,* ed. John L. McCarthy, S.J. (St. Louis, Mo.: Institute of Jesuit Sources, 1995), 283–85 at 284–85.
2. John W. O'Malley, S.J., *The First Jesuits* (Cambridge, Mass.: Harvard University Press, 1993), 200 (brackets by O'Malley).
3. Ibid., 239.
4. Ibid., 209.
5. Ibid., 241.
6. Martin R. Tripole, S.J., *Faith Beyond Justice: Widening the Perspective* (St. Louis, Mo.: Institute of Jesuit Sources, 1994), 25.
7. Séamus Murphy, S.J., "The Many Ways of Justice," *Studies in the Spirituality of Jesuits* 26/2 (March 1994): 19.
8. Ibid., 23.
9. Tripole, *Faith Beyond Justice,* 132.
10. Kenneth L. Pike, *With Heart and Mind: A Personal Synthesis of Scholarship and Devotion* (Duncanville, Tex.: Adult Learning Systems, 1996), 101.
11. Cited in Pedro Arrupe, S.J., "Letter to the Whole Society on Inculturation," *Acta Romana Societatis Iesu* 17 (1978): 230.

Moral and Theological Life and the Mathematical Sciences

Frederick A. Homann, S.J.

ABSTRACT

The author welcomes the words of encouragement that GC 34's Decree 17 on "Jesuits and University Life" gives to the university apostolate. Yet he feels there is need to integrate valuable decrees from General Congregation 31 (GC 31) on education, scholarship, and the arts with the newer challenges of GC 34. The author reviews the strong support for the apostolate of education in GC 31, including references to scientific research and mathematical studies "as a means of aiding the Church in forming social reality." He notes the evangelizing efforts of Jesuits in the pre-Suppression Society. These are "paradigms" for our instruction today. The author sees mathematics as involving both a "dedication to the discipline itself" and to "the apostolic use of the discipline," a balancing act not always easy to maintain. He asks: "Are there apostolic dimensions to the mathematical sciences?" The rest of his paper provides needed and valuable insight on how to handle a question that has proven to be almost intractable for Jesuits since GC 32.

GC 34's Decree 17: "Jesuits and University Life" (JUL) is a welcome affirmation and directive for the Society's long-term involvement in the university apostolate, a spiritual work of mercy that the Society has fostered from its very earliest days, and is today of even greater value for evangelization of the diverse, yet inextricably linked cultures the Society meets in its daily work.

Jesuits missioned to this apostolate deeply appreciate "the warm word of greeting and encouragement to all those Jesuits dedicated to make authentic and currently fresh this long standing but sometimes challenged Jesuit commitment" (JUL 12 [415]).

No less than the theologians, philosophers, economists, linguists, demographers, historians, canonists, and literary critics, do the Jesuits in technology and the natural and mathematical sciences value these words—especially now, at a moment when direct full-time involvement in social causes and the promotion of economic justice seem to preoccupy the Society's interest to the neglect of more hidden, but essential foundation work needed to support appropriate activity. This appreciation is perhaps especially true for the case of the mathematical sciences, where there is a spectrum of specialties ranging from the abstrusities and seeming irrelevancy of algebraic topology and analytic number theory, to classical geometry and calculus, to the alarmingly practical and immediately useful operations research and statistical decision theory.

Jesuits who are professionally engaged in these specialties know (as do all university Jesuits) that Decree 17 is to be understood in the context of all GC 34 documents. But it is also to be read in the light of GC 31, 32, and 33. Decree 1: "United with Christ on Mission" makes that point, which is repeated in JUL 3 [406], 7 [410]. Moreover, for our purposes the Congregation makes an exceedingly valuable if gently stated reference in JUL 3 [406] n. 1 to the "excellent documents" of GC 31 that treat of "The Apostolate of Education" (Decree 28, [495–546]), "Scholarly Work and Research" (Decree 29, [547–52]), and "Cultivating the Arts in the Society" (Decree 30, [553–59]), along with documents of Pope John Paul II and Fathers General Arrupe and Kolvenbach.

GC 31 and Higher Education

These GC 31 documents, in the estimation of many Jesuits who have been involved all of their lives in the higher education apostolate, have not received the attention they deserve. Seemingly, they were set aside and overshadowed by the reception accorded to GC 32. Indeed, many Jesuits would find it difficult to recall a community discussion or province meeting that examined them at any length. Yet these documents offer substantial grounds for Jesuit dedication to cultivating the mathematical sciences (as well as theology, philosophy, literature, and so on) as an integral part of our apostolate. It is then appropriate for each university Jesuit, and in particular those in the mathematical sciences, to review the relevant GC 31 documents and integrate them with the two "relatively fresh challenges to Jesuit universities" that JUL 3 [406] now proposes to us; namely, that from the structure of universities, and another from faith and justice.

GC 31's "The Apostolate of Education" (AE) noted that schools, colleges, universities, and vocational and technical institutes are agencies of "special importance." Their teachers and scholars are "to promote the renewal of the Church and maintain and intensify her . . . presence in the contemporary and particularly the intellectual world" (AE 2 [496]). GC 34 agrees wholeheartedly, recalling "how crucial it is for the whole Church to continue to have dedicated Jesuits engaged in university work" (JUL 12 [415]), and noting that Saint Ignatius was well aware of the impact of the universities of his time, and the opportunity for achieving a more universal good (JUL 1 [404]). Speaking for the Society, GC 31 confirmed the high regard it has for the apostolate of education, and urged Jesuits to keep "unflaggingly" their esteem for this work (AE 4 [498]), despite the well-known problems that beset such an apostolate. In fact, where resources and circumstances allow, the Society should have its own educational institutions, which are to be "outstanding not so much for number and size as for teaching, for the quality of the instruction, and the service rendered to the people of God" (AE 4 [500]). The schools, GC 31 realized, can be "at least one effective instrument for the promotion of our educational purpose, i.e., the synthesizing of faith and culture" (AE 5 [503]), or, as might now be said, inculturation of the Gospel.

The educational apostolate looks "to provide a service of love . . . to educate believers as to make them not only cultured but, in both private and public lives, men who are authentically Christian and able and willing to work for the modern apostolate" (AE 7 [506])—surely an anticipation of the faith-justice mission of GC 32, Decree 4. Our work is not confined to believers only, but "aims to provide non-Christians with a humanistic formation directed towards the welfare of their own nation, and . . . to conduct them by degrees to the knowledge and love of God or at least to the acceptance of moral, and even religious values" (AE 7 [506]).

Coming to the specific case of university activity with its "ever growing importance . . . for the formation of the whole human community," the Congregation wanted that "the Society and its priests [be] present to this work," and that they "should be able not only to teach advanced courses, but also to contribute to scholarly progress by their own research and that of their talented students whom they have trained" (AE 24 [535]).

Theology and philosophy, of course, are first among the disciplines proper to Jesuit institutions, and deserve special place "to whatever extent they contribute . . . to the greater service of God" (AE 24 [536]). Linked with these faculties, the "education of priests, as a work of the highest value, is to be considered one of the chief ministries of the Society" (AE 25 [538]). If the "Apostolate of Education" document has nothing explicitly to say about teaching and research in mathematics and the physical sciences, Decree 29: "Scholarly Work and Research" (SWR) begins by insisting that "Jesuits should have a high regard for scholarly activity, especially scientific research properly so called, . . . as one of the most necessary works of the Society" (SWR 1 [547]). Significantly, it drew attention to documents of the early Society at the time of the formulation of the *Ratio Studiorum* of 1599, and in particular to the recommendations of Father Christopher Clavius, then mathematics professor at the Roman College, which dealt with promotion of the mathematical sciences in the Society as a means of aiding the Church in forming social reality (inculturation!). Decree 29 also significantly drew attention to the subsequent "Ordination on Training Mathematics Teachers," drafted by Father Robert Bellarmine in 1593 and promulgated by authority of Father General Claudio Aquaviva (SWR 1 [547] n. 1).[1]

Now, it should be noted that in the years subsequent to GC 31 there has been an impressive stream of historical studies of the influences of pre-Suppression Jesuit mathematicians and scientists on evangelization-inculturation in China, Europe, and the Americas. The contributions of Cosentino, Baldini, Grant, Crombie, Heilbron, Spence, Wallace, Homann, Lattis, Dear, Moyer, and so on, shed new light on the Jesuit program to deal with the faith-reason problems generated by the Galileo condemnation of 1633 and the subsequent materialist challenge of the eighteenth-century Enlightenment and Encyclopedists, as well as the evangelization opportunities offered by China's interest in Western science and mathematics.[2]

So there are paradigms in the pre-Suppression Society apostolate for our instruction today, even granted the pervasive changes within the disciplines themselves and the ambient university culture.

We shall return to them after hearing GC 31's exhortation that

> *those Jesuits, therefore, who are assigned to this work* [that is, university teaching and research] *by superiors are to give themselves entirely and with a strong and self-denying spirit to this work, which, in one way or another, makes demands upon the whole man. They are to be on guard against the illusion that they will serve God better in other occupations which can seem more pastoral, and they are to offer their whole life as a holocaust to God.* (SWR 2 [549])

Of course this powerful challenge also brings many dangers: intense specialization can isolate a Jesuit from the Society's other apostolic activities, and obscure the essential religious and priestly component of his life as he labors to develop human knowledge (SWR 2 [549]). These dangers can be acute in the highly specialized and often intensely individualistic work of the mathematical sciences. GC 34 adverts to these concerns, although it looks more to the universities (places of "serene and open search for and discussion of the truth") when it notes that "as Jesuits, we seek knowledge for its own sake" but adds, a bit awkwardly, that "[we] must regularly ask, 'Knowledge for what?'" (JUL 6 [409]).

So the problem of university-level scholarship and research, especially in the case of the mathematical sciences, involves both a focused, single-minded dedication to the discipline itself, and a counterpoint consideration of the apostolic use of the discipline. A Jesuit could get so involved in his mathematical research in and for itself that he becomes indistinguishable from a secular academic, a temptation that can be early intensified by the unrelenting demands made by the doctoral programs and peer competition in first-rate graduate schools, and later by the dedication needed for tenure and promotion at a Jesuit university. Such an orientation might accord a value to mathematical knowledge that makes it almost a religion. GC 31's challenge hardly has this scenario in mind. It does recognize that the knowledge of mathematics has value in itself: knowledge indeed perfects the knower. Additionally, the challenge recognizes that the Jesuit mathematician can be credible to his university colleagues, and the intellectual world in general, only if he has a genuine respect, competence, and love for the discipline. An effective, credible presence of the Church will not be had by university Jesuits in any discipline who do not "pay their dues" to the discipline. More concretely, such people may not get tenure, even in a Jesuit-sponsored university. "Publish or perish" has taken up residence in the schools.

Are There Apostolic Dimensions to Mathematics?

The Jesuit's goal, in short, is to maintain a professional level of intensity in the discipline, and at the same time to realize and develop its apostolic potentialities. But are there apostolic dimensions to the mathematical sciences? The General Congregations urge the Jesuit to discern whether these sciences are only logical abstractions in their theoretical divisions, and conveniently compact computational devices for the purposes of technology and statistical analysis of data in their applied modes. Or does mathematical theory touch truth, and do its uses involve moral considerations? Let us see.

APPLIED MATHEMATICAL SCIENCES: OPERATIONS RESEARCH

The moral dimensions and apostolic import of the applied mathematical sciences are readily found in the techniques collected as Operations Research and Optimization Theory, and drawn from algebra, geometry, statistics, and calculus. Basic ideas in Operations Research are regularly taught to first-year university students, and many schools offer specialized programs on both undergraduate and graduate levels. A typical Operations Research problem asks how to allocate limited resources so as to optimize a carefully identified payoff or profit, and, alternately, how to meet selected obligations at minimal cost. A system of equations, an idealized mathematical model to describe the real-life situation, is then proposed. The solutions to the system (the so-called feasible set) can be classified so as to indicate the optimal decision. That decision emerges entirely from the logic and structure of the mathematics, which necessarily embodies only what the mathematician designer judges to be operative in the situation—that is, an expendable resource or a desirable payoff. The model may not take account of human or ecological side effects that cannot be immediately accounted for and assigned quantitative value.

Operations Research is an immensely practical (and profitable) branch of mathematics. Improved algorithms procedure and solution rules for transportation and resource allocation problems can cut yearly costs by billions of dollars for agricultural conglomerates and multinational oil companies. These Operations Research methods are taught, along with other managerial decision methods, in business and mathematics programs at every level. Yet, perusal of the many available texts shows that there is little, if any, attempt made to advise would-be users of such decision processes that there can be side effects touching human lives and involving matters of justice that cannot be reduced to computable quantities.

GAME THEORY

University of Michigan professor and analyst of organizational and international conflict Anatol Rapoport, in particular, has brought these matters to our attention, most of all in connection with the use of the von Neumann–Morgenstern Theory of Games. Starting with the game of poker, von Neumann, the mathematician, and Morgenstern, the mathematical economist, devised a way to model a competition between two players with incomplete knowledge of the other's moves and resources, assuming that what one player won, the other lost—the so-called "zero sum game." Their idea was to develop a rational strategy to ensure that over the long run a player could optimize his "expected payoff" (in the terminology of mathematical probability theory).

Confined to poker, Game Theory is not of great moral concern. However, when it was used to model "games" between Cold War superpowers United States and Soviet Russia, we can then understand Rapoport's dismay at its role, even advisory, in the American decisions and moves of the Cuban Missile Crisis. Under government contract, the RAND Corporation, a California think tank, modeled the United States–Russian confrontation as a zero sum game with rational players making independent moves and responses to achieve chosen objectives. The goal, to be sure, was to aid American strategic military (and diplomatic) decision making in the confrontation. But the "game" was (possible) war, Rapoport observed, and how does one assign quantitative values to loss of human life and mutual nuclear destruction? Does one dead Cuban make one more live American?

Mathematical game theory has built-in ethical and moral assumptions that need to be surfaced before one employs its decision methods. Indeed, as Rapoport noted, "it is the shortcomings of game theory (as originally formulated) which force the consideration of the role of ethics, of the dynamics of social structure and of individual psychology in situations of conflict."[3] Operations Research, then, can serve as a paradigm for the apostolic dimension and ethical component found in the applied mathematical sciences. A competent Jesuit mathematical instructor can, and should, professionally discuss this aspect in all technical presentations, graduate and undergraduate, and influence colleagues teaching in political theory, business, and computer science programs to be aware that what they are teaching cannot be used without consideration of the larger contexts of justice and human welfare. Here too is a way to help implement GC 34's desire that our universities promote interdisciplinary work that comes from a "spirit of cooperation and dialogue among specialists within the university itself . . ." (JUL 10 [413]). We have a concrete example of an area "for research, teaching, and university extension services" where Jesuits in the mathematical sciences "can contribute to the transformation of society towards more profound levels of justice and freedom" (JUL 10 [413]). It can be an "appropriate arena for the encounter with the faith which does justice" (JUL 7 [410]).

Other less-dramatic areas in statistical interpretation of data and applied mathematics can be found that also have moral implications in their use and development. The cases are far, but not completely, removed from Clavius's apostolic use of applied mathematics in the 1582 Gregorian calendar reform or Roger Boscovich's development of geodesy to settle international boundary disputes or the efforts of early Jesuits in Peru and Brazil to teach the computations needed to determine the date of Easter.

MATHEMATICAL SCIENCES IN THEMSELVES: TRACES OF GOD

The applied mathematical sciences have apostolic and moral dimensions. But does mathematics per se show such characteristics? Is there any value, *ad maiorem Dei gloriam,* in the study of algebra or geometry for itself? Does knowledge of mathematics have direct bearing on our "service of faith, directed towards the justice of God's Kingdom" (SCM 16 [41]), a service that includes "proclamation of the Gospel, dialogue, and the evangelization of culture" (SCM 20 [48])?

It might seem not. How can the Quadratic Formula, the Pythagorean Theorem, or the Fundamental Theorem of Calculus speak of Truth, the Word Made Flesh, or the Sermon on the Mount? In practice, our schools and universities teach mathematics as a purely secular discipline, accessible to believers and nonbelievers alike, or at any rate to those who have some aptitude and willingness to apply themselves to this noble discipline. Is mathematics, *pace* Rapoport, value free, and even, if we are to believe mathematician David Hilbert and logician Kurt Gödel, at best the relatively consistent and free creation of the mathematician's imagination? Is mathematics, despite its intrinsic unity, only a formal logical system devoid of any truth content, as their school claims? Admittedly, most active mathematicians pay little attention to questions in the foundations and philosophy (or theology) of mathematics. They are quite content to solve differential equations or develop Riemannian geometry. Jesuit mathematicians could subscribe to this practice; quite likely some do. However, one should also be aware of a Catholic tradition that is more positive, and would claim the possibility of finding traces of God in the theorems, the theoria (insight), of mathematics. The reference, of course, is to the Pythagorean-Platonic tradition as it was interpreted by Clement of Alexandria and Augustine of Hippo, and developed by William of Saint-Thierry and the School of Chartres in the twelfth century.

William, for example, claims that "there are four kinds of reasoning that lead people to knowledge of the Creator, namely, the proofs (*probationes*) of arithmetic and music, or geometry and astronomy. They are to be employed succinctly in this theology, so that both the product of the Creator may be seen in things, and what we have proposed may be intelligently (*rationabiliter*) shown."[4] Geometry, in particular, provided a link between God and the world. Thierry discovered God in creation and explored the mystery of the Trinity in geometric images. Later, in the fifteenth century, Nicholas of Cusa made similar claims about the value of geometry for knowledge of God's attributes and actions: "I claim that because the only way available to us of coming to the divine is through symbols, it follows that we should be able to employ those of mathematics fittingly because of their incorruptible certitude."[5] For Nicholas, the Christian Platonist, geometry is "amor intellectualis Dei."

The tradition did not die with Nicholas. In the mid-twentieth century the charismatic Simone Weil was preoccupied with the Pythagorean-Platonic doctrine of means, or mediation, especially as it occurs in geometric mean proportionals. She started with Plato: "The most beautiful of bonds is that which, to the highest degree, renders itself one with the terms which are bound. It is geometrical proportion, which, by essence, is the most beautiful for such achievement (*Timaeus* 31c)." Weil gave an idiosyncratic interpretation of Plato's attempt to describe mediation between God and man: according to her, in the Incarnation the condition is truly realized when not only the first term, but the link or mean itself is God. She read this in the Johannine texts: "As the Father has sent me, so I send you," and "As the Father has loved me, so have I loved you." Weil asked: "May we suppose that it is because the Greeks saw in geometry the image of the Incarnation (divine images, reflections of reality) that they put into it the amount, the intensity of attention, or religious attention which enabled them to invent the method of demonstration (Logos)? What a staggering thought!" This suggests, and even demands from us a proportionate response: "To restore to science as a whole, (and to) mathematics, the sense of its origin and veritable destiny as a bridge leading to God, not by diminishing, but by increasing precision in demonstration, verification, and supposition, that would indeed be a task worth accomplishing."[6]

Indeed it would. Simone, whose brother André Weil is a world-class theoretical mathematician, was herself a mystic in search of God, a philosopher, and, at times, a social activist. She did not live to accomplish her project, but her concern for the transcendental dimension of classical mathematics was echoed by the Russian mathematician I. R. Shafarevitch, and others. A practicing Russian Orthodox Christian even during the Soviet years, he professed to see in the goal-directed independent growth of world mathematics traces of divine design and direction. In his 1973 Mathematics Prize acceptance address to the Göttingen Academy of Science, he explained how *one is struck by the idea that such a wonderfully puzzling and mysterious activity of mankind . . . must have some goal. . . . More than two thousand years of history have convinced us that mathematics cannot formulate for itself this final goal that can direct its progress. Hence, it must take it from outside. . . . I want to express a hope that . . . mathematics may serve now as model for the solution of the main problem of our epoch: to reveal a supreme religious goal and to follow the meaning of the spiritual activity of mankind."*[7]

Such ideas are not common fare, but neither is his voice a lone one.

Conclusion

But to return to GC 34, which, in effect, challenges Jesuits in the mathematical sciences to look on their discipline as more than an efficient support for technological development and data analysis, or even just as a regimen for training undergraduates to reason and to expound their ideas in clear and succinct form. Mathematics can do that, and this is reason enough to ground the apostolic and educational value of a Jesuit's dedication to university mathematics. Beyond this, Pythagoras, Plato, Augustine, William, Nicholas, Weil, Shafarevitch, and others insist that mathematics need not be a mere auxiliary device for human development. For those who cultivate that faculty of attention whose "highest point . . . makes contact with God," and who realize that "prayer consists of attention," as Weil puts it, for such people mathematics can and should be a light for the intellect, and one that is also a shadow of God. Mathematics does not replace prayer or the sacraments, but with them it can purify the soul. It is not a substitute for the spiritual and corporal works of mercy, but it can be a powerful aid to such Jesuit efforts.

Formal mathematics instruction in Jesuit-related universities will continue in the customary secular mode common to European and American faculties. Jesuit mathematicians will present (create? discover?) new theoretical results. And this can be consistent with the vision of GC 31–34, most of all when the pervasive ethical and moral dimensions of applied mathematics are carefully explored, and the transcendental aspect so dear to the Christian Platonist is attentively reverenced. The task GC 34 gives Jesuits is the ever present one of evangelization and inculturation, but at the same time of drawing from one's own intellectual resources new and old ways of searching for God in all things.

LAUS DEO SEMPER

1. See Frederick A. Homann, S.J., "Christopher Clavius and the Renaissance of Euclidean Geometry," *Archivum Historicum Societatis Iesu* 52 (1983): 233–46; "Institutio Mathematica in Scholis Societatis Iesu Saeculo Sextodecimo," *Hermes Americanus* II (1984): 120–21.

2. Giuseppe Cosentino, "Le matematiche nella 'Ratio Studiorum' della Compagnia di Gesù," *Miscellanea Storica Ligure,* Anno II (Nuova Serie periodica): n. 2, 1970; "L'insegnamento delle matematiche nei collegi Gesuitici nell'Italia settentrionale," *Physis* XIII (1971): Fasc. 2, 205–17.

    Ugo Baldini, *Legem impone subactis: studi su filosophia e scienza dei Gesuiti in Italia, 1540–1632* (Rome: Bulzoni, 1992).

    Edward Grant, "In Defense of the Earth's Centrality and Immobility: Scholastic Reaction to Copernicanism in the 17th Century," *Transactions of the American Philosophical Society* 74/4 (1984).

    A. C. Crombie, "Mathematics and Platonism in the Sixteenth Century Italian Universities and in Jesuit Educational Policy," in *Prismata Festschrift für Willy Hartner,* ed. Y. Maeyanea and W. G. Saltzer (Wiesbaden, 1977), 63–94.

    John Heilbron, *Elements of Early Modern Physics* (Berkeley, Calif.: University of California, 1982).

    Jonathan D. Spence, *The Memory Palace of Matteo Ricci* (New York: Viking, 1984).

    William A. Wallace, *Galileo and His Sources: The Heritage of the Collegio Romano in Galileo's Science* (Princeton, N.J.: Princeton University Press, 1984).

    Frederick A. Homann, S.J., "Faith and Reason in Roger Boscovich's Philosophy of Science," *Faith and Reason* XVIII (1992), 87–93.

    James M. Lattis, *Between Copernicus and Galileo: Christoph Clavius and the Collapse of Ptolemaic Cosmology* (Chicago, Ill.: University of Chicago Press, 1994).

    Peter R. Dear, *Discipline and Experience: The Mathematical Way in the Scientific Revolution* (Chicago, Ill.: University of Chicago Press, 1995), esp. ch. 3: "Experience and Jesuit Mathematical Science: The Practical Importance of Methodology."

    G. V. Coyne, S.J., M. A. Hoskin, and O. Pedersen, eds., "Gregorian Reform of the Calendar," *Proceedings of the Vatican Conference to Commemorate Its 400th Anniversary, 1582–1982* (Rome: Specola Vaticani, 1983).

3. Anatol Rapoport, *Fights, Games, and Debates* (Ann Arbor, Mich.: University of Michigan Press, 1970), xii.

4. Latin text in N. Haring, "The Creation and Creator of the World according to Thierry of Chartres and Clarenbaldus of Arras," *Archives d'histoire doctrinale et littéraire du moyen âge* XXII (1955): 194.

5. Nicolas Cusanus, *Opera omnia,* 14 vols., in *De docta ignorantia,* ed. Ernst Hoffmann and Raymond Klibansky (Leipzig, 1932), I, 11.

6. For an expanded development and source citations of Weil's papers, see Frederick A. Homann, S.J., "Mathematics and Prophecy: Faith and Reason in Simone Weil," *Faith and Reason* XI (1985): 264–79.

7. I. R. Shafarevitch, "Über Einigen Tendenzen in der Entwicklung der Mathematik," *Jahrbuch der Academie der Wissenschaften in Göttingen,* 1973; English excerpts in *The Mathematical Experience,* ed. P. J. Davis and R. Hersh (Boston, Mass.: Houghton Mifflin, 1981), 53–54.

On Being a Medical Geneticist in the Post–GC 34 Era

Robert C. Baumiller, S.J.

ABSTRACT

The author admits, in a rapid survey of his life as a Jesuit, that the documents of General Congregations have not been "of great moment" because "the effects of most decrees have little or no significance" for his life. He supports the "option for the poor" that recent congregations have stressed. He finds that the fear that the Society, in stressing that option, would downplay the importance of the intellectual apostolate has been put to rest by GC 34. The author details his complicated and productive life in medical genetics, especially his work as a pastoral counselor of patients who must make difficult moral choices where genetic disease is a factor. He brings all he is and all he has to offer to his work of service of the Lord.

Apologia

In 1959 I was a scholastic in my sixth year as a Jesuit. In this post-Sputnik era many of us who were scientifically orientated did our doctoral work before our study of theology (the theory being that age and experience enhanced humanistic studies so they could wait; on the other hand, time lessened scientific creativity and the industry needed at the lab bench, so we needed to get trained in these studies early!). I had the advantage of doing graduate work along with the study of philosophy, and so was able to attain the Ph.D. in June of my second year (1961) of what would have been my program of Regency, the period between the study of philosophy and theology. Perplexed at what to do with me and not wanting me to go to our program in theology early, the Society sent me to the University of Wisconsin for a postdoctoral year in the Department of Human Genetics.

During this year I was asked to counsel the abbot of Saint John's College in Minnesota on the practicality of accepting a young man into the Benedictine Abbey at Collegeville. The potential novice's mother had just delivered her eighth child at the University of Wisconsin Hospital where she was brought from an institution where she was being cared for because of advancing Huntington's disease. Huntington's disease is a dominantly inherited condition with late onset and neurological degenerative progression to death over an eight- to ten-year period. The question for the abbot was, "Do you accept into the monastery someone with a 50 percent risk of having the gene?" The onset could be a month or forty years away (average onset is at about thirty-five to forty years of age). Special care would be needed and for a long time. (There were only statistical estimates available at that time; no diagnosis could be made before onset of symptoms. The young man did not know his mother's diagnosis. Today DNA testing could designate not only if the young man would be affected but also at about what age. The ethical problems would be greater today than they were then.) I doubt if the Society would take that risk. The Benedictines did.

While at Collegeville I met with some of their monks in theology and philosophy studies and my natural question to them was, "What are you going to do after ordination?" As a Jesuit I and many of my classmates were already entered into or preparing to enter into a specific field, and those who weren't yet allowed to seek special training were chaffing at the bit to get started. The Benedictines wondered at my question. It was not one they had contemplated. The path they take is one of waiting to be called. The abbot and his consultants decide on the needs of the community and on who has what abilities and what interests, and then call in the monk and tell him that he has been chosen, for example, to go to Harvard and get a doctorate in English.

The somewhat singular approach of Jesuits to search out and to accomplish whatever their capabilities will allow is and was a major factor in my attraction to the Society and our form of religious life. It has become clear to me in an ever-growing way that the only thing I have to give to the Lord and to society in general is myself and whatever talents I may have.

There are different ways of making this offering: passively, as our Benedictine brothers might, or aggressively, as is our Jesuit charism. (My favorite example comes from the Christmas story of the cold, starving juggler who is nursed back to health in the dead of winter at a medieval monastery. From the back of the chapel he sees the monks bringing the fruit of their year's labor to present as a symbolic gift at the manger: a tapestry, vestments, a book copied and/or illustrated. Yet he has nothing! Finally he unfolds his rug and juggles before the delighted Christ child. How terrible a deprivation if he had never been invited to juggle!) So we Jesuits do what we do as best we can. The result measured in overall accomplishment has been excellent, producing a Joe Fitzmyer, a Scripture scholar without peer, and a Walter Ciszek or a Horace McKenna, exemplary pastors to the poor and lost. Each of us with our lesser talents is buoyed up by their excellence.

This rather long introduction and *Apologia* is, I suppose, aimed at the fact that the documents of General Congregations have not been of great moment to me in the past, although they have not been of no moment. Ours is a complicated and yet simple life. All of us have our special area of activity where we spend the bulk of our working time. For me this includes research, a great deal of reading (never enough time to keep up with journals, etc.), writing, teaching, and interacting with patients, colleagues, and students. Then there is time put aside for quiet, for prayer, for Mass. All of these activities I see as actively apostolic. Add to these activities some time for recreation and companionship, and only time for sleep is left.

How much do I, as one who is involved in a single, consuming area of the approved and encouraged apostolates, need to know about the overall governance of the Society, and about its concern about its identity in today's world, and the Society's future allocation of funds and human resources? One needs to know something, of course. Otherwise one becomes totally isolated from the concerns of the body of which he is a part. I want to applaud and support new ways of serving and witnessing within our world. So I read, at least in part, documents issued by the Congregation, and enter into discussion within community, but because I am not directly planning for the formation of new Jesuits or allocating funds toward selected apostolic endeavors, the effects of most decrees have little or no significance for my present life.

The center of the last several congregations and reiterated in the 34th is the Society's call for the "basic option for the poor." The founding of the Fundus Apostolicus Caritativus S.I. in 1976 made practical this option. This program is carried out at higher levels than the individual; it is also a program to which Jesuits in general contribute. The need for social awareness at every moment of history is important; no scholar, however committed to a field, should be out of touch with the reality surrounding him or her. One should support those who are immediately active in bringing about social change that recognizes the dignity and value of each individual.

There has been some concern that the Society was turning from its educational role to a directly social one, working with the people at the community level to bring about change. This concern, namely that our young men would dedicate themselves to peace and justice, to community organizing, and to other social enterprises and forsake the intellectual apostolate, is a concern that has come and gone. GC 34, while replete with the need for standing with the poor and repressed, also goes out of its way again and again to recognize how valuable and germane the intellectual apostolate is. I personally have had the privilege of having four young Jesuits spend time in my laboratory—one as a novice, two as scholastics, and one after ordination—and all four have gone on to finish or are finishing doctorates in genetics or allied biological fields. The list of young men in special studies remains substantial. Any fear that we may become unidimensional should be put to rest. The old joke about the things God doesn't know ends self-servingly with "what a Jesuit will do next." That spirit of adventure still exists, and we have a broad enough vision to allow the competent, inspired, aware person to venture into new and different waters—social, artistic, scientific, theologic, and so on.

The documents of the General Congregations are my documents, after all. My representative goes and reflects in some way my own opinion. The delegates reflect for the Society what can be said institutionally about today's concerns. They must adhere to a political correctness that certainly keeps them far more conservative than many of us whom they represent. But they do an excellent job, and in doing so, set goals for many religious groups in the Church.

Life in Medical Genetics

The life of a Jesuit who is a medical geneticist is and has been interesting. What someone with that vocation does is widely variable. The field has grown exponentially since I became interested more than forty years ago. During my study in theology at Woodstock, Maryland, I was funded by the federal government (Atomic Energy Commission and the National Institutes of Health) to carry on basic research, and so set up laboratories and hired technicians to work in the basement of the old "Science Building." I spent Thursday holiday at Johns Hopkins Hospital, Department of Medicine, Division of Human Genetics. After theology and another postdoctoral year I moved to Georgetown Medical School. At Georgetown basic research continued, and patient-oriented laboratory testing and genetic counseling began to fill the days. The founding of the Kennedy Institute of Bioethics and activity at the national level began to take more time away from the laboratory. In the beginning I and a technician made up the Division of Genetics. By 1990 there were seven professionals and twenty technicians, all supported by grants or funds that I could raise. In the mid-1980s I became founding director of the National Center for Maternal and Child Health, which continues to flourish to this day and now has more than thirty professionals and staff.

For most of my professional lifetime, there was no Catholic priest or religious in the field of medical genetics. Today there is one clinical geneticist who worked with me as a Jesuit scholastic but who left the Society during medical studies. He is active in the field. A Carmelite who did his doctorate with me and who is an excellent teacher is boarded as a clinical cytogeneticist and a medical geneticist as I am, but he rarely attends national meetings. He has an excellent reputation in his home city, Rochester, New York. There is a Jesuit who worked with us at Georgetown. He graduated with his Ph.D. in 1996, and is already making a name at Loyola University Chicago for his ethical opinions in medical genetics. Another Jesuit who worked with us as a novice is finishing his doctorate at Stanford in human molecular genetics. Yet another young Jesuit who spent scholastic time with us is finishing his doctorate in biology at Georgetown. He has interests in genetics but is not specializing in the field. A wonderful lady who was a religious also did her doctoral work in my laboratory. She is presently teaching and administering a good college department of biology in western Maryland. She attends human genetics meetings and is looking to publish a book of genetic conditions presented in art through the ages. Then there is a Paulist who, while getting his Ph.D. in biochemistry at The Catholic University of America, came regularly to our medical genetics seminars and became interested in genetic counseling. He is finishing an M.S. degree in genetic counseling in California in order to qualify for the boards.

There are two Methodist ministers who are active in the field, one at Indiana University and one at Georgetown. Frank Seydel had a Ph.D. in biochemistry and was teaching organic chemistry in Wichita, Kansas, when I was able to persuade him to come to Georgetown and do biochemical testing on bloods and amniotic fluid to determine the well-being of the fetus. He has become an eloquent spokesman on genetic issues in his church and for Protestants in general. With his incorporation into our group we presented a far more ecumenical face.

For many years I have had the privilege of being the only Catholic priest in this fast-moving area, filled with ethical and moral problems. There were and are many Catholics on the professional level who take some encouragement from my professional activity in the field, some of whom may not have entered an area where selective abortion and reproductive technology are part of everyday discussion, or who may have had greater difficulty reconciling their faith and these works and professional interests. It is interesting that many religious Jews and Protestants are likewise pleased to have someone like myself active in a field to which they are contributing. Then there are those many professionally trained ex-Catholics who felt that no priest could ever understand their concerns.

CLINICAL MEDICAL GENETICS

Medical genetics in its clinical manifestation likewise has the patient dimension. The patient in medical genetics is not only the affected child or adult but the whole family, even the extended family. Genetic disease is a special category because its effect is often felt in newborns and young children. The condition of the child is not one caused by a rare, chance situation that occurred and that parents were powerless to avert, but where the parent or parents were the cause. As a geneticist in the Department of Obstetrics and Gynecology at Georgetown University, I constantly saw individuals and couples who were deciding to marry or not, to have children or not, whether to use some reproductive technology to avoid their natural high risk of having an affected child, or whether to continue a pregnancy when serious problems had been discovered *in utero.*

These and other problems, such as paternity, called for presentation of all the scientific information available and all the listening, counseling, and empathizing skills one can muster. Pastoral experience was of the greatest help in making me effective in this most secular (and sacred) of occupations. Those who suffer the anguish of discovering serious problems with their unborn child need special help. This is their child, and yet they have a choice to be heroic and undertake and consciously accept a lifetime of special care, or to cause the death of their child by termination. In many institutions termination is encouraged and continuation is rare. Supporting those who can continue is difficult, helping those who suffer the grief and loss and guilt of termination is particularly challenging, and reconciliation after termination is the most challenging circumstance I have ever experienced. The greatest difficulty is convincing the women that this too can be forgiven.

The lack of pastoral understanding around modern genetics is evident. Every pregnancy among those who have regular prenatal care is offered testing that has ethical and moral consequences. Fifteen percent of pregnancies result in miscarriage or stillbirth, largely ignored by clergy even among those most staunchly pro-life. We lack experience for caring for families with special children at their birth and during their growing years.

In 1981 I convened a meeting of representatives of all the faith groups I could persuade to come to Washington. With the support of the March of Dimes–Birth Defects Foundation, a conference called "Genetic Decision Making and Pastoral Care" was held. Muslim, Jewish, and at least seven Christian denominations were represented. Since that time I have done one-, two-, and three-day conferences in more than forty cities for clergy and health workers. Generally they are interfaith or ecumenical, but a few were presented to single-faith groups.

As one becomes more senior in this exciting and ever-expanding field, one's role changes. As chair of the ethics committee of a national group of care providers heavily identified with state health departments, I have been able to produce a Code of Ethical Principles for Genetic Professionals (Hippocrates never worked with a committee!). This code was unanimously adopted by the 100+ voting delegates at a steering committee meeting and published with an explication in the *American Journal of Medical Genetics*.[1] Continuing committee work includes a National Institutes of Health Drug Monitoring Board for a drug being tested on pediatric patients with sickle-cell anemia, a genetic disease frequent in the African American population.

As a medical geneticist I try to share the multidimensional aspects of this field with my students who now number some ten seniors and juniors who elect to study "Medical Genetics and Its Implications" here at Xavier University in Cincinnati. It is always a joy for those of us who teach to have a student elect to enter the field to which we are dedicated. One of my mainly medical school–bound students this year elected graduate work in human genetics and genetic counseling at the University of Cincinnati. I continue my work at the University of Cincinnati with the university's human geneticist in the biology department, with the division of medical genetics in pediatrics, and with the genetic counseling program.

Reading carefully the decrees of GC 34, I find numerous segments that affirm what I do, but then any Jesuit who reads this essay might smile and say that I would find affirmation even if little were intended. Nonetheless, this is the way I juggle, this is what I have to offer at the manger. I was fortunate in finding the Society and the superiors who have allowed me to do what I do. Each of us brings his limited talents. We pray that they may be accepted, for it is all we have to give. Their value is not in the grandiosity of the accomplishment but in the simplicity of the giving.

ENDNOTES • BAUMILLER

1. Robert C. Baumiller, S.J., et al., "Code of Ethical Principles for Genetics Professionals." Council of Regional Networks for Genetic Services. Adopted April 15, 1994. *American Journal of Medical Genetics* 65 (1996): 177–78; "Code of Ethical Principles for Genetics Professionals: An Explication": 179–83.

Jesuit Hospitality?

James F. Keenan, S.J.

ABSTRACT

The author focuses on the distinctive Jesuit understanding of hospitality where Jesuit spirituality is integrated into the Jesuit mission. Jesuit hospitality is found in going out throughout the world "to those most in need," such as the marginalized, who are present even on our campuses, to invite them "into God's world." Jesuit hospitality is a reflection of God's love and mercy toward humanity, and finds its identity not so much in the traditional way in the receiving Church as in the "sending Church" and its "exemplars," such as "the Good Samaritan."

Moreover, beneath the renewal of our law is a reverence for persons, an effort to make law serve the lived experience of Jesuits, to help the community of the Society become more united in its witness to the Gospel and in its labor. . . . While the term was rarely used, GC 34 was touching upon the Christian virtue of hospitality, of making the Society a symbol of welcome—to the poor, to lay people, to those searching for meaning, to those who want to talk seriously about religious issues. (Decree 1: "United with Christ on Mission" 11 [11])

The assertion that Christian hospitality is the ethical virtue underlying the documents of GC 34 is of incredible significance and deserves sustained consideration. Scripture scholars and church historians have recently studied the virtue and discovered the critical role it played in distinguishing Christianity and its rise. Christian ethicists have reflected on this new data and recognize the normative significance of the apostolic and early Church practice of hospitality. Moreover, reexamining the foundations of Ignatian spirituality reveals a wonderful congruency between apostolic practices of hospitality and the early dynamism of the Society's mission. Finally, these insights together suggest a very distinctive contribution that the Society of Jesus could make both to contemporary spirituality and moral theology in interpreting and promoting this important practice. For that reason, I will pursue these topics in this essay.

Contemporary Research on Hospitality in Scripture, Church History, and Moral Theology

In the field of ethics, hospitality emerges particularly out of scriptural and early Church studies. The Hebrew Bible opens with God creating the first man and woman, placing them in the Garden and giving them all that they need. Whether God walks in the Garden with them or protects them in their exile or, later, leads the descendants of Abraham into the promised land, the God of the Hebrew Bible tends to our needs as a host ministers to a guest. The divine practice of hospitality becomes normative for God's chosen people and is rewarded when, for instance, Abraham welcomes the Lord at Mamre (Gn 18:1–15), Lot provides sanctuary to the angelic guests (Gen 19), Joseph hosts his brothers (Gn 45:4–15), the wealthy woman of Shumen greets Elisha (2 Kgs 4:8–17)[1] and Rahab hides the messengers of Joshua (Jos 2:1–21; 6:17). Because hospitality is normative, any act of inhospitality is an offense to God; nowhere is the offense more clearly described than in the destruction of Sodom (Gn 18:16ff.).[2]

The hospitality of God in the Garden contrasts evidently with the inhospitality of humanity toward Jesus. From start to finish Jesus is rejected and reviled; yet, he is the paradigm of hospitality,[3] whether at Cana (Jn 2:1–11), the Last Supper, or on the beach (Jn 21:4–12). His dying words are themselves an act of hospitality as he assures the good thief of a place of welcome in the world to come (Lk 23:43).

Just as Abraham and his descendants practiced an *imitatio Dei* in their exercise of hospitality, so Christians in the new dispensation practiced an *imitatio Christi.* Wayne Meeks remarks that "the specifically Christian beliefs about Jesus' actions and God's actions through him affected the shape of their moral discourse in a number of ways."[4] One of those ways is hospitality. As in the case of Sodom, the most severe judgment in the New Testament (damnation) is for the inhospitable: whether the rich man who ignored Lazarus (Lk 16:19–31) or those at the Last Judgment (Mt 25:31–46). Jesus does not simply warn us with parables, rather he constantly admonishes those closest to him when they are inhospitable as when they try either to keep the children away (Mk 10:13–16; Mt 19:13–15; Lk 18:15–17) or to send his listeners away hungry (Mk 6:32–44; 8:4–10; Mt 14:13–21; Lk 9:11–17; Jn 6:1–14). In fact, the clearest admonition against inhospitality is directed against Martha for her constant complaining (Lk 10:38–42).[5] Ironically, this passage was long considered (wrongly) an endorsement of the contemplative life, but contemporary writers see in Martha's failure to be hospitable an occasion to reinforce the message of the previous parable of Jesus: the Good Samaritan, the quintessential story of welcoming (Lk 10:29-37). Major theologians from Augustine to the Venerable Bede have commented on this parable's evident Christological structure in which the Samaritan is Christ who encounters the wounded stranger, the exiled Adam, lying on the road outside the city that is Paradise and bears him to the inn that is the Church, where he pays, that is, redeems him and promises to return. The Good Samaritan parable is a story of Christ as the hospitable one who brings us into the Church as a temporary shelter where we await his return.[6]

Hospitality is not simply found in the Gospels. For the itinerant Paul and his coevangelizers, hospitality has a special significance. Throughout his letters we find concrete accounts of the hospitality that he, Timothy, Titus, and others receive (Phlm 22; Rom 16:1–2, 23; 1 Cor 4:17; 16:10–11; 2 Cor 8:16–24; Phil 2:19–23). That hospitality extends into a Philippian financial support group for Paul and his co-workers as they preach in other provinces (2 Cor 11:8–9; Phil 1:5). In particular, the Corinthians are especially praised by Clement I for their hospitality (1 Clem 1:2; 10:37; 11:1; 12:1,3).

The accounts of hospitable practices are paralleled by summons to hospitality that are fairly pervasive in early Christian texts. The Letter to the Hebrews admonishes the reader "Do not neglect hospitality, for by this means some have unwittingly hosted angels" (13:2). In the *Shepherd of Hermas* (38.10) hospitality is promoted as prominent among the Christian virtues. In endorsing hospitality, the early Church identified itself both with the guest preacher and the hosting local community and in both cases considered them "resident aliens" as the Letter of Rome to the Corinthians notes in its opening verse. Likewise, the Letter to the Hebrews reminds us that "we have no enduring city, but we await one that is coming" (Heb 13:14). In turn, this identity led to a sensitivity to all "aliens," as Justin wrote in his *Apology* (1 Apol 67.6).[7]

Hospitality, then, is deeply tied to Christian identity: the patron who hosts welcomes the guest who brings news of the real homeland. This insight played out significantly in the earliest development of the Church, as both a sending and a receiving Church, for the Church that sent out its missionaries knew that the local church would receive them. That local church was little more than an assembly (*ekklesia*) gathered in some patron's home, on whose hospitality the *ekklesia,* in turn, depended. As the *ekklesia* grew, it did so in its ability to receive guests-members.[8] In time, the Church itself took over the role of patron and served as host; that turn from individual to communal patron finally led to the appointment of a bishop for the local church who then served as the community's leader now exercising the hospitality that an individual patron once performed (1 Tim 3:2; Tit 1:8; *Hermas* 104.2).[9]

We cannot overestimate the role that hospitality had in the rise of Christianity. In his brilliant new book, Rodney Stark argues that "Christianity was an urban movement, and the New Testament was set down by urbanites."[10] But those urban areas were dreadful; he describes the conditions as "social chaos and chronic urban misery."[11] This was in part a result of the population density. At the end of the first century, Antioch's population was 150,000 within the city walls, or 117 persons per acre. New York City has a density of 37 persons per acre overall, and Manhattan with its high-rise apartments has 100 persons per acre.[12] Moreover, contrary to early assumptions, Greco-Roman cities were not settled places whose inhabitants descended from previous generations. With high infant mortality and short life expectancy, these cities required "a constant and substantial stream of new-comers" in order to maintain their population levels. As a result, the cities were comprised of strangers.[13] These strangers were well treated by Christians[14] who, again contrary to assumptions, were anything but poor.[15] Through a variety of ways of caring for newcom-ers, financially secure Christians welcomed the newly arrived immigrant.

Moreover, their religion was new. Certainly, ethical demands were imposed by the gods of the pagan religions. But these demands were substantively ritual; they were not neighbor-directed. In addition, while pagan Romans knew generosity, that generosity did not stem from any divine command. Thus a nurse who cared for a victim of an epidemic knew that her life might be lost; if she were a pagan, there was no expectation of divine reward for her generosity; if she were a Christian, this life was but a prelude to the next where the generous were united with God.[16]

Moreover, while the Romans practiced generosity, they did not promote mercy or pity. Because mercy implied "unearned help or relief," it was considered a contradictory of justice. Roman philosophers opposed mercy. "Pity was a defect of character unworthy of the wise and excusable only in those who have not yet grown up. It was an impulsive response based on ignorance."[17] Stark adds:

This was the moral climate in which Christianity taught that mercy is one of the primary virtues—that a merciful God requires humans to be merci-ful. Moreover, the corollary that because *God loves humanity, Christians may not please God unless they* love one another *was something entirely new. Perhaps even more revolutionary was the principle that Christian love and charity must extend beyond the boundaries of family and tribe, that it must extend to "all those who in every place call on the name of our Lord Jesus Christ" (1 Cor. 1:2). . . . This was revolutionary stuff. Indeed, it was the cultural basis for the revitalization of a Roman world groaning under a host of miseries.*[18]

Elsewhere Stark summarizes:

Christianity revitalized life in Greco-Roman cities by providing new norms and new kinds of social relationships able to cope with many urgent urban problems. To cities filled with the homeless and impoverished, Christianity offered charity as well as hope. To cities filled with newcomers and strangers, Christianity offered an immediate basis for attachments. To cities filled with orphans and widows, Christianity provided a new and expanded sense of family.[19]

Meeks and Stark along with many other recent scholars direct us to hospitality as one of the key identifiable traits of early Christians. These studies are congruent with the work of contemporary ethicists who, likewise, turn their interests to hospitality, though often unaware of the data from early Church studies.[20] Thomas Ogletree, for instance, has invoked a variety of philosophical thinkers to awaken the Christian ethicist to the importance of hospitality.[21] Stanley Hauerwas has claimed that the primary ethical task for the Church is to live the Gospel narrative as authentically as possible. The Church, says Hauerwas, is not to preach to the world, but rather is to embody in itself the life of Christ. Thus, rather than being both the sending and receiving Church, Hauerwas's *ekklesia* is singularly receiving and thus hospitality becomes an acutely important virtue.[22] More recently, Christine Pohl takes a critical look at hospitality and analyses the power inequities that occur in any guest/host relationship. But Pohl turns to the Scriptures and discovers in both the Hebrew and Christian Bibles that often the host was once an alien and thus understands the normative significance of being marginal.[23] She captures what so many who write about hospitality miss:[24] that the host must understand the perspective of the alien and that this was precisely the richness of hospitality in both Bibles.

The mention of hospitality in GC 34 is, then, an extraordinarily enlightened one. This virtue plays a critical role in our understanding of God and of Jesus Christ and in the growth of the Church. Likewise it has caught the attention of moral theologians and those interested in New Testament ethics because it provides a normative description of moral conduct that embodies distinctively Christian features. This is an important congruence of data and claims, because currently many moral theologians are looking for ways of expressing the relationship between Christian spirituality and moral theology.[25] Thus the Congregation's writers, in choosing hospitality, pick a virtue that defines us spiritually, ethically, and ecclesially. What we must now do is ask whether that selection is in fact suitable given our identity, our history, and our own particular spirituality.

Roots for Jesuit Hospitality?

The Congregation's identification of hospitality as key for understanding its documents might strike some readers as certainly peculiar, for regardless of the many charisms associated with the Society of Jesus, hospitality is not one of, say, the first dozen descriptions that come to mind. Generally the Society's character is described by evangelization, missiology, ministry, justice, education, advocacy, discernment, spiritual direction, and the service of faith. Hospitality is rarely mentioned.

Recently we see attempts to correct this. For instance, describing his community, Ed Oakes writes in the recent Missouri Province newsletter *Panorama* about "the old joke about Jesuit hospitality. But we here at Regis have had a Benedictine conversion: the Jesuit community has decided to give over the best room in the house to guests." That issue of *Panorama* was solely dedicated to hospitality and profiled the provincial's exhortation that hospitality "is to be a central feature of Jesuit life and a privileged moment in our apostolic mission."

Is this what the Congregation fathers had in mind when they highlighted hospitality? Were they issuing a Benedictine corrective to contemporary Jesuit social practices? Certainly, Jesuits need to be more hospitable, and certainly the Missouri Province, along with other provinces, is right in calling its members to a new realization of their responsibilities for guests. I do not want in any way to diminish new efforts to welcome guests into our community, but was the Congregation really trying to introduce something rooted in Benedictine spirituality as the key for understanding the twenty-six documents? Was the Congregation, by giving a priority to hospitality, directing our spirituality and our practices to a more domesticated and monastic way of life? I think not.

In order to understand the Congregation's claim, we need to locate it within the context of Jesuit identity and spirituality. That identity is caught up in its mission. Whether it is the "First Principle and Foundation" or the *Constitutions,* Jesuit identity is not shaped by where we live but rather by what we do. *The Formula of the Institute* explains in two sentences what we are about:

> *He is a member of a Society founded chiefly for this purpose: to strive especially for the defense and propagation of the faith and for the progress of souls in Christian life and doctrine, by means of public preaching, lectures, and any other ministration whatsoever of the word of God, and further by means of the Spiritual Exercises, the education of children and unlettered persons in Christianity, and the spiritual consolation of Christ's faithful through hearing confessions and administering the other sacraments. Moreover, he should show himself ready to reconcile the estranged, compassionately assist and serve those who are in prisons or hospitals, and indeed to perform any other works of charity, according to what will seem expedient for the glory of God and the common good.*[26]

This extraordinarily extroverted identity of being missioned to the unlettered, the estranged, the imprisoned, and the hospitalized, in a contemporary word to the "marginalized," gives a sense of the type of hospitality to which the contemporary Jesuit is called. If there is no notion of community, of household, of home, whence the hospitality? This is no small problem. If we do not reflect on the nature of our communities, how can we reflect on the nature of our hospitality? For instance, in the recent bibliography of publications in English written in this century on the history of the Jesuits, the 743 entries are divided into six major headings: History, Institute, Spirituality, Pastoral Activities, Cultural and Educational Activities, and Jesuit Images. Not one major heading is dedicated to our community or domestic life. In fact, of the forty subheadings only one is partially dedicated to community, and that entry reads under Spirituality: "Apostolic Community, Priesthood."[27]

Jesuit identity is found in its apostolic mission. That mission is to go anywhere. The *Constitutions* are quite clear about this. Ignatius writes, *"Our vocation is to travel through the world and to live in any part of it where there is hope of greater service to God and of help of souls"* (*Const* [304], p. 128). In the preamble of part 4 we read, *"The aim and end of this Society is, by traveling through the various parts of the world at the order of the supreme vicar of Christ our Lord or of the superior of the Society itself, to preach, hear confessions, and use all the other means it can with the grace of God to help souls"* (*Const* [308], p. 130).[28] Reflecting on these texts, Brian Daley remarks that "every Jesuit, just by being a Jesuit, shares in a brotherhood that is essentially international, intercultural, and commits himself to an essentially international apostolate." Then, Daley adds this astute observation: "The central image of the Jesuit St. Ignatius seems to have had in his own mind, right up to his death, was that of a kind of apostolic vagabond."[29] How can an "apostolic vagabond" be hospitable?

Daley's own writings reflect the influence of John O'Malley. Earlier O'Malley examines the fourth vow "in its historical context"[30] and convincingly demonstrates that the fourth vow means that we can be missioned wherever the pontiff wills (*Const* [605], pp. 276, 278). O'Malley answers the question: "What does the fourth vow mean?" "It is guarantor of that mobility 'for the greater good of souls' for which the order was founded. It is symbol of the universal mission of the Society, which extends, like the papal *cura* itself and under its inspiration, 'to the ends of the earth.'"[31] The fourth vow that so identifies the Jesuit serves then as a guarantor of our mobility! How then is a mobile, apostolic vagabond hospitable?

O'Malley develops his insights on early Jesuit mobility by studying Nadal's understanding of the Jesuit vocation. There he captures Nadal's appreciation of the breadth of Jesuit mission. In 1554 Nadal writes: "It must be noted that in the Society there are different kinds of houses or dwellings. These are: the house of probation, the college, the professed house, and the journey—and by this last the whole world becomes our house."

Nadal's identification of our ministry with our domicile is striking for he reverses what earlier religious founders do: ministry does not expand from Jesuit community; rather, community occurs where Jesuit ministry is. In 1561, Nadal writes: "There are missions, which are for the whole world, which is our house. Wherever there is need or greater utility for our ministries, there is our house." We live wherever those in need live.

In Nadal's writings we find a reason why the Society writes and reflects so rarely on Jesuit communities and Jesuit houses. Eloquently he describes Jesuit identity:

> *The principal and most characteristic dwelling for Jesuits is not in the professed houses, but in journeyings. . . . I declare that the characteristic and most perfect house of the Society is the journeys of the professed, by which they diligently seek to gain for Christ the sheep that are perishing. And this is indeed the distinctive mark of our vocation: That we accept from God and the orthodox Church the care of those for whom nobody is caring, even if there actually is somebody who ought to be caring for them. . . . It is hence that the Society seems somehow to imitate the condition of the Church of the Apostles, in our humility in Christ.*

Jesuit identity is found in journeying toward "those for whom nobody is caring." O'Malley comments that Nadal's description of this journeying as "apostolic" is not casually made, "but with the understanding that in his day the Society was recovering an aspect of the primitive Church."[32] He adds "Like so many of his contemporaries, he seems to have had a sense that the primitive Church was in some way being reborn in his own day." The Society's self-identification of being on mission intentionally reflects the early apostolic sending Church. As Nadal writes in 1557, a year after the death of Ignatius: "Our vocation is similar to the vocation and training of the Apostles: first, we come to know the Society, and then we follow; we are instructed; we receive our commission to be sent; we are sent; we exercise our ministry; we are prepared to die for Christ in fulfilling those ministries."[33]

In summary: our mission is to go to those most in need; we meet them as apostles of the Church; where they are we dwell; and, from that dwelling place, we support those in need.

That journeying forth to meet those in need is, then, an act of hospitality. Jesuit hospitality is then strikingly different from the notion of hospitality we have been examining. For hospitality, even in the early Church was always as a receiving Church, whether it was the patron hosting the *ekklesia* or the *ekklesia* hosting either the apostolic preachers or later the neighbor in need. In all instances, the host was in her domicile. But Jesuit hospitality is not found in its receiving, but in its sending. As one "in the Church" and "in the world" the Jesuit goes to those on the margins of society to welcome them into the Church by preaching, catechizing, and confessing or into the wider society by education or social ministry. If the world is our home as Nadal proclaimed and if our mission is to those "who are perishing," then our call is to bring them into sanctuary.

This journeying forth then is central for understanding Jesuit identity. It is rooted in the *Spiritual Exercises,*[34] where one becomes, as Howard Gray rightly claims, *homo viator,* a person on a journey. Gray writes: "For that reason, I have long felt that the biblical theme of hospitality ought to play a far more important role in the effort to translate the Exercises authentically into the experiences of post-modern retreatants."[35]

The *Exercises* begin with the invitation to reflect on how marginalized we actually are by sin. The first meditation of the first week considers the effects of sin on first the angels who lost heaven (*SpEx,* 50), then on Adam and Eve who lost Paradise (51), and then on myself (52). The effect of sin on those others is the loss of their homeland. Subsequently in turning to myself I likewise "consider my whole composite being as an exile here on earth" (47). Being homeless is the experience of the sinner in the first week.

Geography is important in the *Exercises.* Ignatius wants us to see where we are, where we could be, where we deserve to be. The promise and the curse are localities. Geography becomes more important as the second week begins. After the reconciliation at the end of the first week we are brought to a new "mental representation of the place," that is, "the synagogues, villages, and towns where Jesus preached" (*SpEx,* 91). Here we are to listen to Christ the King as he speaks, "before whom is assembled the whole world" (95). "The whole world" appears then from Christ's perspective. This is reinforced next with a consideration of the Trinity as they look down upon the "whole expanse or circuit of all the earth, filled with human beings" (102). Here the representation of place is now the "great extent of the surface of the earth" (103). The rich first point of this mediation calls us to see first "those on the face of the earth," and then "the throne of the Divine Majesty" as they "look down upon the whole surface of the earth, and behold all nations in great blindness, going down to death and descending into hell" (106). Having been welcomed into discipleship, we see the whole world from the divine vantage point, a perspective thoroughly absent in the first week where we are exiled prisoners of our own sinfulness.

For the Nativity, we are invited to another mental representation of place: "the way from Nazareth to Bethlehem," that is, we are to see that Christ is born *on a road* outside of a town (*SpEx,* 112). Here in that place we are to "look upon them, contemplate them, and serve them in their needs" (114). This is the quintessence of hospitality. For we are to see how we have been rescued from eternal exile by one who has left his homeland to be in this world and who now is born as an exile from his own land and is an exile even among the people he intends to save. Precisely at this point, we are invited to minister to him: we are to be hospitable to him who is doing this for us! This is *imitatio Christi.*

Afterwards in the "Meditation on Two Standards" we are called to see the "great plain about the region of Jerusalem" (*SpEx,* 144) and to consider how "the Lord of all the whole world chooses so many . . . and sends them throughout the whole world" (145). The "whole world" appears in our mediation, but again, from the divine perspective. It is as if we can see the whole world only from the vantage point of the one who saves us.

Both the first and second weeks are shaped then by a dialect of place. On the one hand there is the divine perspective that repeatedly encompasses "the whole world." The divine point of view is absolutely and consistently universally inclusive. Yet the work of the redemption occurs in all the specificity of place that real history requires. That specific place is often either a fixed place from which Christ preaches or commissions or it is a road, like the one on which he was born.

In the third week there is no divine perspective. As "the divinity hides itself" (*SpEx,* 196), it is filled with specific movement. It begins with the exact same composition of place as the second: on a road, here "from Bethany to Jerusalem" (192). This is reinforced in the next mediation where we are to see the place that is the road "from Mt. Sion to the Valley of Josaphat" (202). The Way of the Cross is thematically caught from the beginning of the week's meditations. The one who labors for us journeys to his death and we are to follow him in the Exercises. The *homo viator* is Christ, our Redeemer and prototype.

By the fourth week, we are left finally free to see the Lord, who does not journey, but who appears and infuses particular places with his presence. We are no longer looking at the *homo viator.* But, in the "contemplation to attain the love of God," we finally see the homeland, "in the presence of God our Lord and of His angels and saints" (*SpEx,* 232). There the divine perspective returns as we see the whole "face of the earth" (236) again. As always, the divine vantage point is the same: an ability to see the need to go out to all the world.

Nadal's claim that the world is our home is deeply rooted in the Ignatian *Exercises.* The claim stems from a vision that is a divine one: it does not appear in the first week. In sin, all we see is loss. In the second week, we only glimpse the divine perspective as the Trinity plans our redemption and as Christ calls and commissions us. Otherwise the perspective is distinctively local. In the third week the divine perspective is hidden, and the distinctively local is almost always a road. Like the laborious, exiled birth, the passion begins on a road and ends outside of a town. The entire week is a painful movement in which not only is the journeyer without home, he is without town or village. Yet after the death and resurrection of Jesus the divine perspective of the "whole world" appears for us to see. Likewise a vision of the *patria* complements it: from that homeland we see the whole face of the earth.

Thus Nadal's vision of the whole world is not his imagination, but God's gratuitous gift. It is not a human dream, but an invitation to see the task of redemption from God's point of view: it is universal in its perspective, totally inclusive in its task, and always on the road in its most genuine manifestation.

To be on the road is to be with the one who suffered. To be outside the home, the village, or the town, to be with the exile, is to be the one whose divinity is hidden. Moreover, it is precisely in the movements of exile in Jesus' life that we are invited to serve Jesus: only in the cave where he is born or on the cross beyond the city walls.

Finally, by the end of the *Exercises* the world is no longer a threat. Before the conversion in the first week and before the divine initiative at the beginning of the second week, the world is a place where people are sinning. By the end of the *Exercises* the world is where God is working. The mission then to go out to all the ends of the earth, to embrace homelessness as Nadal suggests, is not so much a decision as an invitation, or better, a response to a commission, like the one the disciples received at the end of Matthew's Gospel (28:19).

The Distinctive Contribution of Jesuit Hospitality

Jesuit hospitality is, then, distinctive in that it is practiced in its sending and not in its receiving: it is practiced by pilgrims rather than by patrons. Yet, in that there is still an abiding identification with the early Church wherein all understood themselves as resident aliens. Still, the Jesuit's understanding of hospitality is found more in the itinerant Paul's actions than in the local churches. For Paul is welcoming his hosts into God's world. That insight must not be lost: our welcome is not into a particular domicile but into a world where God labors.

Read in this way, hospitality is clearly a hermeneutical key to the Jesuit documents. Whether it is interreligious dialogue, listening to women, promoting justice in the world, or ecumenism in the Church, we see ourselves as sent to welcome others into Christ's saving mission. We want those on the margins to be incorporated, those excluded to be included, those perishing to be rescued. Our model for Jesuit hospitality is not found, then, in the Benedictine monastery, though indeed there is much we could learn from that place. Rather, the model for Jesuit hospitality is the refugee camp. For we live where our ministry is and inasmuch as we go out to the whole world we are called especially to those who find no dwelling place in this world. Whether those refugees are without country or church, we go to meet them and welcome them into the world where God works. Where anybody in need is, there is our mission and our hospitality. Our hospitality is not then a domestic one, but a mobile one, mobile not because our communities are mobile, but because those whom we serve are found throughout the whole earth.[36]

This understanding of hospitality achieves at least four noteworthy tasks. First, it provides a way of integrating our spirituality with our mission. It grounds our mission in a discipleship model that seeks out the marginalized: we seek out those who are perishing because we know existentially what it means to be perishing. We are now vagabonds, but we walk through a world where through grace we now see God working. Into that world, and not the world where many are lost, we welcome those in need.

Second, as scriptural and early Church studies are highlighting the importance of hospitality, our contemporary intention to be hospitable locates our mission in apostolic models. Like Nadal, the Congregation fathers invite us to see yet again that our mission and identity have deep ecclesial, indeed "apostolic" roots.

Third, this notion of hospitality redefines a classic religious charism that was generally associated with practices within specific domiciles. One does not think ordinarily of hospitality on the road, but rather in one's home. But our practice of hospitality is on the road because that is where those in need are. We do not wait for them to come to us, rather we go to those who are in need and bring them into the world that is our home. It is our home because it is where God works. Whereas most notions of hospitality are identified with the receiving Church, we identify with the sending Church. Thus we do not look so much to Abraham, Lot, Rahab, Mary Magdalen, or the Corinthian Church as our exemplars, but rather the Good Samaritan.

Fourth, it offers a distinctive alternative not only to Benedictine, Franciscan, or Dominican hospitality, but also to those models of hospitality generally associated with the receiving Church. For instance, in Hauerwas' model, the newcomer is welcomed into an already existing order. As Pohl notes, in such a model it is not always clear how the guest is to become adjusted to an existing order and set of values. In that model the guest is often required to abandon his or her earlier ways in order to become incorporated in the new domicile. In the sending model, the vagabond meets the exile, and the former's world is hardly domesticated. It is rather simply defined as the place where God works.

The Distinctive Impact on Higher Education

If one at a Jesuit school of higher education reads the Congregation documents, then the reader might think that Jesuit hospitality ought to be made visible by the way one is received upon entering the local Jesuit community. Certainly, the reader would be right to expect that after GC 34, Jesuits would be more sensitive to guests whether in the dining room, parlor, or guest room. GC 34's emphasis on hospitality, however, is not found primarily in how Jesuits treat guests who enter their community. Rather, GC 34 prompts Jesuits to be more attentive to those on and beyond their campuses who are marginalized. Jesuits are to help people find hospitality not in Jesuit communities, but rather in the world in which our brothers and sisters live.

Our hospitality means, then, not that we stay in one place and welcome, but rather that we must go out and beyond to those who do not find the world a welcoming place. This does not mean that Jesuits working in higher education must suddenly abandon their apostolates and apply to the missions. It means, instead, that Jesuits must be attentive to those who are marginalized in the university community as well as those who live literally on the margins of the university.

Those who are marginalized on the campus could be persons who are shy and introverted, grieving, or recovering from addictions, among others. That is, Jesuits must be attentive to those whose personal struggles may make their accessing the university community difficult. Likewise, they must also be especially attentive to those students belonging to minority populations on our campuses: persons of color, homosexuals, persons with disabilities, among others. Because our local culture is so inhospitable to these persons, the Jesuits have a particular responsibility to be hospitable to them.

Our universities, moreover, are not in deserts but usually in urban areas. The incorporation of our universities into these cities then provides another context for hospitality. Jesuits have a particular obligation to extend themselves beyond the campus to their neighbors. Those especially on our borders must find that we enliven their world, rather than stand as a contrast to theirs. Jesuits must be sure that the university gates are not impenetrable barriers; they must ensure, instead, that the exchange between the two communities is a sharing of goods. In a word, the Jesuits must be among the guarantors of the quality of neighborliness in their environs.

Inasmuch as the Jesuit charism is so strikingly defined by its mission to go to those in need, the new accent on hospitality ought not to be understood as a call to appreciate and develop a more sensitive sense of domesticity. On the contrary, the new emphasis warns Jesuits against seeing the world as solely the place where they live; rather it calls them to be more attentive to where and how others live.

ENDNOTES • KEENAN

1. T. R. Hobbs, "Man, woman, and hospitality: 2 Kings 4:8–36," *Biblical Theology Bulletin* 23 (1993): 91–100; L. Gregory Jones, "The virtues of hospitality (2 Kgs 4:8–17; Lk 10:38–42)," *Christian Century* 109 (1992): 17–24.

2. Victor Matthews, "Hospitality and Hostility in Genesis 19 and Judges 19," *Biblical Theology Bulletin* 22 (1992): 3–11. See also his "Hospitality and Hostility in Judges 4," *Biblical Theology Bulletin* 21 (1991): 13–21.

3. See my essay, "Hospitality," in James F. Keenan, S.J., *Virtues for Ordinary Christians* (Kansas City, Mo.: Sheed and Ward, 1996), 106–11.

4. Wayne Meeks, *The Origins of Christian Morality* (New Haven, Conn.: Yale University Press, 1993), 87.

5. On Martha and Mary, see Mary Carboy, "Hospitality—Martha and Mary," *Review for Religious* 50 (1991): 387–89; Jones, "The virtues of hospitality"; and John Koenig, "New Testament Hospitality," *America* 155/17 (1986): 372. For other instances of inhospitality, see David Gowler, "Hospitality and Characterization in Luke 11:37–54," *Semeia* 64 (1994): 213–51.

6. On the parable as paradigm for religious life, see Howard Gray, "Shift in Theology," *Way Supplement* 65 (1989): 56–65, esp. 62–63.

7. Meeks, *The Origins of Christian Morality,* 104–6; *The First Urban Christians* (New Haven: Yale University Press, 1983), 109.

8. Ibid., *The Origins of Christian Morality,* 45–51.

9. Ibid., 106. See Abraham Malherbe, *Social Aspects of Early Christianity* (Baton Rouge, La.: Louisiana State University, 1977), 65–68.

10. Rodney Stark, *The Rise of Christianity: A Sociologist Reconsiders History* (Princeton, N.J.: Princeton University Press, 1996), 147.

11. Ibid., 156.

12. Ibid., 149–50.

13. Ibid., 156.

14. Stark narrates, for instance, the effect of Christian nursing during two epidemics in the first three centuries of the Christian era, *The Rise of Christianity,* 73–94.

15. Ibid., 28–47. See also Robin Scroggs, "The Social Interpretation of the New Testament," *New Testament Studies* 26 (1980): 164–79; Marta Sordi, *The Christians and the Roman Empire* (Norman, Okla.: University of Oklahoma Press, 1986).

16. Ibid., 88.

17. E. A. Judge, "The Quest for Mercy in Late Antiquity," in *God Who Is Rich in Mercy,* ed. P. T. O'Brien (Sydney: Macquarie University Press, 1986), 107–21 at 107. As quoted in Stark, *The Rise of Christianity,* 212.

18. Stark, *The Rise of Christianity,* 212.

19. Ibid., 161. On the new social solidarity that Christianity offered to those in strife, see also Jaroslav Pelikan, *The Excellent Empire: The Fall of Rome and the Triumph of the Church* (San Francisco, Calif.: Harper and Row, 1987), 21. See also John Elliott, *A Home for the Homeless: A Sociological Exegesis of 1 Peter, Its Situation and Strategy* (Philadelphia: Fortress, 1981).

20. Besides those below, see Henri Nouwen, *Reaching Out* (New York: Image, 1975); Parker Palmer, *A Company of Strangers* (New York: Crossroad, 1986); John Koenig, *New Testament Hospitality: Partnership with Strangers as Promise and Mission* (Philadelphia: Fortress, 1985); Julia Kristeva, *Strangers to Ourselves* (New York: Columbia University Press, 1991).

21. Thomas Ogletree, *Hospitality to the Stranger: Dimensions of Moral Understanding* (Philadelphia: Fortress, 1985).

22. Stanley Hauerwas, *A Community of Character* (Notre Dame, Ind.: University of Notre Dame Press, 1981).

23. Christine Pohl, "Hospitality from the Edge: The Significance of Marginality in the Practice of Welcome," in *Annual of the Society of Christian Ethics* (Boston, Mass.: Society of Christian Ethics, 1995), 121–36.

24. For instance, Hauerwas, *A Community of Character.*

25. See my essay "Catholic Moral Theology, Ignatian Spirituality, and Virtue Ethics: Strange Bedfellows," *Way Supplement: Spirituality and Ethics* 88 (1997): 36–45. Recent writers on the topic include: Dennis Billy and Donna Orsuto, eds., *Spirituality and Morality: Integrating Prayer and Action* (Mahwah, N.J.: Paulist, 1996); James Keating, "The Good Life," *Church* 11/2 (1995): 15–20; James Keenan, "Rooting Morality in Spirituality," *Church* 12/4 (1996): 38–39; Mark O'Keefe, *Becoming Good, Becoming Holy: On the Relationship of Christian Ethics and Spirituality* (Mahwah, N.J.: Paulist, 1995). Norbert Rigali is the moral theologian who first recognized the importance of pursuing the relationship between the two fields. His essays are numerous; a few salient ones are, "The Unity of the Moral Order," *Chicago Studies* 8 (1969): 125–43; "Christian Ethics and Perfection," *Chicago Studies* 14 (1975): 227–40; "The Future of Christian Morality," *Chicago Studies* 20 (1981): 281–89; and "The Unity of Moral and Pastoral Truth," *Chicago Studies* 25 (1986): 224–32.

26. John W. Padberg, S.J., gen ed., *The Constitutions of the Society of Jesus and Their Complementary Norms* (St. Louis, Mo.: Institute of Jesuit Sources, 1996): "Formula of the Institute," *Exposcit debitum* text: 1, pp. 3–4. Hereafter *Const* in text.

27. Paul Begheyn, "Bibliography on the History of the Jesuits: Publications in English, 1900–1993," *Studies in the Spirituality of Jesuits* 28/1 (1996): 1–50.

28. See also *Const* "General Examen" [82, 92], pp. 41, 43.

29. Brian Daley, "'In Ten Thousand Places': Christian Universality and the Jesuit Mission," *Studies in the Spirituality of Jesuits* 17/2 (1985): 3.

30. The texts can be found in John W. O'Malley, S.J., "The Fourth Vow in Its Ignatian Context: A Historical Study," *Studies in the Spirituality of Jesuits* 15/1 (1983): 46–49. They include excerpts from *Const* [603, 605, 612], pp. 276–80, and the papal bull, *Exposcit debitum*: 3–6, also in *Const,* pp. 6–9.

31. O'Malley, "The Fourth Vow," 33–34.

32. O'Malley, "To Travel to Any Part of the World: Jerónimo Nadal and the Jesuit Vocation," *Studies in the Spirituality of Jesuits* 16/2 (1984): 5–8.

33. Ibid., 12.

34. *The Spiritual Exercises of St. Ignatius,* trans. Louis J. Puhl, S.J. (Westminster, Md.: Newman, 1951). Hereafter *SpEx* in text.

35. Howard Gray, "Changing Structures," *Way Supplement: Person and Society in the Ignatian Exercises* 76 (1993): 79.

36. Certainly, the Jesuit call to mobility so evident in both our spirituality and our historical tradition might be a bit lost in those parts of the world that the Society is institutionally settled. However, even the hospitality exercised in those places ought to derive its meaning from the Jesuit call to mission to those in need.

Meeting God: From Ignatius of Loyola to Michel Foucault

James W. Bernauer, S.J.

A B S T R A C T

Ignatius of Loyola and the French philosopher Michel Foucault have made the greatest contribution to the author's understanding of how to live a philosophical life, of how to speak truthfully about truths. GC 34 called attention to three of the most significant domains for such speech. First, in our institutions there is need for an incarnational education that will enable our students to learn from the wounds of the people with whom they share the world. Second, the author is responding to the Congregation's call for Jewish-Christian dialogue by teaching a course and doing research on the Holocaust. Finally, he is trying to fulfill the suggestion of GC 34 that special concern be shown the situation of women. He has joined a faculty seminar on feminism and Catholicism and is at work on what he regards as a special challenge that comes with careful listening to contemporary voices: How to integrate the Jesuit tradition of *cura personalis* with the new pride that gay and lesbian people have assumed in being who they are.

Introduction: Ignatius and Foucault?

The joining of such different names as Ignatius and Foucault may seem terribly artificial, but their combination is natural if I am to give you, the reader, an accurate understanding of how this contemporary Jesuit is trying to live a philosophical life. Such a life need not necessarily develop from a mere commitment to the study and teaching of philosophy. The wisdom I try to pursue in teaching and writing comes from what I have learned from both the Basque mystic and the French intellectual. When, within weeks of a 1962 high school graduation, I entered the Jesuits, Ignatius of Loyola was for me an admirable but distant and severe figure, a knight of the Lord's Kingdom, a soldier of Christ. His appeal was that of inviting me to enlist in a Great Cause. He was the ideal saint for an era of Cold War, ideological frenzy, and widespread militarism. The attractiveness of that military style was obliterated by many forces: the Vatican Council, the Vietnam War, the cultural shifts of the 1960s and 1970s, the evolution of the Society's practice, and, I like to think, a growth in personal maturity. Ignatius became a figure in a historical museum until I read his autobiography while I was doing my tertianship, or final formative period of study and prayer in the Society. Then I met Ignatius not as soldier, but as he described himself: a pilgrim who knew both that he was on a sacred journey and that he would not arrive at the real Holy Land until after his death. I had developed regard for journeying as a fundamental metaphor for life and I appreciated Ignatius anew, especially how his pivotal "Contemplation to Attain the Love of God" reflected the vision of a pilgrim, acutely sensitive to God's presence in the abundance of the world through which we make our ways, graced by rays of light from the sun and by waters flowing from fountains.[1]

Quite apart from personal feelings about the man, I had long appreciated that the greatest of Ignatian graces for my life was his spirituality of finding God in all things, and it was certainly that vision that motivated the title for my first published book: *Amor Mundi* (Love of the World).[2] Ignatius and his disciples have taught me a love of the world that has had the effect, I now realize, of making me very suspicious of any demonization of people or places. Intellectually, the tendency to demonize would proclaim the failure of our spirituality, of our discernment of God's presence; morally, the tendency would indicate our failure to remember how the Society of Jesus itself had been victimized by such paranoid thinking. I am sure I reflect a common Jesuit consolation in the identity of pilgrim. The Jesuits of 1997 could not be the same as the pre–Vatican II Jesuits for reasons both religious and secular, and I see one of the principal graces of contemporary Jesuit life to be our abandonment of a triumphal identity, of a sense of rightful privilege in the Church. Some of the practices of the current Papacy, especially its suspension of our normal governance at one point, have alerted us to our vulnerable situation and that is a grace to which Father Pedro Arrupe's great suffering witnessed for all of us. There is no reproach of the earlier Society intended, but we are on a pilgrim road again, leaving ethnic and spiritual ghettos and asking very firmly what dimensions of the mentality and practice of nineteenth- and twentieth-century Catholicism we wish to carry into the new millennium. GC 34 recognizes and embraces the "coresponsibility" for Catholicism's renewal that was created by the "prophetic event" of Vatican II (Decree 11: "On Having a Proper Attitude of Service in the Church" 7 [304]).

INFLUENCE OF FOUCAULT

While I have had many brilliant teachers both in the course of my studies in the Society and as a graduate student, Michel Foucault (1926–84) had a singular impact upon me.

While a doctorate student at the State University of New York at Stony Brook, I began a dissertation on his thought and was able to study with him in 1979 and 1980 in Paris. I also had the opportunity of several personal discussions. From time to time religious people have expressed surprise that I have such a high regard for Foucault's thought and I would point to him, as well as to several other so-called postmoderns, as figures who often are demonized in our intellectual culture. While David Halperin expresses an opposite viewpoint in his book *Saint Foucault,* his subtitle, *Towards a Gay Hagiography,* shows that Foucault's canonization is of an unusual type.[3] In an age of death camps and gulags, Foucault made his readers aware of other prisons, not those that are imposed upon us but those that we fashion for ourselves in the ways we think, especially about the human person. He thought of himself as an archaeologist of the human sciences.[4] Although his literary talent created more striking phrases, the most arresting for me when I read it was: "l'âme, prison du corps," "the soul is the prison of the body."[5] I could not help but recall a point that Walter Ong made in his brilliant essay "St. Ignatius' Prison-Cage and the Existentialist Situation." Ong stressed the nuance in a text of Ignatius from the *Spiritual Exercises,* his suggestion that the exercitant "consider my soul to be closed up in this corruptible body as in a prison, and the whole composite as in exile among brute animals. I say the whole composite, soul and body."[6] Ong drew attention to the special functioning of the body, a prison but also a protection from the wild beasts of those passions that surge up from the dark depths of the senses. "When you are surrounded by wild animals, the very next best thing to having them in cages is to be in one yourself."[7] Foucault's "soul as prison of the body" shifts perspectives: how the soul may protect from the passionate depths of human existence only by locking us into the narrow prison of the self. Its bars are formed from the knowledges through which we think of ourselves: how we construct what is reasonable, normal, healthy in opposition to the domains of the unreasonable, abnormal, sick. For Foucault, the prison of soul has exiled our mystery as human beings, and has locked away our differences and strangeness. Foucault and Ignatius are very distant in their views on the soul, and yet show a courageous willingness to renegotiate the traditional boundaries of body and soul, self and other.

Philosopher's Relation to Truth

Although Foucault's analyses are far too complicated to do justice to them here, I would like to mention just one strength in his thought, his view of the philosopher's relationship to truth.[8]

His books explored the territory of how the human sciences actually get constructed as knowledges and how they operate in relation to particular modern institutions: the asylum, the clinic, the prison, and sexuality, the institution that was the domain of his last works.

He described his studies as a history of the political production of truth, and that history distances its readers from the notion of truth as timeless or innocent, that is, as unrelated to the political and cultural problematics that generate the needs for truth. He puts forward a reversal of the Kantian critical questions: "In what is given to us as universal, necessary, obligatory, what place is occupied by whatever is singular, contingent, and the product of arbitrary constraints? The point, in brief, is to transform the critique conducted in the form of necessary limitation into a practical critique that takes the form of a possible transgression."[9] I regard Foucault's most significant transgression to be a form of negative theology or anthropology in which the positive human figure created by the human sciences is subverted and human being is restored to the regions of the yet to be known, of mystery and art. Philosophical life is a guide to these regions to the extent that one becomes a *parrhesiast* (literally, one who speaks frankly or truthfully) rather than a human scientist or a philosopher of systems. The parrhesiast speaks truthfully about the human condition in a way different from other traditional models: not as a prophet claiming insight into destiny, nor as a sage enunciating general principles, nor as a technician offering particular skills. The philosopher as parrhesiast speaks in terms of what he or she has personally discovered to be the case, attempts to describe the present situation and how that situation differs from the past, embraces an ascetic spiritual discipline that enables one to become an ethical critic of contemporary truths and of what those truths do to the actual lives of human beings. Finally, the parrhesiast recognizes that this manner of living the philosophical life is risky and dangerous because today truth is often a privileged vehicle for powerful institutions to determine how we regard human society, how we understand ourselves.[10] My reading of the Congregation is organized under three themes: Incarnational Education; the Jewish-Christian Dialogue; and Listening to Women and Others.

Incarnational Education

I meet God in the searching and loving lives of my students. In order for that meeting to pass from the notional to the real, two steps were required. First, it took me far longer than it should have for me to grasp that I was teaching people and not a field of study. Secondly, I had to find a context where students could learn as full persons. Fortunately, Boston College has had a program since 1969 that provides that personal situation and, consequently, I do most of my undergraduate teaching in a course that integrates theology and philosophy with a student's commitment of ten to twelve hours of service to the local communities. They are engaged in carefully supervised service that includes mentoring for troubled adolescents, a visiting program to the elderly and those living with AIDS, tutoring young children, and working at homeless shelters.

As I have mentioned, Ignatius the soldier is not a very appealing figure for me, but there is one important incident in his military life that my undergraduate students have given me new respect for: the severe wounding that he received fighting at Pamplona in 1521, which slowed him down and forced him to reexamine the direction his life was following.[11] My students have taught me how important a source of education are wounds, those wounds students confront through their placements, in society, and in the broken personal lives of the people they try to assist.

Spiritual growth is visible as the students integrate their experiences through papers and journals with such ancient and contemporary texts as the Book of Job, Frankl's *Man's Search for Meaning,* and Arendt's *The Human Condition.*[12] Working through the suffering of writers searching to capture the meaning of events and through the pain of people confronting raw experiences today, students are brought to the possibility of a choice: a philosophical way of living that separates neither thought from action nor one's personal journey from service to the human family.

This is an incarnational education and the students become worldly, they are better able to accomplish something worthwhile in the world, and, most especially, they develop the parrhesia that enables them to speak authentically about experiences that are far too often turned into ghosts by social analysis, let alone public relations. GC 34's reaffirmation of the Society's commitment to the ideal of a faith that does justice was very important to me both as Jesuit and philosopher, and I see that it was a "particular grace" that GC 32 gave us in that commitment (GC 34, Decree 2: "Servants of Christ's Mission" [SCM] 7 [32]). This faith is the source of the pedagogical conviction of GC 34: "Profound experience is what changes us. We can break out of our habitual way of living and thinking only through physical and emotional proximity to the way of living and thinking of the poor and marginalized" (Decree 9: "Poverty" 14,5 [287]; cf. Decree 13: "Cooperation with the Laity in Mission" 8 [338]). Encountering those experiences continually through my students, I am brought to the central experience of the Spiritual Exercises and of religious conviction: the sublime supremacy of the personal dimension, of our hunger to touch the real, of our passion to make the decision on how to lead our lives only in the presence of God.

The Jewish-Christian Dialogue

A challenging refrain of GC 34 is its call to a pilgrim Society for dialogue with other faiths: the sharing of the joys and sorrows of our common human journey; cooperation in the development and liberation of peoples; and the exchange of spiritual experience and theological insight (Decree 5: "Our Mission and Interreligious Dialogue" [OMID] 4 [131]). For me, the most striking of the dialogues to which the Congregation calls us is that with the Jewish people:

Dialogue with the Jewish people holds a unique place. The first covenant, which is theirs and which Jesus the Messiah came to fulfill, "has never been revoked." A shared history both unites us with and divides us from our elder brothers and sisters, the Jewish people, in whom and through whom God continues to act for the salvation of the world. Dialogue with the Jewish people enables us to become more fully aware of our identity as Christians. (OMID 12 [149])[13]

Several factors give special importance to this call. It represents a step toward the task of accurately understanding the often difficult history of the Society's relationship to the Jewish community. We have much to repent of, preserving, for example, until 1946 an impediment to entrance into the Society of someone of Jewish origin. This long practice was a betrayal of Ignatius' own attitudes, which included his conviction that it would be a special grace to be born into the same physical family as Jesus of Nazareth.[14] In addition, this call establishes a supportive relationship with what to my mind is the single most progressive development of John Paul II's Papacy: its effort to establish a new kinship with the Jewish people, which led him to recognize the State of Israel and which had its most stunning symbolic moment in the Pope's visit to the Synagogue of Rome. On that occasion he declared that the "Church of Christ discovers her 'bond' with Judaism by 'searching into her own mystery.' The Jewish religion is not 'extrinsic' to us, but in a certain way is 'intrinsic' to our own religion. With Judaism, therefore, we have a relationship which we do not have with any other religion."[15]

I was especially pleased by the invitation to dialogue because I have tried to make Jewish-Christian reconciliation a cornerstone of my own ministry as teacher and scholar. For several years I have taught a course on the Holocaust in which I explore the ethical attitudes of the people who experienced this ruinous event. Although Christianity has not turned its back on the Holocaust, as have most other Western institutions, the Church all too often regards the event with far too innocent an eye, a naïveté that should incite a self-doubt. The Christian faith has sustained, throughout its long history, a clear vision of evil as an ineffaceable, ever threatening force. Thus Christianity should have been especially alert to the dynamics of Nazism's mass appeal and, later, it should have been particularly empowered to provide insight into the horrors that exploded from the European heart in this century. Whether we be Jews or Christians, believers or nonbelievers, we are in obvious need of new paths on which understanding might advance in its comprehension of the Holocaust and what was done right or wrong within its shadow.

Such study has become the major task of my current writing and research. I have utilized some of Foucault's work as a way to scrutinize the ethics of that period, most particularly how convinced Nazis thought of ethics. This ethic is not studied in terms of its correspondence to abstract codes of moral principle or the concrete forms of ethical conduct with which our tradition would identify moral life. More basic is the subtler level of how individuals fashion themselves as subjects of moral conduct and, thus, as desirous of certain codes and of conformity to them. This level of ethical self-formation is exposed by a series of questions: What issues are primarily thought of as warranting moral concern? How does a person establish a relationship to a rule of conduct? What specific transformation of oneself is invited by an ethical commitment? Finally, what was regarded as the purpose of moral life? My hope is that the pursuit of these questions will yield a more sophisticated profile of moral awareness at that time than we have created up until now.[16]

I have discovered as a result of attending and speaking at conferences that are dedicated to these themes that one of the most significant of the current dialogues between Christians and Jews is discussion about the Holocaust. I have been able to participate in some of these conversations in Europe and the Middle East as well as in the United States. As I write this essay, I am in the process of finishing a lecture for an international symposium, "Good and Evil After Auschwitz: Ethical Implications for Today," scheduled to take place in Rome in September of 1997 and bring together both Jewish and Christian scholars. My hope is that it will advance both an understanding of the Holocaust and our post-Holocaust dangers as well as the amity between Jewish and Christian communities.[17]

Listening to Women and Others

The statement of the Congregation that evoked the greatest popular response at my university was without doubt Decree 14: "Jesuits and the Situation of Women in Church and Civil Society" (JSW). Although one of my female colleagues mentioned that she did not have the impression that the document had come from the grass roots, it was nevertheless well received and widely discussed at symposia both on campus and at the Jesuit Urban Center in downtown Boston. There was appreciation for the goal of the document, that the Society would regard work for the reconciliation of men and women as integral to a faith that does justice. There was deep regard for the method that was recommended: "In the first place, we invite all Jesuits to listen carefully and courageously to the experience of women." "We do not pretend or claim to speak for women. However, we do speak out of what we have learned from women about ourselves and our relationship with them" (JSW 12 [372], 7 [367]). Moreover, there was particular gratitude for the admission of Jesuit failure in this matter, our support for styles of clericalism that have served male domination, and our neglect of expressions of solidarity with women. We "Jesuits first ask God for the grace of conversion. We have been part of a civil and ecclesial tradition that has offended against women" (9 [369]).

Two of the concrete ways in which I have tried to implement this document is to join a faculty seminar on the question of Catholicism and feminism, which began in September

1996, and to present a course on how the explosion of historical research in the field of sexuality might influence our understanding of ethics. The initiator of the seminar, Dean Mary Brabeck of our School of Education, invited me to join a remarkable group of about twenty faculty and administrators, and we have made a commitment to meet once a month for two hours for at least two years and more likely three. We have the hope of producing a volume of papers on the topic, although this objective is secondary to the mutual enlightenment achieved through the discussions themselves. Our readings have ranged from John Paul II's 1988 Apostolic Letter "On the Dignity and Vocation of Women on the Occasion of the Marian Year" to feminist thinkers such as Julia Kristeva, Elizabeth Johnson, and Judith Evans. We even spent an evening together watching and discussing "The Bells of St. Mary's" with Bing Crosby and Ingrid Bergman! While unsure as to where our seminar will lead, I have no doubt that the discussions have begun to transform their participants and, thus, some corners of Boston College.

Of course, one of the first things one learns from listening to women is that some identify themselves as lesbians. While Michel Foucault had introduced me to the importance of sexuality in historical analysis, my study of National Socialism and my dealings with gay and lesbian people have put it at the top of my academic and moral concerns. Although I am not able to justify this claim here, I would contend that Nazi crimes are unintelligible apart from the sphere of eroticism and sexuality and that, in turn, this domain is incomprehensible apart from the long history of Christian attitudes toward sexuality. In my course I have tried to treat the evolution of the spirit-flesh struggle into the historical field of warring sexual populations.[18] While women have been the principal victims of the sexual violence which culminates in fascism, there are other groups that have suffered terribly as a result of historical Western attitudes, gay and lesbian people among them. While historical research is very early in the process of throwing light on this shadow within our tradition, I have had to confront the issue on a much more personal level.

In June of 1995, the Boston College administration turned down for a second time the application by the college's lesbian, gay, and bisexual community for formal registration as a student organization. Dealing with these students has instructed me in how difficult their situation is on a Catholic campus and how much an issue of love and justice it is. As was the case in GC 34's sensitive acknowledgment of the plight of women, I have come to conclude that only a more profound grasp of the sorrowful damage caused by the Church's teaching on gay people, and of the dangers in which its statements place them, will move Christians beyond many of their traditional prejudices. That damage and danger need recognition. To quote Andrew Sullivan: "The depth of the pain that's been caused [gay] people . . . not only by the laity, but by the clergy too is extraordinary. Honestly and truly, there are few subjects on which the church is now, by virtue of its teaching, inflicting more pain on human beings than this subject—real psychic, spiritual pain."[19] As far as the danger is concerned, please just recall how secure—socially, legally, and economically—were the German Jews on the eve of their annihilation.

Much to my surprise I was presented, in April 1997, with an award at the sixth annual recognition dinner of the association of the gay alumni and lesbian alumnae, the Lambda Association of Boston College Graduates. The award thanked me for the personal care that I had shown students. I was very embarrassed to receive it because I had done almost nothing to deserve it, and so the only way I was able to accept the award was to consider it as a challenge to me to live up to the confidence that the students had placed in me. That challenge is to integrate the Jesuit tradition of *cura personalis,* of personal care of the student, with the new pride that gay and lesbian people have assumed in being who they are. Whatever complex notions are contained in *cura personalis,* it is certainly the refusal to invent the student who is before you. Personal care means accepting who that student is and acknowledging his or her way of loving.

There are many searches in the humanities and the sciences that take place in our Jesuit universities and colleges. As noble as they are, however, they pale next to that hunger and thirst for understanding who one is and for how God has created one to love. It is a real privilege and a major responsibility for us to be with students at that time in their lives. As Jesuits, we have a long tradition of missionary service and so we have gone to all corners of the world to proclaim the Gospel. The new dignity of gay and lesbian people is a continent that invites our exploration and, in that, we need to explore an interior globe of spirit and sexuality, a territory that might be far more frightening than the dangers of vast oceans and uncharted forests presented to other generations.

Conclusion

As is clear by now, this Jesuit feels personally confirmed by GC 34 in my effort to live a philosophical life that is witness both to the grace of God in my own experience and to my desire for a faith that aims to build up a more just social order. I am consoled by the Congregation's willingness to recognize how much of a pilgrim people we continue to be. I have received renewed regard for how, in our Jesuit lives, the "Society of Jesus is the mysterious work of God" (SCM 14 [14]). Moreover, I have a fresh restlessness about how our journeys will move forward and how the next Congregation will capture the calls of Spirit that Jesuits hear now. Will it produce a document on the history of Jewish-Jesuit relations? As a result of listening to women, will there be elaboration of new directions for the Society's relationship to the feminist movement? Will there be a more profound articulation of what personal care of students is in an age more respectful of pluralism, more grateful for the wonders of God's diverse creation, including God's creation of sexual differences? They are all needed. But perhaps most demanded of the next Congregation is the strengthening of our capacity to listen to the unique sounds of our era's struggles and adventures. We know from personal experience with the *Spiritual Exercises* how difficult it is to grow quiet enough so that God might be able to be heard. If some of us are put off at times by the fact that groups seem to be shouting at us rather than speaking in polite tones, perhaps it is because we have so often been deaf to their cries for recognition and assistance. In listening to them we shall encounter the world as it is rather than as it once was.[20] What a blessing!

ENDNOTES • BERNAUER

1. *The Spiritual Exercises of St. Ignatius,* trans. Louis J. Puhl, S.J. (Westminster, Md.: Newman, 1951), 101–3.
2. James Bernauer, S.J., ed., *Amor Mundi: Explorations in the Faith and Thought of Hannah Arendt* (Boston, Mass.: Martinus Nijhoff, 1987).
3. David Halperin, *Saint Foucault* (New York: Oxford University Press, 1995).
4. I am able to mention but a few of his major books: *Madness and Civilization* (New York: Pantheon, 1965); *The Birth of the Clinic* (New York: Pantheon, 1973); *The Order of Things* (New York: Pantheon, 1971); *The Archaeology of Knowledge* (New York: Harper Colophon, 1976); *Discipline and Punish: The Birth of the Prison* (New York: Pantheon, 1977); *The History of Sexuality I: An Introduction* (New York: Pantheon, 1978); *The History of Sexuality II: The Use of Pleasure* (New York: Pantheon, 1985); *The History of Sexuality III: The Care of the Self* (New York: Pantheon, 1986).
5. Foucault, *Discipline and Punish,* 30.
6. "St. Ignatius' Prison-Cage and the Existentialist Situation" in Walter J. Ong, S.J.'s collection *The Barbarian Within* (New York: Macmillan, 1962), 242–59 at 243.
7. Ibid., 246.
8. I have tried to give a comprehensive presentation of his thought in *Michel Foucault's Force of Flight: Toward an Ethics for Thought* (Atlantic Highlands, N.J.: Humanities, 1990). For those who are particularly interested in his relationship to religious thinking, I would suggest my article: "The Prisons of Man: An Introduction to Foucault's Negative Theology," *International Philosophical Quarterly* 27 (December 1987): 365–80.
9. Michel Foucault, "What Is Enlightenment?" in *The Foucault Reader,* ed. Paul Rabinow (New York: Pantheon, 1984), 45.
10. Foucault's last two courses in 1983 and 1984 were taken up with the study of parrhesia. These have not been published but there is one essay that I can recommend that deals with the topic: Thomas Flynn's "Foucault as Parrhesiast: His Last Courses at the Collège de France" in *The Final Foucault,* ed. J. Bernauer and D. Rasmussen (Cambridge, Mass.: MIT, 1988), 102–18.
11. See John C. Olin, ed., *The Autobiography of St. Ignatius Loyola* (New York: Harper Torchbooks, 1974), 21–26.
12. Viktor Frankl, *Man's Search for Meaning* (New York: Washington Square, 1985); H. Arendt, *The Human Condition* (Chicago, Ill.: University of Chicago Press, 1958).
13. Citation is from John Paul II, "Allocution to the Jewish Community" (Mainz, 17 November 1980), *Acta Apostolicae Sedis* 73 (1981): 80.
14. James Reites, "St. Ignatius of Loyola and the Jews," *Studies in the Spirituality of Jesuits* 13/4 (September 1981): 17.
15. "Address by the Pope" (April 13, 1986) in Pope John Paul II, *Spiritual Pilgrimage: Texts on Jews and Judaism 1979–1995,* ed. Eugene Fisher and Leon Klenicki (New York: Crossroad, 1995), 63.
16. I have published but fragments of this work that I hope will become a book. See my "Beyond Life and Death: On Foucault's Post-Auschwitz Ethic," *Philosophy Today* 32 (summer 1988): 128–42; "Nazi Ethics," *Continuum* 1 (autumn 1990): 15–29.

17. I would like to take this opportunity to thank several organizations that have given me the opportunity to pursue my investigations of moral life during the Nazi period: Boston College, which has supported me with a sabbatical and its Jesuit Institute, which invited me to give one of its Institute lectures in October 1996; the Bannan Foundation of Santa Clara University which gave me the opportunity of a full year of residency for my research; the Jesuit Historical Institute in Rome for a semester's residency; Georgetown University, which invited me to give the 1993 Stephen F. McNamee Lecture; Le Moyne College, which honored me with the invitation to present a 1996 Jubilee lecture; and DePaul University, which organized a major 1996 conference on Foucault at which I was able to explore some of these issues.

18. The importance of this spirit-flesh struggle cannot be stressed enough. This is Peter Brown's judgment: "Paul crammed into the notion of the flesh a superabundance of overlapping notions. The charged opacity of his language faced all later ages like a Rorschach test: it is possible to measure, in the repeated exegesis of a mere hundred words of Paul's letters, the future course of Christian thought on the human person." See Peter Brown, *The Body and Society: Men, Women, and Sexual Renunciation in Early Christianity* (New York: Columbia University Press, 1988), 48.

19. Andrew Sullivan, "'I'm Here': An Interview with Andrew Sullivan," interview by Thomas Stahel, *America* 168 (8 May 1993): 5–11 at 7.

20. I do want to thank three of my fellow Boston College Jesuits with whom I have been in special conversation in recent years on the shape of the postmodern world: Ronald Anderson, S.J.; Francis Clooney, S.J.; and Arthur Madigan, S.J.

Navigating Scylla and Charybdis: Contemporary Philosophy and GC 34

Ronald H. McKinney, S.J.

ABSTRACT

This essay tells the story of the author's philosophical journey: a quest to integrate the more traditional ideas of Lonergan with the more postmodern insights of Derrida. The reader will hopefully see this same creative tension between opposites in the author's analysis of the dialogical vision of the documents of GC 34. He concludes by showing how his work in and outside the classroom is also characterized by this same awareness of dialectical tension.

Introduction

I have been asked to write a personal essay on how GC 34 correlates with developments in my field of philosophy and how it impacts my life as a scholar and my work with undergraduates in and outside the classroom. I have decided that the best way to approach this assignment is to tell the "story" of my philosophical and scholarly development as well as to narrate an account of my work here at the University of Scranton. What the reader of this tale will hopefully discover is that the same creative tension between opposed polarities that characterizes my life and the content of my work also underlies the documents of GC 34, or so it seems to me.

The metaphor of Odysseus sailing between the twin dangers of Scylla and Charybdis may appear misleading, because the analogy suggests that my life and work have been a continuous quest to *avoid* the opposing poles of human experience, when the truth has been rather the reverse: I have been *attracted* enormously to both fundamental extremes of the One and the Many throughout my life and work. This metaphor, however, only makes sense if we realize that we can only negotiate the waters of the human condition by striving always to maintain a paradoxical balance between the conflicting desires for unity and multiplicity that constitute our very nature. In other words, my philosophical odyssey has taught me that one must *avoid* presuming that life can be adequately accounted for by only one explanatory pole of experience; on the contrary, such an illusion can only result in a disastrous shipwreck, an experience we scholars and Jesuits have unfortunately undergone all too often in our lives and work.

Creative tension has characterized my consciousness of life from its earliest days. The existence of a fraternal twin brother forced me to deal with the reality of the "other" from the moment of my birth. The fact that I was always aware that I constituted a blending of my father's bookworm tendencies and my mother's practical love for people made me struggle early on for the solution of how to achieve a proper balance in life. When I became a Roman Catholic convert in my senior year in high school, I held onto, instead of rejected, the riches of my Protestant heritage as a preacher's kid. This too posed a challenge of how to integrate two seemingly opposed ways of being a Christian. Finally, it was my attraction to the life and thought of Teilhard de Chardin that made me want to be a Jesuit and continue his task of reconciling science and religion, the sacred and the profane.

My background thus provides the context for understanding why my philosophical journey has been constituted by the ongoing struggle within me between the forces of tradition and innovation. Early on I was an ardent supporter of the transcendental Thomism of the Jesuit Bernard Lonergan, because I felt it constituted a healthy transposition of Thomistic values in the modern world, a kind of balance between old and new needed in our Church. However, later I was led to "deconstruct" the thought of Lonergan in the interests of facing up to the postmodern challenge of Jacques Derrida and others. The reader will hopefully come to understand in what follows that the conflict in loyalties I experienced between Lonergan and Derrida is nothing more than an exemplification of the same creative dialectic that exists *within* both the thought of Lonergan and Derrida themselves.

I shall first explore the dynamics of this debate between two diverging styles of thinking: foundational (Lonergan) and antifoundational (Derrida) philosophy. After showing how I have resolved the conflict between these two rivals for my affection, I will then go on to examine the underlying philosophy of the documents of GC 34. I hope the reader will admire with me the shrewd commitment to the paradoxes of creative tension embodied within these documents. Finally, I will go on to show how my work with my students in and outside the classroom is also characterized by this same fundamental awareness of the dialectical nature of human experience.

The Perennial Problem of the One and the Many

I was originally drawn to the thought of Bernard Lonergan when I was in the novitiate at Wernersville in the early 1970s. Living all my life in an ecumenical family had made me very aware of the fundamental differences that divide human beings religiously and philosophically. I thus longed to become a disciple of a thinker who, though appreciating pluralism, could nonetheless provide a way out of the paralyzing quagmire of relativism. Lonergan's commitment to a traditional Thomism revitalized by the transcendental turn to the subject promoted by modern philosophy seemed the perfect means to satisfy my desire to believe in both a perennial philosophy as well as one open to the riches of ongoing human experience.

Lonergan's two most influential works are *Insight* (1957) and *Method in Theology* (1972). There are those who will refer to the "intellectualist" bias of the former and the greater appreciation for the role of symbolic feeling in the latter as the basis for their distinction between the "early" and "later" Lonergan. However, I have argued elsewhere that there exists a greater continuity than difference between these two works.[1] For, in both, Lonergan is concerned with the same hermeneutical problem of resolving different interpretations of reality by means of a "transcendental method," which appeals to the experience of our "self-appropriation" of our cognitive operations. It is for this reason that many consider Lonergan's thought to be an exemplar of "foundational" discourse: an effort to ground our everyday belief and practice in something more solid than mere everyday belief and practice. Foundationalists hope that such a ground will be an invariant base exempt from the chaos of conflicting historical interests and upon which the latter can be evaluated objectively.

I shall avoid an overly specialized discussion of the battle between foundationalists and their postmodern opponents for the sake of the general reader. However, some suitable summary of Lonergan's enterprise ought to be attempted here. Lonergan's "transcendental method" rests on the premise that not only can the past enlighten us about the present and future, but that contemporary praxis regarding problems of our day provides the sure test for assessing the significance of past contributions. This dialogue between past and present exemplifies what Lonergan means by the critical term "dialectic." For him, "dialectic rests on the concrete unity of opposed principles; the dominance of either principle results in a distortion, and the distortion both weakens the dominance and strengthens the opposed principle to restore an equilibrium."[2]

The term "dialectic" is used by Lonergan in reference to human affairs in which the pure desire to know finds itself in opposition to the other human desires regarding the proper direction of such affairs. This dialectic is "harmonious" and promotes "progress" when one's spontaneous desires and fallible common sense submit to the dictates of pure, disinterested intelligence, but is "distorted" and leads to disintegration and "decline" when such desires refuse to be "patterned" by the wise suggestions of theoretical intelligence.[3] When the needs of each individual are satisfied in conjunction with the good of the whole, then we have the establishment of an ideal community, that is, a "cosmopolis." It is precisely the comprehension of the dynamics of this ideal state of discourse that allows Lonergan to grasp the causes of distortion that lead to misunderstanding and decline in a society. "Dialectical analysis" is thus analogous to psychoanalysis on the individual level, because it allows the philosopher to use the science of the cosmopolis to reveal the biases that destroy the authentic development of a community.

Now Lonergan is well aware that this science of the cosmopolis must be able to justify its own conclusions if it is to function as an adequate critique of ideology. He argues that his "transcendental method" is grounded in his cognitional theory (that is, his analysis of what is involved in the process of knowing) and that such a theory is impervious to radical revision.[4] For all attempts to revise such a basic theory would leave the reformer open to being retorted, that is, the conditions for the possibility of his assertion would be shown to be contradicted by the content of his assertion itself. For example, a person who denies that we can know anything has contradicted himself in this very performance of uttering a truism about our fallible condition.

Lonergan's use of retortion—that is, performative contradiction—to provide the transcendental grounds for his "dialectical analysis" of society is highly controversial. Nevertheless, it reveals his project's bias for the One over the Many. Despite his openness to learning from other philosophers, Lonergan holds himself up as the ultimate arbiter, for it is only the person who has appropriated his own cognitional operations and affirmed himself as a knower who has the Archimedean vantage point to judge the "counterpositions" of those whose cognitional theory is inadequate.

As I read more and more postmodern philosophy, however, I began to see more and more biases in Lonergan's work itself. He always seems to privilege theory over common sense, intellect over feeling, the concept over the symbol, certainty over ambiguity, insight over its linguistic vehicle, and the permanent achievements of the past over the developments of the present. Moreover, this seems to clash with his own definition of dialectic itself in which the dominance of either principle is said to lead to a distortion and reversal. This contradiction in Lonergan's use of his notion of dialectic to privilege pure reason, instead of to question its very power, is what led me to consider the theory and praxis of Derrida.

The basic aim of Derrida's deconstructive enterprise is to undermine the existing hierarchical oppositions within whatever "text" is being considered.[5] It aims to show that what a foundationalist like Lonergan privileges does not deserve to be considered more essential than its opposing concept, as neither pole can do full justice to the infinite complexity of reality itself. A simple affirmation of their equality, however, will not be enough to disrupt a given hierarchy. Rather, the critic must also show how the very affirmation of a hierarchy leads to its own reversal. The marginal, for example, is demonstrated to be of more importance than what was thought to be essential, which results in the very blurring of such distinctions altogether.

The point, however, is not to abolish such distinctions, nor to abandon the first in favor of the second. Nor is the aim to create some dialectical synthesis of opposites, a holistic monism that is neither one nor the other but something new. On the contrary, deconstruction aims at a "double procedure" whereby one relies on one polar concept in order to criticize the other and then reverses the direction as soon as the former has been achieved. Thus, this oscillation between two polar opposites destroys the pretensions of any systematic interpretation at having the last word. For the promotion of one interpretation is shown to be self-destructive, leading to the promotion of its opposite, while its denial is shown to be dependent upon assuming it to begin with. This paradox exemplifies why deconstruction not only cannot do without the principle of noncontradiction, but also why it cannot avoid violating it as well. Indeed, it also explains why describing deconstruction itself is so problematic. For my above portrait, on its own premises, is only one of an infinite number of possible readings of deconstruction.

Consequently, it is not difficult to see why most foundationalists complain that the adoption of deconstruction can only lead to a sheer relativistic chaos, detrimental to the very possibility of rational inquiry and communication. For if every candidate to provide a transcendental ground can be shown to be nothing but a product of historical and contingent forces by deconstructionists, then what possible reason do we have for reforming the status quo? Why presume that any other alternative is necessarily superior to the present social setup? Indeed, postmodernists are hard pressed to refute the charge that, if foundationalists have privileged the One over the Many, they have done the reverse despite their protestations: they have privileged Multiplicity and Change over Unity and Permanence, instead of recognizing their equiprimordiality.

In response to an article in which I deconstructed Lonergan's thought, James Marsh attempted his defense in the following manner:

> *The strong foundationalism that is the proper target of deconstruction Lonergan can claim to evade. His is a chastened foundationalism or critical modernism, claiming to steer between the Scylla of a strict foundationalism and the Charybdis of a post-modern skepticism. . . . I think McKinney misses the extent to which Lonergan's philosophy already contains valid post-modern elements. For example, the canon of residues as Lonergan employs it in science and hermeneutics inviting and requiring us to be open to and recognize inconsistencies, anomalies, and slippages in the data or text is similar to the method of deconstruction as Derrida uses it and McKinney defines it.*[6]

I would readily agree with this observation by Marsh. However, I would ask him to take back his charge that deconstruction fails to do likewise, that in its rage to promote flux it does not incorporate within itself Lonergan's concern to affirm the values of coherence, objective truth, and metaphysical foundations. On the contrary, a good Derridean knows that the One and the Many must both be affirmed in a paradoxical manner.

Linda Hutcheon's marvelous description of postmodernism, based as it is upon postmodern architecture and historical metafiction, reaffirms Derrida's claim that whatever historical tradition deconstruction draws upon is in turn questioned and subverted *but without choosing sides.*[7] According to Hutcheon, for postmodernism, consoling myths may be attractive and necessary, yet they are nonetheless illusory. Thus, its ironic parody of historical materials both incorporates and critiques that which is parodied. She claims that postmodernism is fully aware of even the ideological nature of its own position. It leads to both a vision of interconnectedness as well as to an acceptance of irreconcilable incompatibilities. Postmodernism's enterprise of recontextualization wants both to integrate the past and present as well as to question both in light of each other. It wants to question not only the passions for inspired totalistic visions but the very quest to unmake them as well. Hutcheon thus concludes that this very provisionality of postmodernism, far from making us stop thinking from the despair of it all, is the very guarantee that we will never cease to rethink everything.

What is my conclusion after this survey of my long philosophical journey? That Lonergan and Derrida are really saying the same thing in their desire to balance the One and the Many in their thought? Not exactly. For every *articulation* of the Problem of the One and the Many always ends up being biased in favor of one pole versus the other. A foundationalist's bias always seems to be for the One and their postmodern opponent's for the Many, despite both their attempts to make room for the other pole of experience. After all, every experienced horse rider knows that balance is achieved, not by sitting perfectly still in the middle of one's saddle, but by continually oscillating right and left to the rhythm of the horse's movement. Or, to use our central nautical metaphor, a good sailor knows how to zigzag in the wind by either tacking to the port or starboard to maintain a straight path.

In conclusion, then, I would argue that what characterizes both traditional and postmodern philosophy today is their twin concern for reconciling the One and the Many. This common theme may be played in different keys, but the quest for ordering human experience in a way that is open to "others" is a motif central to both opposing viewpoints, as we shall now see is also the case with those documents that came out of GC 34.

The Dialogical Vision of GC 34

A casual reader of the documents of GC 34 cannot help but observe that in the index, the two most frequently cited topics are "dialogue" and "inculturation"—two terms that refer to the same "dialectical" concerns of both Lonergan and Derrida. *Dialogue* is defined as a "spiritual conversation of equal partners, that opens human beings to the core of their identity" (Decree 4: "Our Mission and Culture" [OMC] 17 [101]). Accordingly, if the theme of previous recent congregations was the faith that does justice, GC 34's primary contribution is that this faith that does justice must be the kind of faith "that engages other traditions in dialogue" as well as "evangelizes culture" (Decree 2: "Servants of Christ's Mission" [SCM] 21 [49]).

The authors of GC 34 are well aware of the Problem of the One and the Many, for they contend that Jesuits have "one mission" even though there are "varied contexts in which we work" (SCM 2 [23]). The different contexts in which Jesuits work are, of course, the many cultures in which they find themselves. This dialogue of the Gospel and culture that Jesuits are called to is predicated upon a "positive approach" to different cultures, characteristic of Jesuits throughout their history (SCM 17 [42]). Indeed, in this mutual dialogue among equals, the Gospel transforms cultures, and is, in turn, transformed by different cultures. GC 34 is adamant on this point that it is not a one-way street as so often was the case in Western Christendom's past. The Gospel both critiques the evil within each culture and embraces the good.

Moreover, the fact that every "particular" expression of justice is itself "inadequate" means that the gospel faith not only "transcends" the limitations of cultural visions of justice, but that particular expressions of the Gospel's vision of justice are also subject to cultural critiques in turn (Decree 3: "Our Mission and Justice" 4 [53]). This dialectic is not only implicit in Lonergan's utopian vision of the "cosmopolis" but also in Derrida's notion of "justice in itself," which transcends its incarnation within every particular set of laws.8

Indeed, GC 34 tackles explicitly the issue of its relationship to postmodernism by arguing for the need for dialogue between the Gospel and postmodern culture (OMC 19–24 [103–8]). That there are so many works relating Derridean and Asian religious philosophies today is reflected in GC 34's insight that what may appear as postmodern agnosticism may be something else entirely: "'Post-Christian culture' witnesses, strangely and implicitly, to a reverence for the God who cannot be imaged by human beings without destroying the divine mystery" (OMC 21 [105]). Thus, a postmodern concern for the paradoxical limitations of expression might well create an enthusiasm for the liberating potential of "negative theology." As GC 34 puts it, "It is never a question of choosing either God *or* the world" (OMC 7 [86]). Rather, postmodern secularism may simply be a strange way of making room for a god of transcendence in an age in which religion has stressed perhaps too much a god of immanence.

GC 34 also promotes a strong need for interreligious dialogue that will result in mutual collaboration to achieve "common goals" (Decree 5: "Our Mission and Interreligious Dialogue" [OMID] 3 [130]). However, it warns that, while dialogue allows us to proclaim our experience of Christ, dialogue also requires us to be open to the working of the

Spirit in others; that is, that we have something to learn as well (OMID 7 [135]). Moreover, GC 34 is careful to add that "no universally valid guidelines can be given" for this dialogical exchange (OMID 9 [137]), advice that any postmodern philosopher would appreciate.

GC 34's vision of a world constituted by the creative tension of opposites is also reflected in its advice to Jesuits as to whom they should be drawn to serve in their ministry. If Derrida seeks to deconstruct privileged positions of power, GC 34 argues that a Jesuit's ministry should be "particularly directed towards . . . those who are at the margins of the Church or of society" (Decree 6: "The Jesuit Priest: Ministerial Priesthood and Jesuit Identity" 12 [169]). Indeed, whatever assignment a Jesuit takes should be always considered "provisional" in order that he be constantly "available" to go anywhere at anytime to those by whom he is needed the most (Decree 8: "Chastity in the Society of Jesus" 11 [238]). Provisionality is, of course, the hallmark of the postmodern creed.

GC 34 adds that Jesuit ministry should also be characterized by a "dialectic of *traditio et progressio*" (Decree 11: "On Having a Proper Attitude of Service in the Church" 6 [303]). We must listen respectfully to the proper ecclesial authorities guarding the deposit of faith, but we must also be willing to speak out for innovative interpretations that we discern may be called for by the Spirit today. This tension between the values of making representation and being obedient is considered a creative one by the authors of GC 34, despite the pain it can cause. It can only be authentically practiced, however, if both sides follow a crucial requirement of all dialogues: seeking "to put the best interpretation on what the other says and does" as Ignatius' preamble to the *Exercises* suggests (Decree 12: "Ecumenism" 3 [328]).

One dialogue that is given special consideration by GC 34 is that between Jesuits and the laity. One radical implication of such a collaboration should shake up the complacency of many a Jesuit: "We must increasingly shift the focus of our attention from the exercise of our own direct ministry to the strengthening of laity in their mission" (Decree 13: "Cooperation with the Laity in Mission" 19 [353]). This subordination of priestly ministry to the ministry of all baptized Christians is merely a needed deconstructive reversal of the privilege priests have all too often had in the past. This same concern to undo past participation in unjust modes of power is reflected in the decree that counsels Jesuits to "listen" to women "in a spirit of partnership and equality" (Decree 14: "Jesuits and the Situation of Women in Church and Civil Society" 12 [372]).

Readers of Lonergan's *Method in Theology* will recognize his influence in Decree 15: "Communication: A New Culture," requiring that Jesuits master the new functional specialty of communication and media education as the primary means today of transmitting the tradition of the gospel faith. Moreover, Jesuits are also expected to respect the autonomy of intellectual disciplines in relation to our faith, to value the creative tension between committing ourselves completely to our work in the world and being able to be critical of the cultures we work within at the same time (Decree 16: "The Intellectual Dimension of Jesuit Ministries"). This implies that "we need consciously to be on guard that both the noun 'university' and the adjective 'Jesuit' always remain fully honored" in our institutions of higher education (Decree 17: "Jesuits and University Life" 5 [408]). Finally, GC 34 urges Jesuits to be aware of the "tension between the local and the universal" that ought to characterize all our apostolic decisions (Decree 21: "Interprovincial and Supraprovincial Cooperation" 3 [435]).

In conclusion, this brief summary of the insights reached by GC 34 should have made clear to the reader how prominent is its vision of a world full of creative tensions requiring honest dialogue as the necessary means for their resolution. Hopefully, the reader could discern the implicit presence of the "dialectic" of Lonergan and the deconstructive tension of opposites described by Derrida in the above summary as well. For it seems to me that most striking in GC 34's portrayal of the postmodern world and the challenges that face our Jesuit mission is precisely its awareness of the Problem of the One and Many. The authors of GC 34 clearly value both opposing poles of human experience as they affirm not only our need for the unity of faith, but our need for the richness of pluralistic experience as well.

Life with Undergraduates

This same dialectical tension is played out in my life as a teacher in and out of the classroom, which I would like to describe in this final section. First, the pedagogy I adopt in the classroom is constituted by a myriad of dialectically related opposites. For me to be successful requires that I not only lecture and summarize the material assigned in an adequate manner but that I also engage my students in a Socratic dialogue that allows me to learn from them as well. Moreover, in this give-and-take approach, the goal cannot be simply their induction into the mysteries of arcane, technical philosophy. Rather, besides introducing them to the history of this academic discipline, I must also show them how all this is relevant to the kind of questioning they must do if their own lives are to have any meaning at all. Thus, failure to engage them where they are will only make the academy all the more irrelevant in the real world, a rising trend that we professors are in part responsible for.

As a Jesuit professor, I also have a responsibility to introduce them to the whole dialectic of *traditio* and *progressio*. In my medical ethics classes, for example, I must ensure that they have a clear, respectful understanding of the Church's positions on abortion, euthanasia, and other related topics to allow them to critique the often antilife culture within which they live. But I also must see to it that they have the necessary tools to challenge possible deficiencies within ecclesial pronouncements from the standpoint of genuine contributions of our postmodern culture. In short, I must give them the freedom to question without encouraging a spirit of mindless relativism.

I also live in a dormitory as a resident counselor, which presents its own share of creative tensions. First, I must constantly be aware of the many different hats I am asked to wear, for my roles can sometimes come into conflict with each other. I am not only my own unique self who can develop friendships (among equals) with some students, but I am also an agent of the Church, an agent of the school working within a team of resident assistants, resident directors, maintenance people, and other student-life personnel, a professor who teaches some of the students in my dorm or surrounding dorms, and at times an advocate for students in their battles with the system in which they find themselves. Each of these roles, for example, requires a different code of confidentiality and, unless I am careful to balance appropriately all my different responsibilities, dialectical reversals and distortions will undoubtedly occur and have occurred.

Finally, I am also the director of the Special Jesuit Liberal Arts Program on the University of Scranton campus. This program that recruits around fifty-five to sixty new freshmen each year is an alternate way of doing their roughly twenty courses of required general education. At the heart of this program is a heavy concentration in philosophy and theology, which aims in part to blur the boundaries between disciplines so that they can see their interconnection. Students in this program are also expected to be involved in extracurriculars and service projects. This requirement aims at trying to bridge the gap between the academy and their lives outside the classroom. However, this brings us to the final dialectical issue I want to raise in this paper.

Several years ago, I attempted to start on our campus a service learning program modeled somewhat on Boston College's famous PULSE Program. We have a great many students who do volunteer work on our campus, and the learning experiences they have in those projects certainly rival what they learn in the classroom. However, there exists as yet no integration between their theoretical and experiential modes of learning. There have been attempts to get them to "reflect" upon their experience in accordance with the Ignatian action/reflection model of learning, but this has not involved to date an inclusion of the textual theory they get in class as the basis for such reflection.

When I proposed my program as a way of alleviating this deficiency several years ago, I was startled by the vehemence displayed by many professors in their contention that the academy's task is simply to present theory, which the students must learn to integrate with their service work on their own. I should not have been so surprised, for what I was asking my colleagues to accept was the mandate of undertaking something they had no expertise in. For most, fostering this dialectic of theory and praxis in our students is as foreign to them as another academic discipline they are not trained in. Surely the dialectical vision of Lonergan and Derrida is needed in our institutions of higher education today, as is indicated by our failure to help bring together the two major opposed worlds of our students: the realm of work and leisure within which many of them spend most of their time *and* the small sphere of involvement they have with the academy itself.

In this essay, I have attempted to share the story of my intellectual and personal journey as a way of demonstrating the crucial relevance GC 34 can have in our world at large today. However, readers can only come to a full understanding of this fact by entering into and appropriating the creative tensions that exist in their own lives. Hopefully, Lonergan and Derrida can serve as complementary mentors in such an enterprise.

ENDNOTES • MCKINNEY

1. Ronald McKinney, S.J., "The Role of 'Conversion' in Lonergan's Insight," *Irish Theological Quarterly* 52 (1986): 268–78.
2. Bernard Lonergan, *Insight: A Study of Human Understanding* (London: Longmans, 1957), 233.
3. Ibid., 217–45.
4. Ibid., 304.
5. This summary is indebted to the masterful and lucid introduction of deconstruction by Jonathan Culler, *On Deconstruction: Theory and Criticism After Structuralism* (Ithaca, N.Y.: Cornell University Press, 1982).
6. James Marsh, "Reply to McKinney on Lonergan: A Deconstruction," *International Philosophical Quarterly* 31 (March 1991): 97–98.
7. Linda Hutcheon, *A Poetics of Postmodernism: History, Theory, and Fiction* (New York: Routledge, 1988), 1–56.
8. Jacques Derrida, "Force of Law: The 'Mystical Foundation of Authority,'" *Cardoza Law Review* 11 (1990): 943–45.

ESSAY 23

The Fingerprints of God

Frank R. Haig, S.J.

ABSTRACT

In a remarkable *tour de force,* the author gives a poetic account of how he faces the challenge of integrating the life of a physicist with the life of a priest. He sees "the fingerprints of God on the universe." For the author, they are found in a world that, in spite of the evil of the Holocaust, is "gloriously alluring, splendidly attractive, and wondrously entrancing," so much so that a scientist who is logically consistent will conclude it is "too good to be an accident."

In the dim dark days of the past when I was only five years old, my family used to go each summer to Atlantic City, New Jersey, for two weeks of vacation. More accurately, my family went to Margate and my mother's sister's family to Ventnor. In the stories that are told around the dinner table, and that so improve with the years, I was one day on the beach when a kindly gentle professor from Notre Dame University, my uncle's college, came to visit my aunt and uncle. I was at my uncle's place that afternoon. The visitor turned to me with the usual question adults use to mildly torture young boys and girls: "What do you want to be when you grow up?" In a statement that sounds straight from the Midrash I replied: "A Jesuit astrophysicist."

At the age I was then, it is difficult to imagine how I could have known what either word meant. Still, I have ended up a Jesuit theoretical physicist so that I can claim some credit as a prophet.

During adolescence I spent a great deal of spare time reading physics and astronomy. Science seemed the direction in which I was going. Because I was also interested in religion and piety, adolescence had its turbulence as I tried to put together the antireligious bias of much of the popular scientific literature I was reading and the antiscientific preaching of many of the priests whose sermons I heard. At times I spent inordinate amounts of energy searching for and going through anti-Darwinian tomes to save my mind from what seemed at the time the evil notion of evolution. I can not remember when I abandoned that pursuit and moved over to the profoundly evolutionary position I have had as an adult. At any rate, the change occurred before I came to realize that evolution involves stars and galaxies and the physical universe as a whole in addition to biology. My public school teachers knew what I was thinking because I spoke with them often. They quietly disagreed with my early fundamentalist leanings but kept a very loose rein and never produced any feeling of rebellion in me. They only kept urging me to go further and read more broadly. They had no fear of either science or religion and engendered none in me.

So after high school I entered the Jesuit Order and began the then-standard early academic training of a Jesuit, which was totally literary and linguistic. After two years of intense study in Latin and Greek, there approached the famous day when the province prefect of studies came to visit the Juniorate at Wernersville, Pennsylvania, where I was studying, and had with me the famous interview that would determine my future studies.

We were told to list three areas of interest. Through the discussion with the province prefect, a choice would then be made. I listed classics, German, and history. The province prefect in those days was Father Stephen McNamee, S.J., a man whom I found I liked immediately. But he made short work of my list.

"As to classics, we have many Jesuits in that area with no pressing need at the moment. As to German, we want a native speaker in such an area. History also has several other candidates. What would you think of physics?" He probably latched onto that choice because we had just finished a summer course in mathematics and I suppose I must have done all right. At any rate, it sounded like my childhood interest, and I immediately accepted. I was to become a physicist.

Shortly thereafter, I met with my sister and told her of the decision. Jean is a brilliant woman, now a noted attorney and successful state politician, but she had done her college work in a largely secular environment. She gasped in disbelief. "But, Frank, how can you be a priest and a scientist at the same time? Science and religion don't mix." "Give me thirty years and I will have an answer," I replied. It is more than thirty years now and I had better be able to say something to the question.

There is, of course, a special reason why I must reply to my sister's puzzlement. The Jesuit Order is peculiar in that it believes in obedience and discipline but does not emphasize the power of its central and supreme control body, which is an international meeting called a *general congregation.* Saint Ignatius usually wanted general congregations only to elect a new general superior of the order. At times, however, events counsel more frequent assemblies. In particular, the recent sea change in the Church has motivated a whole series of general congregations. We are here considering explicitly GC 34 and, from my point of view, its emphasis on the intellectual apostolate. Its concerns must also motivate my reflections and actions.

Perhaps one way of focusing our thoughts is to refer to the survey article in *The Economist* (October 4, 1997), surely the most significant journal commentary on current events in any language in the world today. This survey article treated universities around the world. It maintained that two factors have forced a restructuring of the contemporary university: democracy and science. Democracy I will leave to others, but I had better be able to say something about science and its profoundly centering role in the society of this age.

We might begin with one of the controlling documents of the Catholic and Christian tradition.

A Perfect World and a Perfect Creator

Paul assured the Romans that the presence of God is knowable by a study of the world. He told the Romans: "In fact, whatever can be known about God is clear to [us]; He Himself has made it so. Since the creation of the world, invisible realities, God's eternal power and divinity, have become visible, recognized through the things He has made" (Rom 1:19ff).

Paul does not say how this process of recognition is to be achieved, only that it is possible. Most modern Catholic thinkers would point out that the foundation of belief in the existence of God is not from science itself—it is the contemporary conviction that God did a good job in creation. There are no holes that God has to patch up with special interventions. Put in a simple way, the world is perfectly made. To every scientific question there is a scientific answer. God is not the reply to any scientific inquiry. If we are to find God from the consideration of his creation it will be when we ask a nonscientific question, when we step back from our strictly scientific work and reflect on what we have found out. It will come when we ask something like: "Why is the universe so beautiful?"

At this point it is interesting to turn to a writer such as Steven Weinberg. Weinberg is a great contemporary elementary-particle physicist. He received a Nobel prize for his achievements in the realm of field theory in 1979. But Weinberg is a committed atheist. As a result, even though he insists upon beauty's role in scientific theory, he cannot allow beauty to be asserted of the universe as a whole. Such a position would raise a question he feels dreadfully uncomfortable in answering. Yet, the beauty of the universe is an overpowering experience for any reflective person. How can Weinberg rule it out of his world?

In his recent popular work, *Dreams of a Final Theory*, Weinberg has a whole chapter on God.[1] He starts his text by quoting the nineteenth Psalm: "The heavens declare the glory of God, and the firmament showeth his handiwork" (v. 2). Somehow Weinberg must demolish this text. He does it by interpreting the verse to imply that the psalmist believed that the physics of the heavens is different from the physics of the earth, of the world beneath the moon. The objects in the heavens are eternal, unchanging, of a special magnificence that in a dramatic way reveal the difference between God and the world God is said to have made. In other words, Weinberg interprets the psalmist as a convinced Aristotelian. But Copernicus and all of modern astronomy have shown that the laws of physics are universal. What is true of the sun is true of the dirt beneath our feet. So he can conclude that "the stars tell us nothing more or less about the glory of God than do the stones on the ground around us."[2]

How strange! The psalmist lived hundreds of years before Aristotle. He knew nothing of Aristotle's physics. He is only trying to reflect on the experience that anyone in the Near East has who goes out at night in the clear desert air and is overpowered by the magnificence of the sky. Of course a blade of grass is as beautiful as any star, in fact, in a real sense, more so. But the sky is beautiful, too, even in a startling and almost crushing sense. Weinberg must deny this fact or he will have to face a nonscientific question that his scientific brilliance ill equips him for, the simple question of why the universe is so gorgeous.

At a later point in the chapter even Weinberg is compelled to make a concession to experience. "I have to admit that sometimes nature seems more beautiful than strictly necessary," he admits.[3] But he can counter this concession by reference to the problem of evil. "But the God of birds and trees would have to be the God of birth defects and cancer."[4]

The problem of evil is real. An atheist who points to it has raised a fundamental objection. When the Bible tries to handle it in the one extended discussion of the question that is the Book of Job, it answers merely by appealing to the fact that it is not easy to make a world that is rational and predictable without having aspects we do not like. Unless we are to demand that God intervene repeatedly and erratically, any system of laws would seem to have a downside to it. Any structure with room for human freedom would seem to have the possibility of a Holocaust. Weinberg is really demanding a nonscientific world and does not realize it.

Of course, Weinberg must also get rid of the idea that human beings are special. We must be a meaningless slamming together of blind forces. Otherwise we will end up believing ourselves as "playing a starring role in [some sort] of grand cosmic drama."[5]

Yet, we clearly are. Perhaps there are other actors in our universe also. They have so far proven extraordinarily difficult to detect—but maybe they are there. Moreover, what is wrong with having more than one lead actor in a play? If there is other intelligent life in our universe, then some day we will be able to sit down with it and talk about the problem of God also. And, you know what? I'll bet we will find that some of them believe in God and some do not.

Weinberg and his allies are in a peculiar position. They believe that blind chance and unpatterned necessity can account for the rich, layered variety and magnificence of the physical universe. They believe a world that at every level makes sense and is everywhere and from every point of view patient of logical analysis dissolves into stammering idiocy when viewed at its highest level. Anyone not ideologically compelled to deny the obvious would find this leap of faith valiant in the extreme.

But a physics classroom is no place to impose one's religious ideas on students. It is probably true that the professor's personal views will come out now and then. If so, the freedom of the student must be rigidly protected. This year the editor of the Loyola College yearbook, Kristen M. Aluzzo, wrote to the various department chairs in the college asking them or a member of their department to write a piece for the yearbook. It was to be in the form of a letter to the students. It should tell the students something about how that teacher viewed the experience of teaching his or her subject. My chairman asked me to do the piece. I was delighted to be asked. In the, I hope, gentle way that is appropriate for a teacher in a physics course, I put on paper a hint of how one searches for the fingerprints of God on the universe. Let me conclude by reproducing that letter. Please note that the letter seems to simply trail off at the end. That is a deliberate stylistic device.

Dear Jane and Jim,

I was delighted to hear that you are going to be in my physics class next time around. Naturally, I felt a bit challenged when you asked me in the interview we just had what you could expect to learn from the course. In fact, at one point you both sort of sighed and mournfully asked: "Why am I in physics at all? How am I supposed to be different when this experience is over?"

Of course, one answer is that you will have employable skills and be able to get a job and have the financial resources to move ahead with your plans to get married and start your own family. But you want something more than that. What is that something more?

Let me start by pointing out that physicists have a pronounced tendency to say that a theory which is general and clean and clear is beautiful. In fact, the beauty of a theory is for physicists one sign that it is valuable. We know instinctively that a messy idea is just not a good insight into the world.

But, you know, it is not the beauty of the theory that counts. It is the beauty of the world the theory tries to understand. When you study the peculiar way the planet Mercury spins on its axis as it revolves about the Sun or the enormous quality control in the universe so that every electron can be identical to every other electron throughout all space and time, you can only have a feeling of wonder. We feel the softness of the air against our cheek and do not pause to note that it is composed of billions and billions and billions of molecules speeding on their separate ways about the room moving at some 1500 miles per hour and colliding with each other some four billion times per second and so giving that impression of a gentle pressure against our bodies without themselves showing any sign of wear.

We look at the night sky with its magnificent splendor and seldom stop to ask why the stars keep brilliantly shining night after night. Where does that energy of the sun and the other stars come from? Why do they not burn out, a few each night, like the electric light bulbs in your dorm rooms? When we come to understand that the sun is a great, massive ball of gas with a crushing gravitational field that heats its interior so much that the hydrogen there can burn into helium and other substances, the sun becomes more startlingly impressive than any ancient thinker could ever have imagined it to be.

You are a pretty couple. You may be blessed by being able to bring new life into this world. If so, it is important that you know that the world into which you are bringing such life is dangerous and must be treated with respect.

Nonetheless, in each level of physical reality, the world has its own peculiar enchantments. We will show you those in the physical order and let other programs treat other realms.

Of course, there are those who will tell you that the world is a cold and heartless place that could not care less whether you and those you love are here or not. Let them say it. You will know that the world is gloriously alluring, splendidly attractive, and wondrously entrancing. You may even detect that it is too good to be an accident and must have behind it something of the level of creative intelligence. But, whether you move that far or not, it will be a fabulous place to live and call other life to join you.

And now, there is that question as to whether you know enough mathematics to do the course. . . .

ENDNOTES • HAIG

1. Steven Weinberg, *Dreams of a Final Theory* (New York: Vintage, 1993), 241–61.
2. Ibid., 241.
3. Ibid., 250.
4. Ibid.
5. Ibid., 260.

GC 34 and the Jesuit Political Scientist

Thomas J. Maloney, S.J.

ABSTRACT

The author reflects upon the significance of some of the themes treated in the most recent Jesuit General Congregations, such as faith and justice, the problem of secularism in the modern world, the call of the Jesuits to dangerous apostolates, the role of women in the Church, ecumenism, and the inculturation of the faith in non-Christian cultures. Both intellectually and by providing students with practical experience, Jesuit higher education focuses on these issues, one of the most challenging of which is to promote justice through direct contact with the poor. The author also stresses the importance of preserving the Catholic character of our institutions in the face of pervasive secularism. These Jesuit concerns have been incorporated into the author's own teaching and research in the areas of Latin American politics, Catholic political thought, and immigration to Southern California, where he sees the need to foster sociopolitical activism.

Major Issues Confronted at GC 34

The groundbreaking Second Vatican Council of the Catholic Church took place from 1962 to 1965 in Rome. The Council owed its success to the quiet work of biblical scholars and theologians in this century, the attention to the signs of the times by Catholic bishops throughout the world, and the courage and openness to change of Pope John XXIII, who called the council. The spirit of innovation and change inaugurated by the council empowered subsequent popes, the theologians and bishops of Latin America, synods of bishops meeting in Rome, and national conferences of bishops around the world to build on what was begun at Vatican II.

The Society of Jesus considers Vatican II to be a sea change event in the Catholic Church. GC 34 describes it as ". . . a prophetic event, producing a momentous renewal within Catholicism not witnessed since the Council of Trent" (Decree 11: "On Having a Proper Attitude of Service in the Church" [HPA] 7 [304]). The four most recent general congregations of the Society convened over the past thirty years (1965–95) have been attempts to update the Society in line with the insights and emphases of the council, and the developments in the Church and the world. Three of the general emphases of GC 34 are of particular importance for the Jesuit apostolate of higher education and political science: the faith and justice connection, the prominence of secularism in modern society, and the penchant of the Society of Jesus to choose the most difficult and sensitive apostolates. One of the most striking of the recent developments in the Church is the explicit linking of "faith and justice" and the commitment of the Church to a "preferential option for the poor." The Society of Jesus made an unqualified commitment to these developments at GC 32 in 1974–75. Similar statements in the decrees of GC 34 renew this commitment. GC 32 described the mission of the Society in the contemporary world as ". . . the service of faith, of which the promotion of justice is an absolute requirement" (Decree 4: "Our Mission Today: The Service of Faith and the Promotion of Justice" 2 [48]). GC 34 refers to ". . . the apostolic priority of the service of faith and the promotion of justice with a preferential love of the poor" (Decree 13: "Cooperation with the Laity in Mission" [CLM] 8 [338]). The linking of faith and justice has caused not a little controversy in the Church over the last thirty years. Theologians, priests, and laypeople have been accused of putting too much stress on one to the detriment of the other. One camp is stereotyped as having a pre–Vatican II mentality, putting too much stress on faith, and thus preaching a half-Gospel that has little relevance to people's real problems and needs. The other camp is seen as a group of social and political activists who downplay or forget spirituality, the individual's relationship to God, and the classic concerns of religion.

Some have seen GC 34 as an attempt by the Jesuits to create more of a balance between faith and justice in reaction to a period of overemphasis on justice. The decrees bend over backwards to emphasize the importance of both. Much attention is paid to justice and our obligations to the poor. Decree 11 spells out some of the injustices that the contemporary world is faced with. The list is filled with examples of economic injustice and human rights abuses (HPA 10 [307]). Decree 13 calls on Jesuits to seek justice through involvement with ". . . international organizations, labor unions, ecclesial base communities and grass-roots movements. This cooperation is a way of witnessing to the Gospel and to Ignatian spirituality" (CLM 14 [344]).

But GC 34 gives an equally strong emphasis to faith. In an admission of past problems Decree 3 states, "We also acknowledge our failures on the journey. The promotion of justice has sometimes been separated from its wellspring of faith" (Decree 3: "Our Mission and Justice" [OMJ] 2 [51]). Decree 2 says, "We can now say explicitly that our mission of the service of faith and the promotion of justice must be broadened to include, as integral dimensions, proclamation of the Gospel, dialogue, and the evangelization of culture" (Decree 2: "Servants of Christ's Mission" [SCM] 20 [48]).

The second concern, one familiar to anyone involved with American universities, including Jesuit universities, is secularism. GC 34's Decree 4, "Our Mission and Culture" (OMC), describes the postmodern world in which the Church finds itself today: "Contemporary secular culture, which has developed partly in opposition to the Church, often excludes religious faith from among its accepted values" (OMC 5,1 [80]). The decree calls for a dialogue with secularism, but not one that would compromise the faith. The Gospel of Christ must not be diluted even though it will always provoke resistance (OMC 22 [106], 24 [108]). Through the centuries since its founding the Society of Jesus has sent missionaries to evangelize cultures that are significantly different from the Western and Christian cultures from which they came. In a similar fashion the Society looks on the intellectual world of the contemporary West as mission territory.

The third striking thrust in the decrees of GC 34 is the habit of Jesuits to pick out the most sensitive and difficult apostolates. GC 34 points out that Jesuits are not diocesan priests, those who man the geographical parishes where the Church's normal work takes place. The Jesuit, in contrast, serves the Church in complementary ways: "A Jesuit tries to direct what he does as a priest towards those who are not easily reached by the Church's ordinary ministry" (Decree 6: "The Jesuit Priest: Ministerial Priesthood and Jesuit Identity" [JP] 18 [175]). GC 34 quotes an allocution of Pope John Paul II to the Congregation in which he said that "in today's world the Society is to be engaged 'in the most difficult and extreme fields, in the crossroads of ideologies, in the front line of social conflict'" (HPA 27 [324]). Decree 21 says that "Jesuits are ready to go wherever in the world their service is most needed; . . . mobile, agile, responding to the needs of a fast-changing world" (Decree 21: "Interprovincial and Supraprovincial Cooperation" 1 [433]). Decree 26 uses the terms "holy boldness" and "a certain apostolic aggressivity" in describing the typical Jesuit way of proceeding (Decree 26: "Conclusion: Characteristics of Our Way of Proceeding" [COWP] 27 [561]).

Here are five examples from the decrees of the Congregation choosing sensitive subjects to speak about and areas to work in. One of the most controversial Catholic subjects today is the role of women in the Church. GC 34 devoted a separate decree to the situation of women in the Church and civil society that has garnered considerable attention and a favorable reaction from many Church women (Decree 14: "Jesuits and the Situation of Women in Church and Civil Society").

The second sensitive area is ecumenism. Two different decrees call Jesuits to interreligious dialogue and ecumenism, not only with other Christian denominations but with all the major religious traditions in the world. We are urged to realize that "these religions are graced with an authentic experience of the self-communication of the divine Word and of the saving presence of the divine Spirit" (Decree 5: Our Mission and Interreligious Dialogue" [OMID] 6 [134]). Ecumenism is defined in a most liberal fashion: "It seeks to see things from the other's point of view and to take seriously the other's critique of one's own communion and its historic errors and failings" (Decree 12: "Ecumenism" 3 [328]).

In an age when one religion seems to many as good as another it is not easy to live out these admonitions and still appreciate the uniqueness of the Catholic tradition. Yet that is what these same decrees call on us to do. They call upon Jesuits to proclaim the Gospel, but they express Catholicism's uniqueness in sophisticated language that is probably lost on the average reader (OMID 6 [134]). Some American Catholics see Decree 5 as negating the call of Pope John Paul II for the evangelization of the modern world. Again the Jesuits place themselves in the middle of some of the more challenging ministries.

The third of these ministries is mass communications. For a long time Jesuits have been involved in the print media, enterprises like Vatican Radio, and radio and television in cooperation with bishops in many parts of the world. GC 34 calls on us to deepen that commitment (Decree 15: "Communication: A New Culture"). Again the Congregation thrusts us into the most controversial areas:

> *If the Church appears to be attacked or defamed in the media, we cannot limit ourselves to a dismissive condemnation of such abuses. We must enter the world of communication and defend the truth, while at the same time honestly acknowledging conflicts and polarities within the Church. Though we will do so without sharpening tensions or weakening authority, we cannot avoid issues which, as news, the media will present in any event.* (HPA 25 [322])

The fourth area is culture and the inculturation of the faith. From the time it was founded, the Society of Jesus has been at the forefront of the dialogue between Catholicism and culture, especially non-Christian cultures. GC 34 acknowledges the importance and power of culture when it admits that in the process of its introduction into a new culture "the Gospel comes to be seen in a new light; its meaning is enriched, renewed, even transformed" (SCM 17 [42]). At the same time, in the process of evangelizing a people we seek to transform their cultural and social life (SCM 18 [43]).

The $64,000 question is how do you transform a culture without unnecessarily destroying it; how do you inculturate the Gospel without losing its essence? In a decree devoted to culture (Decree 4), GC 34 calls Jesuits not only to a dialogue with the indigenous cultures of the third world, but to an "inculturated evangelization" of post-Christian secular modernity. Our Jesuit universities are implicated here as the decree mentions that "our educational institutions, in particular, have a crucial role to play in linking Christian faith to the core elements in contemporary and traditional cultures" (OMC 28,7 [125]).

The fifth and last example of difficult, and in this case dangerous, apostolates is the commitment to "faith and justice." GC 34 plunges the Society into those areas "where the human family is most damaged," into "a world still marked by brutality and evil" (SCM 4 [26]). It calls upon us to follow Jesus "in his committed care for the poor, the marginalized, and the abandoned" (Decree 1: "Introduction: United with Christ on Mission" 5 [5]). GC 34 repeats the central position of GC 32 that the promotion of justice is necessarily connected to the service of faith and that this single goal must be at the center of all our ministries (SCM 7 [32], 14 [39]).

GC 34 explicitly rejects a privatized definition of religion when it states that "this faith in God is inescapably social in its implications, because it is directed towards how people relate to one another and how society should be ordered" (SCM 12 [37]). Jesuits are called on to cooperate with labor unions, Christian base communities, and grass-roots movements, all controversial entities in many countries of the world (CLM 14 [344]). GC 34 is not afraid to use the word liberation, a term at the heart of the internal struggle going on in the Catholic Church today over *liberation* theology (OMJ 10 [59], SCM 10 [35]). It is acknowledged that these activities will be dangerous in the future as they have been in the past.

> *We need to recognize that the Gospel of Christ will always provoke resistance.* (OMC 24 [108])

> *Today we bring this countercultural gift of Christ to a world beguiled by self-centered human fulfillment, extravagance, and soft living, a world that prizes prestige, power, and self-sufficiency. In such a world, to preach Christ poor and humble with fidelity and courage is to expect humiliation, persecution, and even death.* (COWP 5 [539])

The University Apostolate and Political Science Research

On November 16, 1989, in the midst of a civil war rebel offensive, a unit of the military of El Salvador entered the Jesuit residence at the University of Central America (UCA) in the middle of the night and assassinated six Jesuits, their housekeeper, and her daughter. They were killed less for their sociopolitical activism and more for their intellectual activities. They were seen by the right-wing government and military as the ideological mentors of the rebels who were reeking havoc on San Salvador, the capital city itself. Those in power, who view peasants and Indians as less than human beings, saw anyone who even talked about equality and the rights of the poor as dangerous radicals out to destroy their way of life.

Nothing could more dramatically illustrate the importance, and danger, of "the intellectual apostolate," Jesuit higher education. Meeting five years after this event, GC 34 wrote with it in mind.

Our Jesuit service can also be the dangerous commitment of witness and struggle against the forces of injustice and persecution, both social and religious, a witness that has been once again sealed by the blood of martyrs. (HPA 4 [301])

The task [of university education] *is possible; it has produced martyrs who have testified that "an institution of higher learning and research can become an instrument of justice in the name of the Gospel."* (Decree 17: "Jesuits and University Life" [JUL] 8 [411])[1]

GC 34 reminds us that Jesuits have always been involved in all fields of university teaching and research. Moreover, it renews the Society's commitment to higher education. "We recognize that universities remain crucial institutional settings in society. For the poor they serve as major channels for social advancement" (JUL 1–2 [404–5]). The twenty-eight Jesuit colleges and universities in the United States have taken seriously this challenge to educate the poor. My own university, Loyola Marymount, has a minority enrollment of 43 percent.

One of the most challenging demands that the Congregation places on Jesuits is to become involved in promoting justice through direct contact with the poor or by "participating in social mobilization for the creation of a more just social order" (OMJ 19 [68]). The liberation theologians, among others, have placed a heavy stress on this point. They are reacting against an armchair theology that is all talk and no action. This demand often places university faculty in a bind because it can take time away from a counterdemand that Jesuit universities now have in place—the demand for professionalism, the demand for published research.

All our universities now have in place a plethora of organized opportunities for students to work and train in the wider community. My own university offers weekend trips to Tijuana, Mexico, to work at an orphanage; mentoring and tutoring local minority junior high school students; work at housing projects and at a food distribution center; and internships in Washington, D.C., for training in advocacy skills. Most of these programs are administered by the Office of Campus Ministry although some academic departments have begun to think about social service requirements for their majors also. These programs would be more effective if more faculty members were directly involved.

One of the duties of a Catholic university is to turn out new generations of Catholic lay leaders whose understanding of their faith is as sophisticated as their understanding of the professions they will move into. Catholic universities as centers of research must also be initiators of a dialogue between the faith on the one hand and culture and the world of secular scholarship on the other. "Our educational institutions, in particular, have a crucial role to play in linking Christian faith to the core elements in contemporary and traditional cultures" (OMC 28,7 [125]). As was discussed above, the secularism that pervades Western intellectual discourse often has little respect for faith and religion. This skepticism is often present in our Jesuit universities as well. Only concerted, vigorous, and often unpopular action will keep them from following the same path taken by many formerly Protestant universities in the United States. GC 34 reasons that it will take hard work to maintain and strengthen each of our institutions so that "both the noun 'university' and the adjective 'Jesuit' always remain fully honored" (JUL 5 [408]). "In order for an institution to call itself Jesuit, periodic evaluation and accountability to the Society are necessary in order to judge whether or not its dynamics are being developed in line with the Jesuit mission" (JUL 9 [412]).

Loyola Marymount University attempts to preserve its Catholic tradition by providing seminars for new faculty and staff and week-long colloquia on the Catholic nature of the university. For a number of years we have been involved in "Western Conversations on Jesuit Higher Education," a faculty exchange effort of the six Jesuit universities in the West.

Some years ago I developed and began teaching a new course called "Catholic Political Thought." It covers the social teachings of the Church over the past century through an examination of papal social encyclicals, statements of international synods of bishops, and pastoral letters of the National Conference of Catholic Bishops of the United States. By covering this literature I emphasize that the Catholic Church holds strong opinions on economic and political models and realities, opinions that are at times different from those of the American mainstream. Just because there is a tradition of the separation of church and state in the United States does not mean that religion has nothing to say about politics and political policy. The course also examines liberation theology, an intellectual movement that not only affected religion in Latin America but the universal Catholic Church and its social thought as well.

As a political scientist I took special note of a statement made by the Congregation as it spoke of the Ignatian tradition and its implications:

> It encourages us to become involved in disciplines which, although they
> may have no explicitly Christian perspective, are nevertheless central to
> the way in which human beings understand themselves and the world
> around them. (JP 20,2 [179])

This is another way of stating the Ignatian goal of "finding God in all things." No matter what his discipline leads him into, whether it be empirical data gathering techniques, survey research, or poring over documents in government archives, the Jesuit political scientist is doing God's work.

About the time of GC 34 the question of immigration became a major public issue in California. Southern California, where Loyola Marymount is located, has become a worldwide center of immigration. In California 26 percent of the population, 8 million people, are now foreign-born immigrants. This is 40 percent of the total in the United

States. Los Angeles County is home to roughly 3.2 million of these immigrants. One-quarter of Los Angeles residents are noncitizens. Although the largest portion (42 percent) comes from Mexico, this immigration has its origins in every corner of the world. The Los Angeles Archdiocese, the largest in the United States, reports that it serves one hundred different national/ethnic groups and provides Mass on any given weekend in sixty different languages.

Many of these immigrants are undocumented. The number is over 2 million or 6.3 percent of the state's population. Most of them reside in Southern California. Estimates are that one-third of the undocumented residents of the United States live in Los Angeles. Cardinal Roger Mahony, the archbishop of Los Angeles, has taken a public pro-immigrant stand, defending not only immigrants in general but the undocumented in particular. In effect he takes the position that people have a right to move across national boundaries for purely economic reasons. While acknowledging the right of nation-states to regulate their borders, he contends that this right is superseded by the right of people to move in order to escape grinding poverty.[2] As countercultural as Cardinal Mahony's statements might be in the context of California in the 1990s, they are in the mainstream of the Catholic social thought tradition.[3]

In November 1994 the voters of California passed Proposition 187, the so-called "Save Our State Initiative," a major attack on illegal immigration. This fueled similar movements in other states and finally to the national level resulting in federal legislation that negatively affects both legal and illegal immigrants. For years the United States Catholic Conference, the administrative arm of the Catholic bishops in Washington, D.C., has been involved in advocacy work on behalf of immigrants by means of government lobbying and supplying practical materials to Catholic parishes for the purpose of aiding immigrants. With the election results in California indicating that a majority of Catholics voted for Proposition 187, it became clear that the Church's position was not getting across to its own members.

Because Latin American politics is my specialty, Latino immigrants are of special interest to me. The Latino component in the immigrant population is significant. Of the foreign-born immigrants in California 42 percent are from Mexico and 9 percent are from Central America. In 1990, 38 percent of the population of Los Angeles County was Latino. It is estimated that, with the continuing flow of immigrants and the high birthrate among Latinos, by 2040, two-thirds of all County residents will be Latino. The vast majority of these Latinos are Catholics. The Church struggles to reach out to this population in its own language and religious culture. To a great extent the struggle has been successful. Sixty-eight percent of the parishes in the archdiocese offer Masses in Spanish on weekends, and 325 priests are involved in one way or another in Hispanic ministry. There are also a significant number of religious women, many of them from Mexico, who serve in a wide variety of ministries.

On the political front, a source of continuing frustration to Latino politicians and activists is the fact that traditionally, Latinos have not enjoyed a political presence and influence commensurate with their numbers. The reasons for the lack of voting and political participation are varied. Many immigrants, poor and in low-paying jobs, have to spend most of their time and energy working to feed their families. Others have been turned off by politics in their countries of origin. Latinos are a younger population statistically and thus there is a lower percentage of them that are of voting age. Finally, a higher percentage of Latinos are noncitizens and thus not eligible to vote no matter what their age.

In response to these immigration controversies and to the thrust of the recent general congregations I redirected my research interests to Latino immigration and the Church in Southern California. Can, and does, the Church play a role in fostering political participation among Latinos? Historically, organized religion has had a profound influence on politics in the United States. Tocqueville pointed this out in the earliest days of the republic, and observers have commented on it ever since.[4] Today there is a growing literature on "civil society" that stresses the importance of societal underpinnings to a healthy political culture. Elaborate networks of prepolitical organizations and groupings seem to be key factors in a society's political success.[5] Churches can play an important role in creating such civil societies. More specifically, religious activists are more likely to be successful political activists.[6]

Religion has been especially important to new immigrants.[7] Churches provide intellectual background, group support, leadership training, and in-place organizations from which newcomers can gain the skills and contacts to negotiate their way in the wider society. However, a recent study suggested that Catholic parishes do not give nearly as many opportunities for skill development and leadership training to their parishioners as do their Protestant counterparts, especially their African American Protestant counterparts. While Catholic parishes are hierarchically structured, in congregationally structured Protestant parishes laypeople have to do more of the organizational work and spend more time each week in church activities. The study argues that because Latinos are disproportionately Catholic, their parish experience is a factor in their relative lack of political participation.[8]

In the light of the questions raised by this research, I have undertaken a study of Latino immigrants in Los Angeles and the role of the Catholic Church in helping to inculturate Latinos to American society and to foster political participation. The research involves a variety of techniques: face-to-face interviews with pastors in heavily Latino parishes, a mail survey of all the parish priests working in the Los Angeles Archdiocese, and face-to-face interviews with lay volunteers in four particularly active Latino parishes. The research seeks answers to the following questions: To what extent are Catholic parishes friendly and welcoming to Latino immigrants? Are religious and social services offered in a cultural setting familiar to the immigrants? How many social service–social justice activities go on in the parish? Are laypeople encouraged and trained to take on leadership positions in the parish?

As crucial figures in the parishes, the priests were asked their personal attitudes and opinions on legal and undocumented immigration, Latinos, multiculturalism, bilingualism, social justice, and the role of women. More than half of the opinion questions were taken from other surveys. This will make possible a comparison between the opinions of the Los Angeles priests and other populations: California residents in general, California Latinos, and Mexican Americans nationally.

My research is also studying two different types of organizations used in Los Angeles Catholic parishes to foster sociopolitical activism. A few parishes have organized Latin American–style ecclesial base communities, small neighborhood gatherings of parishioners meeting in homes weekly to read the Scriptures, pray, and discuss what relevance they have to daily life and local problems. A larger number of parishes have Saul Alinsky/Industrial Areas Foundation community organizations. These organizations are parish based, but they are also hooked into regional and area-wide structures that allow for coordinated campaigns on specific issues.

In 1995–96 these community organizations mounted a well-publicized effort to pressure the Immigration and Nationalization Service to process as many residents seeking citizenship as possible in time to vote in the November 1996 elections. Most of these residents were Latinos. Much of the contacts and organizational work took place through Catholic parishes. Although almost 100,000 new citizens were registered, there was no noticeable effect on the November election. However, in local elections in the spring of 1997 the Latino turnout was considerably higher than it had been in the past. It played a significant part in the passage of a school bond issue that was sorely needed for the physical repair of public schools.

The preliminary results of my research indicate that Catholic parishes in Los Angeles are open and welcoming to Latino immigrants. The opinions of the priests are more pro-immigration and pro-immigrant than the general run of the population, and more pro than even the Mexican American population. They are also positive toward multiculturalism and are generally at ease with Mexican and Latino styles of worship. Because Catholicism is by nature a sacramental religion, much of the Catholic parishes' time and energy is taken up with making the sacraments available and preparing people for their reception. Despite this, almost all parishes put a significant amount of effort into social action activities. Ninety-three percent of the priests surveyed agreed that "action of behalf of justice should have an essential place in the life of every Catholic parish."

The official teachings of the Catholic Church are strongly pro-immigration, sensitive to cultural differences, and supportive of democratic political participation. As a church of immigrants through the centuries the American Catholic Church cannot help but be sensitive to the needs of immigrants. Although earlier, established immigrant groups have often not been open to the differences they find in new immigrants, the contemporary Catholic Church, at least in Los Angeles, seems to be up to the challenge. These preliminary findings picture a religious organization with extensive resources and with a membership cutting across all the major class and ethnic boundaries playing a major role in the slow and difficult process of making room for Latino immigrants and helping them to take their deserved place in American society.

My research into immigration has led me also into a new area of teaching undergraduate students. Our core curriculum, the spectrum of courses that all students must take to assure a well-rounded education, was recently expanded to include a course in multiculturalism. The course can be offered by faculty from any department, and can incorporate a variety of perspectives, as long as it covers at least three American ethnic groups. I developed a course titled "Immigrant Catholic Politics," growing out of my research. The course examines the phenomenon of contemporary Latino and Filipino immigration to Southern California. For historical comparison and contrast I also cover the Irish immigrations to East Coast cities in the last century and their use of the political system to better their social and economic lives. I stress the fact that despite their very different origins in countries in the four corners of the world, the experience of immigration that they all go through is very similar.

In one section of the course I cover the Catholic Church's stance on immigration through readings and lectures.[9] Catholic social teachings in recent times on the subject are prefaced with an analysis of Scripture, both Old and New Testaments, that makes clear how central to the Judeo-Christian tradition is a positive attitude toward strangers in our midst. The course also covers the clash of differing cultures as they mix in the salad bowl called Southern California. Many of the students in the class are themselves first- or second-generation immigrants who have personal stories to tell of prejudice, acceptance, and the frictions that arise within families and in society as the process of acculturation takes place.

My academic specialty is comparative politics, the study of politics and society in countries throughout the world. I teach upper-division courses in Latin America, and Russia and Eastern Europe, as well as courses in the areas I have described here. I feel supported in my work by GC 34's universal thrust. It calls the Society of Jesus to see itself as "united with Christ on mission," boldly moving to all areas of the world and all areas of society, even the most controversial, "finding God in all things." The Congregation has challenged me to move into new areas of teaching and research that I might otherwise have avoided because they were less known or less comfortable. It calls the political scientist in me to pursue justice and equality in a world where the gap between rich and poor grows wider each year. Moreover, it calls the priest and theologian in me to weave the faith dimension into every dimension of the secular realities that I study.

1. Citation from Peter-Hans Kolvenbach, "Address to the Congregation of Provincials," 20 September 1990, *Acta Romana Societatis Iesu* 20 (1990): 452.

2. See for example Archbishop Roger M. Mahony and Los Angeles Archdiocesan Priests Council, "What About Those Who Do Not Qualify for Amnesty?" *Origins* 16 (1987): 826–28.

3. Drew Christiansen, S.J., "Sacrament of Unity: Ethical Issues in Pastoral Care of Migrants and Refugees," in *Today's Immigrants and Refugees: A Christian Understanding,* Office of Pastoral Care of Migrants and Refugees, Bishops' Committee on Migration, National Conference of Catholic Bishops (Washington, D.C.: USCC, 1988), 81–114.

4. Alexis de Tocqueville, *Democracy in America,* 2 vols. (Garden City, N.Y.: Doubleday, 1969); George Gallup, Jr., and Jim Castelli, *The American Catholic People: Their Beliefs, Practices, and Values* (Garden City, N.Y.: Doubleday, 1987); Kenneth D. Wald, *Religion and Politics in the United States,* 2nd ed. (Washington, D.C.: Congressional Quarterly, 1992).

5. Peter L. Berger, *Facing Up to Modernity: Excursions in Society, Politics, and Religion* (New York: Basic, 1977); Berger and Richard John Neuhaus, *To Empower People* (Washington, D.C.: American Enterprise Institute, 1977); Jean Cohen and Andrew Arato, *Civil Society and Political Theory* (Cambridge, Mass.: MIT, 1992).

6. David C. Leege, "Catholics and the Civic Order: Parish Participation, Politics, and Civic Participation," *Review of Politics* 50 (fall 1988): 704–36; cf. also Wald, *Religion and Politics.*

7. James H. Garland, "Congregation-Based Organizations: A Church Model for the 90s," *America* 169 (13 November 1993): 14–16; Will Herberg, *Protestant-Catholic-Jew: An Essay in American Religious Sociology,* 2nd ed. (Garden City, N.Y.: Doubleday, 1960); Raymond Brady Williams, *Religions of Immigrants from India and Pakistan: New Threads in the American Tapestry* (New York: Cambridge University Press, 1988).

8. Sidney Verba, Kay Lehman Schlozman, Henry Brady, and Norman H. Nie, "Race, Ethnicity and Political Resources: Participation in the United States," *British Journal of Political Science* 23 (October 1993): 453–97.

9. An excellent overview, with scriptural background as well as practical applications, of the Church's position on immigration and how to deal with immigrants can be found in: Office of Pastoral Care of Migrants and Refugees, Bishops' Committee on Migration, National Conference of Catholic Bishops, ed., *Today's Immigrants and Refugees: A Christian Understanding* (Washington, D.C.: USCC, 1988).

ESSAY 25

GC 34, Jesuit Higher Education, and Psychology: Growing Respect and Increasing Dialogue

Charles M. Shelton, S.J.

ABSTRACT

The author, while commenting on the decree on chastity, celebrates the role of chastity in the life of a Jesuit, both in the personal satisfaction he receives from it and in the "radical availability" it allows him to have toward others. At the same time, the author enumerates and develops three shortcomings in the decree. He also explains how GC 34's call to justice has focused his work on moral development and the empathy that such development requires. In interdisciplinary study, he urges the students to reflect on their moral center and its application to their daily lives. He sees empathy as the "psychological glue" that helps create "joyfully friendship-filled" communities in the Society, which our students need to see for their own "moral character development." Finally, he calls on Jesuit communities to devote more time to dialogue about corporate commitment and the spiritual and continual growth of each member of the community.

How do the documents of GC 34 influence a Jesuit psychologist's work in the higher education apostolate? My response incorporates insights and experiences gathered in my roles as psychology professor, practicing clinical psychologist, and Jesuit priest. In addition to sharing insights from these roles, my response includes addressing the following question: How do insights from the field of psychological science influence the message of GC 34? As I see it, fully exploring the relationship of psychology with GC 34 requires examining how the discipline of psychology might aid any evaluation of Congregation members' thinking. Thus, we need scrutiny of both the way that the discipline helps convey the message of the Congregation as well as examine the influence the Congregation might offer Jesuits whose work in the university involves the domain of psychology, whether research, teaching, or clinical practice. Moreover, my hope is that the remarks below are of interest not only to Jesuit psychologists, but to the wider audience of Jesuits working in American higher education.

Let's first look at a specific decree where psychological analysis illuminates, I think, the decree's intent and purpose. Decree 8: "Chastity in the Society of Jesus" (CSJ) contains the subject matter most open to psychological insight and principles; as a consequence, I use this document as the focus for discerning psychology's influence.

Some Psychological Reflections on GC 34's Discussion of Chastity

The psychological age in which Jesuits live their lives fuels continuing self-analysis. No doubt the long training program Jesuits undergo encourages prolonged introspection. Such self-scrutiny, when combined with the media's constant focus on increasingly explicit sexual themes and topics, sparks questions of chastity's meaning and its role in Jesuit life. Given this state of affairs, a discussion of chastity by the Congregation appears relevant and needed. All in all, I applaud the Congregation's effort to delineate a more contemporary rendering of the Jesuit's commitment to live the vowed life.

From a psychological perspective, Decree 8 offers several points worth noting. First, as a psychologist I found the document refreshingly honest and direct. As the document notes, advertising, abuse, gender role changes, structural injustices, and more explicit forms of sexual expression require GC 34 "to say something directly and honestly about the meaning of chastity in Jesuit life and our resolve to continue to support it" (CSJ 3 [230]). All in all, statements in the decree are challenging, realistic, and honest.

Second, as I interpret the document, an implicit theme contained in the decree is a personal invitation to every Jesuit to consider the vow of chastity as being a highly prized *personal* statement of profound meaning. What do I mean by this rather abstract statement? As I read the decree, its true purpose is accomplished to the degree that it encourages every Jesuit's awareness that his offering of self to other men and women through his vow is at a *felt* level a freely chosen act of love—an "act" inseparable from who he is, how he defines himself, and what he wishes to convey to the world. Experiencing such identity growth, self-awareness, and desire is the essence of human meaning-making. Pulling together the above comments, chastity actualizes, ideally, the Jesuit's core self by creating for each man, through the interplay of his temperament, talents, and life situation, the opportunity to embrace a more limitless love. The Jesuit actualizes such pervasive love to the degree that he internalizes his acceptance of availability.

According to GC 34, the purpose and role of chastity in Jesuit life calls forth a radical availability—what the Congregation calls "apostolic availability" (CSJ 9 [236]). By embracing such universal openness, the Jesuit lives his chastity "as a means to a greater love, to a more apostolic charity" (CSJ 9 [236]). From the perspective of pastoral and spiritual theology, such statements make sense. But a psychological truth bears mentioning. What I refer to is the "quality" of the Jesuit's availability. In other words, does the

Jesuit find through his everyday encounters with women and men optimal moments where he shares freely and unselfishly the Lord's love and discerns in such sharing not only the satisfaction of personal witness but significant positive feelings that serve to promote personal satisfaction and ratification of his own self-worth?

Let me offer a personal example to make the above concrete. Three years ago I was walking through the Regis Student Center and, while there, stopped to chat with some students from my introductory psychology class. One student, Matt, was on the Regis soccer team, and I jokingly made the remark that I would consider becoming the team's chaplain. I did not think further about my remark, but within the week I received a call from the soccer coach informing me that the team had come to her and requested I be its chaplain! For a few embarrassing moments I was at a loss as to how to respond to the coach's request. I did of course say "yes" and promised to meet with her within the week to go over my role and duties. After hanging up the phone I recall sitting in my chair and saying to myself, "Shelton, you don't even know the rules of soccer! Besides, don't you have enough to do?" The next day I meekly showed up at practice and introduced myself somewhat haltingly to the coach and players.

The result? After three years as chaplain I can truthfully say I have never regretted for a moment my choice to serve the Regis soccer team as its chaplain. My "job" consists simply of periodically stopping at practice and showing up when I can on game days to say a little prayer prior to game time and, to the extent that my schedule allows, watching what I can of the day's match. Even though these requirements are minimal, during the season a day doesn't go by that a soccer player does not say to me, "Father, are you coming to the game [or practice] today?"

Obviously I mention this personal experience for a reason. It is my vow of chastity that makes possible this joy. As I got to know the team members I found many of them approaching me to talk about their majors and career goals. Soon to follow were discussions with many of them about their personal lives, family issues, and romantic relationships. I have received one of them in the Church and was the sponsor of another at his Confirmation. What does all of this have to do with chastity? Everything. If I was not as a Jesuit vowed to chastity I would never have been available to spend such time with these players. If married with wife and children, my preoccupation would be family, and instead of numerous visits to the soccer field, I would be home with my spouse and the kids. I make the effort consciously to call this fact to mind.

Let me say this another way. I would not trade one moment with the players that I have gotten to know as team chaplain for a wife and children. The privileged moments I have had with these student athletes—sharing their laughter, joys, victories, and defeats, as well as the special moments when they have confided to me their hopes, dreams, fears, and hurts—are blessings holding a special place in my heart. I treasure these experiences and relish this time with them. Again, the vow of chastity has made these experiences all possible. As a result, I feel grateful, privileged, and blessed.

I recount the above personal experience because it is instructive, from a psychological perspective, of the attitude we need to have when we consider the chastity the Jesuit is called to proclaim through his availability. Unless a Jesuit creates such treasured moments and truly relishes them, then the vow becomes, simply, a means for more work and bereft of the positive emotions so necessary for happiness and personal contentment. Worse yet, failure to discover such positive moments and feelings renders the Jesuit vulnerable to find the chaste life a more significant and painful burden than otherwise necessary. Speaking as a psychologist, such experiences of intense loneliness, isolation, and workaholism become the breeding ground that engenders dysfunction and impaired living, making life increasingly painful not only for the individual Jesuit, but for the brothers he lives with as well. Every Jesuit working in the higher education apostolate needs to take a proactive stance and seek out moments where he can experience joy and contentment in a healthy manner. Further, he needs to make such moments part of his conscious awareness and incorporate this awareness and the accompanying feelings into his examen.

Are there areas or issues the document should have addressed but didn't? Yes. In my view, three issues come to mind where I would have wished some discussion or at least acknowledgement.

First, the document fails to mention the issue of homosexuality. From discussion with those attending the Congregation, my impression is that this article simply could not be addressed without creating upset with many non-American delegates. I hasten to add that frankly I do not think the Congregation should have dealt with this issue at length. On the contrary, as I have pointed out elsewhere, Jesuit life is about friendship, not sexual orientation.[1] Nonetheless, given that the Congregation produced a document on chastity and Jesuit life, failure at least to note that sexual orientation has at times been a source of tension and misunderstanding among ours and an issue that needs some discussion both in formation and in our apostolic houses renders the document incomplete and perhaps even inadequate to some degree.

The document's tone is the second issue that causes me concern. As the document discusses chastity, I sense the traces of the ascetical language from another era. Several passages stress emphasis on themes of suffering, deprivation, and hardship. This is not to deny the aloneness (or loneliness) that the vow entails and the document itself rightly points out. However, the document is shortsighted in addressing solely this more "negative" feeling side of the vow.

Let me make this criticism more explicit. Like many Jesuits, I am friends with a number of married couples. In one way or another I have heard from these individuals their more or less marvel at the life I live. I have plenty of private time and have wide discretion in how I spend such time. The number of talks and workshops I give annually allow for travel and networking with numerous friends. Moreover, the "gift" of celibate living is friendship, and the vow occasions numerous opportunities for friendship building. Of course at times I get lonely and wish for wife and family and the emotional intimacy it provides. Yet, the life I have constructed (and which chastity allows) is one I find so precious and joyful that I would never trade it for wife and family. In other words, bluntly speaking, chastity is most of the time for me a lot of fun! My question is this: Why can't the document speak directly of such joy and happiness? We shortchange our lives and undercut the benefits of being Jesuits unless we express explicitly *and* celebrate the gains the vow provides. I sometimes wonder if when Jesuits write about the vows (particularly chastity) a tacit assumption is operative. This assumption states that there must always be a "loss" and any advantage the vow provides the Jesuit in terms of joy and contentment must be tempered and discussed cautiously. Perhaps I am being unfair, but my reading of Decree 8 leads me to conclude the document contains, unfortunately, such thinking.

Finally, I wish the document had given more space to the topic of Jesuit friendship. For the Jesuit, the vow of chastity makes no sense unless it is understood under the mantel of Jesuit friendship. To be sure, the document does note the importance of friendship, but so often this discussion is framed in how Jesuit friends help the man live the vow. It is as if this beautiful experience has only an "adjunct" status whose main purpose is to support a Jesuit's being chaste in the midst of personal struggle and loneliness.

I certainly believe that Jesuit friends are indispensable to living a happy, healthy chaste life. But Jesuit friends are more than a means to an end. Jesuit friendship is a wonderful, profound gift I would not trade for a wife and family. The foregoing sentence might appear bold to some, but think about it. Unless such a statement can be made, a Jesuit might be vulnerable to experiencing his life as a second-class emotional status.

I regret the document could not be more direct in acknowledging the joy such friendship offers every vowed man. Friendship is the precious gift chastity offers; it deserves celebration. Again, I go back to the point made earlier. Over my twenty-five years in the Society I have found Jesuit documents failing to celebrate happiness, fun, and contentment. We need to say explicitly there is nothing wrong with such positive feelings. More importantly, if we want to attract men to the Society I strongly suggest we speak about such joy explicitly and with a great deal of pride!

The Decrees' Influence on My Work as a Psychologist

GC 34 calls Jesuits to an awareness of justice's numerous dimensions. Such attentiveness requires every Jesuit to uphold the sanctity of human life, the struggle for human rights, the increasing interdependence of peoples, the care of the global environment, and the connection of every person to community (cf. Decree 3: "Our Mission and Justice").

Furthermore, the decrees emphasize the need for Jesuits to interpret their apostolic engagements as nurturing God's active presence in people's lives. According to GC 34, "Jesuits try to see what God has already done in the lives of individuals, societies, and cultures, and to discern how God will continue that work" (Decree 6: "The Jesuit Priest: Ministerial Priesthood and Jesuit Identity" 20 [177]).

Stressing the theme of justice and appreciating the Lord's active working in human life confirms the path I have worked toward as a writer and researcher in the area of psychological science. More specifically, I have carved out a focus of study stressing human conscience functioning and moral development. The essential argument that GC 34 and previous Congregations have made that calls, indeed demands, Jesuits promote the mission of justice, requires that human beings have the psychological aptitude and skills that insure such moral principles can be internalized and authentically lived. My approach to human moral growth argues that the psychological capacity for empathy—the ability to experience the pains and hurts of others as if they are one's own—is integral to and consonant with the Christian moral vision.[2] Without a meaningful capacity for empathy one is incapable of commitment to the very core principle of justice that the Congregation calls every Jesuit to promote. Moreover, for the Jesuit in higher education to put in practice the Congregation's mandate, at some point in time and at some level of analysis, some experience of empathy must be operable.

Take some commonplace examples Jesuits in higher education encounter on a daily basis. In the classroom a Jesuit professor discusses economic and social variables that affect the lives of a disadvantaged group. Later that day this same professor might carry on a more detailed analysis of a social problem, emphasizing numerous real-life examples that dramatize the plight and pain of the truly disadvantaged. In a parallel fashion, a Jesuit administrator at the same university makes a budgetary decision on the school's future. He continually challenges himself to think how the university's mission takes into account the needs of disadvantaged socioeconomic groups in the surrounding neighborhood and how university programs and policies might benefit the needs of this wider community. Down the hall, a Jesuit in campus ministry is preparing his homily for the upcoming Sunday liturgy and seeks through his words to stimulate the consciousness of students regarding the plight of the powerless and oppressed. Every Jesuit involved in the higher education apostolate most likely identifies with these or similar examples.

Empathy might best be viewed as the "psychological glue" that sustains and promotes Christian community. Speaking personally, lacking empathic triggers that stir me (for example, a hurting student, a confused class), I all too easily slip into a more detached academic mode and run the risk of removing myself from the very desires that brought me to Jesuit higher education. I suggest every Jesuit take time to periodically ask himself several questions:

1. How do I experience empathy in the midst of my daily work?

2. In my daily life in higher education what experiences are most likely to serve as empathic triggers?

3. How do experiences of empathy influence my apostolic service? my work with students? my personal life? my experience of being Jesuit?

A second area identified by GC 34 that influences my work in higher education is the call for interdisciplinary study. "Jesuit universities will promote interdisciplinary work; this implies a spirit of cooperation and dialogue among specialists within the university itself and with those of other universities" (Decree 17: "Jesuits and University Life" [JUL] 10 [413]). At Regis University this document has served to encourage my participation in a university-wide interdisciplinary seminar series. A brief history will prove helpful.

Several years ago the faculty decided that the wide range of knowledge domains required restructuring of the curriculum. As a consequence, four sets of seminars were established, each with a different theme. Freshman seminars introduce students to intensive writing skills around a specific topic chosen by the course's instructor. Sophomore seminars addressed cultural diversity in America. In their junior year, students were exposed to an international theme. The question "How ought I to live?" was addressed in senior seminars. My interest in moral development and young adult psychological growth made this a natural topic of interest. After reading the documents, particularly "Jesuits and University Life" (which I recall was the very first document I read) and its endorsement of interdisciplinary inquiry, I decided to volunteer to teach a senior seminar. The document was not the sole reason I requested to teach a seminar, but it did prove a significant catalyst for volunteering. I teamed with a member of the religious studies department. It so happens that the faculty member I teamed with was my best friend in the Jesuits. Father John Ridgway, S.J., is a member of the Oregon Province and a specialist in New Testament. After several discussions about our individual goals for the course and our mutual interests we decided to entitle the course "The Adult Conscience: Theological and Psychological Perspectives." John addresses the issue of morality from scriptural and theological positions whereas I discuss various psychological theories of moral and human development. Our goals for the course are to help students understand as they prepare to enter the adult world of work that they do indeed possess a moral center (conscience) and that this moral foundation requires something of them. We try to help Regis seniors reflect on their moral principles and how to apply them in their daily lives, as well as help them think through what future moral issues and concerns they might encounter around areas of work and relationship.

The course has proven to be highly popular with students and immensely enjoyable to teach. An unforseen benefit has also occurred. On course evaluations most students remarked that one of the things they found most enjoyable about the course is the relationship John and I display in the classroom. Early on John and I decided to offer a relaxed playful style in the classroom. Included in this "playful style" is questioning of one another in the classroom, commenting upon one another's lectures during classroom discussion, and playful teasing of one another. We have found students resonate with this style, and find such a relaxed (and fun!) classroom environment optimizes learning. Equally important, the relationship John and I exhibit in the classroom serves to promote indirectly student conscience development. To address more fully, the love and respect two Jesuit friends and instructors show one another in front of students communicates to them that (a) conscience does work and is enjoyable; (b) true friendship in life is possible and is immensely satisfying; and (c) being a Jesuit and religious is a joyful experience.

Not surprisingly, this give-and-take with John sparks a sympathetic chord in students. Psychology has become the interpretive lens through which students view life and evaluate themselves. Many of the students we teach today have seen therapists and nearly all of them have been exposed to the current and faddish psychological jargon known through terms such as "dysfunctional family," "toxic parent," and "codependent." Today's undergraduates are products of secondary schools that promote awareness of the danger of drugs and the problem of adolescent suicide. It is remarkable that in a little over several decades the Church has moved from wariness to full embrace of psychological understandings of the human person. Paralleling this trend, students, likewise, have come to accept psychology as part and parcel of their everyday lives. No area exemplifies this fact more than the focus students give their relationships. Relationships are the primary meaning-making experience of the adolescent and young adult years. To lack relationship or be caught in unhealthy relationships creates significant distress for any young person. I am of the firm belief that one significant benefit to which we adults involved in Jesuit education must commit ourselves is helping every student before he or she graduates understand the meaning of "healthy" friendship.

Friendship is critical not only for emotional satisfaction and contentment, as it provides a safe emotional haven in an all too lonely world, but because it serves as a primary force for moral growth. Think about it. As an adult ask yourself this question: How do you grow morally? In other words, what experiences most contribute to your moral growth as an adult? Though a variety of experiences contribute to adult moral development, I am of the firm conviction that adults grow best morally through friendship. Only friends, by their example, challenge, and questions can jolt us or make us reconsider our tacit assumptions about life, the world, and personal self-understandings. Only trusted friends are given the permission to intrude gently into our lives and help us view who we are and where we are going. Think of the last "good" talk you had with a close friend. Chances are you left the conversation somewhat altered. From having had this exchange you might entertain a new perspective on an issue of mutual interest, or perhaps this discussion has increased self-awareness or, at a minimum, served to foster greater emotional contentment.

A primary goal of Jesuit education is to contribute to the growth of student moral character development. I suggest that if we wish to take this task seriously, one of the best ways to provide for this growth is to let students see that we are men who celebrate and live joyfully friendship-filled lives with other Jesuits. We need to let students see that through the respect, joy, and loyalty found in Jesuit friendship we find the call of Jesus and the joy it brings. How to do this? Obviously, team teaching with a brother Jesuit is a wonderful opportunity to convey the joys of Jesuit friendship. I have also found that when lecturing in the classroom, it is helpful periodically to offer at select times examples from my life. Oftentimes I narrate the experience of a Jesuit friend and the value the relationship offers me. Another way to do this is to "build up" other Jesuits with students. If I know of contributions made by Jesuits in my community to the apostolate, I do not hesitate to mention them to students when appropriate. Implicit in GC 34 documents on mission, justice, chastity, and university life is the need for Jesuits to be attached and involved in discerning communities that are truly "friends in the Lord" and to have as our apostolic focus promoting the process of moral conversion of those we minister with and to. I know of no other experience in Jesuit life that better captures its purpose and meaning than the experience of Jesuit friendship.

Reflect on the following:

1. *Who are my Jesuit friends in the university apostolate in which I work?*

2. *Reflect on each of your Jesuit friends at your school. How is your relationship with each of these men of benefit to your spiritual, emotional, moral, and apostolic life? Be as specific as possible when reflecting on each relationship.*

3. *Are there ways your friendship with individual Jesuit friends is made known on campus to student? staff? fellow faculty?*

4. *How do your actions, statements, and so on, "build up" each of these friendships?*

A final area where the documents motivate my actions arises in the holistic nature of Jesuit education's approach to students. We all know that a primary focus of Jesuit education is concern for the whole student. Thus, the document on university life confirms what many other documents have addressed through the years when it states: "A Jesuit university must be outstanding in its human, social, spiritual, and moral formation, as well as for its pastoral attention to its students and to the different groups of people who work in it or are related to it" (JUL 11 [414]). For some students at our universities, before they can truly hear Jesus' saving message of love and conversion, need to address hurts and unresolved, lingering conflicts arising from their life histories. All in all, students attending Jesuit colleges and universities come to our schools with more personal problems and hurts as well as more acutely felt negative feelings than students of previous generations. Studies confirm that college undergraduates not only have more personal problems than students of previous generations, but that these problems are proving more serious.[3]

Yet, even in the midst of their personal concerns, I sense students at our institutions are still desirous of what young adults have always desired—having around them adults who care for them, believe in them, and challenge them to be the best they can be. I often find myself taking a stroll through the student lunchroom or snack bar—taking a few moments to nod or smile or talk briefly with a student even if I do not know his or her name (which is usually the case).

I also find myself increasingly drawn to wearing clerics. Though it probably rubs against current trends, I firmly believe there is something unique about a Jesuit priest's presence on a Jesuit campus. By using the word *unique* I by no means mean that he is "better" than a lay colleague or staff person. Moreover, it is certainly true that the Jesuit mission is increasingly carried out by our lay colleagues, and the Congregation documents themselves support this trend (see Decree 13: "Cooperation with the Laity in Mission"). Nonetheless, a Jesuit priest's attention to students offers something special. I suspect their attraction resides in what we represent and stand for.

In spite of many clergy scandals there still remains for most students a deep sense of trust in the Jesuits affiliated with our schools. However, because of the holistic nature of Jesuit education that we Jesuits take pride in, a Jesuit more than his colleagues is "expected" to be available to students and converse with them on a wide range of topics, running the gamut from spiritual growth and personal problems to academic issues and career choices. This expectation to be available creates a tension not easily resolved, and, to be perfectly honest, one that grows more challenging with diminishing numbers. I have no answer as to how to resolve this issue. The number of Jesuits staffing our higher education institutions continues to decline. Nonetheless, some preventive measures are called for and a few steps in this direction are offered below.

If we are to take seriously the Congregation mandate to be available to students and address their needs, at a minimum, two things are imperative. First, the community of Jesuits at each Jesuit institution of higher learning needs to develop apostolic priorities. More to the point, our communities must increasingly become communities of conversation where serious dialogue takes place among Jesuit brothers regarding corporate commitment and assigning priorities for achieving this commitment. Some communities have made significant progress in furthering this communal discussion, but much more needs to be done. In a related fashion, with the manpower pool for eligible Jesuits in higher education becoming a puddle, attracting young Jesuit faculty and staff will more and more necessitate addressing the *quality* of Jesuit community living, and a vital factor in such quality living is the need for honest, supportive, and challenging conversation among community members.

On an individual level, each Jesuit assigned to Jesuit higher education must come to some understanding of how he is to address personal needs and priorities. How much time to give to teaching, research, counseling, and participating in department and university events must be carefully discerned. For the most part we Jesuits are good-hearted men, but the insidious temptation with declining manpower is for good men to just "do more." This tendency is not only shortsighted but, from a long-term perspective, injurious to a Jesuit's spiritual and emotional health, for it can only lead to burnout and eventual dissatisfaction. My point is that optimal functioning for Jesuit presence and availability in the college/university apostolate in the future must by necessity include communal dialogue whose purpose is to invigorate and ratify every Jesuit's awareness that he is actively engaged in an *enterprise of companionship*. At the same time, this "communal dialogue" serves as a sustaining source of clarity for the Jesuit as he discerns his commitment by sorting through and evaluating workload, interests, challenges, and the daily demands of the apostolate.

Conclusion

In sum, the life of a Jesuit psychologist on the Jesuit campus offers enormous opportunities to be of service to the college/university community. What GC 34 has provided me is clarity of purpose and a realization that "the Risen Christ's call to us to join him in laboring for the Kingdom is always accompanied by his power" (Decree 2: "Servants of Christ's Mission" 7 [32]). More than anything, this "power" becomes operable when the Jesuit cooperates with its immense potential through loving, faithful companionship with his brothers and personal commitment to spiritual and emotional health. Such a stance finds support both in the discipline of psychology as well as the documents of GC 34.

ENDNOTES • SHELTON

1. Charles M. Shelton, S.J., "Friendship in Jesuit Life: The Joys, the Struggles, the Possibilities," *Studies in the Spirituality of Jesuits* 27/5 (November 1995).
2. Ibid., *Morality of the Heart: A Psychology for the Christian Moral Life* (New York: Crossroad, 1997).
3. Ibid., "Helping College Students Make Moral Decisions," *Conversations on Jesuit Higher Education* 2 (fall 1992): 6–21 at 11.

GC 34 and Theology: "Dialogue Is a New Way of Being Church"

Thomas P. Rausch, S.J.

ABSTRACT

The author asks "how is the Society's share in Christ's mission to be understood at this particular moment in history?" He argues that GC 34 can help universities understand their mission as rooted in "theological wisdom"—"the reconciliation of all people to God in Christ Jesus"—and help theology departments "reclaim and clarify" their identity as Catholic departments "at the service of the Church." For theology departments to carry out their mission, they must first make themselves "centers of Catholic theology." The author urges dialogue with other cultures and traditions as a theological experience of "new manifestations of the divine mystery" and the "finding of God in all things."

Introduction

For Jesuits as companions of Jesus, a crucial question must always be, How is the Society's share in Christ's mission to be understood at this particular moment in history? If GC 32 focused our mission in terms of the service of the faith and the promotion of justice, GC 34 broadened that focus to include a dialogue with the many cultures and religions that are so often in conflict.

The fathers of the Congregation saw the Society as "a body more diverse than ever before, engaged in a variety of ministries at the crossroads of cultural conflict, social and economic struggles, religious revivalism, and new opportunities for bringing the Good News to peoples all over the world" (Decree 2: "Servants of Christ's Mission" [SCM] 2 [16]). They acknowledge that GC 32 "speaks of 'our mission to evangelize,' particularly through dialogue with members of other religious traditions and through the engagement with culture which is essential for an effective presentation of the Gospel" (SCM 15 [40]).[1]

Then the fathers of GC 34 conclude: "In the light of Decree 4 [of GC 32] and our present experience, we can now say explicitly that our mission of the service of faith and the promotion of justice must be broadened to include, as integral dimensions, proclamation of the Gospel, dialogue, and the evangelization of culture" (SCM 20 [48]).

It is interesting to see how the Congregation articulates this broadened understanding of mission. The Society's share in Christ's mission is to be expressed *ad extra* in its commitments to the struggle for justice, the evangelization of culture, and interreligious dialogue, each of which merits a separate decree. But as a Society sharing in this mission through its service to the Church, there is also a commitment *ad ecclesiam*. This specifically ecclesial commitment is addressed in the decree on our service to the Church and given contemporary expression in the decrees on Jesuit efforts in ecumenism, on cooperating with the laity in mission, and on seeking to enter into greater solidarity with women in Church and society.

What does this broadened understanding of the contemporary mission of the Society suggest for the teaching of undergraduate theology in Jesuit colleges and universities? I would like to suggest that the values expressed in these documents can help to reclaim and clarify our identity as Catholic departments of theology and religious studies at the service of the Church and give direction to our teaching and research efforts. In the process, a renewed sense of the mission of theology might merit for the discipline its proper place as the integrating discipline within a Jesuit university. Proceeding in reverse order, we will begin by reviewing the place of theology in Jesuit universities and then consider what GC 34 suggests for those teaching theology today, both *ad ecclesiam,* in relation to the Church, and *ad extra,* in relation to the broader human community.

Theology as an Integrating Discipline

From their earliest days Jesuit universities have been concerned with the moral and religious development of their students. Of course, this concern has not been unique to Jesuit schools; it has been true of other Catholic schools as well as of Protestant institutions of higher education. However, as Boston College's William Neenan has observed, the educational philosophies of the two traditions, at least in the United States, have been very different. In nineteenth- and twentieth-century Protestant colleges and universities the curriculum itself did not play a major role in the students' religious development: "The course of studies was not an essential constitutive element of the enterprise but simply the context within which the student's moral and social development occurred."[2] That development was supposed to take place through chapel services, parietal rules, and a capstone course in moral philosophy.

How different is the Jesuit educational philosophy that sees the curriculum itself as essential to the educational process, with philosophy and theology at its center? In Jesuit schools, theology has traditionally taken the first place, at least in theory.

When Saint Ignatius outlined his vision for the Society's colleges and universities, he based it on what he had experienced in his own studies, particularly those at Paris. The *Constitutions* emphasized the importance of theology: "Since the end of the Society and of its studies is to aid our fellowmen to the knowledge and love of God and to the salvation of their souls, and since the subject of theology is the means most suited to this end, in the universities of the Society the principal emphasis ought to be placed upon it."[3] Because the ends or finality of both university studies and of the Society of Jesus itself were best served by theology, Ignatius saw it as an integrating discipline.[4] Michael J. Buckley has described it as "an architectonic wisdom" precisely because it both presumes the other sciences and is able to integrate their striving for the truth in its own.[5] Paul Crowley has summarized the place of theology in Ignatius' view as follows:

> *First, the Ignatian vision, apostolic and world-embracing, is the inspiration of the Jesuit university. Second, the Jesuit university gives theology (though not necessarily the theology department) pride of place because theology is a radically interdisciplinary intellectual wisdom that mediates worldly knowledge and faith; university theology, a university discipline, is foundational and indispensable to achieving the Ignatian vision rooted in the* Exercises, *which is itself highly theological. Third, theology in the Jesuit university is not simply one discipline alongside others; it is rather the discipline that gives coherence and focus to the university. . . . The university's identity as a university depends upon theology's role.*[6]

So much for theory. In practice, from the earliest days of the Society the reality has been considerably more complicated, as Crowley's somewhat hesitant distinction between theology (as an informing vision) and the theology department suggests. According to its *Constitutions,* the Society could operate both colleges and universities [307]. In his chapter on the first Jesuit schools, John O'Malley notes that, "although in theory theology was the discipline toward which the others point, it was not taught in the colleges, that is, the secondary schools," where instead students were instructed in "Christian doctrine" once a week.[7]

The universities included the higher disciplines—philosophy, the sciences, mathematics, and theology. Formal instruction in theology was usually limited to those preparing for the priesthood, though, as George Ganss observes, the very environment meant that the light of theology "filtered down to all the students in various ways."[8] The European model of a university has remained basically the same down to the present day. Theology is present in the university as a faculty or specialty; it is not usually integrated into the general curriculum.

Though universities are differently organized in the United States—divided into undergraduate and graduate divisions—the situation, until recently, was not much different.

In his important study, *The Soul of the American University,* George M. Marsden argues that in Protestant institutions of higher education, theology, though it played an important role in defining intellectual boundaries, had never been well integrated into the curriculum.[9]

> *Already in the eighteenth century, moral philosophy had begun to emerge as the central locus of Christianity in the curriculum, supplemented by periodic revivals intended to enlist student Christian commitment. . . . Some reference to theological principles nonetheless persisted until the age of the universities* [late nineteenth century]. *Early in that era, however, with many pressures working against theology and no formal provision for its presence, it was quickly banished to divinity schools, if not simply banished.*[10]

Similarly, for Catholics prior to the Second Vatican Council, the study of theology took place largely in seminaries. The seminary locus for theology meant that laymen and laywomen were excluded; theology was for priests. Women were unable to do advanced work in theology until 1943, when Sister Madeleva Wolf, C.S.C., established a School of Sacred Theology for women at Saint Mary's College in Notre Dame, Indiana. The first doctoral program open to laymen and laywomen was established at Marquette in September 1963 by Bernard Cooke, though the university had to call the program "Religious Studies" to head off possible objections from Rome.

On the undergraduate level, Catholic colleges and universities in the United States required "religion" courses for their students, but they did not teach theology. Their primary concern was religious formation and doctrinal orthodoxy, and their largely nonelective curricula stressed classical languages and Scholastic philosophy.[11] As Robert Wister has pointed out:

> *Until the 1950s most Catholic colleges did not even offer courses in theology as an academic discipline. They were liberal arts institutions whose curriculum was centered on philosophy, not theology. Most did offer courses in religion, but they were usually of an apologetic nature and in many cases were not offered for credit. Quite often the instructor was not part of the academic faculty and did not possess the academic credentials required by the college.*[12]

The situation Wister describes applied to Jesuit colleges as well. In his study of Catholic higher education in the twentieth century, William P. Leahy notes that in "the 1920s and early 1930s, certain Jesuits and influential alumni . . . judged that philosophy and religion classes were academically weak and poorly taught" in Jesuit colleges.[13] In the *Jesuit Educational Quarterly* for the late 1940s and 1950s one repeatedly finds complaints about the secondary status of "religion" courses in Jesuit colleges. At a 1949 panel discussion on college religion, Eugene B. Gallagher lamented the fact that in Jesuit colleges religion courses were two hours a week rather than the usual three, and received only one semester hour credit, "the same amount they get for public speaking!"[14] Most of the courses were apologetic in nature.

But there were also signs of the coming change. As early as 1939 a symposium sponsored by the National Catholic Alumni Federation called for a "return" of theology to the college curriculum.[15] John Courtney Murray, a participant in the symposium, agreed, but made the case that the kind of theology taught in seminaries would have to be rethought.[16] In an article published in 1944 he argued that the colleges should begin developing theology courses "for the layman."[17] Soon other Jesuits were arguing that "religion or theology" should have "primacy of place" and should be the integrating discipline in the curriculum.[18]

In Jesuit schools the principle of integration had long been philosophy that provided an integrated world view and addressed the basic issue of the human good.[19] Philosophy meant Scholasticism, or more accurately Neoscholasticism, usually Aquinas, though some schools used Suarez well into the Thomistic revival. Undergraduates took a philosophy course almost every semester. As late as 1964 at Loyola University of Los Angeles, all students were required to take, in order, logic, philosophy of nature, philosophy of man, philosophy of knowledge, natural theology, general ethics, and applied ethics. Students also took a one-unit religion course each semester, but the university bulletin does not list a major in religious studies until 1971.

Catholic and Jesuit higher education changed considerably after the Council. Philosophy lost its place as an integrating discipline, partly through the gradual reduction of required courses from what was essentially a minor to, on an average, two required courses, and partly because the disestablishment of Scholasticism in the face of the new pluralism of approaches and methods meant the loss of a unified philosophical outlook. At the same time, Catholic universities began to develop professional theology departments as they began to hire the laymen and laywomen emerging from the graduate schools, eager to teach and do research themselves.

As Jesuit universities today, conscious of the history of their Protestant counterparts, struggle to reaffirm their own religious identity, theology can again play the integrating role in the curriculum that Ignatius envisioned for it, not just in theory, but in practice.

First, theology as a discipline is integrative because of its interdisciplinary nature. In its methods and hermeneutical investigations, theology incorporates the literary analysis of texts, philosophical and historical criticism, sociopolitical and cultural studies, and the disciplined integration of the critical reason used in the sciences with faith. Thus it subsumes and integrates the various disciplines of the academy in its own search for the truth.

Second, and more importantly, the mission that the university seeks to serve is rooted in a theological wisdom, specifically, in the Christian vision of the reconciliation of all people to God in Christ Jesus that one finds in the *Spiritual Exercises*. In the sixteenth century Ignatius articulated the Jesuit mission as "to aid our fellowmen to the knowledge and love of God and to the salvation of their souls" (*Const* [446]). GC 32 reformulated that for the contemporary Society of Jesus as "the service of the faith and the promotion of justice," a formula that most of our universities have incorporated in various ways into their mission statements. It is this theological vision that, in Paul Crowley's words, "gives coherence and focus" to the Jesuit university today.[19] We can now consider how GC 34 has concretized that mission for the Society and thus for Jesuit institutions at the dawn of the Third Millennium.

Theology and Church

What GC 34 says about the ecclesial dimension of our mission has specific implications for Jesuit theology departments as well as for Jesuit theologians. Four documents of GC 34 touch specifically on service to the Church: Decree 11: "On Having a Proper Attitude of Service in the Church" (HPA), Decree 12: "Ecumenism" (E), Decree 13: "Cooperation with the Laity in Mission" (CLM), and Decree 14: "Jesuits and the Situation of Women in Church and Civil Society" (JSW). While each should inform and shape the way we teach theology, Decree 11 is particularly important.

Decree 11 is a nuanced document. It reaffirms the Society's commitment to serving the Church in her teaching, life, and worship, particularly in virtue of the fourth vow of obedience to the Pope in regard to missions (HPA 1 [298]). At the same time, it sketches how the rediscovery of the universal Church as a communion of churches as well as a deepened sense of the coresponsibility of all God's people for the life of the Church can be a source of both vitality and creative tension (8 [305]). Quoting Father General Peter-Hans Kolvenbach, the decree acknowledges frankly that there are "strong tensions within the Church from which the Society may not stand aloof, and through their very apostolic responsibility, Jesuits are inevitably dragged into conflictual, even explosive ecclesiastical situations" (13 [310]).[20]

In wording Decree 11, the Congregation tried to walk a careful line between an obedience that is faithful to the visible, hierarchical Church and, at the same time, a fidelity to God, to the truth, and to a well-formed conscience because this distinction is particularly important for Jesuit theologians (HPA 14–15 [311–12]). The decree does not rule out constructive criticism based on prayerful discernment, and recognizes that Jesuits sometimes must remain silent. In regard to sensitive doctrinal and moral questions, it says the following: "We will not underestimate the possibility of giving scandal, nor forget that between the extremes of premature, ill-considered public criticism and servile silence there exists the alternative of moderate and respectful expression of our views. We will avoid particular interests and bear in mind the greater good of the whole Church" (24 [321]). Moreover, Jesuits will do this with an Ignatian sense of *sentire cum ecclesia* that reveals their love for the Church (26 [323]).

How can Jesuit departments of theology and religious studies carry out this mission of service to the Catholic Church in a way that is both committed and at the same time critical? If they are to do this, they must first have a clear sense of their identity as departments of Catholic theology. This does not mean that they hire only Catholics, or that they teach only Catholic theology. As Charles Curran has observed, "Catholic identity has never defined itself in sectarian terms as over against all other human or secular reality. Catholic always includes catholic with a small c."[22] Indeed, as we shall see below, our departments must be able to engage in the dialogue with other Christian traditions and other religions that the Congregation calls us to. But if they are to do this, they must have a sense of themselves as centers of Catholic theology.

Today that is not always a given. Marsden's book is a powerful testimony to the gradual secularization of the American university system, built on a foundation of Protestant colleges, among them Harvard, Yale, Princeton, Dartmouth, Wellesley, Vassar, Smith, Chicago, and Stanford. He illustrates how their insistence on moving beyond denominational or confessional identities to a "nonsectarian" religious universalism contributed ultimately "to the virtual exclusion of religious perspectives from the most influential centers of American intellectual life."[23]

Most Catholic colleges and universities have not yet lost their religious identity. But they are going through a similar process of secularization, and the danger remains, particularly for their theology departments. While most offer courses in religious studies as well as theology, some have changed their names to religious studies, making it the defining discipline. Notre Dame's Lawrence Cunningham sees this as a "retreat,"[24] and James Heft, provost of the University of Dayton, argues that in Catholic universities, "doing" theology means "a study . . . of religious traditions from a committed stance rooted in a living faith community, the church."[25]

Today that rootedness in the Church is not always apparent. The laicization of theology, with the majority of department members laymen and laywomen, some of whom are non-Catholic, means that university theology operates even more independently of Church authority than in the past when the majority of professors were priests or religious, subject to religious obedience. Some Catholic scholars have expressed concern over the fact that an increasing number of future Catholic scholars are being trained at private or nondenominational Protestant schools, and so are being educated outside their own tradition.[26] Moreover, some theologians today argue that Catholic theology does not need any relation to the Church.[27] At the annual meeting of the chairs of Jesuit departments of theology and religious studies at the American Academy of Religion, some have said that their departments no longer choose to identify themselves as Roman Catholic, or profess that they don't know what such a designation might mean. Thus, it is not surprising that even in Catholic universities, theology has become increasingly specialized and academic, too often cut off from the faith and life of the Church.[28]

Even asking the question of Catholic identity today can be like raising a red flag. It is offensive to some, while others fear an exclusion of non-Catholics or a return to ecclesiastical control. Yet, if our departments are to carry out the mission of committed yet critical service to the Catholic Church for which GC 34 calls, it is an issue that must be faced.

First, there is a distinctive identity to a department of theology rooted in the Catholic tradition. Catholic faith is an ecclesial faith. It would be difficult to describe a department as rooted in the Catholic tradition if it did not regularly offer courses in ecclesiology, sacraments, liturgy, spirituality, and the Church's social doctrine, or if a student was never introduced to the Church Fathers or to figures such as Aquinas, Teresa, Rahner, and Merton.

Second, theology in a Catholic university is not simply a research discipline, making academic comparisons and deconstructing whatever is deemed objectional in the tradition; it is also at the "service of the faith," and so must be evangelical in the sense of proclaiming the Good News to students relatively uninformed about their faith and living in a very secular world. As Heft has said, "The department of theology at a Catholic university hands on the tradition (catechesis), reflects systematically and critically upon that tradition (theology) and recognizes the hierarchy of truths as well as the importance both of official teaching and of being a part of the larger global reality of the church (Catholicism)."[29]

Finally, in an era of diminishing numbers of priests and religious, service to the Church means educating and preparing in the Catholic faith, both in undergraduate and particularly in graduate programs, those who will be tomorrow's lay Catholic leaders and ministers. A 1995 study produced by Georgetown's Center for Applied Research in the Apostolate (CARA) noted that the number of students in United States Catholic lay ministry programs has more than doubled in nine years. In 1986 there were 10,500 students in 206 programs. In 1995 there were 21,800 students in 265 programs. Another study done at Loyola University of New Orleans, tracking the increasing number of laymen and laywomen in these graduate programs, states that Catholic faith will be lived out tomorrow "in an *institutionally different Catholic culture.*"[30]

Our schools, and particularly our theology departments, are already shaping that Catholic culture. Many of those who will be tomorrow's ministers are today among our students. The Congregation recognizes that our own mission is to be shared with these men and women who will be tomorrow's ministers. Decree 13 calls on Jesuits to "shift the focus of our attention from the exercise of our own direct ministry to the strengthening of laity in their mission" (CLM 19 [353]). Decree 14 asks them to work to overcome discrimination against women not only as a matter of social justice, but also because they have much to contribute to both society and the Church. Again, the Congregation calls attention to the fine line that Jesuits must walk: it notes that a change of sensibilities to the situation of women "will inevitably have implications for Church teaching and practice. In this context, we ask Jesuits to live as always, with the tension involved in being faithful to the teachings of the Church while at the same time trying to read the signs of the times" (JSW 14 [382]). Certainly our teaching should incorporate a sense for full partnership with laywomen and laymen in the Church, just as it should educate them in the particular tradition and ethos of the Church in which they will serve.

Third, our service to the Church means a commitment to ecumenism. According to Decree 12, ecumenism is not just a specific work; "it is a new way of being a Christian" (E 3 [328]). Therefore ecumenism should be represented both in the theological curriculum and in the diversity of our faculties. The presence of Christians from other traditions on our theology faculties and of courses in Protestant and eastern Christian theology is important so that the department might be "catholic" in a more inclusive sense.

At the same time, our departments cannot carry out the commitment to ecumenism called for by GC 34 without a clear commitment to Catholic theology. Unfortunately, the word *ecumenism* is sometimes used popularly in an interdenominational sense. To be "ecumenical" is simply to be inclusive. But as Thomas O'Meara points out, there is no "ecumenical" Church. "Theology can be ecumenical only if it is first the theology of a vital church."[31] To do ecumenical work, Catholics must be firmly grounded within their own tradition. Our non-Catholic partners expect that of us; some of them are drawn to our schools precisely because they value its Catholic identity.

Theology and World

The Congregation's broadening of the Society's mission to include the proclamation of the Gospel, dialogue, and the evangelization of cultures also has important implications for the teaching of theology. Three documents attempt to focus the Society's mission in relation to our contemporary world. Decree 3: "Our Mission and Justice" reaffirms the Society's commitment to the promotion of justice as an integral part of our mission. Decree 4: "Our Mission and Culture" (OMC) reminds Jesuits that Pope Paul VI and Pope John Paul II have both placed the issue of the Gospel and culture at the center of the Church's reflection (OMC 1 [75]). Decree 5: "Our Mission and Interreligious Dialogue" (OMID) points out that Pope John Paul has repeatedly asked the Society "to make interreligious dialogue an apostolic priority for the third millennium" (OMID 3 [130]).

In emphasizing the importance of dialogue across cultural and religious differences, the Congregation showed its awareness of the increasingly diverse character of our world. That diversity is increasingly being reflected in our local communities and institutions. To take my own institution as an example, Loyola Marymount is a microcosm of the diversity of Los Angeles, which in turn foreshadows in many ways what is happening in the rest of the country. As of 1997, our supposedly white middle-class school is in reality only 46 percent Caucasian; it includes 8 percent African American, 1 percent American Indian, 15 percent Asian/Pacific Islander, 21 percent Hispanic, with 4 percent international and 5 percent declining to state.

Los Angeles is even more diverse. By conservative estimates, weekend Masses in the archdiocese are celebrated in fifty-five languages. It is estimated that the 1997 population of Los Angeles County will be only 34 percent white, with 42 percent Latino, 9 percent African American (a drop), and 13 percent Asian/Pacific Islander (the fastest growing segment).[32] By 2050 the whole country will be almost half nonwhite; thus, as Dale Maharidge says in his book, *The Coming White Minority,* "California is America's multicultural tomorrow."[33]

In terms of religious diversity, 59 percent of our students identify themselves as Roman Catholic, 8 percent check "Christian," which usually means they are members of evangelical, pentecostal, or fundamentalist churches, and 5 percent belong to mainline Protestant churches. Jewish students represent 1 percent, and 4 percent put down "other," which includes a growing number of students who are Buddhist, Hindu, or Muslim. Significantly, 22 percent decline to state. It is not unusual to find in a theology class students from Buddhist, Taoist, Hindu, or Islamic backgrounds, and of course many with no religious background at all. Nor is this diversity unique to Loyola Marymount. According to Diana Eck, professor of comparative religion at Harvard Divinity School, the United States "is now the most religiously diverse country on earth."[34]

What does this increasing diversity suggest for our teaching of theology? Without compromising the Catholic identity of our departments, it is important to be able to offer courses that will help students from different backgrounds deepen their knowledge of their own traditions, as well as to help all our students learn something about other religions. Thus, the study of the great world religions should be represented in the curriculum.

However, the Congregation's emphasis on dialogue, whether with different cultures in Decree 4 or with other religions in Decree 5, is not just a recognition of the increasing diversity of our schools; it is properly theological. Unlike Christian fundamentalism, which is unable to recognize the Spirit's presence in other religious traditions or the defensiveness of the new Catholic apologetics, GC 34 calls Jesuits to a dialogue that seeks to enter the religious experience of the "Other," whether secular or religious, to find there new manifestations of the divine mystery (OMC 17 [101], OMID 6 [134]). The theological vision that animates these documents is God's ongoing dialogue with the world through the activity of the incarnated and risen Jesus; in terms of traditional Jesuit spirituality, it is "finding

God in all things." Because of this spiritual vision, dialogue and proclamation come together as reciprocal movements in our ministry: "Dialogue reaches out to the mystery of God active in others. Proclamation witnesses to and makes known God's mystery as it has been manifested to us in Christ" (OMID 7 [135]).

If Jesuit universities are to support the dialogue with other cultures and religions that GC 34 calls for, their theology departments need to include courses in the great world religions in their curricula. Indeed, the dialogue with other cultures and religions cannot be effectively carried out without careful theological preparation. Decree 5 on interreligious dialogue states: "Our educational institutions will conscientize their students on the value of interreligious collaboration and instill in them a basic understanding of and respect for the faith vision of the members of the diverse local religious communities, while deepening their own faith response to God" (OMID 9,8 [145]). In its concluding recommendations to Father General, it asks that he explore the possibility of establishing a department for the study of religions at the Gregorian University (19 [156]).

One resource for an interreligious dialogue that is genuinely theological is what Boston College's Francis Clooney and Loyola Marymount's James Fredericks call "comparative theology."[35] A relatively new discipline, comparative theology abandons the attempt to develop a theology of religion based on claims for or against a universal religious experience. Nor does it demand the "pluralist" move of reducing one's own faith to some mutually acceptable common denominator.[36] Instead, it proceeds "by means of limited case studies in which specific elements of the Christian tradition are interpreted in comparison with elements of another religious tradition."[37] In this way, a theologian is enabled to enter sympathetically into dialogue with another religion on its own terms, not seeking to explain it in terms of some more encompassing theory of religion, but respecting it as other and different. In other words, it seeks to view one's own religious tradition through the lens of another.

Conclusion

GC 34 reaffirms our Jesuit service to the Catholic Church while calling for increased dialogue with other Christian traditions, with other religions, and with other cultures. For those of us in higher education, particularly for those of us teaching theology, we cannot fulfill the first part of this call without a strong Catholic identity, both for ourselves and for our theology departments.

At the same time, the *ad extra* dimension of this call has both personal and institutional implications. We are called to dialogue with others, not just because of the increasing diversity of our schools, but because the Spirit is also present in these other traditions. Dialogue is never easy; it can even be "risky," as Pope Paul VI has said.[38] But it is a properly theological task. To enter into dialogue with those different from ourselves is very much in keeping with our Jesuit charism of finding God in all things.

ENDNOTES • RAUSCH

1. Cf. GC 32, Decree 4: "Our Mission Today: The Service of Faith and the Promotion of Justice" 24 [73].
2. William N. Neenan, S.J., "A Catholic/Jesuit University?" in *Finding God in All Things: Essays in Honor of Michael J. Buckley, S.J.,* ed. Michael J. Himes and Stephen J. Pope (New York: Crossroad Herder, 1996), 299–317 at 305.
3. John W. Padberg, S.J., gen ed., *The Constitutions of the Society of Jesus and Their Complementary Norms* (St. Louis, Mo.: Institute of Jesuit Sources, 1996): [446], p. 179. Hereafter *Const* in text.
4. "Theology is the chief source of the scientifically reasoned Christian philosophy of life and the source of integration for the other branches, as their arrangement in ch. 12 indicates;" Saint Ignatius of Loyola, *The Constitutions of the Society of Jesus,* trans. George E. Ganss, S.J. (St. Louis, Mo.: Institute of Jesuit Sources, 1970): 213, n. 2.
5. Michael J. Buckley, S.J., "In Hunc Potissimum . . . : Ignatius' Understanding of the Jesuit University," *Readings in Ignatian Higher Education* 1/1 (spring 1989): 18–27 at 24.
6. Paul G. Crowley, S.J., "Theology in the Jesuit University: Reassessing the Ignatian Vision," in *The Jesuit Tradition in Education and Missions: A 450 Year Perspective,* ed. Christopher Chapple (Scranton, Penn.: University of Scranton Press, 1993), 155–68 at 157.
7. John W. O'Malley, S.J., *The First Jesuits* (Cambridge, Mass.: Harvard University Press, 1993), 218; the Collegio Romano was an exception in that it "taught the full curriculum described in the *Constitutions* and was in effect a 'university,'" 116.
8. See n. 4.
9. George M. Marsden, *The Soul of the American University: From Protestant Establishment to Established Nonbelief* (New York: Oxford University Press, 1994), 99.
10. Ibid., 410.
11. William P. Leahy, S.J., *Adapting to America: Catholics, Jesuits, and Higher Education in the Twentieth Century* (Washington, D.C.: Georgetown University Press, 1991), 55. Leahy's study shows how Catholic schools, suspicious of the secular academic culture, resisted the professionalization taking place in other institutions in the early part of the century.
12. Robert J. Wister, "The Teaching of Theology 1950–1990: The American Catholic Experience," *America* 162 (3 February 1990): 88, 90, 92–93, 106–7, 109 at 92.
13. Leahy, *Adapting to America,* 36.
14. Eugene B. Gallagher, S.J., "A College Religion Course: Problems," *Jesuit Educational Quarterly* 12 (1949): 94–97 at 95.
15. Philip Gleason, *Contending With Modernity: Catholic Higher Education in the Twentieth Century* (New York and Oxford: Oxford University Press, 1995), 164. Gleason notes that the term *return* was used "mistakenly."
16. Ibid., 165.
17. John Courtney Murray, S.J., "Towards a Theology for the Layman—The Problem of Its Finality," *Theological Studies* 5 (1944): 43–75.
18. William A. Huesman, S.J., "Integration of College Studies by Means of Theology," *Jesuit Educational Quarterly* 15 (1952): 29–36 at 30; Gerald van Ackeren, S.J., makes the same point in his "Reflections on the Relation Between Philosophy and Theology," *Theological Studies* 14 (1953): 527–50 at 548.
19. Gleason, *Contending With Modernity,* 264.
20. Crowley, "Theology in the Jesuit University," 157.
21. Cf. Peter-Hans Kolvenbach, S.J., "Final Address to the Congregation of Procurators (8 Sept. 1987)," n. 4, *Acta Romana Societatis Iesu* 19 (1987): 1078–90 at 1079.

22. Charles E. Curran, "The Catholic Identity of Catholic Institutions," *Theological Studies* 58 (1997): 90–108 at 92.

23. Marsden, *The Soul of the American University*, 5.

24. Lawrence S. Cunningham, "Gladly Wolde He Lerne and Gladly Teche: The Catholic Scholar in the New Millennium," *The Cresset* (June 1992): 318; cited by James Heft, S.M., in "Theology in a Catholic University," *Origins* 25 (1995): 243–48 at 244.

25. Ibid.

26. See Thomas F. O'Meara, "Doctoral Programs in Theology at U.S. Catholic Universities," *America* 162/14 (1990): 79–80, 82–84, 101–3 at 84. A recent study indicates that some of the best Protestant graduate programs in theology tend to hire few if any graduates of Catholic programs, while Catholic graduate programs hire a significant numbers of faculty members from nondenominational Protestant graduate programs; see William Ribando, "Top Theological Faculties Lag in Ecumenical Hiring," *Ecumenical Trends* 26/4 (1997): 61–64.

27. Cf. Wister, "The Teaching of Theology," 88–90.

28. Cf. Randy L. Maddox, "The Recovery of Theology as a Practical Discipline," *Theological Studies* 51 (1990): 650–72.

29. Heft, "Theology in a Catholic University," 245.

30. Bernard J. Lee, Barbara Fleischer, and Charles Topper, "A Same and Different Future: A Study of Graduate Ministry Education in Catholic Institutions of Higher Learning in the United States," done for the Association of Graduate Programs in Ministry (Executive Summary), published privately, 1.

31. O'Meara, "Doctoral Programs in Theology," 84.

32. *Los Angeles 1994: State of the County Report* (Los Angeles, Calif.: United Way of Greater Los Angeles).

33. Dale Maharidge, *The Coming White Minority: California's Eruptions and America's Future* (New York: Times Books/Random House, 1996), 21.

34. Cited in the *New York Times*, 23 November 1996, 13.

35. See Francis X. Clooney, S.J., *Theology After Vedanta: An Experiment in Comparative Theology* (Albany, N.Y.: SUNY Press, 1993); James L. Fredericks, "A Universal Religious Experience?: Comparative Theology as an Alternative to a Theology of Religions," *Horizons* 22/1 (1995): 67–87.

36. Cf. John Hick, "The Non-Absoluteness of Christianity," in *The Myth of Christian Uniqueness: Toward a Pluralistic Theology of Religion*, ed. John Hick and Paul F. Knitter (Maryknoll, N.Y.: Orbis, 1987), 16–36 at 22–23.

37. Fredericks, "A Universal Religious Experience?" 83.

38. Paul VI, *Ecclesiam Suam* 88.

ESSAY 27

International Jesuit Higher Education and the Three Dimensions of Our Mission

Charles L. Currie, S.J.

ABSTRACT

Leaders of Jesuit higher education from around the world recently gathered in Santiago, Chile, to discuss how they and their institutions should respond to the mission decrees of GC 34. After discussing the important developments in understanding the Jesuit commitment to faith-justice, now enriched by attention to culture and interreligious dialogue, delegates reviewed the complex economic, social, and cultural context for their work. Common themes included poverty and the growing gap between rich and poor throughout the world; serious questions about "neo-liberalism" and a market economy and their consequences; old and new forms of colonialism; threats to family life and culture; various threats to cultures; and the need to empower people. Particular contextual issues indicated how difficult and complex Jesuit higher education can be. After exploring various possibilities for international cooperation, delegates chose two as both key to their enterprises and realistically achievable: fostering service or experiential learning as a means of raising consciousness of the poor and those of different cultures; and faculty development as a means of fostering the human resources needed to achieve the ambitious agenda of Jesuit higher education today.

Introduction

Mirroring the international and multicultural flavor of GC 34 itself, about 70 presidents, rectors, and principals from 21 countries, representing the approximately 190 Jesuit higher education institutions in 66 countries, met in Santiago, Chile, on October 20–21, 1997. The objectives for the meeting had been set by the International Commission on Jesuit Higher Education, under the leadership of Father Gabriel Codina, S.J., secretary for education at the Jesuit Curia in Rome. The delegates had come (1) to develop a methodology for implementation of the GC 34 decrees in the three dimensions of our mission: justice, culture, and dialogue; and (2) to develop a structure and select a project for international cooperation.

In preparation for the meeting, a representative from each of five geographic regions had been asked to prepare a background paper on the context for Jesuit higher education in that region. Summaries of these papers preceded discussions by the participants, and then small groups discussed two questions: (1) what are the methodologies and structures that will best implement our mission; and (2) what are the most important global concerns that we can jointly address?

Participants stuck amazingly well to their assignments and a masterful piece of chairmanship at the closing session by Father Paul Locatelli, S.J., president of the University of Santa Clara, helped the group to reach consensus on a course of action for the next two years.

This essay highlights the main points of the discussions of these two days, trying to make the account both accurate and readable. Editorial comments will be minimal, but should be obviously distinct from the reporting function. Of course, the highlighting of the presentations is itself somewhat editorial.

Keynote

To establish the context for the meeting, Father Francisco Ivern, S.J., provincial of the Central Eastern Brazilian Province, presented a paper on the challenges posed for the Jesuit university by the three dimensions of the Jesuit mission described by GC 34: justice, culture, and interreligious dialogue.[1] Ivern had earlier critiqued what he considered was the rather unilateral and even simplistic way in which GC 32's Decree 4: "Our Mission Today: The Service of Faith and the Promotion of Justice" (OMT) had been understood and applied.[2] In that piece, he emphasized that much of the opposition to Decree 4 had arisen because it challenged our selfishness or established ways of thinking, behaving, and viewing things. He noted that many good things have followed in the wake of that historic decree. For example, among Jesuits and Jesuit works, there is a greater identification and solidarity with the poor, a simpler lifestyle, and a fuller understanding of gospel values. That being said, the interpretation and application of Decree 4 often failed to achieve an adequate integration between justice and faith. The rather immediate, direct, and excessively action-oriented approach to justice, without sufficient awareness of the complexity of the problems and their historical, ethical, philosophical and anthropological roots and implications, made it difficult to accept the assertion that the faith-justice mission was the responsibility of *all* Jesuits, even more so for those in academic work, many of whom felt excluded from this urgent mission of the Society.

In Ivern's view, GC 34 provided the opportunity to correct past mistakes, and to reformulate, in a fuller and more integrated way, our mission in the world of today, so that all Jesuits and their lay collaborators, indeed all Jesuit-related apostolates and ministries, would be able to embrace this mission.

GC 34 reformulated our mission by introducing, besides justice (Decree 3: "Our Mission and Justice"), two other interrelated dimensions: the cultural (Decree 4: "Our Mission and Culture") and the religious (Decree 5: "Our Mission and Interreligious Dialogue" [OMID]). Instead of one decree—"Our Mission Today"—we have three decrees that are mutually complementary—a single, three-pronged tool to analyze and interpret present-day reality.

The Congregation invited us to look for the roots of today's complex and varied problems, not only in their socioeconomic and sociopolitical components, but also in the cultural and religious substrata, the values on which social structures, institutions, and lifestyles are based. We need to go to a deeper level to change the sociocultural and socioreligious values that are at the base of socioeconomic and sociopolitical structures.

Ivern emphasized that this reformulated mission provides the frame of reference for rethinking the tasks and functions of Jesuit-related universities today. The university should remain always critically open to, and actively inserted in, the concrete reality that surrounds it. (This reminds one of Ignacio Ellacuría's idea of a university focused on the "national reality."[3]) Thus, we cannot ignore the present socioeconomic and sociopolitical system with its global dimensions. This system exercises an enormous influence that goes well beyond economic issues and shapes our social and political life at many different levels. It is also the result of values deeply rooted in our culture.

A Jesuit university cannot remain indifferent or neutral in relation to a system that has such a tremendous influence on our individual and collective existence. Our critique, *both* positive *and* negative, should be concerned primarily with the values underlying the global system, in which economic liberalism is dominant today. The recent "Letter on Neo-liberalism" from the Latin American provincials is one example of starting such a process of reflection and study on that system.[4]

The new perspective of GC 34 thus opens up new opportunities and challenges for Jesuit-related universities. The Congregation also invites Jesuits and their colleagues to make maximum use of the international dimension of Jesuit higher education to create a true exchange network of ideas and experiences, and of reflection and study concerning some of the major problems confronting us in today's world (cf. Decree 17: "Jesuits and University Life" 10 [413]). In a significant intervention at the meeting, Father Xabier Gorostiaga, S.J., the rector of the University of Central America in Managua, Nicaragua, pointed out that the Society is possibly unique in its ability to mobilize simultaneously at the local, national, and international levels.

Regional Analyses of the Context for Jesuit Higher Education

In the spirit of the analysis suggested by GC 34, five regional reports had been prepared to describe the context within which Jesuit colleges and universities operate today. Each report addressed four questions, the first two dealing with contextual analysis, and the second two with proposals for responding to that context. The questions were:

> *1. What is/are the emerging realities of your region (that is, the socio-economic and geopolitical trends affecting "culture")?*

> *2. How can Jesuits in higher education respond to this situation from the perspectives of justice, culture, and dialogue?*

> *3. What characteristics best express the unique identity of Jesuit universities or colleges in your region?*

> *4. What common project(s) exist for international cooperation between Jesuit universities?*

This essay will bring together the answers to these questions from each of the five regions, looking for both commonalities and differences. The five regions chosen to group the nearly two hundred Jesuit higher educational institutions were East Asia and Oceania; South Asia; Africa, Lebanon, and Europe; Latin America; and North America. These regional analyses provide ample evidence for the sobering complexity of the task of Jesuit higher education today, especially if it chooses to be countercultural. Clearly the five reporters find much that is wrong with our societies. They might be accused of neglecting what is right, but it would be difficult not to admit that they identify real problems to be faced by Jesuit higher education. Most importantly, each reporter remains enthusiastic about the enterprise, despite the challenges and difficulties cited.

WHAT IS/ARE THE EMERGING REALITIES OF YOUR REGION (THAT IS, THE SOCIOECONOMIC AND GEOPOLITICAL TRENDS AFFECTING "CULTURE")?

The East Asian report was prepared by Father Daniel Ross, S.J., professor of theology at the Fu Jen University, Hsinchuang, Taiwan.[5] He noted that it is obviously difficult to prepare a comprehensive report for such a wide geographic area that includes many cultures and subcultures. The ten educational institutions are spread over five countries from Japan and Korea, through Taiwan and the Philippines, to Indonesia. There are also Jesuits working in non-Jesuit institutions in Oceania, Australia, Cambodia, Thailand, and China. All of these countries have experienced the effects of colonization, and despite many significant differences, they share something in common.

Socioeconomic trends in the region include a growing rift between the rich and poor (a trend noted in all five reports);[6] the rise of China as a mammoth economic force and market; the growth of consumerism and materialism; the lessening of the belief that Japan can make no economic mistakes; the influence of overseas Chinese as a vast network of international business concerns beyond the control of any country or nation; and, even in the poorest of countries, a very rapid advance in electronic communications.

Underlying these trends is a drive to accumulate wealth, supported for many by a belief in a spiritual world parallel to the one in which we live. Inhabitants of this other world have great control over our world in a relationship of fear and power. Key signs that one is blessed by the gods or spirits are being economically successful, having power, and having one's family protected.

In the economic sector, there is an "idealized" view that sees much money to be made in East and Southeast Asia, while a more "sober" view sees the area facing major energy, resource, and ecological problems. In reality, most emerging nations in the Asia-Pacific region face a drastic choice between the worship of economic growth and a sustained quality of life.

Geopolitically, several trends seem to be emerging: a sense of independence from and disillusionment with the West, and a growing sense that "we can do it ourselves"; the growth of economic regional alliances like ASEAN; and a love/hate relationship with the United States, with the United States seen as the source of many of the region's problems, but also as a military bulwark against a growing China, and one of the largest markets for goods produced in the area.

All of the above affect the culture of the region, often in disastrous ways. The poor are not sharing in whatever progress is being achieved, and the rich are getting richer and more powerful. Tens of thousands of families are being separated as a consequence of bringing foreign labor into the more prosperous countries. In much of East and Southeast Asia, there has been little effort to control environmental pollution and corruption. The search for the cheapest and most easily manipulated labor force can leave sudden and great unemployment when businesses relocate.

Father Ambrose Pinto, S.J., from Bangalore, India, reported on South Asia.[7] In a highly critical fashion, Pinto notes that the long history of colonialism in the region has made Asians critical of their own institutions, and has made others think that Western education has been responsible for whatever is good. In the predominately Hindu society, British educational policy was meant to protect and promote British institutions. Consciously or unconsciously, many of the features of the colonial rulers were maintained after independence. Various institutions, ideas, and practices in these countries are legacies of colonialism.

The state claims to be federal, secular, and transformational. In reality, it is unitary, communal, and exploitative, using bureaucracy, information technology, and socioeconomic and cultural programs to maintain control. Society has rules, regulations, codes, and traditions very different from the state. The state does not enjoy the loyalty of the people when it is perceived as violating their rights.

Today in India, a rightist Hindu group, *Hindtva,* is attempting to capture political power, and is opposed to Muslims, Christians, and the untouchables (*dalits*). In Pakistan, Islamic fundamentalists are equally active in their opposition to Muslims and Christians in Pakistan. The elite or middle-class Brahmans have disproportionate control of public service jobs and other privileges in society, but the backward classes are trying to displace them. Because of the intense competition for power among the dominant castes, efforts to achieve equality for the *dalits* have caused violence in several parts of the country.

At the time of independence, the economic development model dictated mega-projects with the USSR, the United States, and Germany. Then and now, politics have been a central factor in the economic development of India, with the economy correlated with the power relations in society. Land reforms did not succeed, for example, because of rural landlords who scuttled them. In a point we will hear over and over again, in one region after another, Pinto notes that the economy is not working for the benefit of the disadvantaged in society.

In the late 1980s, India turned to globalization to establish a nexus with capitalist countries. This has resulted in the weakening of the public sector, and in reduced investments in the infrastructure, agriculture, and rural development. The whole economy is geared toward the urban upper and middle classes in a country where more than 70 percent live in villages. The market economy has created increasing disparities. For Pinto, the new colonizers are the international organizations such as the International Monetary Fund (IMF) and the World Bank. This was an oft-repeated theme at the meeting.

Father Jacques Berleur, S.J., a member of the Facultés Universitaires, Notre-Dame de la Paix in Belgium, addressed the question from the daunting perspective of Africa, Lebanon, and Europe.[8] Appropriately, he broke down the region into its three components.

Africa today has been progressively shaped by political democratization, freedom of expression, and increasing responsibility. Economically, it is moving from a highly centralized economy to a liberal, privatized system, under pressure from the IMF and World Bank, and from the internal demands of its citizens. Africans know they are more and more marginalized in the global economy. There is a moral crisis in society with the break-up of families, youthful crime, and corruption. Religious movements abound, with lessening confidence in the established churches, and a shift toward sects. The coexistence of Muslims with Christians will probably be a major challenge for the Africa of tomorrow.

In Lebanon, The University of Saint Joseph has been significantly affected by the national and regional crises of recent years. Nationally, Arabic ideology tries to Islamize political thought and legitimize the Syrian presence. Regionally, there are tensions between Israel and Arabs, and the radicalization of integrist movements with the influence of Iran and Syria. Economically, the external debt has grown by 37 percent and the internal deficit by 44 percent. The solution that is being proposed looks to an unrealistic growth rate of 9.3 percent.

On Europe, Berleur writes graphically that "Europe is living in a sad economy for an anxious society, creating a climate of uncertainty, especially for youth." Unemployment ranges from 10 to 20 percent. In a globalized world, competitiveness becomes the law. Political measures have been dictated by the economic convergence criteria of the Treaty of Maastricht and the dominant economic model of neo-liberalism. Universities face a demand for more vocational training, the reality of a violent and harsh society that excludes the less fortunate, and pervasive technology.

Politically, there is a crisis of confidence toward politicians and politics, and tensions between a welfare state and a representative democracy. Europe seems to be losing its concern for the deprived of the third world. On the other hand, new forms of community-based activity like NGOs (nongovernmental organizations) are on the rise. Beneath the surface are questions about the future of employment, about sustainable development, and about social cohesion in an age of individualism.

Berleur was hardly optimistic. Europe is experiencing a very deep change of values, accelerated by postmodernity. This leads to disorientation, if not relativism, where the notion of a lifelong commitment has no meaning. Parents are convinced their children will be worse off than they. People speak of a lost generation, living its own culture, without interest in what is happening globally. The religious context is one of secularization, positivism, disaffection with a Catholic identity, and indifference toward belief in general.

Father Luis Ugalde, S.J., rector of the Universidad Catolica Andrés Bello, Venezuela, described the context for Jesuit higher education in Latin America repeating many of the themes reported above.[9] He noted the all-important difficulty of achieving sustained economic development and the reduction of poverty. A key question is whether we can find inclusive solutions that allow the majority of the population to participate in the determination of their future.

Like the rest of the world, Latin America is experiencing the effects of globalization. Widespread poverty remains all too real, and there is a widening gap between rich and poor. The harsh realities of economic adjustment, dictated by international agencies and markets and administered by inefficient and corrupt governments, have led to a widespread loss of public confidence.

These tendencies have been the subject of studies, research, and reflection in Jesuit universities. More recently (as noted above), the Latin American provincials issued their "Letter on Neo-Liberalism" with its challenge to our universities to develop alternative policies, each in its own country. The Jesuit Centers of Research and Social Action in Latin

America are anxious to get on with this task. Spanish universities are joining with their sister institutions in Latin America, and it is hoped that others will follow. At issue is a true cultural revolution, a struggle for the lives of most of our population. The struggle will include changing the role of government, educating a citizenry, developing greater productive capacity, increasing solidarity, and putting life for the poor before increased riches and power.

Father Joseph P. Daoust, S.J., former P. J. McElroy professor of law at the University of Detroit Mercy and a delegate at GC 34, and currently president of the Jesuit School of Theology at Berkeley, reported on the economic, social, and cultural trends that provide the context for the work of the twenty-eight Jesuit colleges and universities in the United States.

The United States economy has been buoyant through most of this decade, but we have achieved this by entering into a seemingly constant state of restructuring and shifting resources in response to everchanging market forces. Jobs and financial capital have been shifted from one region to another through downsizing, mergers, and acquisitions. The power of multinational corporations is increasing, as is the appeal to free market forces. As in Europe, there is a fear of decline in the standard of living. In fact, over the past twenty years, half of the population has experienced a decline in standard of living, with the lowest third suffering most. The United States joins the rest of the world in experiencing a widening gap between rich and poor. The income earned by the richest 1 percent has more than doubled in the past twenty years.

The United States is a highly urbanized society. Much of urban America is segregated by color and economic class. Half of inner-city men are unemployed, ten times the national figure of 5 percent. National poverty levels remain high, with one in seven living below subsistence levels. Almost one in four children is raised in poverty. Three-quarters of those in poverty are women or those dependent on women, a situation described as the "feminization of poverty." Crime rates are high, and the prison rate has doubled in the last decade.

Some of the country's greatest strengths and weaknesses are derived from cultural diversity. The one million immigrants arriving each year confront increasing anti-immigrant sentiment and racism. Family life is still the center of much of society, even as family life is increasingly problematic. One-half of all marriages end in divorce, and one-fourth of all children are raised by a single parent. The current political mood is one of disillusionment and distrust. Safety nets for society's less fortunate are being drastically reduced.

As a result of the above, United States culture has been undergoing rapid and often confusing change. There are seemingly disconnected paradigm shifts in the values, meaning, and world views, which lie beneath the external manifestations of this change, that make the culture seem fragmented. Moral and ethical relativity can become the norm. Many take refuge in escape of one form or another, for example, a fundamentalist search for answers, or taking care of oneself rather than a commitment to the common good, public virtue, and working together in solidarity.

The challenge of Jesuit higher education is to discern how to build on these latter traditions and counteract the fearfulness and hopelessness that underlie the former. The directions suggested by GC 34 can be most helpful in meeting this challenge.

HOW CAN JESUITS IN HIGHER EDUCATION RESPOND TO THIS SITUATION FROM THE PERSPECTIVES OF JUSTICE, CULTURE, AND DIALOGUE?

Father Ross, answering the question from the perspective of East Asia and Oceania, suggested reexamining what justice means for us in the development of our Jesuit and non-Jesuit teachers. A teacher must have a concern for the whole student. This sounds obvious, but many of our teachers have no idea what this means. Faculty development programs are needed, and have been successful when tried. There is a need continually to analyze what is being done and how we can improve in this crucial area.

Culturally, we can learn from one another, without merely copying what others are doing. We are all ethnocentric to a certain extent, and need to recognize this and avoid stereotypes. We need to be in sincere dialogue with others, not presuming that we know more than they know. We need to be aware of the Holy Spirit at work in non-Christians. At times, pride in our own schools hinders our working together with other Jesuits.

Father Pinto, focusing on South Asia, noted that 48 percent of the population is still illiterate. Sixty percent of those who enter school drop out by fifth standard. Only 8 percent of Indians are in higher education, which is still a luxury.

Jesuit schools were formerly considered elite. Except for the preference shown to Christians, merit was the sole criterion for admission. This was to prepare Christians for leadership roles. In the spirit of Decree 4 of GC 32, priority admission is now granted to depressed castes and classes, first generation learners, with remedial classes to assist them. The emphasis has shifted from academic excellence to "human" excellence, working toward a change of attitude in students. Extension programs have linked colleges with villages and rural communities. Some institutions have established centers for the educational, psychological, and economic uplift of rural communities and urban slums.

Young Jesuits, even those involved in research, are concerned for the environment, human rights, the rights of marginalized groups, service of the poor, and so on.

Seminars, exhibitions, discussions, and reflections on important social issues have helped raise consciousness. All colleges have taken "Ignatian Pedagogy" seriously.

A sad part of higher education in India is that it is highly centralized and state-controlled without any flexibility of courses, thus removing our freedom to be innovative. We have been forced to do innovative things outside the classroom. The country is considering permission for the operation of private universities, and Jesuits are asking whether they should venture in that direction. They would need financial help from an "International Jesuit Monetary Fund."

Father Berleur answered the question from the perspective of Africa, Lebanon, and Europe. In Africa, there is a need to train competent, honest, and clear-thinking men and women for the service of their countries. Teaching and research need to be linked with the social realities of the region.

Education in Lebanon needs to assist students to rise above their religious and cultural differences, to think freely and critically, to discern values, and to have a sense of the universal. Jesuits are challenged to cultivate interreligious dialogue between Muslims and Christians, no easy task in a highly polarized region.

Jesuits in Europe need to provide a holistic formation including theological, philosophical, sociopolitical, cultural, and humanistic education, which is open to the fundamental values of the Gospel. Beyond these academic values, they need to help students adapt to change, to engage in lifelong learning, and to care for the person.

Concerning justice, young men and women need to experience service of the less fortunate, develop the skills for social analysis and reflection, and cultivate a generosity that is nourished by intelligence. The social relevance of our research needs to be evaluated.

Concerning culture, there is a need to integrate specializations within a global perspective, deepen cultural rooting in a globalized world, organize cultural programs for students, and educate them to understand other cultures besides their own.

Concerning faith, through diverse pastoral activities and teaching, there is a need to work on the rupture between the Gospel and culture.

Father Ugalde took up the challenge for Latin America. He noted that the documents of GC 34 provide inspiration for the task we have chosen, especially the reconstruction of our societies in dialogue, social justice, and solidarity. But to have this effect, the documents have to be known and studied as widely as possible in our universities by our students and faculty.

Finally, Father Daoust suggested how North American Jesuits can respond to their context from the perspectives of justice, culture, and dialogue. Students need to come to understand the thirst for justice, and how structural injustice is rooted in the culture and its underlying values. Students can be prepared for lives of technical competence and productivity, but they also can be led toward lives of understanding and commitment, integrating their lives around shared values they can believe in.

Daoust noted that the means to accomplish this mission are suggested by Decree 13: "Cooperation with Laity in Mission" and Decree 17: "Jesuits and University Life." We need the fullest possible incorporation of all those who teach and work at the university into colleagueship. Therefore, we need openness to new kinds and structures of institutional leadership and control by the Society and structures for continuing formation for mission for students and faculty.

The context for this mission is provided by Decree 5 (OMID) and Decree 11: "On Having a Proper Attitude of Service in the Church." We live in a global village. In such an environment, Jesuit higher education has to adopt dialogue as a permanent way of interacting with the "Other," not as a strategy for cooption, but for learning. It also needs to find ways to negotiate between debilitating cultural forces within the Church, and to engage the modern world creatively as part of the Church's mission in today's world.

Jesuit higher education has to continue its mission of bringing in the poor and marginalized of modern America. Traditionally, it has had an urban focus, and American cities continue to be where the Jesuit criteria for mission are probably best met.

We profess to educate "persons for others." Today, that includes preparing students for lives of constant adaptation and sometimes bewildering change. They need to understand their fragmented and relativistic cultural environment, so that they can better integrate their own work and family lives. A commitment to lifelong learning is very important.

Ultimately, faith questions lie at the heart of the postmodern quest. There is a thirst for spirituality, for something to believe in, beyond dogmas and outside of discredited institutions. Jesuit higher education is founded on the belief that one can find God at work in this world.

WHAT CHARACTERISTICS BEST EXPRESS THE UNIQUE IDENTITY OF JESUIT UNIVERSITIES OR COLLEGES IN YOUR REGION?

In East Asia and Oceania, the following characteristics were identified: quality personal relationships with faculty and students (*cura personalis*); humility and a simple lifestyle as a counterbalance to consumerism and materialism; enlightened faculty development; and a focus on our institutions as first-rate educational institutions effectively "leading out" what is in our students.

In South Asia, the commitment to justice has taken concrete form in our preference for students from socially marginalized groups. Efforts are being made to provide a social conscience to our students and faculty through a pedagogy of experience, reflection, and action in courses in religion, social concern, and business ethics. We have been able to provide a much-needed "neutral space" for interaction and dialogue between people of different religions, castes, cultures, and languages. We need to do more in research and in lay collaboration.

In Africa, Jesuit schools are preparing women and men capable of responsible positions in the economic, political, cultural, and social life of their country. The Synod of African Bishops wants Catholic universities to play a role in proclaiming the Gospel. These universities are being asked to serve the Church by preparing people competent in theological and social questions, by helping develop an African theology, by promoting the work of inculturation (especially in the liturgy), and by training in the social doctrine of the Church.

In all our schools we need to insist on academic excellence, quality teaching, *cura personalis,* and interdisciplinary activity. We should teach human rights, sustainable development, justice, and solidarity. We need better to relate theoretical knowledge to social responsibility, developing our capacity for sociocultural analysis and assessing the social relevance of our research choices.

We need better to understand and to stress the importance of Ignatian pedagogy at the university level. Because of the declining numbers of Jesuits, attention needs to be paid to an explicit mission statement that expresses the relationship between the institution and the Society, and addresses the key issues of recruiting personnel and sharing Ignatian pedagogy and spirituality with lay colleagues.

In Latin America, the Ignatian paradigm for seeing, reflecting, and acting needs to be applied to the reality of the continent, and specifically to each country. Jesuit schools need to focus on the total formation of students, the continuing development of our faculty, and the forging of effective links with other Jesuit universities.

In North America, characteristics best identifying the Jesuit character of our schools are integration vs. fragmentation; being distinctively Jesuit and Catholic; an emphasis on the dual importance of discovering and using knowledge; strong theology departments and pastoral ministry programs; teaching the Bishops' "Pastoral on the Economy" (and thus challenging the tenets of a "free market" economy); and ensuring a learning environment that is open to and encouraging of the plurality of cultures.

These characteristics are concretely found in interdisciplinary institutes, experiential learning programs, interdisciplinary courses, research on issues of faith and/or social justice, and leadership development for students.

WHAT COMMON PROJECT(S) EXIST FOR INTERNATIONAL COOPERATION BETWEEN JESUIT UNIVERSITIES?

East Asia and Oceania want to get young Jesuits in common fields working together across provinces as early as possible in their studies.

More could be done with faculty and students exchanges, especially because English is becoming more and more an international language. Other key areas for international cooperation are international business ethics, teaching methodology (including Ignatian pedagogy), and education.

One important example of cooperation is the assistance provided to the University of Phnom Penh in Cambodia by the Ateneo de Manila in the Philippines, Sogang University in Korea, Sophia University in Japan, Fu Jen University in Taiwan, and Sanata Dharma University in Indonesia. This cooperative effort has provided the first master's-level educational program in Cambodia for school principals and administrators.

South Asia argued that Jesuits and Jesuit schools could better influence the policies of organizations like the World Bank and the IMF if they linked together. Each continent needs to study the policies and designs of the World Bank, IMF, the Western bloc and its model of a market economy. We could also take more initiative toward socially marginalized groups that are otherwise becoming more and more difficult to reach. We need to reach the poor, and that means involving ourselves with many of their problems. We also desire to be present to the debates that shape thought on ethics, human rights, values, and the secular fabric.

Africa, Lebanon, and Europe all stress that more explicit cooperation between our institutions is highly welcomed. We really do not use the international potential we have. Already existing cooperative efforts include the meetings of the deans of our business schools, Jesuits in science, and Jesuits in the social sciences. There is significant interest in student-faculty exchanges, and in more mobility for Jesuits, for example, on international sabbaticals.

There are pluses and minuses about the database on current research projects that have been proposed. For example, how do we define strengths without hurting the weaker institutions and individuals? There is significant interest in a common research project related to the more sensitive issues of our time, such as the globalization of the economy and technology. A common project would have to be a real partnership with reciprocal commitment, and be characterized by quality and scientific excellence. The credibility of the project would require the active participation of our most famous institutions. Cooperation via the Internet is already under way, and expansion seems to be feasible. An international form of conversations might also be feasible.

Latin America, through the activities of the Association of Universities Entrusted to the Society of Jesus in Latin America (AUSJAL), already engages in significant cooperative efforts. It participates in international exchange and specialized studies at the master's and doctoral levels in the various Jesuit universities around the world. In addition to the collaborative efforts already underway to address poverty, another project has been proposed; namely, to evaluate the impact of each university's mission statement on the performance of that university. The results, and perhaps even the evaluation instrument itself, could be shared to make comparisons within Latin America, and perhaps even internationally.

The twenty-eight Jesuit colleges and universities in the Association of Jesuit Colleges and Universities (AJCU) in the United States have prepared an extensive directory of the various international and exchange programs for their students and faculty. Most of these exchanges are in first-world countries, but an increasing number of exchanges with third-world countries are being developed. Many of the twenty-eight schools host Jesuits from other countries for language and graduate studies. Several schools have faculty involved in joint teaching and research projects with their colleagues in developing countries. Jesuit business school deans have collaborated to offer an M.B.A. at Beijing University, the latest in a long list of joint academic offerings.

Group Discussions

In an attempt to move toward a plan of action, participants broke into small groups to answer two questions:

> 1. *What are the methodologies and structures that will best implement our mission?*
>
> 2. *What are the most important global concerns that we can jointly address?*

The groups reached an amazing degree of consensus in responding to both questions.

The methodologies and structures seen best to implement the mission of Jesuit higher education today were empowering our lay colleagues and helping them to appropriate the mission; various forms of experiential learning that include experiences of both the poor and those of other cultures; and exchanges of faculty, students, and programs. It was agreed that the Jesuit mission had to be located within the university as university. For example, faculty need to participate as faculty in research and analysis focused on contemporary societal problems; justice concerns and experiential learning need to be integrated within the curriculum.

Conversations/dialogues with our colleagues on our mission and on Ignatian pedagogy have to be sensitive to where they are coming from, have to be in-depth and not merely information sessions, and need to be ongoing. Immersion experiences are important for every constituency: students, faculty, staff, and alumni. Exchanges of various kinds are essential, especially those that involve intercultural sharing and that respond to specific needs of the institutions.

The second question addressed by the small groups was, What are the most important global concerns that could be jointly addressed by Jesuit colleges and universities? After the previous day's recounting of the often daunting challenges facing Jesuit institutions around the globe, this was indeed a difficult question on which to reach some degree of consensus. I personally had in mind Xabier Gorostiaga's challenge to mobilize around the issue of world poverty. In his lecture at Saint Joseph's University in March 1997, he had formed the challenge in these words:

> *I believe that Jesuit universities must confront this scandal* [of world poverty and the widening gap between rich and poor] *in an organized manner. This scandal and our efforts to confront it jointly are the principal*

challenge of our generation as Jesuits, Christians, human persons and cit-
izens of our global village. . . . There probably does not exist another orga-
nization in the world capable of forming a coherent strategy that embraces
the global, the national and the local, i.e., a "gloncal strategy" to confront
this crisis.[10]

The plight of the poor and the marginalized, including the growing gap between rich and poor in all of our societies, was indeed raised as a major issue of global concern. Also discussed were the environment, genetics, the debt crisis, the role of women, migration and employment, the disruption of families and of cultures, and the overarching issue of globalization and its effects.

Gorostiaga himself would admit that the project to which he was challenging his colleagues would probably have to be initiated by a few individuals or groups before it would be possible to mobilize a community of Jesuit universities around such a complex agenda. The Latin American universities (AUSJAL) have already committed themselves to this initial effort.

Thus it was that the small group discussions failed to reach a consensus, in the short time available, on one or two of these mega-issues, but there was broad agreement that there was a need to take at least one exemplary initiative at this meeting as a symbolic beginning. Five specific suggestions for such a beginning were as follows: collaborative efforts with service or experiential learning; Society-wide collaboration on faculty development and exchanges; the Montevideo project on university mission (see above); the project on world poverty with a special emphasis on proposed solutions; and an umbrella study of globalization as embracing most of the issues discussed during the meeting.

Final Session and Recommendations

Looking back, it is indeed amazing that such a diverse group, coming from very diverse backgrounds and institutions, could reach a consensus in the relatively short time of two days, especially considering the broad sweep of topics discussed. This was possible as a result of the seriousness with which delegates approached their task and their concern to respond effectively to the challenges posed by GC 34. It is also a result of the leadership of Father Codina, the genial secretary of education, and his fine group of session chairs. No one of these was better than Father Locatelli, the chair for the final session.

After considering the various options suggested in the small group discussions, the group of delegates agreed on two initiatives for international cooperation. The choice was made to pick something that was clearly important throughout our discussions, and something we are already doing and could share ways to do it more effectively. The choices came down to two:

1. *Encourage, support and develop experiential or service learning that integrates experience with the marginalized and poor, and/or those of different cultures, with intellectually rigorous reflection, which in turn leads to thoughtful, concerned action;*

2. *Foster faculty development, lay and Jesuit, in ways that actualize the Jesuit mission of education today in partnership with our lay colleagues.*

Characteristics of both programs would include:

1. *drawing inspiration from the mission decrees of GC 34 on justice, culture, and interreligious dialogue;*

2. *appreciating the distinctive features of different cultures, North and South, East and West, Christian and non-Christian;*

3. *exchanging information and working together across institutions and regions, sharing information about "best practices";*

4. *improving existing programs or implementing new programs; and*

5. *accepting the assumption that institutions are free to adopt programs or parts of programs from other institutions.*

The secretary of education and the International Commission of Jesuit Higher Education will coordinate the exchange of information and the development of ideas or guidelines for the two common initiatives. Communication and coordination of information on the programs to and within the five regions will be the responsibility of the regional directors.

The twofold action agenda will help raise consciousness to the important issues discussed and help develop the human resources to respond to those issues. When the International Jesuit Rectors/Presidents/Principals gather in 1999 they should be ready for a next step in applying GC 34's decrees on justice, culture, and interreligious dialogue to Jesuit higher education throughout the world.

ENDNOTES • CURRIE

1. Francisco Ivern, S.J., "The Three Dimensions of Our Mission: Justice, Culture and Dialogue: Challenges Which These Dimensions Present for the University," paper presented at the International Jesuit Higher Education (IJHE) Meeting of University Rectors/Presidents/Principals, Santiago, Chile, 20–21 October 1997.

2. Francisco Ivern, S.J., "The Future of Faith and Justice: A Critical Review of Decree Four," *Studies in the Spirituality of Jesuits* 14/5 (November 1982).

3. Ignacio Ellacuría, S.J., "Is a Different Kind of University Possible?" in *Towards a Society That Serves*

Its People: The Intellectual Contribution of El Salvador's Murdered Jesuits, ed. John Hassett and Hugh Lacey (Washington, D.C.: Georgetown University Press, 1991), 177–207.

4. Latin American Provincials of the Society of Jesus, "A Letter on Neo-Liberalism in Latin America." A study document, entitled "Contributions to a Common Reflection," accompanied the letter. Both were finalized and approved by the Latin American Provincials at their October 1996 meeting in Mexico. Both documents are dated November 14, 1996, and are published in *Promotio Iustitiae* 67 (May 1997): 43–47 and 47–60.

5. Daniel Ross, S.J., "East Asia," Regional report prepared for the International Jesuit Higher Education Meeting, Santiago, Chile, October 1997.

6. Xabier Gorostiaga, S.J., in an unpublished lecture entitled "The Role of Universities in Third World Development," delivered at Saint Joseph's University in Philadelphia on March 25, 1997, cited truly alarming documentation of this phenomenon:

    20% of humanity controls 83% of the world's wealth; bottom 20%, 1.4%; the gap is getting worse: in 1960, the richest 20% was 30 times wealthier than the poorest 20%; in 1993, they were 61 times wealthier; 358 people have personal accumulated worth of about $762 billion, 45% of personal capital income of the world's population; the number of billionaires has tripled wealth between 1987 and 1994, with the highest growth rate of billionaires in Mexico.

    Gorostiaga aptly notes that "these figures reflect a crisis in civilization that requires critical reflection by universities which should act as society's critical conscience."

7. Ambrose Pinto, S.J., "South Asia," regional report prepared for the International Jesuit Higher Education Meeting, Santiago, Chile, October 1997.

8. Jacques Berleur, S.J., "Africa, Lebanon, and Europe," regional report prepared for the International Jesuit Higher Education Meeting, Santiago, Chile, October 1997.

9. Luis Ugalde, S.J., "Latin America," regional report prepared for the International Jesuit Higher Education Meeting, Santiago, Chile, October 1997.

10. Xabier Gorostiaga, "The Role of Universities."

Contributors

ROBERT JOHN ARAUJO, S.J., professor of law at Gonzaga University School of Law, is a member of the New England Province. His educational formation took place at Georgetown University, Loyola University of Chicago, Saint Michael's Institute, Weston Jesuit School of Theology, Columbia University, and Oxford University. He began teaching on a part-time basis in 1988, and commenced his full-time teaching in 1994. He also serves as a consultant to the Permanent Observer of the Holy See at the United Nations. Prior to his entry into the Society of Jesus, he practiced law, first with the United States government and then in private practice.

J. ROBERT BARTH, S.J., a member of the New York Province, is in his tenth year as dean of the College of Arts and Sciences at Boston College, after twenty-five years as an English professor at Canisius College, Harvard University, and the University of Missouri-Columbia. His books include *Coleridge and Christian Doctrine, Religious Perspectives in Faulkner's Fiction: Yoknapatawpha and Beyond, The Symbolic Imagination: Coleridge and the Romantic Tradition,* and *Coleridge and the Power of Love.*

ROBERT C. BAUMILLER, S.J., entered the Maryland Province in 1953 after graduating from Loyola College in Baltimore. He obtained his Ph.D. in biology at Saint Louis University in 1961, and did postdoctoral studies at the Universities of Wisconsin, Indiana, and Washington (Seattle). He was assistant in medicine in the Department of Medicine at Johns Hopkins University from 1962 to 1967. He was ordained in 1965 at Woodstock, Maryland. From 1967 to 1990, he was assistant professor at Georgetown University, serving in the Department of Obstetrics and Gynecology as director of the division of genetics and as founding director of the National Center for Education in Maternal and Child Health. From 1990 to 1994, he was dean of the College of Health Sciences at the University of Detroit Mercy. Since 1994, he has been associate dean for Health Education Programs and professor of biology at Xavier University. He is a founding fellow of the American Board of Medical Genetics, and is board certified as a Ph.D. medical geneticist and as a clinical cytogeneticist. He is senior research scholar of the Kennedy Institute of Ethics, and a member of a number of societies of human and medical genetics and of bioethics. He has published over 125 publications.

JAMES W. BERNAUER, S.J., is a professor of philosophy at Boston College. He is a member of the New York Province and was ordained a priest in 1975. He received his B.A. from Fordham University in 1968, an M.A. in philosophy from Saint Louis University in 1970, an M.Div. from Woodstock College in 1975, an S.T.M. in theology from Union Theological Seminary in 1976, and his Ph.D. in philosophy from the State University of New York at Stony Brook in 1981. From 1978 to 1980, he studied with Michel Foucault in Paris. He has been an instructor in philosophy at Le Moyne College in Syracuse and a visiting Bannan professor at Santa Clara University. He is the author of *Michel Foucault's Force of*

Flight: Toward an Ethics for Thought (Humanities, 1990), and editor of *Amor Mundi: Explorations in the Faith and Thought of Hannah Arendt* (Martinus Nijhoff, 1987), as well as, with David Rasmussen, *The Final Foucault* (MIT, 1988). He is currently working on a book that examines moral formation prior to and during the Nazi period.

JOHN B. BRESLIN, S.J., a member of the New York Province, served as a chaplain-in-residence at Georgetown University from 1982 to 1996 and as university chaplain in charge of campus ministry from 1992 to 1996. He is currently rector of the Jesuit community at Le Moyne College where he also teaches in the English department. His anthology of contemporary Catholic fiction, *The Substance of Things Hoped For,* is available from Georgetown University Press.

WILLIAM J. BYRON, S.J., is distinguished professor of management and director of the Center for the Advanced Study of Ethics at Georgetown University, where he serves as rector of the Georgetown Jesuit community. From 1982 to 1992, he was president of The Catholic University of America. Prior assignments include service as president of the University of Scranton (1975–82), dean of arts and sciences at Loyola University of New Orleans (1973–75), and various teaching positions in his field of economics and social ethics. He holds degrees in philosophy and economics from Saint Louis University, a licentiate in theology from Woodstock College, and a doctorate in economics from the University of Maryland. He is author of *Toward Stewardship* (1975), *Quadrangle Considerations* (1989), *Take Your Diploma and Run!* (1992), *Finding Work without Losing Heart* (1995), *The 365 Days of Christmas* (1996), and *Answers from Within* (1997). He also edited *The Causes of World Hunger* (1982) and *Take Courage* (1995).

WALTER A. COOK, S.J., professor emeritus of the linguistics department at Georgetown University and a member of the Maryland Province, served thirteen years in the Jamshedpur Mission in India before acquiring his Ph.D. in linguistics in 1965. He taught linguistics at Georgetown for twenty-seven years, was twice elected chairman of the department, and retired in 1992. During this time he mentored or read seventy-five Ph.D. dissertations in linguistics, and published four linguistics textbooks. He has lectured extensively in Taiwan, Thailand, Indonesia, the Philippines, and South Korea. In 1993 he taught one semester at Sanata Dharma University in Yogyakarta, Indonesia. In 1996 he taught one semester at Sogang University in Seoul, South Korea. He still directs Ph.D. dissertations at Georgetown, and continues to do linguistic research and writing.

CHARLES L. CURRIE, S.J., a member of the Maryland Province, is currently the president of the Association of Jesuit Colleges and Universities (AJCU). In that role, he organized a meeting of the AJCU in Chile prior to the meeting of international presidents, which is the subject of his essay. Before becoming president of AJCU in the summer of 1997, he had served as a faculty member (chemistry) and administrator at Georgetown University, president of Wheeling College (now Wheeling Jesuit University) and Xavier University, and most recently, as rector of the Jesuit Community at Saint Joseph's University. His international experience includes an extended visit to Viet Nam on behalf of Georgetown and many trips to Central America, especially El Salvador.

ANTHONY C. DALY, S.J., is a member of the Missouri Province. Currently he is an associate professor of classical languages (Ph.D. from UCLA) and serves as chair of the Department of Modern and Classical Languages at Saint Louis University. He is a classics generalist and has taught more than thirty different courses, including elementary and upper division Greek and Latin, Greek and Latin literature approached through English translations, courses in myth, women's studies, and theology focused on Greek and Latin sources, and a course in Jesuit education. His research interests include Greek theological terminology, the plays of Sophocles, the ethical theory of Thomas Aquinas, and Greek and Latin pedagogy.

PETER B. ELY, S.J., is a member of the Oregon Province. Most recently, he was president of Rockhurst College in Kansas City, Missouri. He has served as pastor of Saint Joseph Parish in Seattle, Washington, and rector of the Jesuit community, academic vice president, and chair of the religious studies department at Gonzaga University in Spokane, Washington. He has a Ph.D. in theology from Fordham University. His special interest within the field of theology is the development of doctrine. As academic vice president at Gonzaga, he was involved in the beginnings of the university's "Partnership in Mission" program and later served for a time as codirector with one of his lay colleagues. He is now on sabbatical at Seattle University.

JOSEPH J. FEENEY, S.J., a member of the Maryland Province, is professor of English at Saint Joseph's University and has been a visiting professor at Georgetown and Santa Clara Universities. A Hopkins scholar and coeditor of *The Hopkins Quarterly,* he also writes on such contemporaries as Graham Greene, William Golding, Tom Stoppard, Peter Shaffer, Brian Friel, Harold Pinter, Anne Ridler, David Hare, Tom McHale, Andre Dubus, Walker Percy, Pam Gems, and George Mackay Brown. He has lectured on modernism and post-modernism at colleges and art galleries, including the Philadelphia Museum of Art and the National Gallery of Art in Washington. At Saint Joseph's, he served as president of the American Association of University Professors and vice president of the Faculty Senate. In 1983 he won the Lindback Award for Distinguished Teaching. He is currently a trustee of Fordham University.

FRANK R. HAIG, S.J., a member of the Maryland Province, was born in Philadelphia, Pennsylvania. He entered the Society of Jesus in 1946. He received his doctorate in theoretical nuclear physics from The Catholic University of America in 1959 and was ordained in 1960. He served as president of Wheeling College (now Wheeling Jesuit University) from 1966 to 1972, and president of Le Moyne College from 1981 to 1987. While in Syracuse he also served a term as chairman of the board of Syracuse Opera Company. He was president of the Washington Academy of Sciences from 1994 to 1995 and now serves as President of the Maryland Conference of the American Association of University Professors. He is currently professor of physics at Loyola College.

FREDERICK A. HOMANN, S.J., a member of the Maryland Province, was ordained in 1962, and completed his doctoral work at the University of Pennsylvania under the direction of Professor Hans Rademacher. He has been a faculty member at Loyola College, Baltimore, where he was chairman of the mathematics department, and at Saint Joseph's University, where he taught both mathematics and philosophy. He has been published in *Proceedings of the American Mathematical Society, Archivum Historicum Societatis Iesu, Dionysus, Synthesis Philosophica, Records of the American Catholic Historical Society,* and *Faith and Reason.* Marquette University Press published his book *Practical Geometry Attributed to Hugh of St. Victor* (1991).

JAMES F. KEENAN, S.J., associate professor of moral theology, is a New York Province Jesuit teaching at Weston Jesuit School of Theology. He previously taught moral theology at Fordham University. He did his licentiate and doctorate with Fathers Josef Fuchs, S.J., and Klaus Demmer, M.S.C., at the Pontifical Gregorian University in Rome. His books include *Goodness and Rightness in Thomas Aquinas' Summa Theologiae; The Context of Casuistry,* edited with Thomas Shannon; and *Virtues for Ordinary Christians.* His interests include virtue ethics, casuistry, the history of Christian ethics, and the relationship between morality and spirituality. He is working on three main projects: writing a manuscript on the development of British Puritan practical divinity; editing a collection of essays on clergy ethics; and chairing an international commission on AIDS prevention.

THOMAS M. LUCAS, S.J., is assistant professor of fine arts and chair of the fine and performing arts department of the University of San Francisco. He holds a doctorate in theology and the arts from the Graduate Theological Union in Berkeley, California. He designed and supervised architectural restoration of the sixteenth-century rooms of Saint Ignatius Loyola in Rome; curated the Ignatian year exhibit at the Vatican Library; edited the exhibit catalog, *Saint, Site, and Sacred Strategy* (1990); and did archival research on Ignatian letters, which has culminated in *Landmarking: City, Church & Jesuit Urban Strategy* (1997).

THOMAS J. MALONEY, S.J., associate professor of political science, teaches comparative politics at Loyola Maymount University. Upon graduating from The University of Notre Dame, he entered the California Province in 1958. After studies in Saint Louis and Los Gatos, California, he was ordained in 1969. Doctoral studies in political science with a concentration in Latin America followed at The University of Texas at Austin. He joined the faculty at Loyola Marymount in 1974.

ARTHUR F. McGOVERN, S.J., is a professor of philosophy at the University of Detroit Mercy and a member of the Detroit Province. He entered the Jesuits in 1951 after graduation from Georgetown University and obtained his doctorate in philosopohy at the University of Paris in 1967. He has taught at the University of Detroit (Mercy) since 1970. His publications include *Marxism: An American Christian Perspective* (Orbis, 1980), *Ethical Dilemmas in the Modern Corporation* (Prentice-Hall, 1988, coauthored), and *Liberation Theology and Its Critics* (Orbis, 1989). He has contributed chapters to eight other books and numerous articles for periodicals and journals. He served as superior and dean of the Jesuit Collegiate Program in Detroit during much of the 1970s and as rector of the Jesuit Community at the University of Detroit Mercy from 1991 to 1997.

RONALD H. MCKINNEY, S.J., professor of philosophy and a member of the Maryland Province, has been a member of the philosophy department and director of the Special Jesuit Liberal Arts Program at the University of Scranton since 1984. He has over twenty publications in Lonergan and postmodern studies, and also writes poetry, novels, and plays when he has the time. By the time this book reaches press, he will have an article on Christian comedy and tragedy coming out in *Philosophy Today* and a study of Graham Swift's *Waterland* coming out in *New Literary History*.

PAUL D. MCNELIS, S.J., is professor of economics with a joint appointment in the Department of Economics and the Edmund A. Walsh School of Foreign Service. He has been at Georgetown University since 1977. His Ph.D. is from Johns Hopkins University in Baltimore; his undergraduate degree is from Boston College. He regularly teaches courses in international finance and monetary economics. One of his departmental duties is faculty liaison of the Georgetown M.A.–Economics collaborative program with ILADES (Instituto Latinoamericano de Doctrina y Estudios Sociales) in Santiago, Chile. He has worked with this program since its inception in 1987. He has been a consultant to the international development organizations in Washington and to several central banks: the Central Bank of Ireland, the Reserve Bank of Australia, the Reserve Bank of New Zealand, the Bank of Indonesia, and the Bank of Japan. He was visiting professor at Trinity College, Dulbin, from 1986 to 1987 and the first Philips visiting professor at the Vargas Foundation in São Paulo, Brazil during the 1994–95 academic year. He has written in the fields of empirical macroeconomics and international finance, concentrating on problems of adjustment and financial liberalization in Latin America and Asia. His current research is on applications of neural networks and genetic algorithms in macroeconomic models.

JOHN J. PIDERIT, S.J., was elected at age forty-nine as Loyola's twenty-second president in June, and assumed office in August 1993. He is an economist and ethics scholar. Prior to coming to Loyola, he was corporate vice president at Marquette University, Milwaukee; there he served on the board of trustees and as secretary of the corporation. He has experience with university alumni, development, and ministry operations. He has spent most of his career in a variety of academic and administrative positions. These include serving as associate professor of economics and assistant chairperson for graduate studies. He taught economics both at Fordham and Marquette Universities. He holds a Ph.D. and an M.A. in economics from Princeton University, a master's of philosophy and economics from Oxford University, and a licentiate in sacred theology from the Philosophische und Theologische Hochschule Sankt Georgen of Frankfurt, Germany. Father Piderit, born in New York City, entered the New York Province of the Society of Jesus in 1961 and was ordained a priest in 1971. He has been involved in a variety of community related activities in both Milwaukee and New York City. He is the recipient of many fellowships and grants. His book, *The Ethical Foundations of Economics,* was published in 1993 by Georgetown University Press.

THOMAS P. RAUSCH, S.J., received his Ph.D. from Duke University in 1976. He is professor and chair of theological studies at Loyola Marymount University in Los Angeles and a member of the California Province. He serves on the theological commission, the ecumenical commission, and the editorial commission of *The Tidings* for the Archdiocese of Los Angeles. He is also co-chair of the Los Angeles Catholic-Evangelical Dialogue. In 1994 he was appointed to the United States Catholic/Southern Baptist Conversation. His books include *The Roots of the Catholic Tradition* (Glazier, 1986), *The College Student's Introduction to Theology* (Liturgical, 1993), and *Catholicism at the Dawn of the Third Millennium* (Liturgical, 1996).

ROBERT M. SENKEWICZ, S.J., a member of the California Province, is associate professor of history and director of the Bannan Institute for Jesuit Education and Christian Values at Santa Clara University. He has served as director of campus ministry, vice president for student services, and chair of the history department at Santa Clara. He is the author of *Vigilantes in Gold Rush San Francisco* (Stanford Universtiy Press, 1985); editor, with Rose Marie Beebe, of Antonio Maria Osio's *The History of Alta California* (University of Wisconsin Press, 1996); and author of a number of scholarly and popular articles.

CHARLES M. SHELTON, S.J., a member of the Missouri Province, is associate professor of psychology at Regis University, Denver, and a licensed clinical psychologist in private practice. He received his Ph.D. in clinical psychology from Loyola University of Chicago, and did a clinical internship in the Department of Psychiatry at Indiana University School of Medicine. He has published five books and numerous articles and reviews on such topics as moral development, pastoral psychology, adolescent and adult mental health, and psychosocial aspects of adolescent and young adult development. He is a consultant to a number of religious organizations, and is a member of the Archdiocese of Denver's Conduct Response Team. He is currently completing a book on conscience functioning and professional life.

DENNIS C. SMOLARSKI, S.J., associate professor of mathematics at Santa Clara University, is a member of the California Province, and was ordained a priest in 1979. He completed his graduate work in the Department of Computer Science at the University of Illinois in 1982. He is a member of various professional organizations and served as chair of the northern California section of the Mathematical Association of America. He is also known for his work among Eastern Christians (currently the secretary-treasurer of the Jesuits for the Christian East), and his publications in liturgy. He has published review texts in the field of computer science for the Research and Education Association (in FORTRAN and Data Structures) and his best-known liturgical books are *How Not to Say Mass* (1986) and *Sacred Mysteries* (1995).

PAUL A. SOUKUP, S.J., a member of the California Province, is associate professor of communication at Santa Clara University. He received his Ph.D. at The University of Texas at Austin in 1985. He teaches courses in technology and communication, interpersonal communication, and communication and culture. In addition to his teaching, he has served as a member of the communication committee of the United States Catholic Conference and presently works with the American Bible Society's Multimedia Translations Project. He has published *Communication and Theology: An Introduction and Review of the Literature* (WACC, 1983); *Christian Communication: A Bibliographical Survey* (Greenwood, 1989); and edited, with Bruce Gronbeck and Thomas J. Farrell, *Media, Consciousness and Culture* (Sage, 1991); with Thomas J. Farrell, three volumes of *Faith and Contexts* (Scholars, 1992–1995) and *Communication and Lonergan* (Sheed & Ward, 1993); with Philip J. Rossi, *Mass Media and the Moral Imagination* (Sheed & Ward, 1994); and *Media, Culture, and Catholicism* (Sheed & Ward, 1996).

MARTIN R. TRIPOLE, S.J., a member of the New York Province, is an associate professor of theology at Saint Joseph's University, where he has taught since 1972. He received his S.T.D. at the Institut Catholique in Paris, and studied three years in Tübingen under Jürgen Moltmann. He has published numerous articles in theological journals, and two books, the more recent being *Faith Beyond Justice: Widening the Perspective* (Institute of Jesuit Sources, 1994).

KEVIN WATERS, S.J., is a member of the Oregon Province and professor of music and dean emeritus of the College of Arts and Sciences at Gonzaga University. A founding member of the Jesuit Institute for the Arts, panelist with the National Endowment for the Arts, and holder of a doctorate in music theory and composition, he has taught courses in philosophy and music at Seattle University and Gonzaga for the past thirty years. Playwright Ernest Ferlita, S.J., and he were commissioned to create the opera *Dear Ignatius, Dear Isabel* for the 125th anniversary of Loyola College. Following its premiere in Baltimore, the opera was also produced in Seattle, New Orleans, and Spokane. Another opera, *Edith Stein*, awaits its premiere performance. *Psalm 150*, for chorus and symphonic band, was commissioned by the University of Scranton. This year's premieres include *Clare Symphony, Cataldo Trio* for flute, cello, and piano, and *The Lord Is Near: Improvisations for Organ on Advent Plainchants.*

Addresses

REVEREND ROBERT JOHN ARAUJO, S.J.
Professor of Law
Gonzaga University School of Law
Spokane, Washington 99220-3528

REVEREND J. ROBERT BARTH, S.J.
Dean
College of Arts and Sciences
Boston College
Chestnut Hill, Massachusetts 02167-3803

REVEREND ROBERT C. BAUMILLER, S.J.
Associate Dean of Health Education Programs
Xavier University
3800 Victory Parkway
Cincinnati, Ohio 45207-1049

REVEREND JAMES W. BERNAUER, S.J.
Professor of Philosophy
Boston College
Chestnut Hill, Massachusetts 02167-3806

REVEREND JOHN B. BRESLIN, S.J.
Rector
Le Moyne College
Syracuse, New York 13214

REVEREND WILLIAM J. BYRON, S.J.
Director
Center for the Advanced Study of Ethics
Box 571248
Georgetown University
Washington, D.C. 20057-1248

REVEREND WALTER A. COOK, S.J.
Professor Emeritus of Linguistics
Jesuit Community
Georgetown University
37th & O Streets, NW
Washington, D.C. 20057-1735

Reverend Charles L. Currie, S.J.
President
Association of Jesuit Colleges and Universities
1 Dupont Circle, Suite 405
Washington, D.C. 20036

Reverend Anthony C. Daly, S.J.
Professor and Chair
Department of Latin and Greek
Saint Louis University
221 North Grand Boulevard
Saint Louis, Missouri 63103-2097

Reverend Peter B. Ely, S.J.
Jesuit Residence
Seattle University
900 Broadway
Seattle, Washington 98122-4340

Reverend Joseph J. Feeney, S.J.
Professor of English
Saint Joseph's University
5600 City Avenue
Philadelphia, Pennsylvania 19131-1395

Reverend Frank R. Haig, S.J.
Professor of Physics
Loyola College in Maryland
4501 North Charles Street
Baltimore, Maryland 21210

Reverend Frederick A. Homann, S.J.
Loyola Center
Saint Joseph's University
5600 City Avenue
Philadelphia, Pennsylvania 19131-1395

Reverend James F. Keenan, S.J.
Associate Professor of Moral Theology
Weston Jesuit School of Theology
3 Phillips Place
Cambridge, Massachusetts 02138-3495

REVEREND THOMAS M. LUCAS, S.J.
Assistant Professor and Chair
Department of Fine and Performing Arts
University of San Francisco
2130 Fulton Street
San Francisco, California 94117-1080

REVEREND THOMAS J. MALONEY, S.J.
Associate Professor of Political Science
Loyola Marymount University
Loyola Boulevard at West 80th Street
Los Angeles, California 90045-2699

REVEREND ARTHUR F. McGOVERN, S.J.
Professor of Philosophy
University of Detroit Mercy
4001 West McNichols Road
P.O. Box 19900
Detroit, Michigan 48219-0900

REVEREND RONALD H. McKINNEY, S.J.
Professor of Philosophy
University of Scranton
Scranton, Pennsylvania 18510-4623

REVEREND PAUL D. McNELIS, S.J.
Professor of Economics
Georgetown University
Washington, D.C. 20057

REVEREND JOHN J. PIDERIT, S.J.
President
Loyola University of Chicago
6525 North Sheridan Road
Chicago, Illinois 60626-5385

REVEREND THOMAS P. RAUSCH, S.J.
Professor and Chair
Department of Theological Studies
Loyola Marymount University
Loyola Boulevard at West 80th Street
Los Angeles, California 90045-2699

REVEREND ROBERT M. SENKEWICZ, S.J.
Associate Professor of History
Director
Bannan Institute for Jesuit Education
Santa Clara University
500 El Camino Real
Santa Clara, California 95053-0277

REVEREND CHARLES M. SHELTON, S.J.
Professor of Psychology
Regis University
3333 Regis Boulevard
Denver, Colorado 80221-1099

REVEREND DENNIS C. SMOLARSKI, S.J.
Associate Professor of Mathematics
Santa Clara University
500 El Camino Real
Santa Clara, California 95053-0277

REVEREND PAUL A. SOUKUP, S.J.
Associate Professor of Communication
Santa Clara University
500 El Camino Real
Santa Clara, California 95053-0277

REVEREND MARTIN R. TRIPOLE, S.J.
Associate Professor of Theology
Saint Joseph's University
5600 City Avenue
Philadelphia, Pennsylvania 19131-1395

REVEREND KEVIN WATERS, S.J.
Professor of Music
Gonzaga University
502 East Boone Avenue
Spokane, Washington 99258-0001

Bibiography

Abbott, Walter M., S.J., gen. ed. *The Documents of Vatican II.* Trans. ed. Joseph Gallagher. New York: Guild, 1966.

Appleby, Joyce, et al., eds. *Knowledge and Postmodernism in Historical Perspective.* New York and London: Routledge, 1996.

Arendt, H. *The Human Condition.* Chicago, Ill.: University of Chicago Press, 1958.

Arrupe, Pedro, S.J. *Justice with Faith Today, Selected Letters and Addresses II.* Ed. Jerome Aixala, S.J. St. Louis, Mo.: Institute of Jesuit Sources, 1980.

———. "Letter to the Whole Society on Inculturation." *Acta Romana Societatis Iesu* 17 (178): 230.

———. "Report of Father General on the State of the Society." 27 September 1978. *Acta Romana Societatis Iesu* 17 (1978): 451–80.

———. "To a Certain Provincial Superior." *Acta Romana Societatis Iesu* 16 (1976): 1097–98.

———. *Witnessing to Justice.* Vatican City: Pontifical Commission Justice and Peace, 1972.

Augustine, Saint. *Confessions,* Bk 7, Cp 10.16; Bk 10, Cp 27.38. In *The Liturgy of the Hours,* vol. iv. Trans. International Commission on English in the Liturgy. New York: Catholic Book Publishing Co., 1975, 1356–57.

Bailie, Gil. *Violence Unveiled: Humanity at the Crossroads.* New York: Crossroad, 1995.

Baldini, Ugo. *Legem impone subactis: studi su filosophia e scienza dei Gesuiti in Italia, 1540–1632.* Rome: Bulzoni, 1992.

Banke, Arthur S., et al., eds. *Economic Handbook of the World.* 1981. New York: McGraw-Hill, 1981.

Barnes, Julian. *Flaubert's Parrot.* London: Pan, 1985.

Baumiller, Robert C., et. al. "Code of Ethical Principles for Genetics Professionals." *American Journal of Medical Genetics* 65 (1996): 177–78.

———. "Code of Ethical Principles for Genetics Professionals: An Explication." *American Journal of Medical Genetics* 65 (1996): 179–83.

Begheyn, Paul. "Bibliography on the History of the Jesuits: Publications in English, 1900–1993." *Studies in the Spirituality of Jesuits* 28/1 (1996): 1–50.

Berger, Peter L. *Facing Up to Modernity: Excursions in Society, Politics, and Religion.* New York: Basic, 1977.

———, and Richard John Neuhaus. *To Empower People.* Washington, D.C.: American Enterprise Institute, 1977.

Berleur, Jacques, S.J. "Africa, Lebanon, and Europe." Regional report prepared for the International Jesuit Higher Education Meeting, Santiago, Chile, October 1997.

Bernauer, James, S.J., "Beyond Life and Death: On Foucault's Post-Auschwitz Ethic." *Philosophy Today* 32 (summer 1988): 128–42.

———. "Nazi Ethics." *Continuum* 1 (autumn 1990): 15–29.

———. "The Prisons of Man: An Introduction to Foucault's Negative Theology." *International Philosophical Quarterly* 27 (December 1987): 365–80.

———, ed. *Amor Mundi: Explorations in the Faith and Thought of Hannah Arendt.* Boston, Mass.: Martinus Nijhoff, 1987.

———— and D. Rasmussen, eds. *The Final Foucault.* Cambridge, Mass.: MIT, 1988.

Bernstein, Barton J., ed. *Towards a New Past: Dissenting Essays in American History.* New York: Pantheon, 1968.

Billy, Dennis, and Donna Orsuto, eds. *Spirituality and Morality: Integrating Prayer and Action.* Mahwah, N.J.: Paulist, 1996.

Bredbeck, Gregory W. "B/O—Barthes's Text/O'Hara's Trick." *PMLA* 108 (1993): 274.

Brown, Peter. *The Body and Society: Men, Women, and Sexual Renunciation in Early Christianity.* New York: Columbia University Press, 1988.

Brown, Raymond E., S.S. *An Introduction to the New Testament.* New York: Doubleday, 1997.

Bryk, Anthony, Valerie E. Lee, and Peter B. Holland. *Catholic Schools and the Common Good.* Cambridge, Mass.: Harvard University Press, 1993.

Buckley, Michael J., S.J. "In Hunc Potissimum . . . : Ignatius' Understanding of the Jesuit University." *Readings in Ignatian Higher Education* 1/1 (spring 1989): 18–27.

Calvez, Jean-Yves, S.J. *Faith and Justice: The Social Dimension of Evangelization.* Trans. John E. Blewett, S.J. St. Louis, Mo.: Institute of Jesuit Sources, 1991 [1985].

Campion, Donald R., S.J., and Albert C. Louapre, S.J., eds. *Documents of the 33rd General Congregation of the Society of Jesus.* St. Louis, Mo.: Institute of Jesuit Sources, 1984.

Carboy, Mary. "Hospitality—Martha and Mary." *Review for Religious* 50 (1991): 387–89.

Carey, James W. *Communication as Culture: Essays on Media and Society.* Boston, Mass.: Unwin Hyman, 1989 [1975].

Carter, Stephen. *The Culture of Disbelief.* New York: Harvard University Press, 1994.

Catechism of the Catholic Church. Liguori: Liguori Press, 1994.

Chapple, Christopher, ed. *The Jesuit Tradition in Education and Missions: A 450 Year Perspective.* Scranton, Penn.: University of Scranton Press, 1993.

Christiansen, Drew, S.J. "Sacrament of Unity: Ethical Issues in Pastoral Care of Migrants and Refugees." In *Today's Immigrants and Refugees: A Christian Understanding,* Office of Pastoral Care of Migrants and Refugees, Bishops' Committee on Migration, National Conference of Catholic Bishops. Washington, D.C.: USCC, 1988.

Clement I. In *The Epistles of St. Clement of Rome and St. Ignatius of Antioch.* Trans. James A. Kleist, S.J. Westminster, Md.: Newman Bookshop, 1946.

Clooney, Francis X. , S.J. *Theology After Vedanta: An Experiment in Comparative Theology.* Albany, N.Y.: SUNY Press, 1993.

Cohen, Jean, and Andrew Arato. *Civil Society and Political Theory.* Cambridge, Mass.: MIT, 1992.

Connecticut Christian Conference. "Gun Violence Against Children and Youth." *Origins* 25 (25 May 1995): 17, 19–21.

Conwell, Joseph, S.J. *Impelling Spirit.* Chicago, Ill.: Loyola Press, 1997.

Cosentino, Giuseppe. "L'insegnamento delle matematiche nei collegi Gesuitici nell'Italia settentrionale." *Physis* XIII (1971): Fasc. 2, 205–17.

————. "Le matematiche nella 'Ratio Studiorum' della Compagnia di Gesù." *Miscellanea Storica Ligure,* Anno II (Nuova Serie periodica): n.2, 1970.

Coyne, G. V., S.J., M. A. Hoskin, and O. Pedersen, eds. "Gregorian Reform of the Calendar." *Proceedings of the Vatican Conference to Commemorate Its 400th Anniversary, 1582–1982.* Rome: Specola Vaticani, 1983.

Crombie, A. C. "Mathematics and Platonism in the Sixteenth Century Italian Universities and in Jesuit Educational Policy." In *Prismata Festschrift für Willy Hartner,* ed. Y. Maeyanea and W. G. Saltzer. Wiesbaden, 1977.

Crowley, Paul G., S.J. "Theology in the Jesuit University: Reassessing the Ignatian Vision." In *The Jesuit Tradition in Education and Missions: A 450 Year Perspective,* ed. Christopher Chapple. Scranton, Penn.: University of Scranton Press, 1993.

Culler, Jonathan. *On Deconstruction: Theory and Criticism After Structuralism.* Ithaca, N.Y.: Cornell University Press, 1982.

Cunningham, Lawrence S. "Gladly Wolde He Lerne and Gladly Teche: The Catholic Scholar in the New Millennium." *The Cresset* (June 1992): 318.

Curran, Charles E. "The Catholic Identity of Catholic Institutions." *Theological Studies* 58 (1997): 90–108.

Cusanus, Nicolas. *Opera omnia.* 14 vols. In *De docta ignorantia,* ed. Ernst Hoffmann and Raymond Klibansky (Leipzig, 1932).

Czerny, Michael, S.J. "Challenges of Mission Today to Our Minima Societas." *CIS* 75 (1994): 10–19.

———. "Whence the Themes . . . ?" *CIS* 75 (1994): 4–9.

Daley, Brian. "'In Ten Thousand Places': Christian Universality and the Jesuit Mission." *Studies in the Spirituality of Jesuits* 17/2 (1985): 3.

Davis, P. J., and R. Hersh, eds. *The Mathematical Experience.* Boston, Mass.: Houghton Mifflin, 1981.

Dear, Peter R. *Discipline and Experience: The Mathematical Way in the Scientific Revolution.* Chicago, Ill.: University of Chicago Press, 1995.

De Mesa, J., and T. Gisbert. "Bitti, Bernardo." In *The New Catholic Encyclopedia.* New York: McGraw-Hill, 1967.

Derrida, Jacques. "Force of Law: The 'Mystical Foundation of Authority.'" *Cardoza Law Review* 11 (1990): 943–45.

Donahue, John R., S.J. "What Does the Lord Require?: A Bibliographical Essay on the Bible and Social Justice." *Studies in the Spirituality of Jesuits* 25/2 (March 1993): 19–25.

Dulles, Avery, S.J. "Faith, Justice, and the Jesuit Mission." In *Assembly 1989: Jesuit Ministry in Higher Education.* Washington, D.C.: Jesuit Conference, 1990.

Eagleton, Terry. *The Illusions of Postmodernism.* Cambridge, Mass.: Blackwell, 1996.

Eco, Umberto. *The Aesthetics of Thomas Aquinas.* Cambridge, Mass.: Harvard University Press, 1988.

Edwards, Harry T. "The Growing Disjunction Between Legal Education and the Legal Profession." *Michigan Law Review* 91 (1992): 34, 41.

Egan, Gerard. *Adding Value: A Systematic Guide to Business-Driven Management and Leadership.* San Francisco, Calif.: Jossey-Bass, 1993.

Eliot, T. S. *Collected Poems, 1909–1962.* New York: Harcourt, Brace, 1963.

Ellacuría, Ignacio, S.J. "The Historicization of the Concept of Poverty." In *Towards a Society That Serves Its People: The Intellectual Contribution of El Salvador's Murdered Jesuits,* ed. John Hassett and Hugh Lacey. Washington, D.C.: Georgetown University Press, 1991.

———. "Is a Different Kind of University Possible?" In *Towards a Society That Serves Its People: The Intellectual Contribution of El Salvador's Murdered Jesuits,* ed. John Hassett and Hugh Lacey. Washington, D.C.: Georgetown University Press, 1991.

Elliott, John. *A Home for the Homeless: A Sociological Exegesis of 1 Peter, Its Situation and Strategy.* Philadelphia: Fortress, 1981.

Eskridge, William. *Dynamic Statutory Interpretation.* Cambridge, Mass.: Harvard University Press, 1994.

Faase, Thomas Philip. *Making the Jesuits More Modern.* Washington, D.C.: University Press of America, 1981.

Farrell, James F., S.J. *The Jesuit Code of Liberal Education: Development and Scope of the Ratio Studiorum.* Milwaukee, Wis.: Bruce, 1938.

Feeney, Joseph J., S.J. "Can a Worldview Be Healed?: Students and Postmodernism." *America* 177/15 (15 November 1997): 12–16.

———. "Is Literature Still Human? Beyond Politics and Theory." *America* 173/16 (18 November 1995): 26–27.

Fitzmyer, Joseph A., S.J. "Pauline Theology." In *The New Jerome Biblical Commentary,* ed. Raymond E. Brown, S.S., et al. Englewood Cliffs, N.J.: Prentice Hall, 1990.

Flannery, Austin, O.P., ed. *Vatican Council II: The Conciliar and Post Conciliar Documents.* Collegeville, Minn.: Liturgical, 1975 [1971].

Flynn, Thomas. "Foucault as Parrhesiast: His Last Courses at the Collège de France." In *The Final Foucault,* ed. J. Bernauer and D. Rasmussen. Cambridge, Mass.: MIT, 1988.

Foucault, Michel. *The Archaeology of Knowledge.* New York: Harper Colophon, 1976.

———. *The Birth of the Clinic.* New York: Pantheon, 1973.

———. *Discipline and Punish: The Birth of the Prison.* New York: Pantheon, 1977.

———. *Force of Flight: Toward an Ethics for Thought.* Atlantic Highlands, N.J.: Humanities, 1990.

———. *The History of Sexuality I: An Introduction.* New York: Pantheon, 1978.

———. *The History of Sexuality II: The Use of Pleasure.* New York: Pantheon, 1985.

———. *The History of Sexuality III: The Care of the Self.* New York: Pantheon, 1986.

———. *Madness and Civilization.* New York: Pantheon, 1965.

———. *The Order of Things.* New York: Pantheon, 1971.

———. "What Is Enlightenment?" In *The Foucault Reader,* ed. Paul Rabinow. New York: Pantheon, 1984.

Fowles, John. *The French Lieutenant's Woman.* Boston, Mass.: Little, Brown, 1969.

Frankl, Viktor. *Man's Search for Meaning.* New York: Washington Square, 1985.

Fredericks, James L. "A Universal Religious Experience?: Comparative Theology as an Alternative to a Theology of Religions." *Horizons* 22/1 (1995): 67–87.

Gadamer, Hans-Georg. *Truth and Method.* Trans. G. Barden and J. Cumming. New York: Seabury, 1975 [1965].

Gallagher, Eugene B., S.J. "A College Religion Course: Problems." *Jesuit Educational Quarterly* 12 (1949): 94–97.

Gallup, George, Jr., and Jim Castelli. *The American Catholic People: Their Beliefs, Practices, and Values.* Garden City, N.Y.: Doubleday, 1987.

Ganss, George E., S.J. *The Jesuit Educational Tradition and Saint Louis University.* St. Louis, Mo.: Saint Louis University, 1969.

———. *Saint Ignatius' Idea of a Jesuit University.* Milwaukee, Wis.: Marquette University Press, 1954.

———, trans. *The Constitutions of the Society of Jesus.* St. Louis, Mo.: Institute of Jesuit Sources, 1970.

———, trans. *The Spiritual Exercises of Saint Ignatius: A Translation and Commentary.* St. Louis, Mo.: Institute of Jesuit Sources, 1992.

Garland, James H. "Congregation-Based Organizations: A Church Model for the 90s." *America* 169 (13 November 1993): 14–16.

Gates, Henry Louis, Jr. "Canon-Formation, Literary History, and the Afro-American Tradition: From the Seen to the Told." In *Falling into Theory: Conflicting Views on Reading Literature,* ed. David H. Richter. Boston, Mass.: St. Martin's, 1994.

Gleason, Philip. *Contending With Modernity: Catholic Higher Education in the Twentieth Century.* New York and Oxford: Oxford University Press, 1995.

Gorostiaga, Xabier, S.J. "The Role of Universities in Third World Development." Unpublished lecture delivered at Saint Joseph's University in Philadelphia, 25 March 1997.

Gowler, David. "Hospitality and Characterization in Luke 11:37–54." *Semeia* 64 (1994): 213–51.

Grant, Edward. "In Defense of the Earth's Centrality and Immobility: Scholastic Reaction to Copernicanism in the 17th Century." *Transactions of the American Philosophical Society* 74/4 (1984).

Gray, Howard. "Changing Structures." *Way Supplement: Person and Society in the Ignatian Exercises* 76 (1993): 79.

———. "Shift in Theology." *Way Supplement* 65 (1989): 56–65.

Greeley, Andrew. *Religion as Poetry.* New Brunswick, N.J.: Transaction Publishers, 1996.

Gutiérrez, Gustavo. *A Theology of Liberation.* Maryknoll, N.Y.: 1973.

Halperin, David. *Saint Focault.* New York: Oxford University Press, 1995.

Hammarskjöld, Dag. *Markings.* Trans. Leif Sjöberg and W. H. Auden. New York: Knopf, 1964.

Haring, N. "The Creation and Creator of the World according to Thierry of Chartres and Clarenbaldus of Arras." *Archives d'histoire doctrinale et littéraire du moyen âge* XXII (1955): 194.

Harris, Wendell V. "Canonicity." *PMLA* 106 (1991): 110–21.

Harwit, Martin. *An Exhibit Denied: Lobbying the History of Enola Gay.* New York: Copernicus, 1996.

Hassett, John, and Hugh Lacey, eds. *Towards a Society That Serves Its People: The Intellectual Contribution of El Salvador's Murdered Jesuits.* Washington, D.C.: Georgetown University Press, 1991.

Hauerwas, Stanley. *A Community of Character.* Notre Dame, Ind.: University of Notre Dame Press, 1981.

Heft, James, S.M. "Theology in a Catholic University." *Origins* 25 (1995): 243–48.

Heilbron, John. *Elements of Early Modern Physics.* Berkeley, Calif.: University of California, 1982.

Hellwig, Monica. "The Best of Times, The Worst of Times: Catholic Intellectual Life in Today's Academic Setting." *Conversations* 8 (fall 1995):14–19.

Herberg, Will. *Protestant-Catholic-Jew: An Essay in American Religious Sociology.* 2nd ed. Garden City, N.Y.: Doubleday, 1960.

Hick, John, and Paul F. Knitter, eds. *The Myth of Christian Uniqueness: Toward a Pluralistic Theology of Religion.* Maryknoll, N.Y.: Orbis, 1987.

Himes, Michael J., and Stephen J. Pope, eds. *Finding God in All Things: Essays in Honor of Michael J. Buckley, S.J.* New York: Crossroad Herder, 1996.

Hirsch, E. D., Jr. *Cultural Literacy: What Every American Needs to Know.* Boston, Mass.: Houghton Mifflin, 1987.

Hobbs, T. R. "Man, woman, and hospitality: 2 Kings 4:8–36." *Biblical Theology Bulletin* 23 (1993): 91–100.

Hoeffel, Paul Heath. "The Eclipse of the Oligarchy." *The New York Times Magazine* (6 September 1981): 23.

Homann, Frederick A., S.J. "Christopher Clavius and the Renaissance of Euclidean Geometry." *Archivum Historicum Societatis Iesu* 52 (1983): 233–46.

———. "Faith and Reason in Roger Boscovich's Philosophy of Science." *Faith and Reason* XVIII (1992): 87–93.

———. "Institutio Mathematica in Scholis Societatis Iesu Saeculo Sextodecimo." *Hermes Americanus* II (1984): 120–21.

———. "Mathematics and Prophecy: Faith and Reason in Simone Weil." *Faith and Reason* XI (1985): 264–79.

Huesman, William A., S.J. "Integration of College Studies by Means of Theology." *Jesuit Educational Quarterly* 15 (1952): 29–36.

Hutcheon, Linda. *A Poetics of Postmodernism: History, Theory, and Fiction.* New York: Routledge, 1988.

Ivern, Francisco, S.J. "The Future of Faith and Justice: A Critical Review of Decree Four." *Studies in the Spirituality of Jesuits* 14/5 (November 1982).

———. "The Three Dimensions of Our Mission: Justice, Culture and Dialogue: Challenges Which These Dimensions Present for the University." Paper presented at the International Jesuit Higher Education (IJHE) Meeting of University Rectors/Presidents/Principals, Santiago, Chile, 20–21 October 1997.

Jesuits of the Maryland Province. "A Plan for Renewal: A Community of Apostolic Men." II (December 1969): 10.

John Paul II. "Allocution to the Jewish Community." Mainz, 17 November 1980. *Acta Apostolicae Sedis* 73 (1981): 80.

———. "Discourse to the Catholic Institute of Paris." 1 June 1980. *Insegnamenti di Giovanni Paolo II* vol. 3/1 (1980).

———. *Evangelium Vitae.* Vatican trans. Boston, Mass.: Pauline Books, 1995.

———. *Redemptoris Missio.* Washington, D.C.: USCC, 1990.

———. *Spiritual Pilgrimage: Texts on Jews and Judaism 1979–1995.* Ed. Eugene Fisher and Leon Klenicki. New York: Crossroad, 1995.

Jones, L. Gregory. "The virtues of hospitality (2 Kgs 4:8–17; Lk 10:38–42)." *Christian Century* 109 (1992): 17–24.

Judge, E. A. "The Quest for Mercy in Late Antiquity." In *God Who Is Rich in Mercy,* ed. P. T. O'Brien. Sydney: Macquarie University Press, 1986.

Keating, James. "The Good Life." *Church* 11/2 (1995): 15–20.

Keenan, James F., S.J. "Catholic Moral Theology, Ignatian Spirituality, and Virtue Ethics: Strange Bedfellows." *Way Supplement: Spirituality and Ethics* 88 (1997): 36–45.

———. "Rooting Morality in Spirituality." *Church* 12/4 (1996): 38–39.

————. *Virtues for Ordinary Christians.* Kansas City, Mo.: Sheed and Ward, 1996.

Kelly, J. M. *A Short History of Western Legal Theory.* Oxford: Oxford University Press, 1992.

Koenig, John. "New Testament Hospitality." *America* 155/17 (1986): 172.

————. *New Testament Hospitality: Partnership with Strangers as Promise and Mission.* Philadelphia: Fortress, 1985.

Kolvenbach, Peter-Hans, S.J. "Address to the Congregation of Provincials." 20 September 1990. *Acta Romana Societatis Iesu* 20 (1990): 452.

————. "Final Address to the Congregation of Procurators." 8 September 1987. n. 4. *Acta Romana Societatis Iesu* 19 (1987): 1078–90.

————. "To All Major Superiors" (n. 96/16), 8 November 1996.

————. "To All Major Superiors." *National Jesuit News* (October 1993): 8.

————. "To the Whole Society: The 34th General Congregation." *Acta Romana Societatis Iesu* 20 (1994): 788–91.

Korten, David C. *When Corporations Rule the World.* West Hartford, Conn.: Kumarian, 1995.

Kristeva, Julia. *Strangers to Ourselves.* New York: Columbia University Press, 1991.

LaCroix, Wilfred L., S.J. *The Jesuit Spirit of Education: Ignatius, Tradition and Today's Questions.* Kansas City, Mo.: Rockhurst College, 1989.

Latin American Provincials of the Society of Jesus. "A Letter on Neo-Liberalism in Latin America." *Promotio Iustitiae* 67 (May 1997).

Lattis, James M. *Between Copernicus and Galileo: Christoph Clavius and the Collapse of Ptolemaic Cosmology.* Chicago, Ill.: University of Chicago Press, 1994.

Leahy, William P., S.J. *Adapting to America: Catholics, Jesuits, and Higher Education in the Twentieth Century.* Washington, D.C.: Georgetown University Press, 1991.

Lederman, Leon. "On the Record." Interview by Amanda Vogt. *Chicago Tribune,* 6 October 1996, sec. 2, 3.

Lee, Bernard J., Barbara Fleischer, and Charles Topper. "A Same and Different Future: A Study of Graduate Ministry Education in Catholic Institutions of Higher Learning in the United States." Done for the Association of Graduate Programs in Ministry (Executive Summary), published privately.

Leege, David C. "Catholics and the Civic Order: Parish Participation, Politics, and Civic Participation." *Review of Politics* 50 (fall 1988): 704–36.

Lentricchia, Frank. "Last Will and Testament of an Ex-Literary Critic." *Lingua Franca* 6 (1996).

Lewin, Tamar. "Family Decay Global, Study Says." *New York Times,* 30 May 1995, A5.

Lewis, Claude. "Terrorizing of Children Beyond Oklahoma City." *Philadelphia Inquirer,* 24 May 1995, A13.

Linenthal, Edward T., and Tom Engelhardt, eds. *History Wars: The Enola Gay and Other Battles for the American Past.* New York: Metropolitan, 1996.

Lonergan, Bernard. *Insight: A Study of Human Understanding.* London: Longmans, 1957.

————. *Method in Theology.* Toronto: University of Toronto, 1994 [1971].

Los Angeles 1994: State of the County Report. Los Angeles, Calif.: United Way of Greater Los Angeles.

Loyola, Ignatius. *The Constitutions of the Society of Jesus and Their Complementary Norms.* Gen. Ed. John W. Padberg, S.J. St. Louis, Mo.: Institute of Jesuit Sources, 1996.

—————. *The Spiritual Exercises of St. Ignatius: A Translation and Commentary.* Trans. George E. Ganss, S.J. St. Louis, Mo.: Institute of Jesuit Sources, 1992.

—————. *The Spiritual Exercises of St. Ignatius.* Trans. Louis J. Puhl, S.J. Westminster, Md.: Newman, 1951.

MacKenzie, Norman H., ed. *The Poetical Works of Gerard Manley Hopkins.* Oxford: Clarendon, 1990.

Maddox, Randy L. "The Recovery of Theology as a Practical Discipline." *Theological Studies* 51 (1990): 650–72.

Maeyanea, Y., and W. G. Saltzer, eds. *Prismata Festschrift für Willy Hartner.* Wiesbaden, 1977.

Maharidge, Dale. *The Coming White Minority: California's Eruptions and America's Future.* New York: Times Books/Random House, 1996.

Mahony, Roger M., and Los Angeles Archdiocesan Priests Council. "What About Those Who Do Not Qualify for Amnesty?" *Origins* 16 (1987): 826–28.

Malherbe, Abraham. *Social Aspects of Early Christianity.* Baton Rouge, La.: Louisiana State University, 1977.

Maritain, Jacques. *Art and Scholasticism.* Notre Dame, Ind.: University of Notre Dame Press, 1974.

—————. *Creative Intuition in Art and Poetry.* Washington, D.C.: National Gallery of Art, 1952.

Marsden, George M. *The Outrageous Idea of Christian Scholarship.* New York: Oxford University Press, 1997.

—————. *The Soul of the American University: From Protestant Establishment to Established Nonbelief.* New York: Oxford University Press, 1994.

Marsh, James. "Reply to McKinney on Lonergan: A Deconstruction." *International Philosophical Quarterly* 31 (March 1991): 97–98.

Matthews, Victor. "Hospitality and Hostility in Genesis 19 and Judges 19." *Biblical Theology Bulletin* 22 (1992): 3–11.

—————. "Hospitality and Hostility in Judges 4." *Biblical Theology Bulletin* 21 (1991): 13–21.

McCarthy, John L., S.J., ed. *Documents of the Thirty-Fourth General Congregation of the Society of Jesus.* St. Louis, Mo.: Institute of Jesuit Sources, 1995.

McDade, John, S.J. Editorial in *The Month* 28 (May 1995): 170–73.

McFadden, William C., S.J., ed. *Georgetown at Two Hundred: Faculty Reflections on the University's Future.* Washington, D.C.: Georgetown University Press, 1990.

McKinney, Ronald, S.J. "The Role of 'Conversion' in Lonergan's Insight." *Irish Theological Quarterly* 52 (1986): 268–78.

Meeks, Wayne. *The First Urban Christians.* New Haven, Conn.: Yale University Press, 1983.

—————. *The Origins of Christian Morality.* New Haven, Conn.: Yale University Press, 1993.

Messiaen, Oliver. "Preface" to "Quatuor pour la Fin du Temps," reprinted on RCA Victor CD 7845-RG.

Modras, Ronald. *Paul Tillich's Theology of the Church: A Catholic Appraisal.* Detroit: Wayne State University Press, 1976.

Mott, S. C. "The Use of the New Testament for Social Ethics." *The Journal of Religious Ethics* 15/2 (Fall 1987): 225–60.

Murphy, Charles M. "Action for Justice as Constitutive of the Preaching of the Gospel: What Did the 1971 Synod Mean?" *Theological Studies* 44 (June 1983): 298–311.

Murphy, Séamus, S.J. "The Many Ways of Justice." *Studies in the Spirituality of Jesuits* 26/2 (March 1994).

Murray, John Courtney, S.J. "Towards a Theology for the Layman—The Problem of Its Finality." *Theological Studies* 5 (1944): 43–75.

Neenan, William N., S.J. "A Catholic/Jesuit University?" In *Finding God in All Things: Essays in Honor of Michael J. Buckley, S.J.,* ed. Michael J. Himes and Stephen J. Pope. New York: Crossroad Herder, 1996).

Newman, John Henry. *The Idea of a University.* Ed. Frank M. Turner. New Haven, Conn., and London: Yale University Press, 1992.

Niebuhr, H. Richard. *Christ and Culture.* New York: Harper and Row, 1961.

Nouwen, Henri. *Reaching Out.* New York: Image, 1975.

Nussbaum, Martha. *Cultivating Humanity: A Classical Defense of Reform in Liberal Education.* Cambridge, Mass.: Harvard University Press, 1997.

O'Brien, David J. "American Culture Key to Understanding Lay Shifts." *National Catholic Reporter,* 8 October 1993, 30–31.

———. "Conversations On Jesuit (And Catholic?) Higher Education: Jesuit Sì, Catholic . . . Not So Sure." *Conversations* 6 (fall 1994).

——— and Thomas A. Shannon, eds. *Catholic Social Thought.* Maryknoll, N.Y.: Orbis, 1992.

Office of Pastoral Care of Migrants and Refugees, Bishops' Committee on Migration, National Conference of Catholic Bishops, ed. *Today's Immigrants and Refugees: A Christian Understanding.* Washington, D.C.: USCC, 1988.

Ogletree, Thomas. *Hospitality to the Stranger: Dimensions of Moral Understanding.* Philadelphia: Fortress, 1985.

O'Hanlon, Gerry, S.J. "Jesuits Renewed for Mission." *Tablet* 249 (8 April 1995): 473–74.

O'Keefe, Mark. *Becoming Good, Becoming Holy: On the Relationship of Christian Ethics and Spirituality.* Mahwah, N.J.: Paulist, 1995.

Olin, John C., ed. *The Autobiography of St. Ignatius Loyola.* New York: Harper Torchbooks, 1974.

———, ed. *The Autobiography of St. Ignatius Loyola, with Related Documents.* Trans. Joseph F. O'Callaghan. New York: Fordham University Press, 1992.

O'Malley, John W., S.J. *The First Jesuits.* Cambridge, Mass.: Harvard University Press, 1993.

———. "The Fourth Vow in Its Ignatian Context: A Historical Study." *Studies in the Spirituality of Jesuits* 15/1 (1983): 46–49.

———. "To Travel to Any Part of the World: Jerónimo Nadal and the Jesuit Vocation." *Studies in the Spirituality of Jesuits* 16/2 (1984): 5–8.

O'Meara, Thomas F. "Doctoral Programs in Theology at U.S. Catholic Universities." *America* 162 (1990).

Ong, Walter J., S.J. *The Barbarian Within.* New York: Macmillan, 1962.

Padberg, John W., S.J. "The Society True to Itself: A Brief History of the 32nd General Congregation of the Society of Jesus (December 2, 1974–March 7, 1975)." *Studies in the Spirituality of Jesuits* 15/3–4 (May–September 1983): 20–26.

————, gen. ed. *The Constitutions of the Society of Jesus and Their Complementary Norms.* St. Louis, Mo.: Institute of Jesuit Sources, 1996.

————, ed. *Documents of the 31st and 32nd General Congregations of the Society of Jesus.* St. Louis, Mo.: Institute of Jesuit Sources, 1977.

Palmer, Parker. *A Company of Strangers.* New York: Crossroad, 1986.

Paul VI. *Ecclesiam Suam.* Washington, D.C.: NC Welfare Conference, 1964.

————. *Evangelii Nuntiandi.* Washington, D.C.: USCC, 1976.

Pelikan, Jaroslav. *The Excellent Empire: The Fall of Rome and the Triumph of the Church.* San Francisco, Calif.: Harper and Row, 1987.

Pike, Kenneth L. *With Heart and Mind: A Personal Synthesis of Scholarship and Devotion.* Duncanville, Tex.: Adult Learning Systems, 1996.

Pinto, Ambrose, S.J. "South Asia." Regional report prepared for the International Jesuit Higher Education Meeting, Santiago, Chile, October 1997.

Pohl, Christine. "Hospitality from the Edge: The Significance of Marginality in the Practice of Welcome." In *Annual of the Society of Christian Ethics.* Boston, Mass.: Society of Christian Ethics, 1995.

Pontifical Council for Social Communications. *Aetatis Novae.* (A New Era: Pastoral Instruction on Social Communications on the 20th Anniversary of *Communio et Progressio*). Vatican City: Libreria Editrice Vaticana, 1992.

————. *Communio et Progressio.* (Pastoral Instruction on the Means of Social Communication). In *Vatican Council II: The Conciliar and Post Conciliar Documents,* ed. Austin Flannery, O.P. Collegeville, Minn.: Liturgical, 1975 [1971].

"The Practice of American History: A Special Issue." *The Journal of American History* 8/3 (December 1994).

Puhl, Louis J., S.J., trans. *The Spiritual Exercises of St. Ignatius.* Westminster, Md.: Newman, 1951.

Rahner, Hugo. *Ignatius: The Man and the Priest.* Rome: CIS, 1977.

Rakove, Jack N. *Original Meanings: Politics and Ideas in the Making of the Constitution.* New York: Knopf, 1996.

Rapoport, Anatol. *Fights, Games, and Debates.* Ann Arbor, Mich.: University of Michigan Press, 1970.

Reites, James. "St. Ignatius of Loyola and the Jews." *Studies in the Spirituality of Jesuits* 13/4 (September 1981): 17.

Revel, Jacques, and Lynn Hunt, eds. *Histories: French Constructions of the Past.* New York: New Press, 1995.

Ribando, William. "Top Theological Faculties Lag in Ecumenical Hiring." *Ecumenical Trends* 26/4 (1997): 61–64.

Richter, David H., ed. *Falling into Theory: Conflicting Views on Reading Literature.* Boston, Mass.: St. Martin's, 1994.

Rigali, Norbert. "Christian Ethics and Perfection." *Chicago Studies* 14 (1975): 227–40.

————. "The Future of Christian Morality." *Chicago Studies* 20 (1981): 281–89.

————. "The Unity of Moral and Pastoral Truth." *Chicago Studies* 25 (1986): 224–32.

————. "The Unity of the Moral Order." *Chicago Studies* 8 (1969): 125–43.

Rock, Judith. *Terpsichore at Louis-le-Grand: Baroque Dance on the Jesuit Stage in Paris.* St. Louis, Mo.: Institute of Jesuit Sources, 1997.

Rosen, Marie Simonetti. "Professor Alfred Blumstein of Carnegie Mellon University: A LEN Interview." *Law Enforcement News* (30 April 1995): 10–13.

Ross, Daniel, S.J. "East Asia." Regional report prepared for the International Jesuit Higher Education Meeting, Santiago, Chile, October 1997.

Sandos, James A. "Junípero Serra's Canonization and the Historical Record." *American Historical Review* 93/5 (December 1988): 1253–69.

Schweickart, Patrocinio P. "Reading Ourselves: Toward a Feminist Theory of Reading." In *Falling into Theory: Conflicting Views on Reading Literature,* ed. David H. Richter. Boston, Mass.: St. Martin's, 1994.

Scroggs, Robin. "The Social Interpretation of the New Testament." *New Testament Studies* 26 (1980): 164–79.

Selden, Raman, and Peter Widdowson. *A Reader's Guide to Contemporary Literary Theory.* Lexington, Ky.: University Press of Kentucky, 1993.

Shafarevitch, I. R. "Über Einigen Tendenzen in der Entwicklung der Mathematik." *Jahrbuch der Academie der Wissenschaften in Göttingen* (1973). English excerpts in *The Mathematical Experience,* ed. P. J. Davis and R. Hersh. Boston, Mass.: Houghton Mifflin, 1981.

Shelton, Charles M., S.J. "Friendship in Jesuit Life: The Joys, the Struggles, the Possibilities." *Studies in the Spirituality of Jesuits* 27/5 (November 1995).

———. "Helping College Students Make Moral Decisions." *Conversations on Jesuit Higher Education* 2 (fall 1992): 6–21.

———. *Morality of the Heart: A Psychology for the Christian Moral Life.* New York: Crossroad, 1997.

Sigmund, Barbara Boggs. "Five Minutes with the Pope." *America* 157/6 (19 September 1987): 30–31.

Sobrino, Jon. *Christology at the Crossroads.* Maryknoll, N.Y.: Orbis, 1978.

Sordi, Marta. *The Christians and the Roman Empire.* Norman, Okla.: University of Oklahoma Press, 1986.

Soros, George. "The Capitalist Threat." *Atlantic Monthly* 279/2 (February 1997).

Spence, Jonathan D. *The Memory Palace of Matteo Ricci.* New York: Viking, 1984.

Stark, Rodney. *The Rise of Christianity: A Sociologist Reconsiders History.* Princeton, N.J.: Princeton University Press, 1996.

Steinberg, Laurence. *Beyond the Classroom: Why School Reform Has Failed and What Parents Need to Do.* New York: Simon and Schuster, 1996.

Steinfels, Margaret. "The Catholic Intellectual Tradition." *Origins* 25 (24 August 1995): 169, 171–73.

Sullivan, Andrew. "'I'm Here': An Interview with Andrew Sullivan." By Thomas Stahel. *America* 168 (8 May 1993): 5–11.

Thurow, Lester C. *The Future of Capitalism: How Today's Economic Forces Shape Tomorrow's World.* New York: Morrow, 1996.

Tocqueville, Alexis de. *Democracy in America.* 2 vols. Garden City, N.Y.: Doubleday, 1969.

Tripole, Martin R., S.J. *Faith Beyond Justice: Widening the Perspective.* St. Louis, Mo.: Institute of Jesuit Sources, 1994.

Tushnet, Mark. "Catholic Legal Education at a National Law School: Reflections on the Georgetown Experience." In *Georgetown at Two Hundred: Faculty Reflections on the University's Future,* ed. William C. McFadden, S.J. Washington, D.C.: Georgetown University Press, 1990.

Ugalde, Luis, S.J. "Latin America." Regional report prepared for the International Jesuit Higher Education Meeting, Santiago, Chile, October 1997.

van Ackeren, Gerald, S.J. "Reflections on the Relation Between Philosophy and Theology." *Theological Studies* 14 (1953): 527–50.

Verba, Sidney, Kay Lehman Schlozman, Henry Brady, and Norman H. Nie. "Race, Ethnicity and Political Resources: Participation in the United States." *British Journal of Political Science* 23 (October 1993): 453–97.

Wald, Kenneth D. *Religion and Politics in the United States.* 2nd ed. Washington, D.C.: Congressional Quarterly, 1992.

Wallace, William A. *Galileo and His Sources: The Heritage of the Collegio Romano in Galileo's Science.* Princeton, N.J.: Princeton University Press, 1984.

Walsh, J. P. M., S.J. *The Mighty from Their Thrones.* Philadelphia: Fortress, 1987.

Weakland, Rembert G. "Economic Justice for All: Ten Years Later." *America* 176/9 (22 March 1997): 8–22.

Weinberg, Steven. *Dreams of a Final Theory.* New York: Vintage, 1993.

Williams, Raymond Brady. *Religions of Immigrants from India and Pakistan: New Threads in the American Tapestry.* New York: Cambridge University Press, 1988.

Wister, Robert J. "The Teaching of Theology 1950–1990: The American Catholic Experience." *America* 162 (3 February 1990).

Wuthnow, Robert. *God and Mammon in America.* New York: Free, 1994.

————. *Poor Richard's Principle: Recovering the American Dream Through the Moral Dimension of Work, Business, and Money.* Princeton, N.J.: Princeton University Press, 1996.

Zonneveld, Sjaak. *The Random Grim Forge: A Study of Social Ideas in the Work of Gerard Manley Hopkins.* Assen/Maastricht: Van Gorcum, 1992.

Document Index

Subject Index

Islam (Muslims), 30, 36, 75, 80, 206, 210, 228, 305, 314, 318
Ivern, Francisco, 310–11

Jesuit Institute (BC), 33, 36, 38, 39, 41
John XXIII, 273
John Paul II,
    and communication, 101
    and culture, 84, 98
    and general congregations, 9, 214
    and interreligious dialogue, 17, 30, 38, 250, 276, 304
    and justice, 11, 146
    and laity, 178, 250
    and sacredness of life, 14, 20
John the Evangelist, 80
Johnson, Elizabeth, 252
Joseph, 231
Joshua, 231
Joyce, James, 138
JRS (Jesuit Refugee Service), 19
Judaism (Jews), 30, 36, 49–50, 75, 80, 206, 227, 228, 249–51, 305
justice. See also education, faith-justice, GC 34 Decree 3 (OMJ)
    biblical notions of, 7–9
    and law profession, 189–99
    meaning of in GC 34, 2, 3, 9–17
Justin, 232
JVC (Jesuit Volunteer Corps), 185

Kelly, J. M., 192
Kersten, Kevin, 41
Keynes, John Maynard, 129
Kolvenbach, Peter-Hans, 1, 2–4, 18, 30, 32, 138, 141, 202–3, 214, 301
Kristeva, Julia, 252

Lacan, Jacques, 135
LaCroix, Wilfred, 163–65
Lainez, Diego, 81
laity, 32, 37–39, 54–57. See also GC 34 Decree 13 (CLM)
    formation of, 181–83
    Jesuit partnership with, 2, 30, 177–87
    and justice, 18–20
    as university faculty, 52–54, 177–87, 303
Landy, Tom, 183
law, 189–99
Leahy, William, 299
Lederman, Leon, 115

Le Moyne College, 106
liberation theology, 277–79
linguistics, 206–10
literary criticism, 133–36
literature, 89–92, 133–36
Locatelli, Paul, 310, 323
Locke, John, 194
Lonergan, Bernard, 256–57
Louis-le-Grand, 165
Loyola Marymount Los Angeles, 278–79, 300, 305
Loyola School (Jamshedpur, India), 203
Loyola University Chicago, 203
Loyola University New Orleans, 165, 303
Lubbers, Lee, 41
Lyotard, Jean-François, 135

magis, 112, 203
Mahoney, John, 38
Mahoney, Roger, 280
Mamet, David, 133
"marginalized" persons, 235, 237–38, 241–42
Maritain, Jacques, 163–64, 166–67
Marquette University, 299
Marsden, George, 299, 302
Marsh, James, 260–61
Martha, 231
Marxism, 145–47
Mary, 70
math, 213–21
McKenna, Horace, 224
McNamee, Stephen, 268
medical genetics, 223–29
Meeks, Wayne, 231
Men for Others, 8, 15
Messiaen, Oliver, 160–61
moral theology, 230–42
More, Sir Thomas, 199
Murphy, Séamus, 148, 204
Murray, John Courtney, 300

Nadal, Jerome, 31, 236–40
NAWCHE (National Association for Women in Catholic Higher Education), 40
Nazism, 250–51, 252
Neenan, William, 297
Newman, John Henry, 28
Nicholas of Cusa, 220, 221
Niebuhr, H. Richard, 73
Notre-Dame de la Paix University (Belgium), 314
Nussbaum, Martha, 35, 36

CPSIA information can be obtained at www.ICGtesting.com
Printed in the USA
BVOW051803030512

289378BV00001B/1/A